Lonely Planet Publications
Melbourne | Oakland | London

Duncan Garwood &
Josephine Quintero

Naples
& the Amalfi Coast

The Top Five

1 Palazzo Reale di Capodimonte
Feast on magnificant art at this impressive museum (p79)

2 Museo Archeologico Nazionale
Get your art and history fix here (p66)

3 Ravello
Enjoy spectacular views overlooking the Amalfi Coast (p199)

4 Pompeii
Visit the ruins of this ancient city, a victim of Vesuvius' wrath (p181)

5 Certosa di San Martino
Revel in one of Naples' must-see sites (p75)

Contents

Published by Lonely Planet Publications Pty Ltd
ABN 36 005 607 983

Australia Head Office, Locked Bag 1, Footscray,
Victoria 3011, ☎ 03 8379 8000, fax 03 8379 8111,
talk2us@lonelyplanet.com.au

USA 150 Linden St, Oakland, CA 94607,
☎ 510 893 8555, toll free 800 275 8555,
fax 510 893 8572, info@lonelyplanet.com

UK 72–82 Rosebery Ave, Clerkenwell, London,
EC1R 4RW, ☎ 020 7841 9000, fax 020 7841 9001,
go@lonelyplanet.co.uk

Printed through The Bookmaker International Ltd
Printed in China

The Authors

DUNCAN GARWOOD

Duncan currently lives in the wine-rich hills overlooking Rome. He is an Italian speaker, and over the years has travelled extensively throughout the peninsula enjoying the disarming beauty of the country and its hidden complexities.

Duncan's first trip to Naples and the Amalfi Coast was something of an eye-opener and left a deep impression. A big fan of the city, he returned to research the area for Lonely Planet's *Italy* guide. This latest assignment provided him with a great excuse to explore Naples further and to eat plate loads of its finest food.

Duncan researched and wrote the introductory chapters, Quarters, Walking Tours, Entertainment and Sleeping.

JOSEPHINE QUINTERO

Born in England, Josephine started travelling with a backpack and guitar in the late '60s (didn't everyone?), stopping off in Israel on a kibbutz for a year. Her next stop was California, where she graduated from UC Berkeley and worked for several Bay Area newspapers and glossy magazines. Further travels took her to Kuwait, where she was editor of the *Kuwaiti Digest* and from where she made several side trips, including to Yemen and India. She was held hostage during the Iraqi invasion of Kuwait and moved to the relaxed shores of Andalucía in Spain shortly after. Josephine has made numerous trips to Italy to visit family and deepen her appreciation of the finer things in life. She has contributed to more than 25 travel guidebooks, including Lonely Planet's *Tuscany & Umbria*, and considers Naples the most compelling Italian city she has lived in to date. Josephine wrote the Eating and Shopping chapters, as well as the Bay of Naples & the Amalfi Coast chapter.

PHOTOGRAPHER
JEAN-BERNARD CARILLET

A Paris-based author and photographer, Jean-Bernard has contributed to numerous Lonely Planet guides in both French and English. When not shooting crystal-clear lagoons in the tropics or markets in eastern Africa, he travels regularly to the east of France and the Ruhr in Germany to work on a darker subject – the industrial wasteland. After his stay in Naples, Jean-Bernard confirms that Neapolitan pizzas are the best in the world.

Introducing Naples & the Amalfi Coast

Nowhere can prepare you for the manic in-your-face vitality of Naples. A highly charged mix of screaming humanity and teeming streets, it's an unrelenting assault on your senses.

Raucous, polluted, unruly, deafening and with many of its historical buildings filthy and crumbling, Naples is a city that polarises opinion like no other. Tell an Italian you're going to Naples and they'll either wax lyrical about the city's artistic heritage, wonderful food and fantastic natural setting, or they'll warn you to avoid vast swathes of the city centre – a Neapolitan will cheerfully do both.

Beautifully positioned on the bay and with the far-from-extinct Mt Vesuvius looming menacingly in the background, southern Italy's one true metropolis is a city of many faces.

It's in the dark streets of the *centro storico* (historic centre) that you'll meet the Naples of folklore – cocky kids playing football in grubby piazzas, overloaded Vespas screeching past street vendors and students thronging narrow alleyways. Once the heart of the Graeco-Roman Neopolis, this atmospheric and claustrophobic area is crammed full of ancient churches, underground tunnels, a medieval university and countless eateries and cafés.

In complete contrast, the vast Piazza del Plebiscito stands at the heart of one of Italy's most monumental square miles. The result of more than 600 years of royal history, the Palazzo Reale, Teatro San Carlo and Castel Nuovo continue to dominate the cityscape. Further north the sumptuous collections of the Palazzo Reale di Capodimonte, the Museo Archeologico Nazionale and the Certosa di San Martino, constitute an artistic legacy that the city's reputation does little to highlight.

Naples is one of the Mediterranean's great ports, and like many working ports it's a little rough round the edges. Neapolitans share a deep-rooted distrust of authority, and regulations are observed with absolute discretion; petty thievery is common and organised crime a fact of life (although unlikely to interfere with your stay in town). The Neapolitan Mafia, the Camorra, thrives, controlling the fruit-and-vegetable markets, the drugs trade and the massive *toto nero* (illegal football pools). The Camorra also has hands in the booming black market in fake designer clothes and pirated CDs.

The city has, however, undergone something of a facelift in the last decade. Since left-wing mayor Antonio Bassolino instigated a massive clean-up for the 1994 G7 summit, many churches, museums and monuments that had been off-limits for decades were reopened and tourist areas were made safer. It was a good time that led, in 2000, to Bassolino being booted upstairs to the presidency of the Campania region.

Lowdown

Population 1,008,419
Population in the Vesuvius danger zone 700,000
Last Vesuvius eruption 1944
Ferry ticket to Capri €5.60
Cup of coffee €0.65
Three-star hotel room From €75
Bus ticket €1
Pizza From €3.50
Time zone Central European Time (GMT plus one hour)

His shoes were filled by Naples' first-ever female mayor, Rosa Russo Jervolino. Striving to continue the politics of her predecessor, she has inevitably suffered from succeeding such a charismatic leader. She has struggled to maintain the pace of change that Bassolino set, and while he was able to hit an immediate chord with his programme of high-profile measures, Jervolino has had to deal with many of the less glamorous elements of city life. Managing the city's precarious finances and allocating refuse-disposal contracts are never going to set hearts racing as much as hosting G7 summits or announcing major cultural initiatives.

Essential Naples

- Museo Archeologico Nazionale (p66)
- Piazza del Gesù Nuovo (p58)
- Cappella Sansevero (p56)
- Certosa di San Martino (p75)
- Palazzo Reale di Capodimonte (p79)

Naples is a year-round destination, even if some months are better than others. May is the busiest time of the year. The annual Maggio dei Monumenti (p9) attracts thousands of visitors to the city for a month-long cultural programme of open-air concerts, extended opening hours and art exhibitions. Similarly, the period leading up to Christmas is very busy as Italians flock to Via San Gregorio Armeno in the *centro storico* to buy their traditional *presepi* (nativity scenes; p138). The best time to visit is spring, when the sun shines and the flowers begin to bloom. It's also not too hot – whereas if you come in August you'll find the city half-closed as Neapolitans flee to the sea.

You don't have to go very far out of Naples to find scenery that has been seducing travellers for millennia. Legends tell how sirens lured sailors to their deaths off Sorrento, and of islands inhabited by mermaids. Travel down the bewitching Amalfi Coast or out to the magical islands of the Bay of Naples and maybe all this will start to make more sense – high prices and holidaymakers allowing, of course.

Of the towns that nestle into the craggy Amalfi coastline, it is Amalfi itself that attracts the biggest crowds, even if Positano is more picturesque and Ravello more refined. Out in the Bay of Naples, Capri pulls the celebs and day-trippers, while Ischia is famous for its thermal baths. The smallest of the three islands, Procida is, however, the prettiest.

Myth meets history in Pompeii, Italy's biggest tourist attraction. Destroyed by Mt Vesuvius in AD 79, the Roman city provides a fascinating glimpse of ancient life buried in time. Further down the coast, the Greek temples of Paestum are among the best preserved in the world. To the west of Naples the Campi Flegrei boasts the oldest Greek remains in Italy, as well as some sulphurous volcanic scenery and the ancient entrance to Hades (Lago di Averno, according to Homer and Virgil).

Legends of Campania also include a number of gastronomic highlights: some time around the 10th century the water buffalo was introduced to Campania and *mozzarella di bufala* was conceived; in 1840 the first industrial pasta plant was opened in Torre Annunziata; and in 1889 the pizza margherita was created by a Neapolitan *pizzaiola* (pizza maker). Needless to say the food in these parts is sensational. The pizza's the original article, the seafood is abundant and tasty, and the fast food is among the best there is.

DUNCAN'S TOP NAPLES DAY

Before anything I dip into a bar in the *centro storico* – any bar'll do – for an early coffee and *cornetto* (croissant). The streets are showing signs of life but the students aren't up yet and the atmosphere is muted. After wandering along Via San Biagio dei Librai for a bit I head up to the Museo Archeologico Nazionale (p66). I still can't get over the mosaics – how patient do you have to be to prepare thousands of tiny stone pieces and then fit them together like a giant jigsaw?

For lunch I know exactly what I want – pizza. Some of the best are served back in the centro storico (p111) so that's where I go.

I can't help having a siesta; I'm sleepy after lunch and it's hot. Around 5pm I emerge ready to join the early evening throng. From Piazza Dante (p67) I head down Via Toledo, munching on a *sfogliatella* (pastry filled with ricotta) as I go. The animation of the place never ceases to amaze me and to think it's like this *every day*. A beer beckons and from my favourite spot I watch the small boats pootle around off Borgo Marinaro (p68). Now, where to eat tonight?

City Life

City Life

NAPLES TODAY

Naples is not what it once was. It's no longer the city of barefoot urchins scrimping a living on the mean streets or of gangland bosses partying with football stars. Nor, however, is it the Naples that so impressed world leaders at the 1994 G7 summit. Today Naples is a city struggling to maintain the momentum of its recent past.

Under the leadership of the charismatic mayor Antonio Bassolino, Naples underwent a drastic transformation in the 1990s. Italians began to look on the city in a new light and tourists began to return. But the pace was unsustainable – things had to slow down, and they have.

One of the most frequent grumbles in Naples today is that optimism and hope have given way to indifference and cynicism, and that the political forces of inertia have returned to the fore. Some blame Bassolino's successor Rosa Russo Jervolino, others maintain that after such an intense period of change, a lull was inevitable.

Neapolitans point out that construction work on the new metro stations in **Piazza del Municipio** (p73) and **Piazza Bovio** (p91) is far from complete and that public transport is struggling. In the *centro storico* (historic centre) shopkeepers complain that shoplifting is once again an issue and curse the punks who beg on their cobbled streets. A regionwide rubbish crisis and the saga of Napoli football team have also done the city few favours.

But through all this the most striking feature is the resilience of the Neapolitans themselves. Cynical and cheerful by nature, they make this city what it is. Visit Naples today and you'll be struck by their sheer energy. Wherever you look there are people on the move. The Neapolitans may complain that the city is idling in neutral but if they hadn't told you, you'd never have guessed.

Hot Conversation Topics

Here are some of the things you may overhear locals talking about in Naples:

- I hope they're going to collect the rubbish this week.
- I know the winning lottery numbers, I dreamt them last night.
- Prices gone up again, I see.
- I could have sworn there was smoke coming out of Vesuvius.
- It's not Jervolino's politics I mind, I just can't stand her voice.
- There was a time when our footballers put fear into the rest of Europe, now we can't even stay in the second division!

CITY CALENDAR

Naples' calendar of annual events spans religious processions, international rock festivals, firework bonanzas and pizza parties.

Naples' biggest festival month is May when long-closed museum and church doors are opened and concerts, exhibitions and performances are held in many of the city's picturesque piazzas.

Throughout the summer, from June to September, events are organised in Naples and in many spectacular venues along the Amalfi Coast and on the islands in the bay (see p163 for further details). Christmas, New Year and Easter are also celebrated with a spate of concerts and popular processions.

For an updated timetable of events consult the monthly *Qui Napoli*, or go online at www.inaples.it. For music, film and theatre listings, see p124; for a list of public holidays, see p213.

High season in Naples is generally regarded as mid-April through to June, and then all of December. Late spring is the best time to visit, as the weather is not too hot and is more suitable for pounding the streets. In August, Naples becomes unbearably hot and many bars and restaurants close down until September. Party animals looking for a good time in the height of the Neapolitan summer would do well to follow local habits and head out to the Bay of Naples islands or down to the Amalfi Coast.

The following is a list of the major annual events and festivals in Naples.

JANUARY
O CIPPO 'E SANT'ANTONIO
Held on 17 January, this is the traditional date for a post-Christmas clearout. Throughout the city people heap everything they want to throw out into huge piles and then torch the lot.

FEBRUARY
CARNEVALE
During the period before Ash Wednesday, kids dress up in fancy costumes and throw coloured confetti over each other as Neapolitans enjoy their last opportunity to indulge before Lent.

MARCH & APRIL
SETTIMANA SANTA
Easter Week in Naples and the surrounding area is marked by solemn processions and Passion plays. Particularly famous are the processions of **Procida** (p178) and **Sorrento** (p188).

SETTIMANA PER LA CULTURA
www.beniculturali.it
A nationwide initiative celebrating Italy's national heritage. For a week, entry to publicly owned galleries and museums is free.

MAY
FESTA DI SAN GENNARO
Via Duomo 147; bus CS to Via Duomo
On the first Sunday of May, thousands gather in the **Duomo** (p60) to witness the saint's blood (held in two phials) liquefy – a miracle said to save the city from potential disasters.

MAGGIO DEI MONUMENTI
☎ 081 247 11 23
The city's premier cultural event offers a month-long menu of exhibitions, concerts, dance performances, guided tours and much more. Many buildings that are otherwise closed open their doors to the public.

JUNE
PALIO DELLE QUATTRO ANTICHE REPUBBLICHE MARINARE
Held on the first Sunday of June, this is a procession of boats and a race between the four historical maritime rivals: Pisa, Venice, Amalfi and Genoa. The event rotates between the four towns: Amalfi in 2005, Pisa in 2006, Venice in 2007 and Genoa in 2008.

ESTATE A NAPOLI
☎ 081 247 11 23; www.napolioggi.it in Italian
All the city's a stage as music, film and dance take to the streets from June to September.

JULY
MADONNA DEL CARMINE
Piazza del Carmine; bus C55 to Corso G Garibaldi
The traditional celebration of the Madonna del Carmine, held in Piazza del Carmine on 16 July, culminates in a spectacular fireworks display.

NEAPOLIS ROCK FESTIVAL
Arenile di Bagnoli, Via Nuova Bagnoli 10; www.neapolis .it in Italian; metro Bagnoli
Southern Italy's largest rock fest attracts top international acts. It's held west of town, down by the beach at **Arenile di Bagnoli** (p130).

AUGUST
FERRAGOSTO
The busiest day of the beach year, the Feast of the Assumption is celebrated on 15 August with concerts and local events.

SEPTEMBER
FESTA DI PIEDIGROTTA
Metro Mergellina
Dedicated to the Madonna, this once-popular song festival (8 September) is being revived. The centre of events is the **Chiesa Santa Maria di Piedigrotta** (p96) in Mergellina.

FESTA DI SAN GENNARO
Via Duomo 147; bus CS to Via Duomo
Repeat performance of San Gennaro's powder-to-blood miracle, held on 19 September.

NAPOLI STRIT FESTIVAL
☎ 338 622 60 47
Street artists perform in the narrow alleyways and packed squares of the *centro storico*.

PIZZAFEST
☎ 081 420 12 05; www.pizzafest.info/2004 in Italian
Homage is paid to the city's most famous export as *pizzaoili* (pizza makers) from all over the country perform in various pizza-based events.

DECEMBER

FESTA DI SAN GENNARO
Via Duomo 147; bus CS to Via Duomo
The third running of the San Gennaro blood miracle on 16 December.

NATALE
Church concerts, exhibitions and shopping frenzy leading up to Christmas Day, particularly around the *presepi* (nativity scenes) shops in **Via San Gregorio Armeno** (p59).

CAPODANNO
31 December; Piazza del Plebiscito; bus CS to Piazza Trieste e Trento
Tens of thousands of Neapolitans pile into **Piazza del Plebiscito** (p73) for the traditional New Year's Eve concert.

Piazza del Plebiscito (p73) dominated by Chiesa di San Francesco di Paola (p70)

CULTURE

IDENTITY

For a Neapolitan, wherever they are – in Naples or New York, Melbourne or Milan – Naples is the greatest city in the world. They might have spent 40 years churning out pizzas in Argentina or cutting sugarcane in Queensland, but a Neapolitan will still regard Naples as home.

Tough times have forced Neapolitans to become what they are. For much of its history the city was fought over, occupied and invaded by foreign powers whose interests were purely selfish. The lot of the city's population was irrelevant as long as they paid their taxes. Consequently the Neapolitans learned early to fend for themselves and to get by on what they had. The art of *arrangiarsi* (getting by) is not a uniquely Neapolitan skill, but it's one at which they excel.

Consummate performers and as *furbo* (cunning) as they come, Neapolitans are justifiably famous for their ingenuity. Where else would you hear of street entrepreneurs selling second-hand newspapers to lovers so that they can cover their car windows? Or of vendors flogging T-shirts imprinted with a diagonal seatbelt design so as to fool short-sighted traffic cops?

Neapolitans are very much aware of their image. They know that many of the stereotypes foreigners hold of Italians – noisy, theatrical, food-loving, passionate and proud – refer to them. And they revel in it. Nowhere else in Italy are the people so conscious of their role in the theatre of everyday life. They know they've been cast as the loveable rogue; the rough diamond who'll always try it on but with a smile and a quip. In many respects they encourage it. But while this persona has its comic sides, it also hides some uncomfortable truths.

Like most Italians, Neapolitans share a strong distrust of authority. The state has done little for them and they feel justified in doing nothing in return. Tax evasion is widespread and *abusivismo* (illegal building) rampant. And where the state hasn't provided, the Camorra (see opposite) has stepped in. Organised crime is a fact of life in Naples. It's something that lurks behind the scenes, emerging occasionally as gangs violently settle their accounts, but otherwise

---

Top Five Naples Events

- **Festa di San Gennaro** (p9 & above) Tri-annual miracle wards off misfortune. If it happens!
- **Maggio dei Monumenti** (p9) Month-long cultural bonanza.
- **Madonna del Carmine** (p9) Dramatic pyrotechnic display in a historic piazza.
- **Pizzafest** (p9) Celebration of Naples' great contribution to world cuisine.
- **December shopping** (above) Thousands head for the *presepi* (nativity scenes) in Via San Gregorio Armeno.

it silently gets on with its business of making money. Neapolitans are not proud of this but they know it exists and they accept it as they've accepted many of their historic ills – with a resigned shrug and a melancholy nod of the head. Life goes on.

LIFESTYLE

The province of Naples is not a great place to live, according to the Milan-based newspaper *Il Sole 24 Ore*. In its 2002 annual survey on the quality of life in Italy's 103 provinces, Naples only managed 83rd position. The results were based on a set of criteria ranging from rates of employment to leisure facilities, environmental management and public-service provision. The survey made grim reading for the 91 municipal areas that constitute the province.

But what is it actually like to live in a city where the population density of 2613 people per sq km is nearly 14 times higher than the national average? 'Cramped' is the obvious answer. In many apartment blocks you can hear the family in the adjacent flat as clearly as if they were in the next room.

It's not surprising then that Neapolitans pass a lot of their time on the streets. Office workers saunter up and down on their lunch breaks; old grannies sit on the streets glaring at passers-by, while their husbands play cards on the piazza. Privacy is a luxury which many Neapolitans can't afford, even if they wanted it.

In Naples, as in the rest of Italy, it's still the norm for young people to stay at home until they marry. This is partly a fact of economics – rents are relatively high and unemployment is a major problem – and partly tradition. Renting is not a Neapolitan habit and young couples will often delay marriage until they can afford to buy a place.

On the whole, the system seems to work well – young Neapolitans are free to spend their parents' money on cars, clothes and going out, and the parents can keep tabs on their precious offspring. Occasionally, however, differences of opinion arise. In April 2002 Italy's highest appeals court ruled that a Neapolitan doctor continue to pay for his son's keep. A law graduate in his mid-thirties, the son had a trust fund of US$220,000 and had previously rejected a number of job offers.

The role of the family is a well-documented feature of Italian life, and Neapolitan families are thriving. The size of the typical Neapolitan family is 3.23, which is larger than the national average of 2.6, and the city's birth rate is the highest in Italy. Much debate, however, rages as to why 51.4% of these births are by Caesarean section. Certainly some women choose them, but many do not, and, as there are no clinical reasons to explain the situation, critics point to the economic case: the more surgical procedures a hospital carries out, the more it earns.

Financially, the Neapolitans don't fare well either. Their per-capita income of around €12,500 is well below the Italian average of €20,000, but they still manage to go out late, enjoy the theatre, love their food and drive like maniacs.

The Camorra

Fans of the Fascist dictator Benito Mussolini still talk about one of his great successes – the eradication of the Mafia. However, although the great criminal organisations of the south had a tough time of it under the Fascist regime, they weren't quite destroyed for good. Down but not out, they were quick to grasp the window of opportunity that WWII provided. Following the 1943 Allied invasion, the British and American command turned to the flourishing underworld as the best way to get things done. The black market thrived and slowly the Camorra began to re-spread its roots. Post-war reconstruction provided plenty of business as the need for cheap housing ran roughshod over such niceties as planning permission and the law.

The earthquake of 1980 heralded a boom period. By now skilled in the art of siphoning off government and European grants, the Camorra made a lot of money – and they flaunted it. Bosses Carmine and Luigi Giuliano, for example, became famous for their lavish parties.

Nowadays, the bosses prefer to keep a lower profile but the coffers continue to swell. To their core activities of racketeering, drug smuggling and control of the city's fruit-and-veg markets, the families have added the lucrative business of counterfeiting (CDs, designer clothes etc) and waste disposal. There's a lot of money to be made in running illegal landfill sites, especially when the bosses are not too fussy about what sort of rubbish they take. According to 2002 figures, the market in illegal waste was worth €2500 million.

Lottery Dreams

Every year thousands of Neapolitans cram into the **Duomo** (p60) to witness the blood of their patron saint, San Gennaro, miraculously liquefy. Of course, very few actually believe that it's a real miracle and science has a ready explanation. Apparently, it's all to do with thixotrophy, or the property of certain compounds to liquefy when shaken and then return to their original form when left to stand. To verify this, though, scientists would have to analyse the blood, something the Church has effectively blocked by refusing permission to open the phial.

Still, the fact remains that when the blood liquefies the city breathes a sigh of relief – another year safe from disaster. A coincidence maybe, but when the miracle failed in 1944 Mt Vesuvius erupted and when it happened (or didn't happen) again in 1980 an earthquake struck the city.

The whole miracle scenario illustrates the way in which religion and superstition have become entangled in this most superstitious of cities. Many Neapolitans believe in the *malocchio* (evil eye) and will make the sign of the horns (by extending their thumb, index finger and little finger) to ward off bad luck. Alternatively they'll *tocca ferro* (touch iron).

But the Neapolitans are best known for their lottery superstitions. In every visible aspect the Neapolitan lottery is the same as every other lottery – tickets are bought, numbers marked and the winning numbers pulled out of a tightly guarded hat. Where it differs, however, is in the way that Neapolitans select their numbers. They dream them, or rather they interpret their dreams with the aid of *La Smorfia*, a kind of dream dictionary. According to the good book, dream of God or Italy and you should pick number one; for a football player choose 42 (Maradona, a football-playing God, is 43). Other numbers include dancing 37, crying 21, fear 90 and a woman's hair 55.

FASHION

Neapolitans, like most Italians, hang out in groups. And it's your group that dictates what you wear. In the *centro storico*, for example, the student look is to a greater or lesser degree grunge, give or take various subsets. The anti-globalisation/punks opt for the alternative military look – heavy boots, matted hair and body piercing. The rap and hip-hop brigade wear low-slung baggy trousers, while the rastas sport dreads and the usual reggae paraphernalia.

Cross town to Chiaia and you're in designer country. The streets are lined with big-name designer boutiques (see p144), the look is label-conscious and expensive jewellery is worn to dazzle. In summer smart casual outfits are studiously selected to complement tanned flesh.

There are one or two constants, however. Tattoos are popular everywhere. Currently, the number-one design is Che Guevara. In true Neapolitan style this is not a homage to the Cuban revolutionary but rather to the footballer Maradona, who famously has Che engraved on his arm. Mobile phones are universal, too. Children talk to their mums by mobile, teenagers compare designs and grandparents shout into them, suspicious that something so small can possibly be a phone.

Naples is not a city that stands out on the Italian fashion map. It can't compete with Milan, Florence or Rome, and it has no Dolce e Gabbana (from Sicily) or Versace (originally from Calabria). Its most famous designer was Salvatore Ferragamo, who after a period in America returned to Italy in 1936, set up shop in Florence and became a shoemaker to the stars. Past clients included Queen Elizabeth II and her sister Queen Margaret. He is also said to have invented the platform heel.

But what Naples lacks in big-name designers it makes up for in graft. Some 5500 clothing, leather and shoe factories operate within the province, as well as scores of illegal sweatshops.

SPORT

Olympic champion Massimiliano Rosolino is not your average Neapolitan. At six foot two, the blonde swimmer became a national hero when he won gold at the Sydney Olympics in 2000. For a short period he was the face of Italian sport. At least he was until the football season started and all other sports were instantly forgotten.

Napoli football club has the third-largest following in Italy (after Juventus and Milan) and yet the team is wallowing in the depths of *Serie C1* (Italy's third division). How they came to be there makes sorry reading (see p134). In short, Napoli finished the 2003–04 campaign mid-table in *Serie B* and completely broke. Bankruptcy proceedings followed and after a lengthy courtroom battle the club was relegated on a legal technicality and bought by a famous film producer.

The club's fortunes can only get better. However, whether or not they reach the heady days of the late 1980s remains to be seen.

In 1984 Napoli made world headlines when it bought the world's most famous footballer, the Argentinian genius Diego Armando Maradona. The stocky number 10 proved to be a natural Neapolitan and before long was worshipped alongside the Madonna and San Gennaro. Success on the pitch (championships in 1987 and 1990, the UEFA Cup in 1989) led authorities to turn a blind eye to his friendship with Camorra bosses and a cocaine habit that continues to plague him more than 20 years later.

Perhaps the most emblematic moment of Maradona's Italian adventure came in the 1990 World Cup. Leading Argentina to victory over Italy in the semifinals, Maradona was hailed by the Stadio San Paolo as a hero. The national team had lost but the Neapolitans identified Maradona's victory as their own; they had finally shown the world what one of their own could do. It was a victory for Naples over the rest of Italy.

MEDIA

Italy's media is centred in two cities, Milan and Rome, and is in two hands – those of Silvio Berlusconi. Milan is the operational base of Berlusconi's media empire, which comprises TV, Italy's largest publishing house, newspapers and advertising companies; and Rome is home to the state broadcaster Rai. On this national stage Naples doesn't feature. True, Rai has had a production centre in Naples for more than 40 years, but in terms of editorial influence it counts for little.

Yet Neapolitans are highly creative. Small publishers (eg Intra Moenia and Eva Luna) abound; graffiti is widespread, and is usually political and sometimes artistic; and art is universally appreciated (viz the modern art in the metro stations). The city also produces an inordinate amount of truly appalling TV. There are any number of local channels and the output is comically bad – a mix of cheap soft porn, homemade adverts and South American soap operas.

Naples' daily newspaper is the middle-of-the-road *Il Mattino*, while *Corriere della Sera* and *La Repubblica* both print Naples editions. For more on publications in Naples; see p216.

LANGUAGE

True Neapolitans will tell you that *Nnapulitano* is not a dialect, it's a language. Certainly, the fact that you can buy Neapolitan dictionaries and that it has its own distinct grammar weigh in their favour. For example, in *Nnapulitano* neutral nouns exist, whereas they don't in Italian; there are also no plural articles and many words have a unique plural form rather than masculine and feminine variants.

Both Italian and *Nnapulitano* grew from popular spoken Latin. But while Italian is largely based on the Tuscan dialect, Neapolitan is a hybrid of various different influences. As each new wave of foreign rulers took control of the city, so the native language developed. You'll find words borrowed from Arabic, from Spanish, French and German, even from English. Two examples: the Neapolitan word for moustache is *mustàccio*, while *stocco*, meaning salted cod, is taken from the English noun 'stock fish'.

Local Lore

Nnapulitano (Neapolitan dialect) has some rich and colourful proverbs. Here's five typical examples, with their Italian and English translations, respectively:

'A léngua nun tène òsso ma ròmpe ll'òssa' (La lingua non ha osso ma spezza le ossa) The tongue has no bone but it breaks bones.

'A mughièra 'e ll'àte é sèmpe cchiù bbòna' (La moglie degli altri è sempre più bella) Other people's wives are always more beautiful.

'Ògne scarafóne è bbèllo 'a màmma sóia' (Anche lo scarafaggio è bello per la sua mamma) Even a beetle is beautiful to its mother.

'E pariénte so còmme 'e scàrpe: cchiù so strìtte e cchiù te fànno màle' (I parenti sono come le scarpe: più sono strette e più fanno male) Relatives are like shoes: the tighter they are the more they hurt.

'Si 'a fatica fósse bbòna, 'e priévete faticàssero' (Se lavorarae fosse cosa buona, i preti lavorerebbero) If it were a good thing to work, priests would work.

Although there are no official figures, it was estimated that in the late 1970s that around 7.5 million people spoke *Nnapulitano*. It was, and is, the most widespread of Italy's regional tongues even if it has no legal status. In 2003 an attempt to introduce a degree course in *Nnapulitano* failed.

Part of its popularity dates to the great era of Neapolitan song at the end of the 19th century. Many of the classic songs, including 'O Sole Mio', were written in dialect and as their popularity grew so did the language. Later, in the 20th century, Totò performed in dialect and Eduardo de Filippo often used it in his plays. Massimo Troisi of *Il Postino* fame was famous for his mumbling part-Neapolitan, part-Italian dialect.

Today a southern Italian might understand a little Neapolitan, but a northerner probably wouldn't. A foreigner who's learnt Italian as a second language will have no chance.

ECONOMY & COSTS

Naples is a city of small businesses. Although some 30% of the province's workforce is employed in the public-service and administration sector, of the 250,000 registered private companies, 54% employ no more than 19 people.

Traditional mainstays of the economy include manufacturing and commerce, with more than 56,000 retail outlets present in the province. Naples' port is also a major employer, providing jobs for around 5000 people. Tourism is particularly important along the Amalfi Coast and in the Bay of Naples islands. In 2001 more than 10 million tourists visited the area. From the central tax pool Naples receives €524 per resident, some 3½ times more than Rome.

Unemployment is a major problem. In 2002 the rate of unemployment in the province of Naples was 24.7%, compared to a national average of 9%. Especially worrying is that more than half of Naples' 25- to 29-year-olds are out of work. It's a depressing fact, but economic migration is still a way of life for many young Neapolitans. For confirmation, you need only go to Stazione Centrale late on a Sunday night to find crowds of workers catching the trains north after a weekend at home.

How Much?
Taxi from the airport to Stazione Centrale €12.50
Litre of petrol €0.90
Half-litre of bottled water €1
Large Peroni (beer) €1 in a supermarket
Slice of pizza From €1
T-shirt About €8
Funicular ticket €1
Entry to Museo Archeologico Nazionale €6.50
Espresso €0.60
Ticket for the opera at Teatro San Carlo €35-90

According to figures published by Naples' financial newspaper *il Denaro*, the cost of living in Naples rose by 3.29% in 2003. But compared to Rome and the north of Italy, the city remains relatively cheap. Hotel prices vary enormously but you can expect to pay from €45 for a double room in a two-star pad to €300 for a four-star room. Similarly for food, you can pay as little as €3 for a pizza in the *centro storico,* while a full meal in one of the smart seafront restaurants will cost about €30.

Museum entry costs no more than €7.50 (for the Palazzo Reale di Capodimonte), while the hundreds of churches in the city are free. Under-18s and over-65s often qualify for a reduced fare or enter free. If you're planning on visiting the major museums you may save yourself money with the Campania artecard (p212). Transport is generally cheap.

GOVERNMENT & POLITICS

Life in Italy is political, and a politician's life is a good one. The highest-paid politicians in Europe, they enjoy a list of free benefits that for some reason includes cinema tickets and entrance to any football stadium in the country. Unsurprisingly many Italians are highly cynical about politicians.

The *sindaco* (mayor) of Naples is Rosa Russo Jervolino. A former Interior Minister, the Naples-born lawyer is unfairly known more for her voice than her politics. Her politics are, in fact, moderately left-wing – she represents the centre-left Ulivo coalition. Elected in

2001, she leads the city *giunta*, a group of 16 *assessori* (councillors), who hold ministerial positions as heads of municipal departments. The *assessori* are appointed from the *consiglio comunale*, a kind of city parliament.

The mayor has her office in Palazzo San Giacomo in Piazza del Plebiscito, while meetings of the *consiglio comunale* are held in the Castel Nuovo. The meetings, in the **Sala dei Baroni** (p69), are open to the public and make entertaining, if incomprehensible, viewing.

Issues which Jervolino has been facing since she replaced Antonio Bassolino, now Regional President of Campania, include traffic, *abusivismo* (illegal construction), waste disposal and crime.

ENVIRONMENT

THE LAND

Naples enjoys a fabulous natural setting. From Parco Virgiliano on the westernmost tip of Posillipo you can look east over the Bay of Naples, and round to Vesuvius and the Sorrento Peninsula; to the west lie the Bay of Pozzuoli and the Campi Flegrei. But while nature has blessed with one hand, she's cursed with the other. Looming 10km east of Naples, Mt Vesuvius is a constant threat; while underground, geological faults make earthquakes a continual possibility.

The only active volcano on the European mainland, Vesuvius (1281m) exploded into history in AD 79. At the time, however, it was not technically Vesuvius that erupted, but Mt Somma. Standing at more than twice the current height of Vesuvius, Mt Somma's peak exploded with such violence that it destroyed much of the upper mountain. Out of the shattered crater emerged the cone that today tops Mt Vesuvius.

Vesuvius last erupted in 1944. When she'll blow next is impossible to tell but scientists insist that it will happen. And when it does it'll be catastrophic. The upper reaches of the mountain are barren but the lower slopes are highly fertile and are heavily cultivated. They are also densely populated – some 700,000 people live within a 7km radius of the volcano (see p16).

On the other side of the city, the **Campi Flegrei** (p98) is a volcanic area of spectacular geological instability. The slow upward and downward movement of the earth's crust, known as *bradeyism*, has afflicted the 150 sq km area for millennia and explains why so many Roman ruins are under water. The area was originally created after a massive volcanic eruption 35,000 years ago forced magma to the earth's surface. On cooling, the magma reacted with the air to form tufa rock.

In such a geologically complex area, earthquakes remain a threat. Particularly at risk is the east of Campania where geological fault lines pass under the Apennines. The last major quake in 1980 killed 3000 people.

GREEN NAPLES

Rampant post-WWII urban development and the earthquake of 1980 haven't helped the green cause in Naples. However, things are looking up and in the last decade or so, the city's parks have been treated to a major makeover. Today there are more than 20 parks covering an area of 300 hectares. The main historic parks are the **Parco di Capodimonte** (p80), **Villa Floridiana** (p76), **Villa Comunale** (p94) and the **Parco Virgiliano** (p97).

Villa Comunale (p94)

Paid to Leave Vesuvius

In July 2004 the region of Campania paid the Vignola family of San Giorgio a Cremano €30,000 to move house.

The payout was the first to be awarded as part of the Progetto Vesuvia, a regional plan to persuade locals to move from the dangerous slopes of Mt Vesuvius.

Launched in 2003, the initiative is aimed specifically at the 700,000 people who live within the 7km radius of the volcano's crater, in the so-called 'red zone'. Under the terms of the project anyone who wants to move from the area can apply for a re-housing grant.

To meet its promises the region has budgeted €90 million for the 2003–05 period. So far it has received 3276 grant applications.

News of the Vignola move was met with relief by project organisers who had been worried that even with a €30,000 incentive people would be reluctant to move from their homes. Apart from the obvious emotional ties, many people would still face considerable financial problems in moving house. This fact was acknowledged by Assessore Marco Di Lello, the man behind the scheme, when he said that the money he was offering would only cover about quarter of the cost of a new two-bedroom flat.

To give further publicity to the project, the scheme was featured in three episodes of Italy's popular police drama La Squadra in September 2004.

The major environmental issue in Naples today is waste disposal. The subject first made headlines in May 2003, when residents set fire to some 20,000 tons of uncollected rubbish, then in summer 2004 it reared its smelly head again. This time, angry demonstrators blocked Italy's main north–south rail line to protest against plans to build two new incinerator plants. The authorities claimed that behind the protests lay the Camorra whose interests in illegal rubbish dumps would be threatened by any new incinerator plants.

However, although attention was centred on the south, the rubbish crisis is not a uniquely Neapolitan issue. Experts estimate that problems relating to waste disposal will cost Italy €350 million over the next 10 years.

URBAN PLANNING & DEVELOPMENT

The most alarming feature of Naples' post-WWII urban planning has been the lack of it. Certainly, the war left the city in urgent need of housing but not even the most pessimistic of forecasters could have predicted the lawlessness and speed with which Naples spread. Today the third-largest city in Italy (after Rome and Milan), it lies at the centre of a vast urban sprawl that extends from the Campi Flegrei in the west to the Vesuvian suburbs in the east.

Naples has always been a cramped city and today has one of the highest population densities in the world (see p11). In the constant search for new breathing space authorities turned eastwards. In the 1980s the high-tech Centro Direzionale area of glass and concrete skyscrapers seemed a stunning solution to many problems. However, 20 years on it remains unfinished and unwelcoming.

More recently, plans to assign 25,000 hectares of agricultural land for urban use have met with opposition but do at least show a willingness by the mayor to front a problem that so many of her predecessors ignored.

Arts & Architecture

Arts & Architecture

Artists in Naples have never been short of inspiration. Cursed with a turbulent past and a natural backdrop that's as deadly as it is beautiful, Naples has provided food for thought for painters, sculptors, filmmakers, writers and musicians. Over the centuries the city has been bombed, battered by earthquake, spat on by Vesuvius, crippled by disease and fought over by foreign powers. Yet nothing can dampen the creativity of its fiercely proud population. If ever proof were needed that turmoil breeds great art, Naples is it.

What follows is not intended as a chronological cultural history, rather as a look at the salient features of the city's artistic development.

PAINTING & SCULPTURE

For a city so steeped in history, the contemporary art scene in Naples is flourishing. Thanks to the efforts of former mayor Antonio Bassolino and his successor Rosa Russo Jervolino, the city council has supported art initiatives throughout the city. Most visible of all are many of Naples' new metro stations, adorned with specially commissioned works by local and international artists.

UNDERGROUND ART

Travelling by metro is never much fun, but step down into Naples' underground art stations and you'll be pleasantly surprised at what you see. The line between Piazza Dante and Vanvitelli boasts five originally and colourfully decorated stations.

In the station under Piazza Dante, the works are inspired by Italy's great 13th-century poet and his *Divine Comedy*. From Dante the line leads to Museo where the reproductions of the sculptures **Toro Farnese** (Farnese Bull; p67) and *Testa Carafa*, the black-and-white photographs by Mimmo Jodice and the bronze horse's head all pack a visual impact.

The Martedei station is a cheerful mix of mosaics, reliefs and brightly coloured panels. However, it's the next stop, Salvator Rosa, that's something special. Situated on the choking road that leads from Piazza Museo Nazionale up to Vomero, the station is an explosion of colour in an otherwise grim area. It's worth the trip just to see Mimmo and Salvatore Paladino's landscaped garden – with its free-standing sculptures, steel-and-glass spire and Roman remains – and the highly charged interior. Inside you'll find mosaics by Gianni Pisani, sculptures, murals and a row of four covered cars by Perino and Vele.

The last of the five stations, Quattro Giornate, pays homage to the *quattro giornate napoletane*, the four days in September 1943 when popular uprisings in the city drove out the German occupiers.

THE ROMANS

First founded by Greek colonialists and later adopted by Roman holidaymakers, Naples has a rich heritage of ancient art.

The Romans used painting and mosaic work, both legacies from the Etruscans and Greeks, to decorate homes from about the 2nd century BC. Many of the mosaics from Pompeii date from this period, created by skilled craftsmen from Alexandria. Although many of Pompeii's treasures are now in the **Museo Archeologico Nazionale** (p66) you can still see one of the ancient world's largest Roman paintings, the *Dionysiac Frieze*, in Pompeii's **Villa dei Misteri** (p184).

Just as many Roman mosaics were the work of foreign artists, so were early Roman sculptures which were either made by Greek sculptors or were copies of imported Greek works. A classic example is the 3rd-century **Toro Farnese** (p67) in the Museo Archeologico Nazionale.

Unlike the Greeks, who liked nothing better than a muscled nude to depict the virtues of their leaders, the Romans usually portrayed their heroes with at least a toga on. However, they still went in for art that owed more to propaganda than reality. The main exception was the portrait sculpture, which took its lead from the Etruscan warts-and-all school of artistic reality.

FROM CATACOMBS TO CATALONIA

Art in Naples really took off in a big way in the 17th century when a generation of talented artists painted the city onto the artistic map. Up until then, however, it had struggled to establish a tradition it could call its own.

Early Christian art was influenced more by its covert character than by any single artistic influence. Largely limited to secret symbols and underground paintings, the Christian painters took to the catacombs to express themselves. Some of the best and earliest examples of Neapolitan Christian art are to be found in the Catacomba di San Gennaro (p77), where San Gennaro's body is interred.

The onset of foreign rule did little to encourage home-grown artistic talent. The Angevins, for example, transformed Naples into a thriving cultural centre by importing the greatest artists of the day. Giotto worked in town between 1328 and 1334, painting Castel Capuano, Castel Nuovo and the Basilica di Santa Chiara.

Later, in the 15th century the Aragonese added their Catalan contribution to the cultural cauldron. Of the artists working in the city at the time, the best known was the Neapolitan Niccoló Antonio Colantonio (c 1420–70), whose work can be admired in the Chiesa di San Lorenzo Maggiore and San Domenico Maggiore.

GREATS OF THE 17TH CENTURY

Thanks to a dramatic population increase in the 16th century, Naples was the biggest city in Europe by 1600. To meet the demand for housing, new quarters were built and hundreds of new churches sprang up. Inevitably, there was no shortage of work for Naples' newly in-demand artists.

Certosa di San Martino (p75)

The main influence on 17th-century Neapolitan art was Caravaggio (1573–1610). A controversial character, he escaped to Naples in 1606 after killing a man in Rome and although he only stayed for a year in the city his impact was huge. His dramatic depiction of light and shade, his supreme draughtsmanship and his naturalist style had an electrifying effect on many of the city's younger artists. Take a look at his works *Flagellazione*

(Flagellation) in the Palazzo Reale di Capodimonte (p79) or *Le sette opere di Misericordia* (Seven Acts of Mercy) in the Pio Monte della Misericordia (p63) and you'll easily understand why he is still held in such high regard.

A deeply unpleasant character, Giuseppe de Ribera (1591–1654) was one of Caravaggio's main fans. A Spaniard who arrived in Naples nine years after his hero had left, Ribera was almost as well known for his violent temper and ruthless behaviour as he was for his paintings. He is said, for example, to have won a commission for the Cappella del Tesoro in the Duomo by poisoning his rival Domenichino (1581–1641) and wounding the assistant of a second competitor, Guido Reni (1575–1642).

However, he did attain artistic recognition for his elegant naturalistic style and use of colour. His *Pietà* in the Certosa di San Martino (p75) is considered a masterly example. Building on Ribera's naturalism, Naples-born Luca Giordano (1632–1705) took it further and added his own vibrant touch. An exceptionally prolific artist, Giordano's works can be seen in churches throughout the city, including the Certosa di San Martino and the Chiesa del Gesù Nuovo.

A contemporary of Giordano, Francesco Solimena (1657–1747) was also influenced by Ribera, although his use of shadow showed a clearer link with Caravaggio.

Artists continued to be in demand after the accession of the Bourbons to the Neapolitan throne in 1734. As Charles VII set about building a palace in Caserta and refurbishing the Palazzo Reale, his wife Maria Amalia began decorating the family properties. To do this she turned to a willing group of painters, including Francesco de Mura (1696–1782), Domenico Antonio Vaccaro (1678–1775) and Giuseppe Bonito (1707–89).

The master sculptor of the age was Giuseppe Sanmartino (1720–93), whose technical brilliance reached its apogee in the sensational *Cristo Velato* (Veiled Christ; 1753), now in the Cappella Sansevero (p56).

Ancient Porn Provokes Church Reaction

The Catholic Church's role in the history of Italian art is an important one. A major historical patron, today it's still a force in the art world. The Vatican's collection is among the most spectacular in Italy and the wealth of art housed in the nation's churches is staggering.

Naturally, though, the Church's tastes are conservative and the cassocked authorities take a dim view of anything they consider corrupting, which is exactly how they regarded the opening of the *Gabinetto Segreto* (Secret Chamber) in the Museo Archeologico Nazionale (p66) in 2000.

Central to the controversy was the museum's collection of 250 works of erotic art. Pillaged from Pompeii and Herculaneum, it includes a number of paintings depicting sex acts, numerous figurines of small men with large phalluses, and a small but perfectly formed statue of Pan caught in flagrante with a goat. Originally unearthed in the mid-19th century, the collection had been kept under royal lock and key for some 170 years – and if the Church had had its way it would have remained so. The decision to display it was met with ecclesiastical outrage and condemned as an obscene affront to decency.

A year later and the Church was once again spluttering with fury. In December 2001 a series of seven explicit panels were revealed to the public for the first time. The frescoes, which had been discovered in the 1950s in the Terme Suburbane in Pompeii where they remain to this day, depict perhaps the only lesbian sex scene in ancient art.

Originally situated in the unisex changing room of the bath complex, the frescoes are still the subject of debate. Some maintain that they were a taster for the 1st-floor brothel, others that they were simply put there as decoration. Whatever their purpose, the Church was not amused.

THE CITY ON CANVAS

The first panoramic painting of the city is the anonymous *Tavola Strozzi*, a depiction of Ferdinand of Aragon's fleet returning to Naples after the battle of Ischia in 1465. The frontal presentation of the city clearly shows the 15th-century cityscape dominated by the Castel Nuovo, Castel Sant'Elmo and the Certosa di San Martino.

But it wasn't until the 18th century that landscape painting came into its own. Inspired by the 1631 eruption of Mt Vesuvius, *Eruzione del Vesuvio dal ponte Maddalena* by Pierre Jacques Volaire (1729–1802) is a superb example of the emotional style that Romanticism aimed for. Hanging in the **Palazzo Reale di Capodimonte** (p79), it's a dramatic study in contrasts, combining the colours of the violent eruption with a scene of nocturnal stillness. It's a picture designed to provoke a reaction.

In contrast, the landscapes of the latter part of the century aimed for reality rather than emotion. A typical example is the visually cold but geographically exact *Campi Flegrei dal monte Epomeo* by Pietro Fabris (in Naples 1754–1804).

The 19th century saw something of a return to a more atmospheric and less formal style. Anton Sminck Pitloo (1791–1837) led the way with a lyrical and romantic touch which provided inspiration for the Posillipo school. The leading light of this movement was Giacinto Gigante (1806–76).

ARCHITECTURE

Striking modern architecture in Naples is largely noticeable by its absence. The vast number of housing blocks and council estates that sprung up in the lawless post-WWII building frenzy were grim concrete constructions designed with speed and cost in mind. Very little attention was paid to architectural finesse.

The one striking exception is the Centro Direzionale, the area of glass-and-steel skyscrapers to the east of Stazione Centrale. Today, an unattractive windswept place, it did at least represent an attempt to innovate. Designed by the Japanese architect Kenzo Tange in the 1980s, the area is home to the regional government and numerous companies and corporate bodies.

Despite Naples' sad recent record, however, the city remains rich for those interested in architecture.

THE ANCIENTS

No study of ancient architecture would be complete without a close look at southern Italy. The Greek ruins at **Cuma** (p99) tell of a thriving settlement, while the temples at **Paestum** (p203) are considered among the best surviving examples of classical Greek architecture in Italy.

In Naples itself the *centro storico* (historic centre; p54) is based on the three *decumani* (main streets) of the Graeco-Roman city of Neapolis. You can still see plenty of evidence of the ancient city, especially if you head under the ground. Dive down under the **Chiesa di San Lorenzo Maggiore** (p61) and you will find yourself walking down an eerily quiet Roman street. Similarly, the **Duomo** (p60) stands atop a series of Graeco-Roman remains and the network of tunnels that extends beneath Piazza San Gaetano dates back to ancient times.

Further afield, the **amphitheatre** (p98) in Pozzuoli is the third largest in Italy, while in Cuma the **Antro della Sibilla Cumana** (Cave of the Cumaean Sybil; p100) is steeped in legend. **Pompeii** (p181) and **Herculaneum** (p179), of course, need no introduction.

> **Top Five Arts Reads**
> - *Palaces of Naples* by Donatella Mazzoleni (2003)
> - *Art and Architecture in Italy 1600–1750* by Rudolf Wittkower (2000)
> - *In the Shadow of Vesuvius: Views of Naples from Baroque to Romanticism 1631–1830* edited by Silvia Cassani (1990)
> - *Eros in Pompeii: The Erotic Art Collection of the Museum of Naples* by Michael Grant (1975)
> - *Baroque Naples 1600–1800* edited by Jeanne Chenault Porter

ANGEVIN GOTHIC

When Charles I of Anjou took the Neapolitan throne in 1266 he was determined to transform the city into a shining example of cutting-edge culture. He called on French architects and the Angevin period was marked by the construction of the Castel Nuovo, the Chiesa di San Lorenzo, the Basilica di Santa Chiara and the Duomo.

Although largely destroyed by Allied bombs in 1943, the Basilica di Santa Chiara (p55) has been lovingly restored to its Gothic origins. Inspired by concepts of Franciscan poverty, Gagliardo Primario's original design was a classic of its time, featuring high-vaulted arches and a simplicity of décor that led Robert of Anjou's son Charles to dismiss it as a stable.

Much Angevin Gothic architecture was radically revamped by the baroque boys of the 17th century. A case in point is the 14th-century Certosa di San Martino (p75), which owes its baroque look to Cosimo Fanzago and its Angevin origins to Francesco de Vito and Tino da Camaino.

THE BAROQUE

In the centuries between the Angevins and the onset of Naples' 17th-century baroque makeover, the Aragonese extended the city walls westwards, added an Arco di Trionfo to the Castel Nuovo and worshipped at the Chiesa di Sant'Anna dei Lombardi. Continuing the city's expansion west the Spanish viceroy Don Pedro de Toledo built the Quartieri Spagnoli and Via Toledo.

But Naples owes much of its look to the extravagant skills of the baroque artists. As the city grew, so did the increasing number of religious orders seeking to use the theatrical art of the era to showcase their increasing wealth and power. A famous example is the Guglia dell'Immacolata (p57), in Piazza del Gesù Nuovo. Standing at 30m, the ornate spire was designed to be as elaborate as possible to demonstrate the power of the Jesuits who commissioned it.

The undisputed master of Neapolitan baroque was Cosimo Fanzago (1591–1678). His hand is visible in hundreds of works throughout the city. These include the Certosa di San Martino, the Guglia di San Gennaro and San Domenico, and the Basilica di San Giorgio Maggiore.

BOURBON NEOCLASSICISM

Under the Bourbons, Naples became one of Europe's most glamorous capitals. Neoclassicism was the fashionable architectural style, marking a return to the symmetrical lines and colonnades so beloved of the ancients. Piazza del Plebiscito (p73) and the Chiesa di San Francesco di Paola (p70) clearly reflect the style.

Chief among Naples' architects was Luigi Vanvitelli (1700–73), whose work in the city included the Foro Carolino, now known as Piazza Dante, and Palazzo D'Angri. He's best remembered, however, for the monumental Reggia at Caserta.

His contemporaries were also a talented, and busy, group. The leading lights included Ferdinando Fuga (1699–1788), the man responsible for the Albergo dei Poveri; Giovanni Antonio Medrano (1703–date unknown), the brains behind the Teatro San Carlo and the Palazzo Reale di Capodimonte; Ferdinando Sanfelice (1675–1748), best known for his trademark open staircases; and Domenico Antonio Vaccaro (1678–1745), whose Chiostro di Santa Chiara is an oasis of peace in the *centro storico*.

POST-UNIFICATION

The late 19th century was a period of urban renewal. Following the crippling cholera epidemic of 1884 swathes of slums were destroyed, Corso Umberto I was bulldozed through the city centre, and the upmarket residential district of Vomero was born.

Inspired by the industrial influences sweeping through Europe, Naples' two glass-and-steel shopping arcades were built as monuments to the city's modernising spirit. The more famous of the two, Galleria Umberto I (1900; p71) covers about 1000 sq metres

Galleria Umberto I (p71)

and has a glass roof that curves up to a height of 57m. A fashionable hang-out for the *belle époque* bohemian set, it was almost identical to its twin, the **Galleria Principe di Napoli** (1870–83; p65).

The turn of the century heralded in Art Nouveau, known in Italy as Liberty. The florid decoration, wrought iron and stained glass was used to good effect in many of the smart *palazzi* (mansions) in Vomero. But it was a style that the Fascists abhorred – it was too effeminate, not macho enough. Naples' Fascist architecture is centred on the area around the **Palazzo delle Poste** (p67) in Piazza G Matteotti. All hunky bare walls and linear forms, it was a style absolutely suited to the ideals of the regime.

MUSIC

Naples prides itself on its musical heritage, and well it might: its opera house is one of the most important in the world, the tradition of *la canzone napoletana* (Neapolitan song) has produced any number of classic tunes, and Italy's most famous bluesman is a Neapolitan.

Pino Daniele (1955–) started his career as a long-haired protest singer, hitting a popular chord in the late 1970s with his brand of Neapolitan blues. He has since left his city of birth to build a mainstream fortune elsewhere, but his soft high-pitched voice is still a crowd pleaser. Contemporaries Edoardo Bennato (1949–) and Daniele Sepe (1960–) are also very popular.

But these artists are not the modern face of Neapolitan music. Rather they are the forerunners of a number of local groups who have achieved national success on the back of their Neapolitan origins. The rap group 99 Posse started belting out their left-wing lyrics in the Officina 99 *centro sociale* (organised squat), while the dialect-singing dub-and-techno outfit Almamegretta collaborated with internationally famous Massive Attack on the track *Karmacoma*.

For the golden age of Neapolitan music, however, you have to turn back the clock.

Top Five Neapolitan Tracks

- 'Facendo La Storia' – 99 Posse
- 'Sempre' – Almamegretta
- 'Il Rock di Capitano Uncino' – Edoardo Bennato
- 'Napul é' – Pino Daniele
- ''O Sole Mio' – Giovanni Capurro

LA CANZONE NAPOLETANA

Anyone who's ever seen an ice-cream advert on TV has probably heard a Neapolitan song. Let's face it, who hasn't hummed along to Giovanni Capurro's 1898 classic 'O Sole Mio?' But while this is the most famous example, it is only one of the many songs that the early-20th-century Italian immigrants took with them to the far corners of the world.

No-one knows for sure when *la canzone napoletana* was born. The most credible theory is that it derives from songs sung by 13th-century washerwomen in Vomero. However, the defining moment came in 1839 when the song 'Te voglio bene assaje' (roughly translated as 'I love you loads') was released. Written by Raffaele Sacco and set to music by Donizetti, it became an instant smash hit. More than 180,000 printed copies of the song's lyrics were sold and witnesses tell of pandemonium verging on mass hysteria.

The song also launched the habit of releasing new titles at the Festa di Piedigrotta. Among subsequent songs to win universal acclaim were 'O Sole Mio' and 'Funiculì funiculà', which was released in 1881 for the inauguration of the Mt Vesuvius funicular railway.

The success of the songs was largely based on their catchy melodies and lyrics, generally in dialect, which spoke of love and death, passion and longing. They were popular, but many serious writers, including Salvatore Di Giacomo (see p26) were big fans.

The genre is still flourishing. Kept alive thanks to the likes of Roberto Murolo (1912–2003) and Sergio Bruni (1921–), it's been given a commercial pop touch by pint-sized Nino D'Angelo (1957–) and Gigi Alessio (1967–). As a visitor, though, you're more likely to hear it performed by one of the army who traipse round the city's restaurants doing a lucrative trade in tableside concerts.

OPERA

Emotional and highly theatrical, opera has always been close to the Neapolitan heart. In fact, in the 18th century Naples was the capital of the opera world. The sparkling **Teatro San Carlo** (p73) stood at the centre of the Bourbon's glittering city, attracting Europe's greatest composers. Inaugurated in 1737, the theatre has staged all the greats, including Gioachino Rossini (1792–1868), Gaetano Donizetti (1797–1848), Giuseppe Verdi (1813–1901) and Vincenzo Bellini (1801–35).

Teatro San Carlo (p73)

Considered Naples' greatest composer, Alessandro Scarlatti (1660–1725) was one of the most prolific composers of the early 18th century. He wrote some 100 operas, and as one of the leading lights of the Neapolitan school he helped establish the conventions of *opera seria* (serious opera). Opera buffs owe the *aria da capo* and the three-part overture to Scarlatti and company.

Running parallel to the formal and classical *opera seria* was the more popular *opera buffa*. Taking its cue from the Neapolitan *commedia dell'arte* (see below) much *opera buffa* was written in dialect with the emphasis on comedy rather than the love, duty and honour so favoured by *opera seria*. Classics of the genre include Mozart's *The Marriage of Figaro* (1786) and Rossini's *Barber of Seville* (1816).

THEATRE

Naples is the most theatrical city in Italy. Its streets are famously entertaining and its actors universally acclaimed – both Totò and Massimo Troisi (see p126) got their initial breaks working the city's cabaret circuit. But Naples' greatest gift to the stage is its unique theatrical heritage: playwrights Eduardo De Filippo and Roberto De Simone have achieved international recognition while remaining firmly rooted in the city's culture; *commedia dell'arte* was born in Naples in the 16th century while the music-hall tradition of *la sceneggiata* is making a modern comeback.

The most famous figure of 20th-century theatre in Naples was Eduardo De Filippo (1900–84). The son of a famous Neapolitan actor, Eduardo Scarpetta (1853–1925), he made his stage debut at the age of four and over the next 80 years became a hugely successful actor, impresario (he brought mime artist Marcel Marceau to Naples in 1965) and playwright. His body of often bittersweet work includes such classics as *Il sindaco del rione Sanità* (The Mayor of the Sanità Quarter) and *Sabato, Domenica e Lunedì* (Saturday, Sunday and Monday). The latter, a story of family jealousy around the Sunday lunch table, brilliantly depicts the lengthy preparation of a real Neapolitan *ragù* (tomato and meat sauce). Today Eduardo's son Luca (1948–) is a highly regarded theatre actor.

Roberto De Simone (1933–) is another great Neapolitan playwright and composer. He's made less of an international impact than De Filippo as much of his work is in dialect and so loses something in the translation. However, his masterpiece *La Gatta Cenerentola* (The Cat Cinderella) enjoyed a successful run in London in 1999.

Of the new generation of theatrical talent Enzo Moscato (1948–) is the leading light. Fusing a physical style with skilful use of local dialect and music, Moscato's works often provoke debate. Of his numerous plays, the most famous is the multiple award-winning *Rasoi* (Razors; 1991).

COMMEDIA DELL'ARTE

With its origins in the earthy Roman comedy theatre of *fabula Atellana*, *commedia dell'arte* dates to the 16th century. Like its Roman inspiration, it featured a set of stock characters in masks acting out a series of semi-standard situations. Based on a recipe of adultery, jealousy, old age and love, performances were often used to satirise local situations.

Popular and accessible – it was performed on temporary streetside stages by troupes of travelling actors – *commedia dell'arte* gave birth to a number of legendary characters. Chief among them was the Harlequin, whose multicoloured costume has inspired a thousand subsequent designs, and the Pulcinella.

Nowadays, the ubiquitous symbol of Naples, the Pulcinella is a complex figure who combines many of the contradictions inherent in the Neapolitan character. In his white costume and black, beak-nosed mask, he is exuberant and optimistic, cynical, lazy and melancholic. A street philosopher, he is anti-authoritarian and is often to be seen beating the local copper with a stick (hence the term slapstick). At home, however, his wife's the beater and he's the victim, much like his English descendant Mr Punch.

Naples' great tradition of popular theatre grew out of the *commedia dell'arte*. It was a tradition in which Raffaele Viviani (1888–1950) was firmly rooted. Born into a poor family,

Viviani became Naples' greatest 19th-century dramatist. His use of dialect and his subject matter – the Neapolitan working class – won him local success and the enmity of the Mussolini regime.

Running parallel to the theatrical tradition was that of *la canzone napoletana*. The two came together in the music-hall style of *la sceneggiata*, developed between WWI and WWII. Performances were based on a typical mix of Neapolitan themes – family, honour, injustice – and were unashamedly sentimental. It's now enjoying something of a renaissance, and the main man on the scene is the chubby crooner Mario Merola (1934–).

For a more eclectic musical extravaganza, Peppe Barra (1944–) combines modern electronic sounds, traditional songs and stunning visuals to produce a distinct and unnerving style.

LITERATURE

Writers and poets have long enjoyed a fruitful relationship with Naples. From the 17th century onwards European authors have been falling over themselves to praise the city. In 1663 the great Spanish poet Cervantes described Naples as the best city in the world; a sentiment that Stendhal echoed 200 years later when he judged it the most beautiful in the world. In 1775 the Marquis de Sade claimed, a little unbelievably, to be shocked by the habits of the Neapolitans, while in the mid-19th century Charles Dickens wrote of the theatrical life of the city's squalid streets.

EARLY WRITINGS

Accounts of Naples' early days are steeped in legend. Much of this myth was due to the writings of Virgil (70–19 BC). The Roman spent a happy period in Naples and is buried in the city (at least his tomb is here). His rollicking *Aeneid* tells of how Aeneas escapes from Troy, visits the Sybil in Cuma, pops down into the underworld via Lago di Averno and finishes up founding Rome.

Some 300 years later Naples was a thriving cultural centre. Among the crowd of Angevin courtiers were Francesco Petrarch (1304–74) and Giovanni Boccaccio (1313–75). Boccaccio, who is said to have based his character Fiammetta on Mary of Anjou, set his most famous work, *The Decameron*, near Naples. A kind of Italian *Canterbury Tales*, the book tells how a group of seven women and three men avoid a plague epidemic by escaping to a rural villa. To while away the time each person tells a story on each of the 10 days they spend in the villa. And like Chaucer's stories, many of the tales were a little too spicy for the Church's tastes.

Fast forward another 300 years and you find Giambattista Basile (1575–1642) doing his best to amuse the 17th-century reading public. Considered the father of Neapolitan literature, Basile wrote predominantly in dialect and is best known for his masterpiece *Lu cunto de li cunti* (*Il racconto dei racconti* in Italian, or a 'Tale of Tales'). Translated into Italian, English and German and beloved of the Brothers Grimm, the book was the first written collection of the tales traditionally told by Neapolitan storytellers in the 10 days following Epiphany.

POETRY

Although not a Neapolitan, Giacomo Leopardi (1798–1837) is buried in Naples, alongside Virgil in the Parco Vergiliano. Inspired by Naples' violent nature, his poem *La Ginestra* tells of a fragile but beautiful flower's vain attempts to resist the onslaught of lava from the mountain destroyer Vesuvius. An allegory of man's dignified but ultimately futile struggle against the destructive forces of nature, the poem is typical of Leopardi's melancholic existential style.

More jolly by far is the work of Naples' greatest poet, Salvatore Di Giacomo (1860–1934). A one-time medical student and journalist, Di Giacomo is well known for his verse set to music, although he also wrote short stories, plays, operas and histories. Often written in dialect, his work inevitably loses in translation, although his volume *Poesie e Novelle* (Poems and Stories) still provides an interesting glimpse into how he saw his city and its people.

THE ISLANDS

The beautiful islands that rise out of the Bay of Naples are a feature of many literary works. A Roman by birth, Elsa Morante (1912–85) set *L'Isola di Arturo* (Arturo's Island) on Procida. The magnificent colours, the sea and its smells provide the wonderfully vivid backdrop to the story of young Arturo's harsh life on the island.

In contrast, everything's a breeze for the Swedish doctor, writer and animal-lover Axel Munthe, whose autobiography *The Story of San Michele* has become a classic Capri read. The doctor spent a long time on the island and was an enthusiastic advocate of its simple pleasures. Fellow fans of the island included Maxim Gorky, Graham Greene and Norman Douglas. WH Auden, meanwhile, ruled the roost over Ischia's gay expat colony.

> **Top Five Neapolitan Reads**
> - *The Aeneid* by Virgil (19 BC)
> - *La Virtù de Checchina* by Matilde Serao (1884)
> - *The Story of San Michele* by Axel Munthe (1929)
> - *L'Isola di Arturo* by Elsa Morante (1957)
> - *Così Fan Tutti* by Michael Dibdin (1996)

MODERN DAYS

A rival of the Sardinian author Grazia Deledda for the Nobel Prize for Literature, Greek-born Matilde Serao (1856–1927) is considered to be one of Naples' great writers. A journalist, Serao specialised in chronicling the lives of the long-suffering Neapolitans. In her short story *La Virtù de Checchina* (Checchina's Virtue), she lyrically describes the torment of Checchina as she struggles to reconcile the squalor of her everyday life with her rich fantasies.

In recent times, Naples has become a fashionable setting for detective thrillers. One of the best is *Così Fan Tutti* by Michael Dibdin (1996), written in English. Featuring Italy's most imaginatively named detective, Aurelio Zen, and an operatic cast of gangsters, prostitutes, sailors and rubbish collectors, it's a murder mystery that unashamedly plays on every stereotype of Naples' grimy underworld.

CINEMA & TV

As Sophia Loren celebrated her 70th birthday in 2004 she couldn't help but look back on her illustrious career. Born and brought up in Pozzuoli, the diva starred in many of Italy's classic post-war films, often acting alongside Marcello Mastroianni (1924–96). A prize example is the part she played in *Ieri, Oggi, Domani* (Yesterday, Today, Tomorrow; 1963) as a black-market cigarette seller who is forced to get pregnant at least five times to avoid prison. Mastroianni is the exhausted father and Vittorio De Sica (1901–74) the director. Born in Naples, De Sica is better known, however, for his 1948 neorealist masterpiece *Ladri di Biciclette* (Bicycle Thieves).

Although Naples' cinematic history can't compare with the city's vibrant theatrical tradition, it's not without its greats. Dominating Italy's comedic output, Totò (1898–1967) is a Neapolitan legend. A workaholic impoverished aristocrat, nobody was better able to embody Italy's post-war struggles.

The portrayal of struggle is central to much of Naples' cinema. In his debut film *Ricomincio da Tre* (I'm Starting from Three; 1980) Massimo Troisi humorously tackles the problems faced by Neapolitans forced to head north for work. Troisi was the first of a new wave of Neapolitan directors keen to explore the city and its difficulties. Antonio Capuano (1945–), Mario Martone (1959–) and Pappi Corsicato (1960–) have all turned their cameras onto the city's grim urban realities.

In contrast, Naples and its environs have often been used by foreign directors to provide a colourful Mediterranean backdrop: *The Talented Mr Ripley* was partly filmed in Procida, Billy Wilder chose Ischia for his comedy *Avanti!*, while the Reggia in Caserta was used by George Lucas for *Star Wars 1: The Phantom Menace*.

As to TV, the less said the better. Naples' most famous small-screen production is Italy's top soap *Un Posto al Sole* (A Place in the Sun), which tells of life in an upmarket block of flats in Posillipo. Otherwise, local channels pump out a steady stream of junk which will not appeal unless you like middle-aged magicians with big hair or bored-looking bikini models.

For a brief introduction to Neapolitan cinema try these films:

L'Oro di Napoli (The Gold of Naples; 1954; Vittorio De Sica) A who's who cast of Neapolitan greats – Totò, Sophia Loren, Eduardo De Filippo and Vittorio De Sica – star in five episodes of city life. The second episode combines Sophia Loren and pizza in a tasty tale of love and a lost ring.

Le Mani Sulla Città (Hands Over the City; 1963; Francesco Rosi) This powerful condemnation of Naples' corrupt post-war building boom won the Leone d'Oro prize at the Venice film festival. The cast of amateur actors is headed by Rod Steiger.

Ricomincio da Tre (I'm Starting from Three; 1980; Massimo Troisi) Starring alongside his chum in comedy Lello Arena, Troisi plays a Neapolitan floundering in Florence. The humour is bittersweet Troisi and the message sadly relevant.

Un Complicato Intrigo Di Donne, Vicoli e Delitti (Camorra: A Story of Streets, Women and Crime; 1986; Lina Wertmüller) Roman-born Wertmüller's aggressive and angry take on the Camorra and Naples. The story centres on an uprising led by the mothers of the local Mafia's drug-addled lower echelons.

Libera (Free; 1992; Pappi Corsicato) Often compared to Pedro Almodòvar, Corsicato is flamboyant, bizarre and colourful. This, his debut film, features a cast of transsexual parents, unwitting porn stars and wedding singers in three short stories.

L'Amore Molesto (Nasty Love; 1995; Mario Martone) A harrowing mystery set against Naples' cruel underbelly. At the heart of the story is the relationship between a daughter and her murdered mother.

Luna Rossa (Red Moon; 2001; Antonio Capuano) Claustrophobic, edgy and oppressive, Capuano's study of a Camorra family trapped in conflict makes grim viewing. Critically acclaimed on its release, it tells of murder, incest and betrayal.

Food & Drink

Food & Drink

To a Neapolitan there's no such thing as Italian food. There's Neapolitan food and Roman food. Piedmont has a strong gastronomic tradition, and Puglia's diet is trendy and healthy, but Italian food? There's no such thing. Italy's food map remains obstinately regional and foodies tied to their territory.

But there are some constants that even the most locally minded chef would acknowledge: all Italians eat pasta and tomato sauce, pizza is served everywhere from Milan to Palermo, and coffee is the Italian drink of choice. Put this to a Neapolitan though, and they'll tell you that the best tomato sauce is made in Campania, that pizza is a Neapolitan invention and that there's no decent coffee served anywhere north of Naples' *tangenziale* (ring road).

This typically partisan view contributes to the role that food plays in Italian life. It's about taking pride in what you do, celebrating your traditions and sharing your table with friends and family; but above all it's about pure, unrefined pleasure. The simple fact is that Neapolitans enjoy food with a passion that is both uniquely Neapolitan and very Italian.

HISTORY

Naples has been a jewel in many crowns. In its 3000-year history it's been a Roman holiday resort, a cosmopolitan centre of medieval culture and a glittering European capital. And as the foreign rulers came and went so they left their mark – on the art and architecture, on the local dialect and on the food.

In the very early days, it was the Greeks who introduced olive trees, vines and durum wheat to Italy. Later on, the Byzantines and Arabs from nearby Sicily brought with them the pine nuts and almonds, raisins and honey that they used to stuff their vegetables. Pasta arrived in the 12th century courtesy of Arab traders, while the 16th-century Spanish rulers imported the tomato from their New World colonies.

During Naples' Bourbon period (1734–1860), two parallel gastronomic cultures developed – that of the opulent Spanish monarchy and that of the streets, the *cucina povera*. And just as the former was elaborate and rich, so the latter was simple and healthy.

The food of the poor was largely based on vegetables grown on the fertile volcanic plains around Naples. Aubergines (eggplants), artichokes, courgettes (zucchini), tomatoes and peppers were among the staples, while milk from sheep, cows and goats was used to make cheese. Flat breads imported from Greek and Arab lands were also popular. Meat and fish, however, were expensive and reserved for special occasions.

Meanwhile in the court kitchens, the top French cooks of the day were working to feed the insatiable appetites of the Bourbon monarchy. History tells how Maria Carolina, the headstrong wife of King Ferdinand I, was so impressed by her sister Marie Antoinette's court in Versailles that she asked to borrow some chefs. The French cooks obviously took to the Neapolitan air, creating among other things *babà* (a sponge soaked in rum), *sfogliatelle* (puff pastry filled with ricotta and candied fruit) and *zeppole* (fried dough served with custard cream).

A Pizza History

To watch a Neapolitan *pizzaiola* (pizza maker) in action is to watch a master at work. Dressed from head to toe in white, the *pizzaiola* dances with an economy of movement that comes from endlessly repeating the same actions. The ball of dough is taken from the pre-prepared collection and slapped onto the floured marble surface. It's prodded and pulled into a circular shape, hung over the forearm and slapped around a bit, tossed up into the air and then laid down ready for the topping. To the dough a spoonful of tomato sauce, a handful of chopped mozzarella and a few leaves of fresh basil are added. Olive oil is splashed on before the floppy disc is placed in the *forgno a legna* (wood-fired oven). After one minute and 15 seconds the *pizzaiola* reaches into the oven with his wooden paddle, extracts the bubbling pizza and slides it onto a waiting plate.

Naples' most famous contribution to world cuisine is startlingly simple. A derivation of the flat breads of ancient Greece and Egypt, the pizza was already a popular street snack by the time the 16th-century Spanish colonialists introduced the tomato to Italy.

The modern pizza, however, dates to 1889 and a royal visit to Naples. In order to impress the visiting King Umberto I and his wife Queen Margherita, Raffaelle Esposito based his creation of tomato, mozzarella and basil on the red, white and green flag of the newly unified Italy. The resulting topping met with the queen's approval and was subsequently named in her honour.

Today there are hundreds of pizza toppings but traditionalists claim you really can't top the original pizza margherita made by a true Neapolitan *pizzaiola*. So it's anyone's guess what they'd make of the fact that in 2003, the man voted the best pizza maker in Naples was Japanese.

But while Maria Carolina was toying with the exquisite experiments of her French cooks, her husband was stuffing his face with *maccheroni* (macaroni) and tomato sauce. A renowned boor, King Ferdinand I apparently took great delight in being served pasta during opera performances at the Teatro San Carlo. Foregoing cutlery, he would use his hands to shovel in the *maccheroni,* trying as best he could to shower the sparkling uniforms of his attending courtiers.

CULTURE

To the Neapolitans, food is one of the great joys of life. And in Naples it need not cost a bomb to eat well. In fact, many of the things the locals cook best are simple street snacks. A slice of freshly cooked focaccia, a bag of crispy fried vegetables, a *palla di riso* (rice ball) are all delicious and all can be eaten on the hoof. But that's not to say that Neapolitan cuisine is all about snacking. Certainly fast food in Naples is among the best in the world, but it's only one side of the gastronomic coin.

To really get the full taste of the Neapolitan art of cooking you need to step into a local home, preferably on a Sunday. Here you'll find the great pasta dishes – the *pasta al ragù* (pasta with tomato and meat sauce) – and magnificent main courses such as the wonderfully rich *parmigiana di melanzane* (baked aubergine with cheese). It's also here that you'll see the uninhibited pleasure that the locals take in eating a good meal in good company.

Come to Naples looking to lose weight, however, and you could be disappointed. To many the south of Italy is synonymous with the Mediterranean diet – that healthy combination of fruit, vegetables and olive oil. And yes, the quantity and quality of the fruit and veg served in Naples is impressive, but it takes an iron will to choose the boiled veg over the fried version or to turn down the selection of artfully decorated desserts put there just to tempt you.

Restraint is not a Neapolitan characteristic, and when confronted with such temptations the locals know which choice to make. Unfortunately, the results are showing. According to a survey carried out by local education authorities in the 2004 summer, 38% of Neapolitan children are overweight or, to put it another way, they're the fattest in Europe.

ETIQUETTE

As a foreigner any faux pas you make will be forgiven as long as you've enjoyed your meal and done so visibly. The rule that you must enjoy is one of the few that you break at your peril, especially if you're eating with an Italian family.

In general, though, eating etiquette in Naples provides few surprises to Westerners. The rules regarding which knife and fork to use, talking with your mouth full and so on are the same here as they are in New York, London or Melbourne; see the boxed text (above) for a list.

Business meals are an artform in Italy. Generally, little business is done and the chat is friendly and relaxed. There's plenty of time to finish your work later.

One thing about which there is no consensus, however, is smoking. Technically, there is a law banning smoking in all public places but it is hardly respected. Everywhere you'll see people smoking and restaurants are no exception.

HOW NEAPOLITANS EAT

Neapolitans eat with gusto. They eat fast and they eat a lot. They also like to eat in company. Mealtimes are social occasions and it's not uncommon to see three generations of a family sitting around a table together.

The main meal of the Italian day is traditionally *pranzo* (lunch). While this is changing because of modern working practices, it's still common for office workers to return home at lunchtime. On Sunday, however, *pranzo* remains the main highlight of the day. There'll be a pasta dish, meat and/or fish, pastries, fruit and liberal helpings of wine. During the week though, many people simply grab a piece of pizza or a *panino* (bread roll).

But if lunches are big, breakfasts are not. The usual *primo colazione* (breakfast) consists of little more than a cappuccino or espresso and a *cornetto*, basically a less flaky croissant filled with *cioccolata* (chocolate), *marmellata* (marmalade) or *crema* (custard cream).

The evening meal, *cena*, is traditionally smaller than *pranzo* although, again, this is changing. In the old days, it probably consisted of a single plate of pasta or some ham with salad or vegetables.

Neapolitans eat later than those in northern climes, especially when eating out. You'll often see queues outside popular restaurants at 11pm while the same place at 7pm would be half empty. Pizzerie also attract huge crowds, although the turnover is quicker and the clientele often younger. On Saturday nights, in particular, pizzerie are full of adolescent couples enjoying a romantic meal out before joining their mates at the disco.

STAPLES & SPECIALITIES

A typical Italian meal consists of an antipasto, a *primo piatto*, a *secondo piatto* with *contorno*, *dolci*, fruit, coffee and liqueur.

ANTIPASTO

Antipasto includes a dazzling array of dishes which can often constitute meals in themselves. A popular dish is *verdure sott'olio* (vegetables in olive oil), usually peppers, courgettes or aubergines. Peppers and tomatoes might also be served stuffed with a mix of capers, olives, anchovies, bread crumbs, garlic, basil and parsley. Seafood antipasti range from *acciughe/alici marinata* (marinated anchovies) to *insalata di polpo* (octopus salad) and *impepata di cozze* (peppered mussels). You'll also often find a selection of fried nibbles that might include *palle di riso*, various fried vegetables and *mozzarelle in carrozza*, small deep-fried mozzarella sandwiches to which anchovies are added.

PRIMO PIATTO

The *primo piatto* is generally a pasta or rice dish. Not surprisingly for a city that gave the world spaghetti and boasts the tastiest tomatoes in Italy, many *primo piatti* are based on a combination of pasta and tomato. A classic is *maccheroni al ragù* (macaroni in a tomato and meat sauce), with the *ragù* left to simmer for hours prior to serving. Another favourite is *pasta al forno* (baked pasta), a combination of macaroni, tomato sauce, mozzarella and, depending on the recipe, hard-boiled egg, meatballs and sausage. The most colourfully named pasta dish in Naples is *spaghetti alla puttanesca* (whore's spaghetti) – spaghetti served with a sauce of tomatoes, black olives, capers and anchovies. Some cooks like to tart this up with a dash of red chilli.

Two other dishes to try are *spaghetti alla vongole* (spaghetti with clams) and *sartù di riso*, rice baked with mince, mozzarella, peas, chicken giblets, mushrooms, sausage and ham.

SECONDO PIATTO

Naples is less famous for its meat and fish main courses than for its pasta. Fish is served baked, grilled or fried, and is usually as fresh as the morning's catch. Two favourite seafood dishes are *polpi alla luciana*, essentially baby octopuses cooked in tomatoes, garlic and olive oil, and *baccalà alla partenopea*, fried dried cod served with a Neapolitan sauce of tomatoes, capers and black olives.

Meat dishes tend to be the stock Italian mainstays – steaks, *costolette* (usually a piece of veal cooked in breadcrumbs) and sausage.

INSALATI & CONTORNI

If you haven't had any stuffed vegetables as an antipasto you can try them as a *contorno* (side dish). Classics include *pepperoni imbottiti* (peppers), *pomodori ripieni* (tomatoes) and *melanzane ripiene* (aubergines).

Of the salads, the one absolutely not to miss is the *insalata caprese*. How a simple mix of sliced tomato, mozzarella, olive oil, salt and a couple of basil leaves can taste so good is a mystery that goes well beyond the realms of science.

STAPLES

Pasta

The stereotype is true – Italians eat pasta in enormous quantities. Supermarkets dedicate entire aisles to it, while TV cooks repeatedly demonstrate how it should be cooked in salted water and served so that it is slightly crunchy when you bite into it – *al dente*. There is no greater crime to an Italian cook than unsalted, overcooked pasta.

Pasta is divided into *pasta fresca* (fresh pasta), which is eaten within a few days of

Pasta comes in all shapes and sizes

Travel Your Tastebuds

To taste the best of Naples, you could try:

- **Pizza** Where better to taste pizza than in the city that created it.
- **Mozzarella di bufala** The ethereally perfumed, freshest-tasting cheese imaginable. The most memorable way to eat it is in *insalata caprese*, a salad with tomato, basil and just a touch of olive oil.
- **Spaghetti alla vongole** A classic Neapolitan dish of tiny clams with *al dente* spaghetti and garlic.
- **Sfogliatella** Naples' classic *dolce* of pastry, ricotta and cinnamon.
- **Limoncello** This sweet lemon liqueur is the signature drink of the Amalfi Coast.

purchase, and *pasta secca* (dried pasta), which can be stored for as long as you want. Naples is famous for its *pasta secca*, the most obvious examples of which are spaghetti, *maccheroni*, *penne* (smallish tubes cut at an angle) and *rigatoni* (similar to penne but with ridges on them).

Although the Neapolitans claim to have invented spaghetti, no-one knows who first created pasta. *Pasta secca* was first introduced into Sicily in the 12th century by Arab traders who'd developed it for use on their desert caravans. From Sicily it came to Naples where, in the 17th century, it took off in a big way.

During the 17th century the population of Naples increased dramatically, putting pressure on the food supply. At the same time the invention of a mechanised press meant that pasta could be produced in greater quantities at lower costs. The dry windy Campania climate provided the ideal conditions for drying pasta, and it soon became the popular food of choice.

But it wasn't until Gennaro Spadaccini invented the four-pronged fork in the early 18th century that the nobility started eating pasta. A century later it was first combined with tomato and its place in the pantheon of world cuisine was ensured. The first industrial pasta plant opened just south of Naples in Torre Annunziata in 1840.

Pasta secca is, and always has been, made from *semolino* (durum wheat) flour and water and is often served with vegetable-based sauces, which are generally less rich than the traditional *pasta fresca* sauces.

Fruit & Vegetables

Until pasta became readily available in the 17th century the Neapolitans were known as *mangiafoglie* (leaf eaters). Their diet was based on the rich fruit and vegetable crops of the volcanic plains that surround Naples. It still is to a large degree, with the tomato providing the perfect partner for pasta.

The most famous and most cultivated tomato of all is the San Marzano. Its sauce, *conserva di pomodoro*, is made from super-ripe tomatoes, cut and left to dry in the sun for at least two days to concentrate the flavour. This is the sauce that perfumes the world's best pizzas and makes the *parmigiana di melanzane* indecently good.

Other vegetables that are cultivated in Campania include artichokes, asparagus, fennel, aubergines and peppers. Fruit is equally abundant. The most widespread is the lemon, which grows on the steep slopes of the Amalfi Coast and Sorrento Peninsula.

Cheese

Water buffalo are not indigenous to Italy. But *mozzarella di bufala* is, and the best you'll ever taste is made in Campania. It's the high fat and protein in the buffalo milk that gives it its distinctive pungent flavour, so often absent in the versions sold abroad. Mozzarella made from cow's milk has a milder taste and is known as *fior di latte* (flower of milk).

For something completely different, *caciocavallo*, a bulbous pear-shaped cheese made from ewe's milk, is often to be found hanging in delis, while *scamorze* is a cow's-milk cheese that is usually sold smoked.

Seafood

This port town has always had a close attachment to the sea, and despite overfishing the Tyrrhenian Sea still provides an abundance of edible goodies. The best *insalata di mare* (seafood salad) is found here, although versions exist all over Italy. Besides a large variety of fish, including grouper, sea bass and swordfish, the *aragoste* (crayfish) are highly regarded, as are the *cozze* (mussels) and *vongole* (clams). *Acciughe* (anchovies) also crop up in a number of dishes.

Dolci

Naples' most famous *dolce* (sweet) is the flaky pastry *sfogliatella*, similar to a Danish pastry. Filled with ricotta and candied fruit and scented with cinnamon, it's delicious when eaten hot off the baker's tray. *Sfogliatelle* come in a few forms: a softer, doughier one, a deep-fried version and the justifiably popular crispy version. Sweet-toothed travellers should also give the rum-soaked sponge *babà* a go, or try the deep-fried *zeppole*.

DRINKS

COFFEE

Neapolitans are justly proud of their coffee. They'll tell you it's the best in Italy and they may have a point. Although many bars and cafés use the same coffee machines that are used in the rest of the country, the espresso that drips out of the Neapolitan models seems somehow darker and richer than everyone else's. They're certainly dangerously addictive.

There are many combinations of coffee served in Naples but the most common are: *un caffè* (an espresso), *un caffè macchiato* (an espresso with a drop of milk) and a cappuccino. For a more watered down coffee ask for a *caffè lungo* or a *caffè Americano*. In summer a *cappuccino freddo* (a cold cappuccino) is a wonderfully refreshing drink.

WATER

Italians are the biggest consumers of bottled water in the world. It's a modern habit that in Naples has its roots in the *aquafrescai* (fresh water) stalls and the folkloristic figure of the wandering water seller with a terracotta tank slung over his shoulder.

However, tap water is fine to drink. Water from street fountains is OK, too, and the wonderful lemon- or coffee-flavoured crushed ice drinks, *granite*, are a speciality.

Un caffè

WINE

Campania's wine-making traditions go back to ancient times, and Renaissance writers apparently loved the local vintages. The modern wines, however, are noted more for their quantity than quality. Still, the best of the bunch are produced for the local market and make very pleasant drinking.

The most important are Greco di Tufo, a crisp fruit-flavoured white; Lacryma Christi (Christ's Tears), a once great white that has suffered through overproduction; and the region's top red, Taurasi, sometimes referred to as the Barolo of the south.

LIMONCELLO

Limoncello is a yellow lemon-based drink that either has a zestful taste and mild kick, or a sickly sweet chemical flavour. The best is made with lemons from the Amalfi Coast, water, alcohol and sugar. It's traditionally served in a frozen glass after dinner.

CELEBRATING WITH FOOD

Neapolitans love to celebrate and they love to eat so it's only natural that the two go hand in hand. At an Italian party there's always a huge amount of food and a host would rather run out of booze than have guests go hungry. Christenings, first communions and weddings are big events and are often celebrated with an extravagance that would impress a Roman emperor.

Italy's annual festival calendar is a full one and throughout the year you will find an inordinate number of festivals dedicated to everything from patron saints to artichokes. The big religious events are celebrated with traditional dishes: fish is served on *La Vigilia* (Christmas Eve), while *Pasqua* (Easter) is the time for a dove-shaped cake called *la colomba* and mountains of chocolate eggs. In Naples, celebrations of the Festa di San Giuseppe (19 March; also Father's Day in Italy) are accompanied with copious quantities of *zeppole*.

While just about every festival has food involved, many are dedicated entirely to food. These are called *sagre* and are usually celebrations of local specialities such as hazelnuts, sausages, white wine, fish and broad beans.

WHERE TO EAT & DRINK

Eateries are divided into several categories. At the most basic level a *tavola calda* serves pre-prepared pasta, meat and vegetable dishes canteen-style. The quality is usually fine, although dishes tend to be heavy on the olive oil. A pizzeria obviously specialises in pizza, but might also offer a range of antipasti and pasta. On the whole pizzerie are more informal than restaurants and the turnaround is quick. These are not places to go and linger lovingly over your post-meal coffee, as you'll soon have a waiter asking if you'd like the bill.

For a glass of wine your best bet is an *enoteca*, a wine bar that usually offers a choice of delicatessen-type snacks or a couple of hot dishes. Similarly cafés will often have a menu of light meals and *panini*.

For a sit-down meal of pasta and meat or fish you'll want a trattoria or a *ristorante* (restaurant). The difference between the two is now fairly blurred, although as a general rule you'll pay more at a *ristorante*. Traditionally, trattorie were simple, family-run places that offered a basic menu of local dishes at affordable prices. Thankfully many still are. For gastronomic innovation and artistic presentation head for a *ristorante*.

Trattorie and *ristoranti* should legally post their menus outside the front door. However, an absence of one doesn't mean much. In fact, much of the best food is served in places that don't even have a menu on the inside either. The waiter will simply explain what's on the menu. Patience and goodwill are the keys to a good meal here. Still, it's always worth asking for a menu even if one's not immediately offered.

There is not a big drinking culture in Naples, although there are plenty of bars and cafés. These range from smart designer places to hole-in-the-wall drinking dens. For an ice cream *gelaterie* abound, while the sweet-toothed will have fun in the well-stocked *pasticcerie*.

Restaurants and trattorie usually open for lunch from noon to 3pm and in the evening from about 7pm to 11pm. Many cafés are open all day from early to late, while the fashionable drinking bars often open around 6pm for aperitifs and stay open until the early hours.

VEGETARIANS & VEGANS

Although vegetarianism is not specifically catered to in Naples, vegetarians shouldn't have too many problems. The abundant choice of high-quality vegetables means that many pasta dishes, pizzas and antipasti feature veg in some form or other. Similarly, salads are tasty and served in most places. However, you'll need to watch out that there isn't an anchovy or two hidden away somewhere or that a piece of ham hasn't slipped in. Also check that your tomato sauce hasn't been cooked with meat in it. Ask for *senza carne o pesce* (without meat or fish).

Vegans, however, are in for a tougher time. Cheese is widespread – to avoid it request *senza formaggio* (without cheese) – and pasta fresca is made with eggs.

CHILDREN

Neapolitans love children and they're welcome just about everywhere. In very few places, however, will you find a special children's menu. Most parents simply order a *mezzo piatto* (half plate) of something on the regular menu. If you find nothing suitable most places will do a simple *pasta e pomodori* (pasta and tomato sauce) on request or will tailor a dish to suit your child's tastes. Neapolitans are never afraid to say exactly how they want their food prepared, and nor should you be.

Many places have a highchair on request, although check in advance to make sure. For more on travelling with kids, see p210.

QUICK EATS

Snacking is a true pleasure in Naples. The quality of takeaway pizza and deep-fried nibbles is excellent and the number of outlets high. Be warned though, popular takeaway places get very crowded at meal times. For a tasty and inexpensive lunch you could do a lot worse than picking up a €3/4 bag of fried goodies or a slice of pizza and a bottle of beer.

Fried nibbles for sale

EAT YOUR WORDS

For pronunciation guidelines, see p224.

Useful Phrases

Following are some phrases you may need while dining out in Naples.

I'd like to reserve a table.
   vo-ray ree-ser-*va*-re oon *ta*-vo-lo

Vorrei riservare un tavolo.

I'd like the menu, please.
   vo-ray eel me-*noo* per fa-*vo*-re

Vorrei il menù, per favore.

Do you have a menu in English?
   a-*ve*-te oon me-*noo* (*skree*-to) een een-*gle*-ze

Avete un menù (scritto) in inglese?

What would you recommend?
   ko-za mee kon-*see*-lya

Cosa mi consiglia?

I'd like a local speciality.
   vo-ray *oo*-na spe-cha-lee-*ta* dee *kwe*-sta re-*jo*-ne

Vorrei una specialità di questa regione.

Please bring the bill.
   mee *por*-ta eel *kon*-to per fa-*vo*-re

Mi porta il conto, per favore?

I'm a vegetarian/vegan.
   so-no ve-je-ta-*lya*-no/a

Sono vegetaliano/a.

History

History

The history of Naples spans the history of Western civilisation. From the time a settlement was founded on the site of a siren's grave to the modern-day metropolis that Naples is today, some 3000 years have passed – three millennia in which the Neapolitans have lived under numerous foreign masters and endured earthquakes, volcanoes and disease. Naples has been Europe's largest city, a glamorous capital of aristocrats, artists and poets. It has also been a city of crime, corruption and scandal, a byword for anarchy.

THE RECENT PAST

In May 2003 images of black smoke billowing through the streets of Naples made the Italian front pages. Angry residents, fed up with the inability of the city's refuse services to clean the streets, had decided *basta* (enough) and set fire to the rotting rubbish piled up on street corners. Commentators muttered darkly about criminal tactics linked to the lucrative waste-disposal business; residents screamed that they just wanted their streets clean again. It was a very Neapolitan drama.

The rubbish crisis, which was still making news more than 12 months later, is just one of the major headaches that Rosa Russo Jervolino has had to contend with since becoming Naples' first woman mayor in 2001. Representing the centre-left *Ulivo* (Olive Branch) coalition, her election was a rare victory for the left wing in the year that Silvio Berlusconi and his right-wing *Casa della Libertà* (House of Liberty) romped to victory in Italy's general election. A former Interior Minister with a piercing voice, Jervolino was stepping into the very big shoes of Antonio Bassolino, a key figure in Naples' recent past.

THE RENAISSANCE

A former Communist, Bassolino was the driving force behind the so-called Neapolitan Renaissance of the mid-1990s. But what is now history must have looked impossible when he took the reins of civic power in 1993. Naples was in a mess.

Already weakened by decades of crime and mismanagement, Campania was hit by a devastating earthquake on 27 November 1980. Three thousand people were killed and thousands more left homeless. The response was rapid and soon billions of lire were pouring into the region. But just as quickly as the money arrived it was siphoned off by the rapacious Camorra, the Neapolitan Mafia (see p11 for more information). In the decade that followed *abusivismo* (illegal construction) flourished and public services virtually ceased to exist.

It couldn't go on and in 1992 the *Mani Pulite* (Clean Hands) campaign kicked into gear. What had started as an investigation into bribery at an old-peoples' home in Milan quickly grew into a nationwide crusade against corruption. Industry bosses and politicians were investigated, some imprisoned, and former prime minister Bettino Craxi fled Italy to avoid prosecution. In Naples, the city voted its approval by electing Bassolino whose promises to smarten up the city and fight corruption were exactly what the weary Neapolitans wanted to hear.

In the seven years that followed Naples began to clean up its act. After being used as a huge car park for years, Piazza del Plebiscito was pedestrianised; a new arts festival, the Maggio dei Monumenti, was inaugurated; and Naples' new metro stations were brightened up with a dash of modern art. In 1994 world leaders met in Naples for the G7 summit. It was one of the city's finest hours and today Bill Clinton is still remembered with affection by many Neapolitans.

TIMELINE	8th century BC	680 BC	474 BC
	Greeks establish colony at Cuma	Parthenope founded	Cumans found Neapolis (New Town)

Top Five History Reads

- *Naples'44: An Intelligence Officer in the Italian Labyrinth* by Norman Lewis (2002) – umpteenth reprinting of Lewis' much quoted account of wartime Naples
- *See Naples and Die: The Camorra and Organized Crime* by Tom Behan (2002) – Mafia junkies can mainline on Naples' criminal history
- *Modern Naples 1799–1999* edited by John Santore (2000) – collection of travellers' accounts, newspaper articles, diary entries and illustrations
- *Italian Journey* by Goethe (1992) – WH Auden's translation of Goethe's travel journal
- *The Bourbons of Naples* by Harold Acton (1956) – classic account of Naples' Bourbon monarchy

Winning a second term in 1997, Bassolino couldn't keep up the amazing momentum he'd started, and things began to slow down. In 2000 he was elected president of the Campania region in a move which many people considered a political fudge to remove him from the day-to-day running of the city.

The four years since Jervolino succeeded Bassolino have not been easy. In April 2002 eight policemen were arrested on charges of torture. According to prosecutors they had abused up to 80 anti-globalisation protestors arrested after rioting at a 2001 government conference. Political chaos ensued as right-wing leaders leapt to defend the police, accusing prosecutors of left-wing bias. As if that wasn't enough, a year later, in 2003, the rubbish crisis exploded into the headlines.

The woes of the city football team (see p12) have also been making life tough for Jervolino. Following a long and bitter bankruptcy proceeding, a Naples court ruled that Napoli could contest the 2004–05 season in Italy's third division and not, as the fans had demanded, in *Serie* B (the second division). This is a decision that can only augur tough times ahead for the mayor. As another high-profile Italian politician knows only too well, if your football team does well the fans vote for you. Silvio Berlusconi's Milan are the current champions of Italy.

FROM THE BEGINNING

A GREEK COLONY

According to Homer, Ulysses survived the seductive voice of the sirens by having his sailors block their ears with wax and tying himself to his ship's mast. The sirens were outraged at this act of cunning; Parthenope, in particular, was so distraught that she threw herself into the sea and drowned. The waves carried her body to a small volcanic island a few metres off the Italian mainland. It was here on the island of Megaris (where today the Castel dell'Ovo stands) that Naples was founded.

Originally named Parthenope in honour of the suicidal siren, the settlement was established in about 680 BC by Greek traders from the nearby town of Cuma (or Cumae as it was then known). About 10km up the coast from Naples, Cuma had become the first Greek settlement in Italy when travellers from the Aegean island of Euboea had set up camp there in the 8th century BC. En route they'd also founded the colony of Pithekoussai on the island of Ischia.

The colony of Parthenope, which covered the island of Megaris and Mt Echia (also known as Mt Pizzofalcone), was destined to remain in the shadow of Cuma. A thriving commercial city, Cuma caught the attention of the marauding Etruscans who twice invaded and were twice repelled. Following the second of these battles, in 474 BC, the Cumans founded Neapolis (New Town, to distinguish it from Paleopolis, Old Town, the name by which Parthenope was then known) on the land that is now Naples' *centro storico* (historic centre).

But where the Etruscans failed the Romans succeeded. Eager for new land and ever ready for a good war, the Romans launched themselves against the Samnites who, in 421 BC, had captured Cuma. The Samnites fell and in 326 BC the legionnaires marched into Neapolis after a two-year siege.

326 BC	AD 79	476	536
Romans conquer Neapolis	Mt Vesuvius erupts burying Pompeii and Herculaneum	The last Roman emperor Romulus Augustus dies	Naples becomes a Byzantine duchy

ROMANS RULE

Displaying early signs of the Neapolitan disdain for authority, the Greek citizens of Neapolis never became completely Romanised. They refused, for example, to give up their own language, traces of which remain in modern-day Neapolitan dialect. But as Roman rule established itself, so the two cultures began to fuse and before long Neapolis had become a trendy Roman holiday resort.

But even with Roman money pouring into the area, the citizens remained quite a contrary lot. During the Roman Civil War (88–82 BC) they opposed Rome, invoking the wrath of Cornelius Sulla who promptly took the city and slaughtered thousands of its citizens. Not surprisingly, anti-Roman feeling continued to run high and, in 73 BC, slave leader Spartacus based his rebel army on the slopes of Mt Vesuvius.

Pompeii (p181)

Campania's fabled volcano exploded onto the stage in AD 79, drowning nearby Pompeii and Herculaneum in a mix of molten lava, mud and ash. Coming just 19 years after a massive earthquake, Vesuvius was a massive blow for an area that was in rapid decline. Within the city walls, however, Neapolis was enjoying a boom period. General Lucullus built a massive villa on the spot where the Castel dell'Ovo now stands and Virgil moved to the town for a period; the famously debauched Emperor Tiberius went further and transferred his entire court to the island of Capri.

Roman civilisation (or lack of it) had arrived and the welfare of Neapolis was now tied to that of the Roman Empire. So, when the last Roman emperor Romulus Augustus died in 476, as a prisoner of the Goth king Odoacer, the city passed into barbarian hands.

THE DUKES OF NAPLES

The Goths' Neapolitan adventure didn't last long, however. Besieged by the Byzantines, the city fell to the men from Constantinople in 536 and became a duchy.

The Byzantines ruled well and the city flourished. Industry thrived, schools were founded and Christianity caught on with the population in a big way. In 645 Basilio became the first native-born Neapolitan to be appointed duke of the city.

But trouble lay outside the walls. By now in control of much of Campania, the northern Lombards were a constant thorn, laying siege to the city three times in the last two decades of the 6th century. From the sea, the north African Saracens launched periodic attacks, tempted by Naples' considerable wealth. Yet the city held out and the uneasy status quo stood.

The situation started to change in the 9th century. And ironically it was a split in Lombard unity that signalled the beginning of the end for the dukes of Naples. Although the natural enemies of the Neapolitans, the united Lombards were at least a familiar foe. It was when divisions started appearing in the Germanic ranks that events took a turn for the worse. In the 9th century the two main Lombard cities, Benevento and Salerno fought and split, each forming an independent principality. Capua followed suit in the 10th century, while Amalfi increasingly began to follow its own path. Watching developments closely, the Normans were biding their time, waiting for the right moment to play their hand.

1073	1139	1224	1279
The Normans conquer Amalfi	Naples becomes the Norman capital of the Kingdom of the Two Sicilies	Frederick II of Swabia founds Naples University	Charles of Anjou builds Castel Nuovo

THE NORMANS

The Normans had arrived in southern Italy in the 10th century. Initially they were just passing through, pilgrims on their way home from Jerusalem. It was the successive bands of mercenaries who stayed, attracted by the money to be made fighting for the rival principalities or against the Arab Muslims in Sicily.

At the beginning of the 11th century the Duke of Naples Sergio IV employed a Norman, Rainulfo Drengot, to drive the Lombards out of Capua. It was a decision that was to cost Naples dearly.

To give a spurious legitimacy to his decision, Sergio made Drengot Duke of Aversa in 1038. It was enough to give the Normans a base in Campania, and in the years that followed the small town grew from a toehold into a stronghold. Mercenaries poured in, eager to cash in on the never-ending circle of factional fighting. The town became rich and Norman minds began to turn to conquest.

In 1062 Drengot fulfilled his contract and took Capua. What was not written in the agreement was that the Normans should also take Amalfi, which they did in 1073, and four years later they took Salerno. Over the water in Sicily, Robert Guiscard and his brother Roger of Hauteville were busy kicking the Arabs off the island. By 1130 most of southern Italy was in Norman hands and Robert's son was crowned King Roger II of Sicily.

Surrounded on all sides it was only a question of time before Naples gave in to the inevitable. It did so in 1139. The Kingdom of the Two Sicilies was now complete.

The Normans kept their capital in Sicily and Palermo began to outshine Naples. Wealth moved out to the island and the Norman rulers took to the lifestyle that the palaces of Palermo afforded. Surprisingly, however, the Neapolitans seemed happy with their rulers and when, in 1194, the last of the Norman kings, Tancred, was succeeded by his enemy Henry Hohenstaufen of Swabia, the mood turned ugly.

The Neapolitans despised the new Swabian interlopers. Henry managed to further alienate himself by knocking down the city walls as punishment for the city's lack of support. His death in 1197 did little to appease the groundswell of hatred and not even his successor Frederick II could win the city over despite investing in the infrastructure and founding a university.

The end came for the Swabians in February 1265 when King Manfred was routed by Charles I of Anjou at the battle of Benevento. Head of the French Angevin dynasty, Charles took control of the Kingdom of the Two Sicilies with the full blessing of the Pope, who had agreed to back the Angevins if they'd do the dirty (and expensive) work of removing the Swabians.

Three years later Conrad, the son of Frederick II, tried one last time to assert Swabian control. He was defeated at the battle of Tagliacozzo and for his trouble was beheaded on Piazza del Mercato.

THE ANGEVIN ERA

Perhaps suspecting treachery in Sicily, or perhaps to break with the past, Charles of Anjou moved his capital back from Palermo to Naples. It was a precipitous move as treason was, in fact, in the Sicilian air.

In league with the powerful Sicilian barons, the Spanish Aragonese had already begun to plot against the Angevins when events came to a climax on Easter Monday 1282. In an eruption of pent-up violence, the Sicilians killed more than 2000 French people. Remembered as the Sicilian Vespers, the massacres were the first act in a rebellion that was to last until 1302. Worn down by years of fighting, Charles II of Anjou finally gave up the island to Peter III of Aragon.

Back on the mainland, it was a completely different story. The Angevins were determined to make Naples a sparkling artistic and intellectual centre. Charles built the Castel Nuovo in 1279, the port was enlarged, and in the early 14th century the third Angevin king, Robert

1282	1442	1485	1501
Massacres, known as the Sicilian Vespers, occur	Alfonso of Aragon claims Naples	Barons rebel against Ferdinand I	Joint Franco–Spanish forces invade

of Anjou, constructed Castel Sant'Elmo. Known as *il Saggio* (The Wise), Robert also invited the top artists and writers of the day to visit Naples. Giotto, Petrarch and Boccaccio were among those who took up the invitation.

The last century of Angevin rule was marked by complex and often bloody politicking between family factions. Queen Joan I was suspected of murdering her husband and fled the city between 1348 and 1352, leaving her vengeful Hungarian in-laws to occupy Naples. Some 70-odd years later her namesake Queen Joan II could only stop her husband stealing the crown thanks to substantial popular support.

Weakened by in-fighting, the Angevins were rapidly losing their grasp. The time had come for the Aragonese to step in.

THE ARAGONESE

After vicious fighting, Alfonso of Aragon took control of Naples in 1442. Bitterly opposed by the pro-Angevin Neapolitans, he quickly installed himself as king and set about ensuring that his son Ferdinand would succeed him, which he did in 1458.

Alfonso, who went under the title *il Magnanimo* (The Magnanimous), did a lot for Naples, promoting art and science and introducing institutional reforms. But he could never live down the fact that he'd overthrown the popular Angevins. Naples may have been prospering, but the situation was anything but secure and Angevin support anything but dead.

In 1485 the city's barons raised their heads and took up arms against Ferdinand I. Within a year, however, the king had executed the ringleaders (in the Sala dei Baroni in Castel Nuovo) and made peace with the rest. It was not a lasting peace though and in 1495 King Charles VIII of France invaded. Supported by a small group of barons but fiercely opposed by the population at large, the French monarch occupied the city for four months. When he was forced out, the Neapolitans replaced him with the Aragonese Ferdinand II.

After Ferdinand II's death in 1496, the mutinous barons once again flexed their muscles, this time by crowning Ferdinand's uncle, Frederick, as king. This angered everyone – the Neapolitans, the French and the Spanish, who had all wanted Ferdinand II's widow Joan to succeed him. The upshot was the joint Franco–Spanish invasion of 1501. Frederick tried to hang on to power, but facing almost total opposition he skulked off, leaving Naples to the Spanish general Consalvo di Cordoba. Thus King Ferdinand of Spain became King Ferdinand III of Naples.

DON PEDRO & THE VICEROYS

For two centuries, between 1503 and 1707, Naples was part of the Spanish Empire. Ruled by a succession of hated viceroys, the city flourished artistically acquiring much of its splendour.

The 16th century was one of Naples' golden eras. Spain, wealthy on the back of its silver-rich colonies in the New World, was enjoying a period of hitherto-unseen prosperity, and confidence was running high throughout the empire. In Naples, the unruly barons were brought into line, order was imposed and the population continued to grow. In fact, by 1600 Naples was the biggest city in Europe with a population of 300,000. To house the ever-increasing masses, expansion became a priority.

To deal with the situation, viceroy Don Pedro de Toledo took drastic measures. Deciding that the only way to build was westwards, he set himself the onerous task of moving the city walls and building an entire new quarter. The result was Via Toledo, and, to its immediate west, the Quartieri Spagnoli. Housing was not enough though; the new Neapolitans had spiritual needs to satisfy. Hundreds of new churches and monasteries sprung up, many of them decorated by the city's new wave of architects and artists.

The most prolific of all Naples' architects was Cosimo Fanzago (1591–1678). A master of the baroque, his hand is visible in many of the city's historic churches. Other big-name sculptors

1532–53	1600	1606	1647
Don Pedro de Toledo rules as Spanish viceroy	Naples is the biggest city in Europe	Artist Caravaggio arrives in town	Masaniello revolt

included Giovanni di Nola and Pietro Bernini, father of the more famous Gian Lorenzo. Painters were also having a rich time of it. Caravaggio arrived in town in 1606, running from a murder rap in Rome. Inspired by his revolutionary style, Giuseppe de Ribera, Massimo Stanzione, Luca Giordano and Francesco Solimena all made their names in this fruitful time.

But as is often the way, this burst of creativity coincided with a period of economic turmoil. If the 16th century had been good to Naples, the 17th century was decidedly not.

The first big blow came in 1622 when the Genoese economy collapsed. Both Spain and Naples had close business connections with the Ligurian city-state and the repercussions were felt deeply. At the same time, Spain's expensive wars were putting increasing strain on the empire's finances. To sustain their military costs, the Spanish began to impose widespread tax hikes. And it was this that drove the Neapolitans to rebellion.

The Masaniello Revolt

Already crippled by the sheer weight of taxes, the Neapolitans were becoming increasingly mutinous when in January 1647 the Spanish introduced a levy on fresh fruit. It was one tax too many and on 7 July 1647 events took a nasty turn.

Roused by the refusal of the Pozzuoli fruit traders to pay the tax and harangued by an illiterate fisherman from Amalfi, Tommaso Aniello, aka Masaniello, the angry mob exploded into violence. Fighting broke out between protesters and soldiers sent down from Castel Nuovo.

From his command post in Piazza del Mercato, Masaniello spelled out his demands, or rather demand, as he asked only that the fruit tax be abolished. He was not anti-monarchist and had no desire to overthrow the Spanish rulers, but for a Neapolitan rebel this was a dangerously moderate line to take and ultimately proved his downfall. Extremists within the rebel camp became disillusioned with his stance and when the chance came to get rid of him, albeit with the tacit support of the Spanish viceroy, they took it. Masaniello was murdered on 16 July in the **Chiesa di Santa Maria del Carmine** (p82).

But by now the revolt had snowballed and become a serious political crisis. Where before the rebels had fought for a single cause, now everyone with a grievance was trying to exploit the anarchic situation. The French even tried to cash in by sending the Duke of Giusa down to try and wrest control of the city. He failed, and on 6 April 1648 he was captured by the new Spanish viceroy, the Count of Oñate. Order was soon re-established, the rebel leaders executed and life in Naples resumed a semblance of normality.

An Earthquake, Eruption & the Plague

Naples' woes in the 17th century were not all man made, however; nature played her hand to the full, striking three times in the space of 60 years.

The first of the unholy trio was the eruption of Mt Vesuvius in 1631. After almost 500 years of inactivity, she blew her top on the morning of 16 December following 24 hours of earth tremors. Seismic activity reached a peak a day later when a molten mass of ash, gas and stone shot out of the crater and, according to witnesses, rushed down the mountainside like a torrent of water, killing some 3500 people.

It was a death toll that paled into comparison with that of the devastating plague epidemic that hit Naples and Campania in 1656. In a six-month period up to three-quarters of Naples' population was killed and any hopes of economic recovery were buried with the dead. The horror that infected the city's squalid streets is graphically depicted in the paintings that hang in Room 37 of the **Certosa di San Martino** (p75).

The *coup de grâce* arrived 32 years later in the form of an earthquake. Although Naples was some distance from the epicentre in Benevento, the shockwaves were clearly felt and the damage to the city was considerable. More than 10,000 people died in the Benevento area and the psychological effects on the superstitious population can only be imagined.

1656	1707	1734	1737
Plague epidemic	Austrians rule for 27 years	Charles becomes first Bourbon king of Naples	Teatro San Carlo built

Vesuvius looms over the Castel dell'Ovo (p68)

THE BOURBONS
The Golden Age

Many of Naples' most famous buildings date from the Bourbon period. From Charles' accession to the Neapolitan throne in 1734 until Italian unification in 1860, Naples underwent a transformation. The 16th-century Palazzo Reale was enlarged, Teatro San Carlo became Europe's grandest opera house and the Palazzo Reale di Capodimonte was built as a royal hunting lodge. In fact, so glamorous did Naples become that aristocrats rushed from all corners of the continent to live on Via Toledo.

Charles' journey to Naples had not, however, been an easy one. It started in 1700 when the childless Charles V of Naples (Charles II of Spain) died, sparking off a continent-wide succession crisis. Up for grabs were Spain's European possessions. Europe divided into two camps: the English and Dutch backed the Austrian Habsburgs, while the Spanish and French allied to defend their Bourbon claims. In the meantime Philip, the grandson of Charles V's brother-in-law, had taken the Spanish throne (and therefore the Neapolitan throne) as King Philip V.

Given the complexity of the European situation the wishes of the Neapolitans didn't count for a whole hill of beans. And in a clear case of better the devil you know, they supported the Spanish. But stronger forces were at work, and in 1707 Austrian troops marched into Naples. In effect though, this changed little for the city – it was still ruled by hated foreign viceroys, this time Austrian rather than Spanish, and taxes remained high.

Meanwhile in the north, Charles, the Bourbon son of King Philip V and his grasping second wife Elisabetta Farnese, was dutifully watching over the family's Italian duchies, Parma and Piacenza. Elisabetta, a voracious collector, had set her eyes on Naples and ordered her boy to head down the peninsula and take the city. With surprisingly little trouble he did exactly that and in 1734 he was crowned King Charles VII of Naples. A year later, after defeating the Austrians in Sicily, he added the crown of Sicily to his name.

From all accounts Charles was not a brilliant man. Neither a general – he apparently hated wearing a uniform – nor a great politician, he was nevertheless dutiful and felt honour-bound to do his best by Naples. Ruling through a Council of State, whose ministers were appointed by Charles' dominating parents, he embarked on a grand building spree. Royal palaces were built, a *Biblioteca Nazionale* (National Library) was founded and the Albergo dei Poveri became Europe's largest poorhouse (indeed Europe's largest building).

1768	1799	1806–15	1820 & 1848
Maria Carolina marries Ferdinand I	The Parthenopean Republic is proclaimed	The French decade	Ferdinand grants and revokes a constitution

Being his mother's son, he also inherited an appetite for art. Pompeii and Herculaneum were systematically ransacked and the Farnese art collection was housed in the gleaming **Palazzo Reale di Capodimonte** (p79).

Ferdinand & Maria

In 1759 Charles returned to Spain to succeed his father as King Charles III. According to the European law of the time, he couldn't hold three crowns at the same time (Naples, Sicily and Spain) so he left Naples to his eight-year-old son Ferdinand. In effect, he left power to his prime minister, Bernardo Tanucci (see below).

But Tanucci's days were numbered and when in 1768 the Austrian Maria Carolina arrived in town to marry Ferdinand, his time had come. Maria was one of 16 children of the Habsburg Empress of Austria (the very person who Tanucci had opposed in the 1740 crisis of Austrian succession). She was beautiful, clever and ruthless; a ready match for Tanucci and an unlikely partner for the famously dim, dialect-speaking Ferdinand. She soon had her husband wrapped round her little finger; to eliminate Tanucci took a tad longer – nine years in fact.

In accordance with her marriage agreement Maria Carolina joined the Council of State on the birth of her first son in 1777. It was the position she'd been waiting for to oust Tanucci, and out he promptly went. Into his shoes stepped a French-born English aristocrat, John Acton.

Acton's reputation as a brilliant seaman, earned during a stint with the Tuscan navy, led to a commission to reorganise the Neapolitan navy. A smooth and paranoid operator, Acton quickly realised where the real power in Naples lay and wasted no time in ingratiating himself with Maria. He managed to win her over completely and after a series of promotions became prime minister.

Part of his appeal for Maria was his decidedly anti-Bourbon politics. Maria, herself an Austrian, was delighted at Acton's support in ridding the Neapolitan court of Spanish influence and forging closer links with Austria and Britain. But just as things began to go smoothly with the English, France erupted in revolution.

The Man Behind the Throne

In the context of 18th-century Europe, Bernardo Tanucci (1698–1793) was a liberal. In other words, he stood against the Church and feudal nobility in favour of the state.

A former professor of law at Pisa University, he arrived in Naples in 1734 alongside the soon-to-be king, Charles. The two men had met in Tuscany where, on the advice of Cosimo Medici, Charles had offered Tanucci a job. Once in Naples, Tanucci never looked back.

His anti-clerical measures, including reducing tax revenue to the Church and abolishing the feudal privileges enjoyed by the papacy, won him few friends in the Vatican. And following the expulsion of the Jesuits from Naples in 1767, he was duly excommunicated by Pope Clement XIII.

In foreign affairs, he was more moderate. He tried to steer Naples clear of war and was generally successful. His closest shave came in the 1740 crisis of Austrian succession. To try to prevent Maria Teresa succeeding to the Austrian throne, Charles (for which you can read Tanucci) had reluctantly sent an army to Lombardy. This didn't please the British who dispatched a fleet to the south of Italy. The commanding admiral threatened to bombard Naples unless the Neapolitan troops were withdrawn. Charles took the man at his word and ordered the retreat. It was a rare defeat for Tanucci.

Throughout his career, Tanucci was generally honest and his objectives largely honourable – he wanted Naples to be a model of modern efficiency. But as a man of power he was well versed in the murky arts of political survival. And when the eight-year-old Ferdinand became king, he sensed danger. The solution as Tanucci saw it was to deny the young Ferdinand an education, and encourage his sporting pleasures. An ignorant oaf was less likely to pose a threat and Ferdinand duly became a thick boor. But Tanucci had been right – danger was to come from Ferdinand's direction. His wife Maria Carolina clashed with Tanucci and had him dismissed from the ruling Council of State in 1777. He died 16 years later.

1860	1884	1889	1898
Garibaldi is given a hero's welcome	Mass cholera epidemic	Raffaele Esposito invents pizza margherita	Popular song 'O Sole Mio' is copyrighted

The Neapolitan government remained surprisingly sanguine when news filtered south of the 1789 revolution. It didn't stay so for long. The execution of Maria Carolina's sister Marie Antoinette was enough to send Naples rushing to join the anti-French coalition.

Troops from revolutionary France and Naples first clashed in French-occupied Rome in 1798 when the Neapolitans victoriously claimed the city. Within 11 days, however, they were scurrying back south with the French in hot pursuit.

The Parthenopean Republic

Frightened by the prospect of an army of anti-monarchist revolutionaries descending on Naples, Ferdinand and Maria Carolina escaped to Palermo on Nelson's ship *Vanguard*, leaving the ever-faithful monarchist poor to defend the city.

Bitterly opposed by most of the population, the French were nevertheless welcomed by the nobility and bourgeoisie, many of whom had adopted similar fashionable republican ideas. It was therefore with the full backing of the French that the liberals proclaimed the Parthenopean Republic on 23 January 1799.

But it wasn't a success. The leaders were an ideological rather than practical lot, and were soon in financial straits. Their efforts to democratise the city failed and the army was a shambles.

Over the water, the exiles in Palermo had not been sitting idle. They dispatched Cardinal Fabrizio Ruffo to Calabria to organise an uprising. The crusading cardinal soon assembled a motley army of crooks and peasants and began to climb north. On 13 June he entered Naples and all hell broke loose. He was unwilling, or unable, to control his men, and Naples became a slaughterhouse. But the rebels, holed up in the city's impregnable castles, were able to hold out for a negotiated peace guaranteeing their safe passage. The return of the royals put an end to that.

On 8 July Ferdinand and Maria returned from Sicily and embarked on a systematic extermination of Republican sympathisers. More than 200 were summarily executed.

The French Decade

By the beginning of the 19th century the whole of Europe was at war. Napoleon had emerged from France's post-revolutionary anarchy intent on carving out an empire for himself. After victory over the Austrians at the Battle of Austerlitz in December 1805, he sent an army south, towards Naples.

Led by Napoleon's brother Joseph Bonaparte, French forces once again entered Naples. And once again Ferdinand and family hotfooted it over to Sicily. Although nominally the King of Sicily, Ferdinand was pretty much ignored by the British ambassador Lord William Bentinck, who became the island's de facto ruler. Maria Carolina was less easy to ignore, so Bentinck had her exiled to Austria where she died three years later in 1814.

In Naples, Joseph was replaced as king by Joachim Murat in 1808. From his residence in the Palazzo Reale di Capodimonte, Murat launched a series of what should have been popular measures: he abolished feudalism and initiated a series of land redistribution programmes; he brought in foreign investment and kickstarted local industry. And yet still he was hated. As a Frenchman and a revolutionary he could do no right in the eyes of the royalist masses.

As a self-made man, Murat knew when to abandon a sinking ship. When the tide turned against his brother-in-law, Napoleon, he felt the time right to jump. Desperate to keep control of Naples, he cut a deal with the Austrians and the British allowing him to retain his position. Unfortunately for him, they reneged. In 1815 Murat was ousted from Naples, and Ferdinand returned to claim his throne.

1934	1936	1943	1944
Sophia Loren is born	Naples airport is built	Allied bombing raids wreak havoc on the city	Mt Vesuvius erupts

Towards Unification

Post-Napoleonic Europe saw a short-lived resurgence of absolutism. On his return to Naples Ferdinand awarded himself the new title of Ferdinand I of the Kingdom of the Two Sicilies; up until then he'd been Ferdinand IV of Naples and Ferdinand III of Sicily.

But the French revolution had stirred up too many ideas for a return to the great age of absolutism. In Naples, the ruthless and secretive Carbonari society forced Ferdinand to grant the city a constitution in 1820. A year later, however, it was abandoned as Ferdinand called in Austrian troops.

In 1848 a wave of rebellion hit a number of European capitals and Ferdinand once again granted his parliament a constitution. Yet again he changed his mind, this time by dissolving parliament. He was as blind to the changing times as his equally obstinate son, who succeeded him in 1859. The last of the Bourbon monarchs, Francesco II was to rule for less than a year.

GARIBALDI & UNIFICATION

Giuseppe Garibaldi is Italy's most famous guerrilla fighter. A natural-born nationalist, he was instrumental in the unification of Italy and in the consequent demise of the Kingdom of the Two Sicilies.

After a period commanding Uruguayan forces in a war against Argentina, Garibaldi returned to Italy in 1848. Forced to flee the country for six years, he reappeared in Piedmont champing for rebellion. Fighting soon broke out between Piedmontese rebels loyal to Garibaldi's vision of a united Italy and the Austrian army. Buoyed by victory, he set sail for Sicily in May 1860 with a volunteer army of 1000 Red Shirts.

Waiting for him in Sicily, however, was Ferdinand's 25,000-strong Neapolitan army. But the mood on the ground was beginning to change. The Bourbon monarchy had long enjoyed popular support in Naples but its consistent refusal to grant any constitutional concessions was beginning to cost it goodwill.

In Sicily, Garibaldi stunned the Neapolitan royals with the speed of his advances. With an army that had swelled to 5000 men he managed to defeat the full-strength but half-hearted Bourbon forces and declare himself dictator in the name of King Vittorio Emanuele II.

Terrified for his future, King Francesco II agreed to a constitution in June 1860. But by this time Garibaldi had crossed over to the Italian mainland and was marching relentlessly up Calabria towards Naples. True to the family spirit, Francesco fled the city, taking refuge with 4000 loyalists behind the River Volturno, about 30km north of Naples. On 7 September Garibaldi marched unopposed into Naples, welcomed as a hero.

But it wasn't quite over for Francesco. More in hope than anything else, the Bourbon loyalists launched a series of last-ditch attacks on the rebel army, only to be defeated on 1 and 2 October at the Battle of Volturno. Naples was now well and truly in Garibaldi's hands and on 21 October the city voted overwhelmingly to join a united Italy under the Savoy monarchy.

Thanks to its royal past Naples was a serious contender for capital of Italy. But when Rome was eventually wrested from the French in 1870, the newly formed Italian parliament transferred from its temporary home in Florence to the Eternal City.

DARK DAYS: POST-UNIFICATION

The shock of unification was immediately apparent. From being the grand capital of a Bourbon kingdom, an international player, Naples suddenly became a lowly regional capital. Unable to adapt to its new role and ill-supported by a national government intent on boosting industrial development in the north, Naples turned to nostalgia as an escape.

The myth of beautiful Naples grew in this period. Neapolitans began to present themselves as a bunch of cheerful scallywags, who are ready to burst into song at any moment.

1946	1980	1987	1992
Largo di Palazzo is renamed Piazza del Plebiscito	A devastating earthquake kills 3000	Under Maradona Napoli wins the Italian football championship	The anti-corruption campaign known as *Mani Pulite* kickstarts

The tradition of Neapolitan song was born and exported around the world by thousands of immigrants fleeing the poverty of the city. Migrants fled to the north to find jobs in the factories or overseas to America. Between 1880 and 1914, it's estimated that around 2½ million Italians left for America, most of them from the poor south.

A rare period of optimism appeared following the massive cholera epidemic of 1884. Realising the need for a citywide clean-up, authorities launched a number of urban-renewal projects. The worst slums near the port were destroyed, new housing areas were built and Corso Umberto I was bulldozed. At the top of the Vomero hill developers constructed a sparkling new residential quarter, while lower down, Galleria Umberto 1 (p71) and Caffè Gambrinus (p113) became stylish new landmarks. But however much the face of the city changed, the underlying problems remained – poverty, corruption and the growth of organised crime.

FASCISM & WWII

Naples was largely untouched by WWI. The same cannot be said for Italy as a whole. Not only did the nation lose 600,000 men but the war economy had produced a small number of super-rich industrial barons and left the bulk of the population in penury. It was a situation made for a determined and charismatic leader.

Benito Mussolini took full control of Italy in 1925. Determined to beef up Italy's international credibility, he charged into a colonial war in Ethiopia and allied himself with Hitler in Europe. On the domestic front, he embarked on a nationwide building spree. In Naples, an airport was built in 1936, railway and metro lines were laid and the Vomero funicular was completed. The Mostra d'Oltremare was inaugurated in 1937 to celebrate Italy's great colonial victories.

But if Mussolini's domestic policies left a legacy of robust public buildings, his foreign affairs brought nothing but destruction. During WWII, Naples suffered horrendously. Heavy aerial bombing left more than 20,000 people dead and destroyed large swathes of the city centre.

Events came to a head in 1943. Bombardments were at their worst in preparation for the Allied invasion of the mainland and the Germans had taken the city. They didn't stay long though and were forced out by a series of popular uprisings between 26 and 30 September. Known as the *quattro giorni napoletane* (the four days of Naples), the street battles paved the way for Allied troops to enter the city on 1 October.

Greeted as liberators, the Allies set up their provisional government in Naples. By this stage, though, the city has become an anarchic mass of humanity, with Allied troops pouring in, German prisoners of war and bands of Italian fascists all competing with the city's starving population for food. Then, as if it couldn't get any worse, Mt Vesuvius erupted in 1944.

Faced with such a situation the Allied authorities continued to turn to the underworld for assistance. Willing to help, in return for the Allies turning a blind eye towards their black-market activities, criminal organisations began to flourish.

THE POST-WAR PERIOD

The post-war years were not kind to Naples. Corruption thrived, nepotism became the order of the day and the Camorra grew into an international crime organisation.

Naples' immediate post-war problem was to rehouse its population. And while the frantic reconstruction of the 1950s and 1960s provided plenty of cheap, ugly housing, it also gave ample cover for a whole host of crimes. Under the banner of housing for the poor an entire generation of dodgy politicians and crime bosses became rich. The Camorra had a field day, making money hand over fist on property speculation, money laundering, drugs and racketeering.

In 1971 a public report officially admitted that most building work carried out since the war had been illegal. Nobody was surprised. Naples had reached rock bottom.

1993	1994	2001	2003
Antonio Bassolino is voted mayor	Naples hosts the G7 summit	Rosa Russo Jervolino becomes the first woman mayor	The Rubbish crisis hits

Quarters

Quarters

First impressions of Naples are not promising. The overwhelming sense of chaos, the dodgy street life and filthy buildings aren't attractive prospects. But Naples is, in fact, a highly cultured city with a sumptuous artistic heritage. To appreciate it you simply need to acclimatise.

For many people the first port of call is the *centro storico* (historic centre), the oldest of Naples' *quartieri* (districts). A fascinating area of dark narrow streets and hidden treasures, this is the ancient heart of the city. Easily reached from Stazione Centrale, either on foot or by public transport, the two central streets, Via San Biagio dei Librai (which becomes Via Benedetto Croce at its western end) and Via dei Tribunali, date back to ancient Greek times.

Marking the western boundary of the *centro storico*, Via Toledo is Naples' main shopping drag. A busy and once elegant boulevard, it undergoes three name changes as it climbs from Piazza Trieste e Trento in the south up to the Parco di Capodimonte in the far north of the city. No longer the refined road that so impressed 19th-century tourists, it is especially anarchic in the stretch from Piazza Dante to the Museo Archeologico Nazionale. To its immediate west lies the Quartieri Spagnoli, with Naples' most notorious inner-city streets.

At Via Toledo's south end, the royal district of Santa Lucia boasts the city's most visually impressive square mile. Flanking the mighty Piazza del Plebiscito, the Palazzo Reale adjoins Teatro San Carlo, Naples' world-famous opera house, while a few hundred metres to the northeast Castel Nuovo (known locally as the Maschio Angioino) dominates Piazza del Municipio.

Looking down on all of this is the middle-class residential district of Vomero, a natural balcony with grand views across the city to Mt Vesuvius.

Heading west from Piazza del Plebiscito you come to the upmarket quarter of Chiaia. Centred on Piazza dei Martiri, this area of designer boutiques and trendy bars stretches west along the Riviera di Chiaia to Mergellina. Continue around the waterfront and you reach Posillipo, home of the seriously rich.

Back at the opposite end of the seafront, the Mercato district is poor, uncared-for and grim. Sprawling south from Stazione Centrale and the enormous, unwelcoming transport terminus that is Piazza Garibaldi, it's as far removed from the affluent seafront suburbs in the west as a Ferrari is from a pair of second-hand roller skates.

Although the city covers a large area, most of the major sights are best covered on foot. The appalling traffic makes travelling by bus (or heaven forbid, a car) a tortuous process that is best avoided unless absolutely necessary.

ITINERARIES
One Day

Start with an espresso and *sfogliatella* (pastry) on **Piazza del Gesù Nuovo** (p58) before popping into the **Basilica di Santa Chiara** (p55). Famed for its beautiful cloisters, it provides one of central Naples' few quiet spots. Continue down Via Benedetto Croce and Via San Biagio dei Librai, taking time to explore the densely packed palazzi (mansions) and churches. At the end of the road turn left up Via Duomo to the **Duomo** (p60), before turning back into Via dei Tribunali and more of the *centro storico*. Before you emerge be sure not to miss the incredible **Cappella Sansevero** (p56). Lunch on pizza, before making for the **Museo Archeologico Nazionale** (p66) and its spectacular collection of sculpture and ancient mosaics. Late afternoon is the best time for a walk down Via Toledo to **Piazza Trieste e Trento** (p73). Round off the day in one of the many trattorie or bars in **Chiaia** (p120).

Campania Artecard

If you're planning on spending three days or more in Naples, it's worth getting the **Campania artecard** (☎ 800 600 601; www.campaniartecard.it in Italian). For more details on this museum-and-transport ticket see p212.

Three Days

Add a visit to the fabulous art collection in the **Palazzo Reale di Capodimonte** (p79). If you've still not had your fill of art, the 2nd-century **Catacomba di San Gennaro** (p77) is nearby. Alternatively, give Capodimonte a miss and head up to Vomero to explore the stunning **Certosa di San Martino** (p75).

In the afternoon wander down to the seafront where you can pop over to the **Borgo Marinaro** (p68) for a quick drink before some serious shopping (real or window) in the designer boutiques around **Piazza dei Martiri** (p94).

On the third day take a trip out of town to **Mt Vesuvius** (p181) and **Pompeii** (p181) – both are absolutely unique and within easy reach of the city.

It's Free Top Five

- Villa Comunale (p94)
- Duomo (p60)
- Chiesa di Sant'Anna dei Lombardi (p65)
- Views from Largo San Martino in front of the Certosa di San Martino (p75)
- Museo Nazionale Ferroviario Pietrarsa (p100)

One Week

With a week you can pretty much do it all. After you've explored the *centro storico* and visited the major museums, including all of the above plus the **Palazzo Reale** (p72) and **Museo Civico di Castel Nuovo** (p69), you might want to spread your wings. To the immediate west of the city the **Campi Flegrei** (p98) merits a day trip. A volcanic area of archaeological interest, it was, according to Homer, the entrance to Hades. Nearby in **Cuma** (p99), the ancient oracle Sybil is said to have lived in a cave.

On the other side of the city, beyond Herculaneum, the **Amalfi Coast** (p191) is not to be missed. Further south, the remarkable Greek ruins at **Paestum** (p203) are also well worth a visit.

You'll also have time to visit one or more of Naples' famous islands. The best known and most visited are **Capri** (p164) and **Ischia** (p171), but it's the third, **Procida** (p176), that is the most atmospheric.

ORGANISED TOURS

Outside of the city, **Cima Tours** (Map pp244–6; ☎ 081 20 10 52; cimatour@tin.it; Piazza Garibaldi 114) and **Tourcar** (Map pp244–6; ☎ 081 552 04 29; Piazza G Matteotti 1) both organise excursions to the islands of the Bay of Naples, the Amalfi Coast and Pompeii, Herculaneum and Vesuvius. A half-day tour to Pompeii costs about €40, which includes admission costs.

CITY SIGHTSEEING NAPOLI Map pp244-6
☎ 081 551 72 79; infonapoli@city-sightseeing.it; Via Parco del Castello, Piazza del Municipio; adult/child/family €18/9/54

City Sightseeing Napoli operates a hop-on, hop-off bus service for tourists. There are three routes, all of which depart from Piazza del Municipio Parco Castello. Route A (*I Luoghi dell'Arte*, or Art Tour) covers the city's major art sites including Piazza del Gesù Nuovo, Piazza Dante, the Museo Archeologico Nazionale, Museo di Capodimonte, the Catacomba di San Gennaro, Piazza Bellini, Porta Capuana and Piazza Bovio. The 1¼-hour circular tour departs daily every 45 minutes between 9.45am and 6.45pm.

Route B (*Le Vedute del Golfo*, or Bay of Naples) follows the sea west passing through Santa Lucia, Piazza Vittoria, Villa Pignatelli, Mergellina and Posillipo. Departures are every 45 minutes between 9.30am and 7.30pm on Thursday, Friday and Saturday, and every 30 minutes between 9.30am and 7.15pm on Sunday. The tour takes 1¼ hours.

Route C (San Martino) runs up to Vomero, with stops in Via Santa Lucia, Piazza dei Martiri, Piazza Amedeo, Piazza Vanvitelli, Largo San Martino (for the Certosa di San Martino), Via Salvator Rosa and Piazza Dante. Tours last 1¾ hours and depart every two hours between 10am and 6pm on Saturday and Sunday.

Tickets, which are available on the bus, are valid for 24 hours for each of the three routes. Commentaries are provided in eight languages including English.

NAPOLI SOTTERRANEA Map pp244-6
Underground Naples; ☎ 081 29 69 44; www.napoli sotterranea.org; Piazza San Gaetano 68; tours €9.30; ☯ 1½-hr tours noon, 2pm & 4pm Mon-Fri, extra tours 10am & 6pm Sat & Sun

This company organises guided underground tours that take you 40m below the city to explore the network of ancient passages and caves. The passages were originally hewn by the Greeks to extract the soft tufa stone for construction, then extended by the Romans as water conduits. Clogged up with illegally dumped refuse over the centuries, they were used as air-raid shelters in WWII.

LEGAMBIENTE Map pp244-6
☎ 081 420 31 61; www.napolisworld.it in Italian; Vico della Quercia 7
A national environmental organisation offering made-to-measure tours in the *centro storico* and in less explored areas like the Sanità district.

NAPOLIJAMM Map pp242-3
☎ 081 562 13 13, 393 916 45 47; www.napolijamm.it; Via Sannio 9; adult/child €27/free
Napolijamm runs four walking tours covering the *centro storico* (red tour); castles and historic palazzi (green tour); sites of famous miracles and mysteries (blue tour); and the *centro storico* by night (pink tour).

With the exception of the three-hour pink tour, all tours last four hours. Departure is at 9.30am from one of two meeting points: Borgo Marinaro (outside Zi Teresa restaurant) or outside Caffè Gambrinus in Piazza Trieste e Trento. You should book at least 24 hours in advance.

CENTRO STORICO

Eating pp111–2; Shopping pp137–8; Sleeping pp150-2; Walking Tours pp102–4

As you join the tourists, ball-kicking kids, street vendors and students that throng the narrow streets of the *centro storico* you become part of a daily circus that has changed little in hundreds of years. The area may be a Unesco-listed World Heritage Site, but there's no place for sentiment here as history is pushed aside to make way for the here and now: precariously loaded scooters weave quickly through the narrow streets to make deliveries and fishmongers struggle to keep the flies off their wares, while bored policemen smoke menacingly.

However, look beyond this and you'll find more than 2000 years of history. The area was first inhabited in the 1st century BC when the ancient Greeks and Romans established Neapolis (New Town), setting down a street plan that is still evident today. Running dead straight from east to west, the three *decumani*, or main streets, form the foundations on which the area has grown. The most famous of the three is the *decumanus inferior* or, to give it its common name, Spaccanapoli (Break Naples). Comprising Via Benedetto Croce, Via San Biagio dei Librai and Via Vicaria Vecchia, it cuts right through the heart of the old city. One block to the north, Via dei Tribunali is the ancient *decumanus maior*. Most of the major sites are grouped around these two parallel streets. The northernmost of the three ancient roads, the *decumanus superior*, is made up of Via Sapienza, Via Anticaglia and Via Santissimi Apostoli.

Successive rulers left their mark on this ancient structure. In particular, the late 13th and early 14th centuries saw a flurry of construction activity: the Duomo dates to this period, as do both the Chiesa di San Domenico Maggiore and the Basilica di Santa Chiara. Centuries later 17th-century baroque artists went to work, adding a fancy façade here and a rococo *guglia* (obelisk) there.

SPACCANAPOLI

The main street in the *centro storico* is Via San Biagio dei Librai. Lined with historic churches and palazzi, it's here you'll find the Ospedale delle Bambole (Dolls' Hospital; Map pp244–6), a famous landmark and one of the many artisan shops on this street and its continuation, Via Benedetto Croce; see p138 for more information.

At No 39, two blocks west of the Dolls' Hospital, is Palazzo Marigliano (Map pp244–6), behind whose grubby façade is a magnificent Renaissance entrance hall. Carrying on west you pass the Palazzo di Carafa di Maddaloni (Map pp244–6) and the Chiesa di SS Filippo e Giacomo (Map pp244–6) with their contrasting baroque and classical styles.

ARCHIVIO DI STATO Map pp244-6
☎ 081 563 81 11; www.archivi.beniculturali.it/ASNA in Italian; Piazzetta Grande Archivio 5, Via Grande Archivio; ☽ 9am-6pm Mon-Fri, 9am-1pm Sat; bus CS to Via Duomo
Housed in a 15th-century ex-Benedictine monastery, the State Archive was founded in 1835 by the Bourbon King Ferdinand IV. Despite

bomb damage sustained in 1943, it remains one of the biggest archives in Europe – some 300 rooms hold up to one million documents and about 10,000 parchments.

BASILICA DI SANTA CHIARA Map pp244-6
☎ 081 552 62 09; Via Benedetto Croce; cloisters €4, basilica free; basilica ⏱ 7am-12.30pm & 4.30-7pm, cloisters ⏱ 9.30am-1pm & 2.30-5.30pm Mon-Sat, 9.30am-1pm Sun; bus CD to Via Monteoliveto

Simple, severe and vast, the Basilica di Santa Chiara is a spectacular monument to the ability of Italy's restoration experts. The bare Gothic interior that you see today is not the genuine 14th-century article, but a brilliant recreation of Gagliardo Primario's original design. Commissioned by Robert of Anjou for his wife Sancia di Maiorca, the hulking complex was built to house 200 monks and the tombs of the Angevin royal family. Adhering to the Gothic principles of the day that equated height with vicinity to God, the original design met with a lukewarm reaction in some quarters – Robert's son Charles of Anjou brusquely dismissed it as nothing more than a 'stable'. Four centuries later, however, it was given a complete baroque makeover.

Tragedy struck though on 4 August 1943. During an Allied air raid, the church took a direct hit from an incendiary bomb and burned out of control for more than 48 hours. Virtually the entire baroque interior was gutted, along with the main roof and various Angevin

Transport
Bus CD, CS, C55, R2 along Corso Umberto I; E1 along Via Santa Maria di Costantinopoli
Metro Line 1 Piazza Dante

tombs. However, thanks to the skill and dedication of a small army of experts it has been largely restored to its original form. Features that survived the fire include part of a 15th-century fresco to the left of the main door and a chapel containing the tombs of the Bourbon kings from Ferdinand I to Francesco II.

To the left of the church, the famous tiled **cloisters** provide one of the few quiet spots in central Naples. Although dating back to the 14th century, the cloisters took on their current look in the 18th century thanks to the landscaping work of Domenico Antonio Vaccaro. The walkways that divide the central garden are lined with 72 ceramic-tiled octagonal columns connected by benches. Painted by Donato e Giuseppe Massa, the red, blue and yellow majolica tiles depict various scenes from rural life, including numerous images of animals being shot, speared and fished. The four internal walls are covered with colourful frescoes.

Adjacent to the cloisters there is a small **museum** which has various ecclesiastical bits and bobs, including some impressive 14th-century busts and 16th-century liturgical volumes.

Tiled cloister, Basilica di Santa Chiara (above)

Top Five Centro Storico

- Basilica di Santa Chiara (p55)
- Cappella Sansevero (below)
- Pio Monte della Misericordia (p63)
- Duomo (p60)
- Chiesa e Scavi di San Lorenzo Maggiore (p61)

CAPPELLA E MUSEO DEL MONTE DI PIETÀ Map pp244-6

☎ 081 580 71 11; Via San Biagio dei Librai 114;
🕐 9am-7pm Sat, 9am-2pm Sun; bus CS to Via Duomo

An imposing 16th-century complex, the Cappella e Museo del Monte di Pietà was originally home to the Pio Monte di Pietà, an organisation set up to issue interest-free loans to impoverished debtors. Today it houses part of the Banco di Napoli's considerable art collection. Displayed in three rooms to the right of the courtyard, you'll find a mixed bag of paintings, sumptuous embroidery and antique silverware. More impressive, however, is the **chapel** itself and its four richly decorated side rooms. Flanking the entrance to the single-nave chapel are two sculptures by Pietro Bernini, while above sits Michelangelo Naccherino's *Pietà*. Inside, it's the frescoes by Belisario Corenzio that make the biggest impression.

CAPPELLA SANSEVERO Map pp244-6

☎ 081 551 84 70; Via de Sanctis 19; admission €5;
🕐 10am-6pm Mon & Wed-Sat, 10am-1.30pm Sun May-Oct, 10am-5pm Mon & Wed-Sat, 10am-1pm Sun Nov-Apr; bus CD to Via Monteoliveto

For sheer 'how the hell did he do that' impact, the **Cristo Velato** (Veiled Christ) sculpture takes some beating. Giuseppe Sanmartino's incredible depiction of Jesus lying covered by a thin sheet is so realistic that it's tempting to try to lift the veil and look at Christ underneath. The magnificent centrepiece of this opulent chapel is one of three works that defy belief. Similarly lifelike, Francesco Queirolo's *Disinganno* (Disillusion) shows a man trying to untangle himself from a net, while *Pudicizia* (Modesty) by Antonio Corradini is a deliciously salacious veiled nude.

Hidden away in a narrow alley east of San Domenico Maggiore, the Cappella Sansevero, also known as the Cappella di Santa Maria della Pietà dei Sangro, is something of an ecclesiastical curiosity. Originally built around the end of the 16th century to house the tombs of the de Sangro family, it was only when the bizarre

Prince Raimondo de Sangro decided to restyle it that it got its current baroque look. Between 1749 and 1766 he commissioned the top artists of the day to decorate the chapel, while he quietly got on with the task of embalming his dead servants. Determined to crack the art of human preservation, Raimondo was regarded with considerable fear by the local population. You can judge for yourself whether they were right by going down the stairs to the lower floor and checking out the two meticulously preserved human arterial systems.

CHIESA DEL GESÙ NUOVO Map pp244-6

☎ 081 551 86 13; Piazza del Gesù Nuovo;
🕐 6.45am-1pm & 4-7.30pm; bus CD to Via Monteoliveto

The Chiesa del Gesù Nuovo, on the northern side of the piazza, is one of the city's greatest examples of Renaissance architecture. Consecrated in the 16th century, the church is actually the result of a spectacular conversion job. Whether or not it was the peculiar façade of grey, diamond-shaped stones that originally persuaded the Jesuits to buy the 15th-century Palazzo Sanseverino is not known. Still, the fact remains that once they got their hands on it they embarked on some pretty serious decoration. Architect Giuseppe Valeriani designed the church's exterior, while a series of big-name baroque artists, including Francesco Solimena, Luca Giordano and Cosimo Fanzago, transformed the barrel-vaulted interior into the frescoed wonder that you see today.

In sharp contrast to the opulence of the main church is a small **chapel** dedicated to the much-loved local saint Giuseppe Moscati. In here you'll find walls covered with *ex votos* and a recreation of his study, complete with the armchair in which he died. Canonised in 1977, Moscati (1880–1927) was a local doctor who spent his life helping the city's poor.

CHIESA DEL GESÙ VECCHIO

Map pp244-6

☎ 081 552 66 39; Via Giovanni Paladino 38;
🕐 7.30am-noon & 3.45-6pm Mon-Sat, 7.30am-12.30pm Sun; bus R2 to Corso Umberto I

Hidden away down a small sidestreet off Via San Biagio dei Librai, Chiesa del Gesù Vecchio (not to be confused with the more famous Gesù Nuovo) is the oldest Jesuit church in the city. Established in 1570, it was completely rebuilt in the 17th century and in 1777 was taken over by the university. The interior is classical baroque with plenty of gold, statues by Cosimo Fanzago, and frescoes by Francesco

Solimena and Battista Caracciolo. In the midst of all this extravagance it's strange to spot a simple stone from Lourdes exhibited alongside a photo of the French sanctuary.

CHIESA DI SAN DOMENICO MAGGIORE Map pp244-6

☎ 081 45 91 88; Piazza San Domenico Maggiore 8a; ☾ 7.30am-noon & 5-7pm Mon-Sat, 9am-1pm Sun; bus CD to Via Monteoliveto

The Gothic Chiesa di San Domenico Maggiore was completed in 1324 on the orders of Charles of Anjou. Connected to the piazza by a grand marble staircase, the castle-like construction was built on top of the already existing church of Sant'Angelo a Morfisa. The royal church of the Angevins, it was also the city base of the Dominican order.

The church's interior, a cross between baroque and 19th-century neo-Gothic, has undergone various facelifts, leaving very little of the original Gothic design. Of the few remnants of the 14th century, the frescoes by Pietro Cavallini in the **Cappella Brancaccio** stand out. In the **Cappellone del Crocifisso**, the 13th-century *Crocifisso tra La Vergine e San Giovanni* is said to have spoken to St Thomas Aquinas. Legend has it that the good saint was praying before the painting when he heard a voice saying: *'Bene scripsisti di me, Thoma; quam recipies a me pro tu labore mercedem?'* ('You've written good things about me, Thomas, what are you going to get in return?') – *'Domine non aliam nisi te'* ('Nothing if not you, O Lord'), Thomas replied.

In the sacristy there are 45 coffins of the princes of Aragon and other nobles. Curiously enough, the first bishop of New York, Richard Luke Concanen (1747–1810), is also buried here.

CHIESA DI SANT'ANGELO A NILO

Map pp244-6

☎ 081 420 12 22; entrance at Vico Donnaromita 15; ☾ 9am-1pm & 4.30-7pm Mon-Sat, 9am-1pm Sun; bus CD to Via Monteoliveto

Benignly presided over by a quartet of tubby gilt cherubs, this modest 14th-century church contains one of the first great works of art to grace the Neapolitan Renaissance – the majestic tomb of Cardinal Brancaccio, the church's founder. Although considered a part of Naples' artistic heritage, the great sarcophagus was, in fact, sculpted by a crack team of artists in Pisa. Donatello, Michelozzo and Pagno di Lapo Partigiani spent a year chipping away at it before shipping it down to Naples in 1427.

CHIESA E CHIOSTRO DI SAN GREGORIO ARMENO Map pp244-6

☎ 081 552 01 86; Via San Gregorio Armeno 44; church ☾ 9am-noon Mon & Wed-Sat, 9.30am-12.30pm Tue & Sun, cloisters ☾ 9.30am-noon Mon-Fri & Sun, 9.30am-12.30pm Sat; bus CS to Via Duomo

Baroque décor and legend are combined in this fascinating religious complex. Comprising a convent and a small 16th-century church, it was originally founded in the 13th century by a group of nuns fleeing persecution in Constantinople. The sisters named the church after the Bishop of Armenia, San Gregorio, whose earthly remains they were carrying with them. More famously, though, they also kept the relics and dried blood of Santa Patrizia (St Patricia) who, having escaped from Constantinople, died in Naples sometime between the 4th and 8th centuries. Patricia's powdered blood is said to liquefy every Tuesday, unlike that of Naples' patron saint San Gennaro, who can only manage it three times a year.

The church itself is currently undergoing restoration but when it's finished it'll be quite a sight. A spectacular ensemble of baroque opulence, it boasts works by artists such as Luca Giordano and Dionisio Lazzari. The cloisters are accessible by a gate on nearby Via Maffei.

CHIESA SAN GIOVANNI PAPPACODA

Map pp244-6

☎ 081 552 69 48; Largo San Giovanni Maggiore; bus R2 to Corso Umberto I

This small yellow-fronted church owes its name to Artusio Pappacoda, a nobleman and councillor at the court of the Angevin King Ladislas. Like so many of Naples' churches, its original 15th-century structure barely survived the attentions of a later makeover, in this case in the 18th century. Antonio Baboccio's Gothic portal remains, along with a bell tower constructed out of tufa, marble and *piperno*, a hard volcanic rock from the Campi Flegrei.

GUGLIA DELL'IMMACOLATA

Map pp244-6

Piazza del Gesù Nuovo; bus CD to Via Monteoliveto

Standing in the centre of the Piazza del Gesù Nuovo, this highly ornate baroque *guglia* is regarded as one of Naple's finest examples of 18th-century sculpture. Commissioned by the Jesuits and dedicated to the Madonna (who stands at the top of the 30m-high extravaganza), it was built between 1747 and 1750 to a design by Giuseppe Genuino. Inspired by ancient Egyptian obelisks, it owes much of its

A Man for all Seasons

Benedetto Croce was Italy's leading 20th-century intellect. A gentleman scholar, Croce never held a university position, nor completed his degree, yet he was a hugely influential critic, philosopher and historian.

Born in 1866 to a wealthy landowning family in Abruzzo, Croce was to spend the best part of his life in Naples. After the death of his parents and sisters in an earthquake in 1883, he briefly moved to Rome to study law, but never completed his studies. Returning to Naples, he set up camp in Palazzo Filomarino (right) where he lived for the rest of his life.

A man of conservative tastes, Croce was also politically active. In 1910 he was made a senator for life and 10 years later he became the Minister for Education. An arch critic of Fascism, he was president of the Italian Liberal Party (1943–47) and a major advocate for the Italian constitution.

Philosophically, Croce is best known as an idealist. He believed that the spirit was the only reality and that artistic expression was the logical outcome of intuition.

Croce died in 1952.

intricate beauty to the Jesuits whose insistence on a flamboyant design was fuelled by propagandistic aims. Envisaged as a symbol of their power, it was financed according to a simple maxim – the more spectacular the design, the more powerful they would seem to be.

GUGLIA DI SAN DOMENICO Map pp244-6
Piazza San Domenico Maggiore; bus CD to Via Monteoliveto

The baroque *guglia* in Piazza San Domenico was commissioned by Naples' elected citizens in 1656. A token of gratitude to San Domenico for his help in ridding the city of the plague epidemic, the *guglia* was decorated by Cosimo Fanzago and completed in 1737 by Domenico Antonio Vaccaro, better known for his work on the cloisters at Santa Chiara.

It's a reminder of the infamous 17th-century plague epidemic that swept through the entire Campania region, leaving up to 75% of Naples' population dead.

LARGO SAN GIOVANNI MAGGIORE
Map pp244-6
Largo San Giovanni Maggiore; bus R2 to Corso Umberto I

Much frequented by students, Largo San Giovanni Maggiore is an attractive square on the *centro storico*'s southern fringes. Dominating

the western flank is the impressive Palazzo Giusso, now home to the Istituto Universitario Orientale. The imposing palace was built in 1549 to designs by Giovanni da Nola, and for a period in the 17th century it was home to Cardinal Filomarino. Facing this is the Chiesa San Giovanni Pappacoda and tucked into the corner of the piazza, the popular bar Vibes (p129).

PALAZZO FILOMARINO Map pp244-6
Via Benedetto Croce 12; bus CD to Via Monteoliveto

It would be easy to miss this historic palazzo. Like many of Naples' grand buildings it's in pretty poor nick, with the dirty façade in urgent need of a thorough going over. Palazzo Filomarino owes its fame to Benedetto Croce, Italy's foremost 20th-century philosopher and historian, who lived here until his death in 1952. The original building dates to the 13th century but underwent alterations in the 16th century and again after it was damaged during the 17th-century revolt of Masaniello (see p45). The doorway was a later addition, designed by architect Sanfelice in the 18th century. The building now houses the Istituto Studi Storici and the 40,000-volume library that Croce (see opposite) bequeathed to the institute.

PIAZZA DEL GESÙ NUOVO Map pp244-6
Bus CD to Via Monteoliveto

Flanked by the Chiesa del Gesù Nuovo (p56) and the Basilica di Santa Chiara (p55), this lively square is one of Spaccanapoli's most impressive spaces. Dominated by its baroque guglia, for hundreds of years it was the principal western entrance to the city. But it wasn't until two major modifications in the 16th century that the piazza took on its current proportions. Firstly, Ferrante Sanseverino decided to knock down the houses that were blocking his beautiful 15th-century palazzo (later to become the Chiesa del Gesù Nuovo) and in one fell swoop cleared the square's northern flank. Some years later and in order to clear a path to his brand new Quartieri Spagnoli, Spanish viceroy Don Pedro de Toledo demolished the Angevin city gate and once again moved the city walls westwards.

PIAZZA SAN DOMENICO MAGGIORE
Map pp244-6
Bus CD to Via Monteoliveto

Most evenings, this vivacious square hums with activity as crowds of all ages gather to hang out with a bottle of beer, or share a cigarette with friends. Headed by the Chiesa di San Domenico Maggiore (p57) and flanked by

Chiesa del Gesù Nuovo (p56)

imposing **palazzi**, the piazza didn't become an important site until the 15th century. Up until then it had been largely covered by gardens, but when the Aragonese decided to make San Domenico their royal church the gardens were flattened. Later, in the 17th century, various aristocrats built their townhouses around the square and a **guglia** was added.

STATUA DEL NILO Map pp244-6
Piazzetta Nilo, Via Nilo; bus CD to Via Monteoliveto
This rather grim statue of the ancient Egyptian river god Nilo was put up by the city's

Alessandrian community during Roman times. When they moved out of town, however, the statue disappeared. It eventually turned up minus its head in the 15th century. Renamed *Il Corpo di Napoli* (The Body of Naples), it remained headless until the end of the 18th century when a great big bearded bonce was added.

VIA SAN GREGORIO ARMENO
Map pp244-6
Bus CS to Via Duomo
Naples is famous for its traditional *presepi* (nativity scenes) and Via San Gregorio Armeno is the street where people from all over Italy come to buy theirs. Running north off Spaccanapoli, the street is lined with shops crammed full of thousands of figurines, ranging from traditional religious characters to caricatures of well-known film stars and politicians. You can buy grinning Berlusconis and grotesque Laurels and Hardys, sweet little lambs and flying angels.

> ### Altar to the Maradona
>
> Opposite the Statua del Nilo there is an altar to an altogether more temporal deity. Argentine football player Diego Armando Maradona is worshipped throughout the city and so it's only natural that he should have his own small corner. Displayed on the wall outside the Bar Nilo, the **Maradona altar** (Map pp244–6) a small glass case containing a number of artefacts relating to the great man. Stuck to an epic poem written in his honour is a small wiry black hair – 'Kapel Original of Maradona' reads the English label, a direct translation of the Italian *Capello originale di Maradona*. You can also admire a small container full of genuine Maradona tears. And shame on anyone who suggests it's only water.

VIA DUOMO
Built as part of the late 19th-century *Risanamento* (slum-clearance programme), Via Duomo connects Corso Umberto I with Via Foria and more or less runs parallel to Via Toledo.

BASILICA DI SAN GIORGIO MAGGIORE Map pp244-6

☎ 081 28 79 32; Via Duomo 237; ⊗ 8am-noon & 5-7.30pm Mon-Sat, 8.30am-1.30pm Sun; bus CS to Via Duomo

One of the oldest churches in Naples, the Basilica di San Giorgio Maggiore dates back to the 4th century. It was built by St Severus but took on its modern form in the mid–17th century when Cosimo Fanzago oversaw a thorough restyling. Two hundred years later the right-hand wing of the church was demolished to make way for Via Duomo.

The church merits a quick look for its classical and relatively austere – by Neapolitan standards – interior.

CHIESA E PINACOTECA DEI GIROLAMINI Map pp244-6

☎ 081 44 91 39; Via Duomo 142; ⊗ pinacoteca 9am-12.50pm Mon-Sat; bus CS to Via Duomo

Opposite the Duomo is the entrance to the Chiesa dei Girolamini, also called San Filippo Neri, a rich baroque church of two façades. The more imposing 18th-century façade, facing Via dei Tribunali, is now closed for restoration. A small **picture gallery** on the 1st floor of the adjoining convent has mainly local works from the 16th to the 18th centuries. Artists represented include Luca Giordano, Battista Caracciolo and Giuseppe de Ribera. The convent also houses a 60,000-volume library which, unfortunately, is also closed to the public.

DUOMO Map pp244-6

☎ 081 44 90 97; www.duomodinapoli.com; Via Duomo 147; ⊗ 8am-12.30pm & 4.30-7pm Mon-Sat, 8am-1.30pm & 5-7.30pm Sun; bus CS to Via Duomo

Built on the site of earlier churches, which were themselves preceded by a temple to the god Neptune, this cathedral was begun in 1272 by King Charles I of Anjou and consecrated in 1315. Largely destroyed in 1456 by an earthquake, it's undergone numerous alterations. The neo-Gothic façade is the result of late-19th-century cosmetic surgery. Inside, above the huge central nave, is an ornately decorated coffered ceiling.

Central to Naples' religious (some would say superstitious) life is the 17th-century baroque **Cappella di San Gennaro** (Chapel of St Januarius; also known as Cappella del Tesoro, or the Chapel of the Treasury). Designed by Giovanni Cola di Franco and featuring frescoes by Giovanni Lanfranco and a painting by Giuseppe de Ribera, it was completed in 1637 to house the skull and blood of San Gennaro, the city's patron saint.

Also on display is an impressive collection of silver busts and bronze statues depicting all the saints of Naples' churches.

San Gennaro was martyred at Pozzuoli, in AD 305 and tradition holds that the phials of his blood liquefied when his body was taken back to Naples. Every year in May, September and December thousands gather here to pray for a miracle – that the blood will again liquefy and save Naples from potential disaster. The saint is said to have saved the city from calamity numerous times – although the miracle failed to occur in 1944 when Vesuvius erupted.

The next chapel eastwards contains an urn with the saint's bones, cupboards full of femurs, tibias and fibulas and a stash of other relics. Below the high altar is the **Cappella Carafa**, also known as the Crypt of San Gennaro, a Renaissance chapel built to house yet more of the saint's earthly remains.

On the north aisle the **Basilica di Santa Restituta** is one of Naples' oldest basilicas, dating to the 4th century. Incorporated into the main cathedral, it was subject to an almost complete makeover following damage incurred in an earthquake in 1688. Beyond this is the **archaeological zone** (admission €3; ⊗ 9am-12.30pm & 4.30-7pm Mon-Sat, 9am-1pm Sun). The tunnels beneath lead you deep into the remains of the site's original Greek and Roman buildings. Here, too, is the baptistry, the oldest in Western Europe, with its remarkably fresh 4th-century mosaics.

MUSEO DEL TESORO DI SAN GENNARO Map pp244-6

☎ 081 29 49 80; Via Duomo 149; admission €5.50; ⊗ 9am-6.30pm Mon-Sat, 9.30am-7pm Sun; bus CS to Via Duomo

Situated on the southern side of the Duomo, this recently inaugurated museum contains an impressive collection of 13th- to 18th-century silverware. Donated over a period of seven centuries, the pieces all belong to the San Gennaro treasure – a rich collection of jewellery, busts, statues and paintings. Included in the price of the ticket is a multilingual audioguide.

PALAZZO CUOMO & MUSEO CIVICO FILANGIERI Map pp244-6

☎ 081 20 31 75; Via Duomo 288; ⊗ currently closed for restoration

Housed in the 15th-century Palazzo Cuomo, this museum was founded in 1882 by Gaetano Filangieri to showcase his collection of sculpture, paintings, porcelain, medieval weapons, precious coins and historical manuscripts.

Originally built by Tuscan craftsmen, Palazzo Cuomo was moved 20m down the hill to its current position in 1881 after it was knocked down to make space for Via Duomo.

VIA DEI TRIBUNALI

The Roman *decumanus maior*, Via dei Tribunali parallels Via San Biagio dei Librai one block to the north.

CASTEL CAPUANO Map pp244-6

☎ 081 223 72 44; Piazza Enrico De Nicola; metro Garibaldi

Scenes of chaos around Castel Capuano are a daily occurrence. The Norman castle has been the seat of the city's civil courts since 1540, and the crowd of lawyers, noisy families and menacing police around the main entrance is a permanent feature. The fort was built in 1165 by William I, known as *Il Malo* (The Wicked; see below), to guard the nearby city gate Porta Capuana. Later enlarged by the Swabian king Frederick II and fortified by Charles I of Anjou, it remained a royal residence until the 16th century when Don Pedro de Toledo made it the city court.

The castle is not open to the public.

William the Wicked

William's role in history was not a great one. The fourth son of the highly charismatic Norman king Roger II, he would never have succeeded his father to the throne if his three elder brothers hadn't all died between 1138 and 1158. Unprepared for power, he did not make a great impression on the people of Naples, or indeed on anyone.

King of Sicily between 1154 and 1166 – at the time Naples was part of the Kingdom of Sicily – William took to the languid lifestyle of a pampered king with gusto. The pleasures afforded him by the palaces of Palermo were, according to the historians, much to his taste. The onerous business of ruling he left to his lieutenant Maio of Bari.

An unscrupulous wielder of power, Maio continued Roger II's policy of excluding the powerful barons from the ruling administration. It was a tactic that William was happy enough to go along with, earning himself the nickname *Il Malo* (The Wicked) and Maio an early grave; the Machiavellian politician was murdered in Palermo in November 1160. William saw out the rest of his years in relative peace, secure (a relative term in the bloody politics of 12th-century Italy) in the support of Pope Adrian IV.

CHIESA DI SAN PAOLO MAGGIORE

Map pp244-6

☎ 081 45 40 48; Piazza San Gaetano 76; ☺ 9am-1pm Mon-Sat, 11am-noon Sun; bus CS to Via Duomo

The Chiesa di San Paolo Maggiore stands at the head of tiny Piazza San Gaetano. Leading up to the entrance is a grand double staircase built by baroque master Francesco Grimaldi in 1603. Situated on the site of a Roman temple, of which the only two columns flanking the entrance are the only visible sign, the church dates to the 9th century but was virtually entirely rebuilt at the end of the 16th century. The interior is huge and typically baroque, with paintings by Massimo Stanzione and Paolo De Matteis. Particularly beautiful are Francesco Solimena's frescoes in the sacristy, to the right of the altar.

CHIESA E SCAVI DI SAN LORENZO MAGGIORE Map pp244-6

☎ 081 29 05 80; Via dei Tribunali 316; excavations adult/child €4/2; ☺ 9am-5pm Mon-Sat, 9.30am-1.30pm Sun; bus CS to Via Duomo

One of the highlights of the *centro storico*, the Chiesa di San Lorenzo Maggiore is a cathedral of calm in one of Naples' noisiest areas. Magnificently bare, the French Gothic interior is huge, with massive arches stretching up to the sky and streams of light beaming down onto the stone floor. Catherine of Austria, who died in 1323, is buried here and her mosaic-covered tomb is among the most eye-catching. Legend has it that this was where Boccaccio first fell for Mary of Anjou, the inspiration for his character Fiammetta, while history records that Petrarch lived in the adjoining convent in 1345.

Beneath the complex are some extraordinary **scavi** (excavations) of the original Graeco-Roman city. As you go down into the dark it's as if someone switches off the volume, so silent are the dimly lit passageways. There are very few signs to explain the patchwork of crumbling walls and alleyways but this takes little away from the experience – simply let your imagination do the job. (You can, however, buy a glossy leaflet that explains the excavations in Italian or English for €1.50.)

Stretching the length of the underground area is a 54m-long road paved with *piperno*, a hard volcanic rock from the nearby Campi Flegrei. On to this open a series of bakeries, wineries and laundries, as well as a number of communal washbasins used for washing and dying clothes. At the far end of the *cardo* (road) there's a *cryptoporticus* (covered market) with seven barrel-vaulted rooms.

CHIESA SANTA CATERINA A FORMIELLO Map pp242-3

☎ 081 44 42 97; Piazza Enrico De Nicola 65;
🕒 8.30am-8pm Mon-Sat, 8.30am-2pm Sun;
metro Garibaldi

This richly decorated Renaissance church may be considered one of the most beautiful in Naples, but it's difficult to tell as you struggle to detect the artwork through the thick layers of grime. The décor is decidedly baroque, and under the dust there are a series of exceptional frescoes by Luigi Garzi, as well as the relics of the martyrs of Otranto. The martyrs were all killed in 1480 when Turkish invaders swept into the Puglian coastal town after a lengthy siege and vented their bloody fury by killing 800 citizens. The relics were brought to Naples on the express wishes of Alfonso II of Aragon.

Dedicated to Santa Caterina, a martyr from Alessandria, the church was commissioned in 1510 and completed in 1593. For 300 years it belonged to the Dominicans, but in the 19th century they moved out and the military moved in, transforming it into a wool factory.

CHIESA SANTA MARIA MAGGIORE

Map pp244-6
Via dei Tribunali 16; 🕒 9am-1pm Mon-Sat; bus CS to Via Duomo

Santa Maria Maggiore alla Pietrasanta, the full title of this church, is a reference to a 17th-century practice of kissing the church's *pietrasanta* (holy stone) to gain indulgences. Dating to the 6th century, the church was originally built by San Pomponio, the Bishop of Naples, on the ruins of an earlier Roman building. It was later modified in the 17th century by Cosimo Fanzago, whose dome is visible from miles around. The church suffered severe damage during WWII but fortunately the Romanesque **campanile** (bell tower) was not damaged. Built sometime between the 10th and 11th centuries, it is one of Naples' oldest.

CHIESA SANTA MARIA DELLE ANIME PURGATORIO AD ARCO Map pp244-6

☎ 081 29 26 22; Via dei Tribunali 39; 🕒 9am-2pm Mon-Sat; bus CS to Via Duomo

Guarded by three bronze skulls, this 17th-century church is a macabre place. The sinister motif continues inside where two winged skulls stare out from either side of the main altar. Built by a congregation dedicated to praying for souls in purgatory, the church became a centre for the Neapolitan cult of the

---

For Children

- Anfiteatro Flavio, Pozzuoli (opposite)
- Catacomba di San Gennaro (p100)
- Città della Scienza (p100)
- Edenlandia (p94)
- Museo di Mineralogia, Zoologia e Antropologia (p77)
- Solfatara crater, Pozzuoli (p98)
- Stazione Zoologica (p98)

---

dead which, although officially banned, is said to be far from extinct. Cult practices included lavishing care and gifts on a skull as a means of keeping in touch with an absent loved one. Below the church in the **hypogeum** (currently closed) you can still see a dusty hoard of skulls and bones.

On a lighter note, the church boasts some fine paintings by Massimo Stanzione and Luca Giordano.

CHIESA SAN PIETRO A MAIELLA

Map pp244-6
☎ 081 45 90 08; Via San Pietro a Maiella 4;
🕒 7.30am-noon & 5.30-7.30pm Sun-Fri, 5-7.30pm Sat; bus CD to Via Santa Maria di Costantinopoli

Not many churches are dedicated to hermits. But not many hermits go on to become popes as Pietro Angeleri da Monone did when, in 1294, he was named Pope Celestine V. The typically Gothic interior dates to the 14th century, but the ceiling is pure baroque with 10 round paintings by Mattia Preti and some impressively intricate woodwork. Further baroque touches are provided by Cosimo Fanzago and Massimo Stanzione, whose *Madonna Appearing to Celestine V* hangs in one of the side chapels on the right.

Since 1826, Naples' Conservatory, one of the most important music schools in Italy, has been housed in the **convent** adjacent to the church.

GUGLIA DI SAN GENNARO pp244-6

Piazza Riario Sforza; bus CS to Via Duomo

The oldest of the three obelisks in the *centro storico*, the Guglia di San Gennaro was dedicated to the city's patron saint in 1636. And like the Guglia di San Domenico it was a token of gratitude, only this time to San Gennaro for protecting the city from the 1631 eruption of Mt Vesuvius. The stonework is by Cosimo Fanzago, the statue at the top by Tommaso Montani.

MUSEO DI MINERALOGIA, ZOOLOGIA E ANTROPOLOGIA Map pp244-6

☎ 081 253 51 60; www.unina.it in Italian; Via Mezzocannone 8; admission for each museum €0.70; 🕙 9am-1.30pm Mon-Sat, 9am-1pm Sun; bus R2 to Corso Umberto I

Within the university is a museum complex, the Museo di Mineralogia, Zoologia e Antropologia. The Museo della Mineralogia is considered the most important museum of its type in Italy. Founded by the Bourbon king Ferdinand II, it features some 30,000 minerals, meteorites and quartz crystals collected from the Vesuvius region and as far afield as Madagascar.

The Museo della Zoologia is the most child-friendly of the three, with its collections of birds, butterflies and insects. The elephant skeleton also makes a dramatic sight. The third of the three museums, the Museo della Antropologia, across the courtyard, contains a collection of prehistoric relics including a Palaeolithic skeleton from the southern region of Puglia and a Bolivian mummy.

PALAZZO SPINELLI DI LAURINO

Map pp244-6

Via dei Tribunali 362; bus CS to Via Duomo

Dodge past the porter patrolling the entrance to this Renaissance palazzo and you'll find that the cars are parked on an unusual oval-shaped courtyard. This, together with the imposing double staircase, was the work of architect Ferdinando Sanfelice, whose hallmark staircase design became something of a novelty among the 18th-century Neapolitan nobility.

PIAZZA BELLINI Map pp244-6

bus CD to Via Santa Maria di Costantinopoli

Just to the north of the western end of Via dei Tribunali, Piazza Bellini is one of the historic centre's most vibrant squares. A favourite of the jazz-loving, left-wing bohemian set, its lively ivy-clad cafés and bars hum until late into the night. In the centre of the square, virtually hidden by the trees and foliage, you can see sections of the original Greek **city walls**. Until the mid-16th century the square actually lay outside the walls; it was only when Don Pedro de Toledo, the Spanish viceroy, moved them further west that the piazza was incorporated into the city proper.

PIO MONTE DELLA MISERICORDIA

Map pp244-6

☎ 081 44 69 44; Via dei Tribunali 253; church admission free, gallery €5; church 🕙 9.30am-12.30pm Mon-Sat, gallery 🕙 8.30am-2.30pm Tue, Thu & Sat; bus CS to Via Duomo

Caravaggio's masterpiece *Le sette opere di Misericordia* (The Seven Acts of Mercy) is considered by many to be the single most important painting in Naples. And it's here that you will see it, hung above the main altar of this

Chilling out in a café, Piazza Bellini (above)

small eight-sided church. The painting magnificently demonstrates Caravaggio's unique style that had such a revolutionary impact in Naples (see p20 for more information). A disturbing image, it depicts two angels reaching down towards a group of shadowy Neapolitan characters, while on the right a young woman feeds her exposed breast to a hungry grey-bearded man.

On the 1st floor of the 17th-century church is a small **art gallery** that displays the art collection of the Pio Monte, a city institution founded in 1601 to help the poor.

PORTA CAPUANA Map pp242-3
Piazza Enrico de Nicola; metro Garibaldi
Standing across the square from Castel Capuano and alongside the Chiesa Santa Caterina a Formiello, the imposing Porta Capuana was one of the city's main medieval gates. Built on the orders of Ferdinand II of Aragon in 1484, the two cylindrical towers, named Honour and Virtue, flank a white marble–clad triumphal arch. Giuliano da Maiano oversaw the intricate decoration centred on Charles V's coat of arms.

PORT'ALBA Map pp244-6
Via Port'Alba; metro Piazza Dante
The area around this medieval city gate is particularly atmospheric. It's best known for the bookshops and second-hand bookstalls that line the street, selling everything from Lonely Planet guides to obscure 1950s sci-fi novels. The gate, which leads through to Piazza Dante, was opened in 1625 by Antonio Alvárez, the Spanish viceroy of Naples.

DECUMANUS SUPERIOR
The most northern of the *decumani*, the *superior* comprises Via Sapienza, Via Anticaglia and Via Santissimi Apostoli.

CHIESA SANTA MARIA DONNAREGINA NUOVA Map pp242-3
☎ 081 44 18 06; Largo Donnaregina 7; bus CS to Via Duomo
Undergoing one mighty slow restoration – the church has been closed to the public since 1972 – Santa Maria Donnaregina Nuova was built in the 17th century to give the nuns of the adjacent convent more room to pray. The design of the church was assigned to Giovanni Guarino, while Francesco de Benedictis and Francesco Solimena looked after the painting. The façade features the statues of Sant'Andrea and San Bartolomeo.

CHIESA SANTA MARIA DONNAREGINA VECCHIA Map pp242-3
☎ 081 44 18 06; Vico Donnaregina 25;
☯ 9am-12.30pm Sat by appointment only; bus CS to Via Duomo
The older of the two Donnaregina churches, the Vecchia (Old) dates back to the 8th century when it was annexed onto an existing convent. Built at the behest of Mary of Hungary, wife of Charles II of Anjou, it was seriously damaged in an earthquake in 1293 and later in the 14th century by a fire. However, Mary's spectacular marble tomb (created by Tina da Camaino between 1326 and 1327) survives, along with some magnificent frescoes by Pietro Cavallini.

TOLEDO & QUARTIERI SPAGNOLI
Eating pp112–5; Shopping pp139–41; Sleeping p153

After the cramped alleyways of the *centro storico*, Via Toledo can come as a relief – although if you're hoping to escape the crowds, forget it. The nearest thing Naples has to a high street, it's not only the city's main shopping strip but also the Neapolitans' favourite spot for an afternoon stroll. People flock to the department stores or to grab an ice cream; impromptu football games spring up in the lower pedestrianised section, while further up white-helmeted traffic wardens whistle into the wind as they woefully fail to direct the anarchic traffic.

Via Toledo connects Piazza Trieste e Trento with Piazza Dante, at which point it becomes Via Enrico Pessina as it continues north to the Museo Archeologico Nazionale and beyond. It is named after Don Pedro de Toledo, the Spanish viceroy of Naples between 1532 and 1553. An enthusiastic town planner, Don Pedro had great designs for Naples, central to which was his plan to extend the city westwards. When he decided to build a new quarter to house his Spanish troops, he naturally turned west.

The resulting Quartieri Spagnoli, which lies to the west of Via Toledo, is an area of narrow, criss-crossing streets that over the centuries has earned notoriety as a hotbed of crime and urban malaise. The infamous *bassi* (one room, ground-floor houses) became, and still are, home to entire families, while the mean streets provided fertile ground for the spread of organised crime. It is said that the area is still controlled by the Camorra (the Neapolitan Mafia; see p11 for more information), although as a visitor this probably won't affect you. You should, however, keep a close eye on your valuables if you visit the area which, despite a lack of sites per se, has a certain menacing appeal. You're unlikely to get mugged but bag-snatchers are at work.

The centuries have, in contrast, been kinder to Via Toledo. Constructed along the lines of the Aragonese city walls, Don Pedro's great boulevard became one of Europe's great streets and the address of choice for many aristocrats. Today you can still see the grand 17th- to 19th-century palazzi even if many are showing increasing signs of wear and tear. The colossal Fascist buildings, such as the Palazzo della Poste, are, however, looking as brutal and solid as ever.

In 1860 Via Toledo was renamed Via Roma to celebrate the birth of the new Italian republic and, although it has recently reverted to its original name, you'll still see it labelled Via Roma on some maps.

ACCADEMIA DI BELLE ARTI

Map ppp244-6

☎ 081 444 25; Via Santa Maria di Costantinopoli 107; ☽ 9am-2pm Mon-Fri; bus CD to Via Santa Maria di Costantinopoli

The Accademia di Belle Arti transferred to its current 17th-century home shortly after Italian unification in 1860. Formerly the convent of San Giovanni Battista delle Monache, the building was given a thorough makeover in 1864. Architect Enrico Alvino followed the fashions of the day and gave the academy a neoclassical façade and a grand staircase, along with two noble lions to guard the main entrance. Today the academy houses an important collection consisting mainly of 18th-century Neapolitan and French paintings. There is also another entrance to the academy on Via Bellini.

CHIESA DI SANT'ANNA
DEI LOMBARDI Map pp244-6

☎ 081 551 33 33; Piazza Monteoliveto; ☽ 8.30am-12.30pm Tue-Sat; bus CD to Via Monteoliveto

Despite the ugly scaffolding, you can still see enough of the interior to appreciate that the Chiesa di Sant'Anna dei Lombardi is one of the most beautiful churches in all of Naples. In fact, it's often spoken about as being more a museum of Renaissance art than a church; a fact that owes much to the close links that existed between the Neapolitan Aragonese and the Florentine Medici dynasty. It also houses some elegant tombs.

The main, but by no means only attraction of the church is Guido Mazzoni's spectacular

Transport

Bus CD, CS, C55, R1, R2, 24, 201
Metro Line 1 Piazza Dante; Line 2 Cavour & Montesanto
Funicular Centrale Toledo; Montesanto

work *Pietà*. Dating back to 1492, the terracotta ensemble is made up of eight life-size figures surrounding the dead body of Christ. Originally the figures were painted, but even though time has faded away the colours they still make quite an impression.

The **Sacrestia** is a work of art in itself. The walls are lined with gloriously inlaid wood panels by Giovanni da Verona, while the ceiling is covered by Giorgio Vasaari's 16th-century frescoes depicting the Allegories and Symbols of Faith.

Across Via Monteoliveto from the church is the 16th-century **Palazzo Gravina** (Map pp244–6), today the seat of the university's architecture faculty.

GALLERIA PRINCIPE DI NAPOLI

Map pp244-6

Piazza Museo Nazionale; bus CD to Via Santa Maria di Costantinopoli

In a pretty sorry state today, the Galleria Principe di Napoli, is an abandoned neoclassical shopping arcade. Built between 1870 and 1883, its structure of iron and glass is almost identical to that of the much more famous Galleria Umberto I, located at the lower end of Via Toledo.

MUSEO ARCHEOLOGICO NAZIONALE

Map pp244-6

☎ 081 44 01 66; www.cib.na.cnr.it/mann/museo1 /mann.html in Italian; Piazza Museo Nazionale 19; admission €6.50; 🕙 9am-7.30pm Wed-Mon; metro Museo

Naples' top attraction, this spectacular archaeological museum is considered by many the most important in Europe. And even if the idea of an archaeology museum usually sends you to sleep, this place will amaze you. With many of the best finds from Pompeii and Herculaneum on display, as well as hundreds of classical sculptures and a treasure trove of ancient Roman pornography, the Museo Archeologico Nazionale's collection of Graeco-Roman artefacts is considered one of the most comprehensive in the world.

Originally a cavalry barracks and later the seat of the city's university (Palazzo dei Regi Studi), the museum was established by the Bourbon king Charles VII in the late 18th century to house the rich collection of antiquities he had inherited from his mother, Elisabetta Farnese. However, he never lived to see its inauguration; he died in 1788, 28 years before the Reale Museo Borbonico (Royal Bourbon Museum) was opened by his successor

Ferdinand IV. Forty-four years later, in 1860, the museum became the property of the new Italian state.

Before you venture into the galleries – numbered in Roman numerals – it's worth arming yourself with some navigational aids: invest €7.50 in the green quick guide *National Archaeological Museum of Naples* or, to concentrate upon the highlights, €4 for an audioguide in English.

The museum is spread out over four floors. In the basement you will find the Borgia collection of Etruscan and Egyptian relics, while it is on the ground floor that the great Greek and Roman sculptures are displayed; the world-famous *Toro Farnese* (Farnese Bull) is in Room XVI. Continuing up the grand staircase, the mezzanine floor houses the intricate mosaics from Pompeii and the ancient smut in the Gabinetto Segreto (Secret Chamber). Centred round the massive Sala Meridiana (Great Hall of the Sundial), the 1st-floor rooms contain further artefacts from Pompeii, as well as a scale model of the ancient city. In the rooms on the 2nd floor there are various engraved coppers and Greek vases.

You could easily spend a couple of days exploring the museum, although it is possible to do an abridged tour in a morning.

Museo Archeologico Nazionale (above)

The two highlights of the Farnese collection of classical sculpture are the *Toro Farnese* and the gigantic *Ercole* (Hercules). Sculpted in the early 3rd century AD and noted in the writings of Pliny, the *Toro Farnese*, probably a Roman copy of a Greek original, depicts the death of Dirce, Queen of Thebes. According to Greek mythology she was tied to a wild bull by Zeto and Amphion as punishment for her treatment of their mother Antiope, the first wife of King Lykos of Thebes. Carved from a single colossal block of marble, the sculpture was discovered in 1545 near the Baths of Caracalla in Rome and after restoration by Michelangelo, it was shipped to Naples in 1787.

Ercole (Room XI) was discovered in the same Roman dig and like the *Toro Farnese* remained in Rome until 1787. Originally without legs, Ercole had a new pair made for him by Guglielmo della Porta. In fact, the story goes that the Farnese were so impressed with della Porta's work that they refused to reinstate the original legs when they were subsequently found. The Bourbons, however, had no such qualms and later attached the originals to their rightful place. You can see the della Porta legs displayed on the wall behind *Ercole*.

On the mezzanine floor, the collection of mosaics is incredible. Of the series taken from the Casa del Fauno in Pompeii, it is *La Battaglia di Alessandro contro Dario* (The Battle of Alexander against Darius) in Room LXI that stands out. The best-known depiction of Alexander the Great, the 20-sq-metre mosaic was probably made by Alexandrian craftsmen working in Italy around the end of the 2nd century BC. Of the other mosaics in the collection, that of a cat killing a duck in Room LX impresses with its portrayal of feline ferocity, while in Room LXIII, the study of Nile River animals combines art with zoology.

Beyond the mosaics is the **Gabinetto Segreto** and its small but much studied collection of ancient porn. The room was only reopened to the public in 2000 after decades of being accessible only to the seriously scientific (see boxed text, p20). Guarding the entrance is a marble statue of a decidedly lascivious-looking Pan draped over a very coy Daphne. Pan is then caught in the act, this time with a nanny goat, in the collection's most famous piece – a small and surprisingly sophisticated statue taken from the Villa dei Papri in Herculaneum. There are also nine paintings depicting erotic positions, which served as a menu for brothel clients.

Originally the royal library, the **Sala Meridiana** is enormous. Measuring 54m long and 20m high, it contains the Farnese *Atlante*, a statue of Atlas carrying a globe on his shoulders, and various paintings from the Farnese collection. The rest of the 1st floor is largely devoted to a treasure trove of discoveries from Pompeii, Herculaneum, Stabiae and Cuma. Items range from huge murals and frescoes to a pair of gladiator's helmets, household items, ceramics and glassware – even eggcups. Rooms LXXXVI and LXXXVII house an extraordinary collection of vases of mixed origins, many of which have been carefully reassembled from fragments.

PALAZZO DELLE POSTE Map pp244-6
☎ 081 551 14 56; Piazza G Matteotti 3;
🕑 8.15am-7pm Mon-Fri, 8.15am-noon Sat; bus CD to Via Monteoliveto

Naples' main post office is housed in one of the city's best examples of Fascist architecture. Designed in 1935 by Giuseppe Vaccaro as part of a drive to modernise the area around Piazza G Matteotti, it features a number of Fascist architectural hallmarks: most noticeably its monumental size and the writing on the curved façade.

PIAZZA DANTE Map pp244-6
Metro Piazza Dante

Piazza Dante is one of the best places in the city to people-watch. On warm summer evenings entire families decamp here to walk, smoke, play cards, kick a ball round, chase balloons, feed the pigeons, have dinner, get drunk, or simply sit and stare.

The eastern flank of the square is taken up by the enormous façade of the **Convitto Nazionale**. A huge building, which now houses schools, shops and cafés, it was the highlight of Luigi Vanvitelli's spectacular 18th-century square. Dedicated to the Bourbon king Charles VII, it was known as the Foro Carolino until Italian unification in 1860 when it was renamed Piazza Dante. At the centre of the square, a marble Dante stands looking out over Via Toledo.

PIAZZA MONTEOLIVETO Map pp244-6
Bus CD to Via Monteoliveto

A small piazza to the east of Via Toledo, Piazza Monteoliveto is headed by the regional command station of the *carabiniere* (military police) and the Chiesa di Sant'Anna dei Lombardi. The lower end of the square opens on to Via Monteoliveto and features a baroque statue of Bourbon King Charles VII standing atop an ensemble of spewing lions and elaborately carved eagles.

SANTA LUCIA

Eating pp115–6; Shopping p141; Sleeping pp153-4;
Walking Tours pp104–8

Santa Lucia is an area of grand buildings and vast squares; it's where you'll find the city's most recognisable landmarks and smartest hotels. At its heart, the vast Piazza del Plebiscito is the obvious centrepoint. To the northeast, beyond the Palazzo Reale and Teatro San Carlo, is Piazza del Municipio and Castel Nuovo (Maschio Angioino). Across the busy seafront road, the ferries dock at the Stazione Marittima. To the southwest, Via Santa Lucia, the so-called street of fishermen, leads down to elegant Via Partenope and the Borgo Marinaro.

Less explored is the Pizzofalcone district above Piazza del Plebiscito. Draped over Monte Echia, this is the city's oldest inhabited area, dating back to the 7th century BC. A warren of hilltop streets, it's home to an important military academy and offers some great views over the city's rooftops. Descend the steep hairpin road that leads down to the southern side of the hill and you'll see houses gouged into the sheer volcanic rock face.

Lending its name to the area, Via Santa Lucia is a lively street with an interesting past. Today a wide parade of elegant 19th-century palazzi, pizzerie and bars, it was originally a poor street of fishermen – to see how they must have lived look up at the houses cut into the side of Monte Echia. Named after the 16th-century Chiesa di Santa Lucia a Mare, Via Santa Lucia became, in the mid-20th century, the centre of the Neapolitan *dolce vita* (sweet life). Well-to-do tourists from upmarket cruise ships flocked to the street's expensive jewellery shops or to eat in the characteristic trattorie or simply to walk up and down. Locals remember Prince Rainier of Monte Carlo strolling arm-in-arm with Princess Grace, and mafia boss Lucky Luciano dropping by for a spot of dinner (apparently he was a perfect gent), accompanied as always by a couple of huge bodyguards.

It was a good time that didn't last. The double whammy of a citywide cholera epidemic in 1974 and the massive earthquake of 1980 put pay to the area's wellbeing. Fishermen were forced out of work as the consumption of fish was drastically reduced due to cholera, while the destruction of the earthquake forced many families to relocate. Today, the area is looking good, and tourism is once again returning, but the locals are not convinced. It'll never be like it was, they wistfully say.

ACQUEDOTTO Map pp248-9

www.lanapolisotterranea.it in Italian; Piazza Trieste e Trento; bus CS to Piazza Trieste e Trento

Deep below Naples' royal quarter lies a series of Graeco-Roman tunnels that were once part of the city's aqueduct system. Used as air-raid shelters in WWII, the tunnels, cut out of the tufa rock, run below Via Chiaia.

Guided tours are organised by Napoli Sotterranea (see p53) and depart from Caffè Gambrinus at 10am, noon and 6pm on Saturday and Sunday. The 90-minute visits cost €6 and are in Italian.

BORGO MARINARO Map pp248-9

Bus C25 to Via Partenope

Opposite the luxury hotels on Via Partenope and dominated by the stark Castel dell'Ovo, the Borgo Marinaro is a small island of volcanic rock. Known to the ancient Greeks as Megaris, it was a fishing centre in the 19th and early 20th century, but today is an area of bars and restaurants.

A few fishermen remain but they are considerably outnumbered by the tourists and fun seekers who flock here on warm summer nights.

CASTEL DELL'OVO Map pp248-9

☎ 081 764 05 90; Borgo Marinaro; ☺ 9am-6pm Mon-Fri, 9am-1pm Sat & Sun; bus C25 to Via Partenope

Legend surrounds the Castel dell'Ovo. According to myth, the castle owes its name – Castle of the Egg – to Virgil. The Roman poet was said to have buried an egg on the site where the castle now stands, ominously warning that when the egg breaks the castle will fall. A second legend has it that under the castle the siren Partenope is buried. Killjoys prefer to say that the name of the castle is due to its oval shape.

Built in the 12th century by the Normans, the castle is the oldest in Naples. Its particular position had long been appreciated – originally by the Roman general Lucullus, who had his villa here – and it became a key fortress in the defence of the Campania region. It was subsequently used by various rulers, including the Swabians, Angevins and Aragonese. Curiously, as you walk across the castle, you will see a couple of cannons facing inland – perhaps ready to fire on the fiery Neapolitan masses who, in 1799, did actually occupy the castle for a time.

Today the Castel dell'Ovo is used for exhibitions and to house the **Museo di Etnopreistoria** (Map pp248–9; ☎ 081 764 53 43; ☯ 10am-1pm by appointment only). Founded in 1971, the museum has a display of prehistoric tools, fossils and ceramics.

CASTEL NUOVO
(MASCHIO ANGIOINO) Map pp244-6
Museo Civico ☎ 081 795 58 77; admission €5;
☯ 9am-7pm Mon-Sat, 9am-2pm Sun; bus R2 to Piazza del Municipio

Known to Neapolitans as the Maschio Angioino (Angevin Keep) and to everyone else as the Castel Nuovo, this 13th-century castle is one of Naples' most striking buildings.

When Charles I of Anjou took over Naples and the Swabians' Sicilian kingdom, he found himself in control not only of his new southern Italian acquisitions, but also of possessions in Tuscany, northern Italy and Provence (France). It made sense to base the new dynasty in Naples, rather than in Palermo in Sicily, and Charles launched an ambitious construction programme to expand the port and city walls. His plans included converting a Franciscan convent into the castle that is still standing in Piazza del Municipio.

Christened the Castrum Novum (Castel Nuovo, or New Castle) to help distinguish it from the older Castel dell'Ovo and the Castel Capuano, it was erected in only three years from 1279. A favourite residence of royalty, it was frequented by the leading intellectuals and artists of the time. Petrarch, Boccaccio and Giotto all stayed here, with Giotto repaying his hosts by painting much of the castle's interior. However, of the original structure only the Cappella Palatina remains; the rest is the result of renovations by the Aragonese two centuries later, as well as a meticulous restoration effort that occurred prior to WWII. The heavy grey stone that dominates the castle was imported from Mallorca. The two-storey

Top Five Santa Lucia
- Palazzo Reale (p72)
- Teatro San Carlo (p73)
- Castel Nuovo (p69)
- Borgo Marinaro & Castel dell'Ovo (p68)
- Piazza del Plebiscito (p73)

Renaissance triumphal arch at the entrance, the Torre della Guardia, commemorates the triumphal entry of Alfonso I of Aragon into Naples in 1443.

To reach the Museo Civico you have to pass through the 15th-century **Sala dei Baroni** (Hall of the Barons). Now the venue of city council meetings, this stark stone hall is named after the barons who were slaughtered here in 1486. The duplicitous knights paid the penalty for plotting against King Ferdinand I of Aragon.

The **museum** is spread across several halls on three floors. The 14th- and 15th-century frescoes and sculptures on the ground floor are of the most interest. The other two floors display paintings, either by Neapolitan artists, or with Naples or Campania as subjects, covering the 17th to the early 20th centuries. Worth looking out for though is Guglielmo Monaco's 15th-century bronze door, complete with a cannonball embedded in it.

In the summer months the castle's courtyard is often used for outdoor concerts, including some productions from the nearby Teatro San Carlo.

CHIESA DELLA PIETÀ DEI TURCHINI
Map pp244-6
☎ 081 552 04 57; Via Medina 19;
☯ 7-11am & 5-7pm Mon-Fri, 9.30am-1.30pm Sun; bus R2 to Via Medina

Better known as a historic conservatory than as a place of worship, this late 16th-century church is the birthplace of one of Naples' best-known musical organisations. The Pietà dei Turchini group still regularly performs a programme of baroque music at a deconsecrated chapel located in the Chiaia district (see p133).

Built between 1592 and 1607 by the priests of the Bianchi di Santa Maria Incoronatella religious order, the church takes its name from the *turchino* (deep blue) uniforms the children used to wear. One of the conservatory's most famous alumni was the Neapolitan composer Alessandro Scarlatti (1660–1725).

Virgil & the Egg

Legend doesn't record why Virgil decided to bury an egg in the **Castel dell'Ovo** (p68). Still, that's what they say he did, warning as he did so that when the egg breaks the castle will fall. If the legend is to be believed the egg must still be there.

The story may have no basis in history but it was fervently believed by the medieval Neapolitans. A superstitious lot, they regarded Virgil as a sorcerer as much as a poet. It was a belief that the Christian scholars of the day apparently supported, claiming that Virgil had prophesied the birth of Christ some 42 years before Jesus was born. In the *Eclogue No 4*, Virgil writes of a new age of peace to be heralded by the birth of a baby boy. The Christians took this to be a reference to Jesus. Alternative theories, however, suggest that Virgil was referring to Scribonia, the pregnant wife of the Roman emperor Octavian, who subsequently gave birth to a son.

Yet further mystery surrounds the fate of Virgil's body. Although he died in Brindisi, on Italy's southeast coast, he is said to be buried in Naples. At least his tomb is in Naples; whether or not his remains are inside is an unresolved matter. The tomb sits in a tiny park in Mergellina (see p96) at the entrance to the Crypta Neapolitana, a Roman tunnel that connected Naples with Pozzuoli.

CHIESA DI SAN FERDINANDO

Map pp248-9

☎ 081 41 81 18; Piazza Trieste e Trento 1; ☉ 8am-noon Mon-Sat, 9.30am-1pm Sun; bus CS to Piazza Trieste e Trento

When the Jesuits were kicked out of Naples in 1767 the Chiesa di San Francesco Saverio became the Chiesa di San Ferdinando. Behind the name change were the Knights of Constantine, an ancient Catholic order charged with protecting the Christian faith. The knights, who today still have their Chancellery in Naples, named the church after King Ferdinand's namesake, an 8th-century Spanish saint.

The church originally dates to 1622 when construction began on Giovan Giacomo di Conforto's designs, although it was not actually consecrated until 1665, following some last-minute modifications by Cosimo Fanzago. Worth looking out for in the transept is Tito Angelini's tomb of Lucia Migliaccio, the Duchessa di Floridia and wife of King Ferdinand I.

CHIESA DI SAN FRANCESCO DI PAOLA Map pp248-9

☎ 081 764 51 33; Piazza del Plebiscito; ☉ 8am-noon & 3.30-6pm Mon-Sat, 8am-1pm Sun; bus CS to Piazza Trieste e Trento

Dominating Piazza del Plebiscito, this imposing neoclassical copy of the Pantheon in Rome strikes more for its size than any artistic merit – the church's focal feature, the dome, measures 34m in diameter and 53m in height. Designed by architect Pietro Banchini, it was commissioned by Ferdinand I in 1817 to celebrate the restoration of his kingdom after the Napoleonic interlude. Today, it's a popular venue for weddings.

CHIESA DI SANTA LUCIA A MARE

Map pp248-9

☎ 081 764 09 43; Via Santa Lucia 3; ☉ 7am-12.15pm & 5-7pm Mon-Sat, 7am-1.45pm & 5-7pm Sun; bus C25 to Via Partenope

Although of little architectural or artistic note, it's nevertheless this small and unremarkable church that gives its name to the street on which it stands and the surrounding quarter. Dedicated to Santa Lucia, the protector of mariners, Chiesa di Santa Lucia a Mare has long been, and indeed still is, a much-loved place of worship. It originally dates to the 9th century, although over the intervening centuries it's undergone a series of facelifts. The most recent restoration was carried out after the church sustained bomb damage during WWII in 1943.

CHIESA SAN GIACOMO DEGLI SPAGNOLI Map pp244-6

☎ 081 552 37 59; Piazza del Municipio 27; ☉ 7.30-11.20am Mon-Fri, 10.20am-1pm Sun; bus R2 to Piazza del Municipio

Don Pedro de Toledo, the Spanish viceroy who did more than most to change the face of Naples, is buried in this small 16th-century church. Alongside his wife Maria, he lies in a great stone sarcophagus, which was designed by Giovanni da Nola.

Originally a hospital for Spanish officials serving in Naples, the Chiesa San Giacomo degli Spagnoli was consecrated in 1547 and later modified in 1819.

The Spanish connection is further strengthened by the presence of a chapel dedicated to San Josemariá Escrivá, the controversial founder of Opus Dei.

CHIESA SANTA MARIA INCORONATA

Map pp244-6
Via Medina 60; bus R2 to Via Medina
The beautiful Gothic arches of the Chiesa Santa Maria Incoronata date to the mid-14th century. Situated on the sunken site that Charles I of Anjou had earmarked for his planned Castel Nuovo, the church was built on the wishes of Giovanna of Anjou, who wanted somewhere to conserve a fragment of her most precious relic – Jesus' crown of thorns.

Although it has recently been restored for the umpteenth time, it is only open to the public when there's an exhibition on. Still, if you get the chance, get in there to admire the cycle of 14th-century frescoes by Roberto Oderisi.

FONTANA DELL'IMMACOLATELLA

Map pp248-9
Via Partenope; bus C25 to Via Partenope
Marking the point at which Via Partenope becomes Via Nazario Sauro, the Fontana dell' Immacolatella is a dramatic three-arched affair. Known also as the Fontana del Gigante, it was built by Michelangelo Naccherino and Pietro Bernini in 1601. Two minor arches, under which stand statues of river gods, flank a grand central arch topped by an impressive collection of obelisks, cherubs and coats of arms.

Originally displayed outside the Palazzo Reale, the fountain has stood on its current spot since 1905.

FONTANA DI NETTUNO Map pp244-6

Via Medina; bus R2 to Via Medina
This fountain of the god Neptune, standing aloft a baroque ensemble of lions and spewing creatures, is the work of three artists: Cosimo Fanzago, Michelangelo Naccherino and Pietro Bernini, father of the more famous Gian Lorenzo Bernini. Much loved by the city, the fountain has stood in various spots since it was built in 1601. Its last move was when work on the metro forced a transfer from Piazza Bovio to its current position at the foot of Via Medina. Whether it stays here remains to be seen.

GALLERIA UMBERTO I Map ppp244-6

Via San Carlo; bus R2 to Via San Carlo
Opposite the Teatro San Carlo is one of the four entrances to the imposing steel-and-glass atrium of the Galleria Umberto I (1900). A twin to the Galleria Vittorio Emanuele II in Milan, it's worth a look for its impressive marble floor and structural engineering but will probably not detain you long. A favoured haunt of street vendors, and housing a few anonymous shops and cafés, it retains little of the refined air that it breathed in the early 20th century.

Fontana di Nettuno (above)

NAPOLI NELLA RACCOLTA DE MURA

Map pp248-9

Piazza Trieste e Trento; admission free; 🕒 9am-7pm **Mon-Sat; bus CS to Piazza Trieste e Trento**

Hidden among the chairs of the Bar del Professore (next to the Caffè Gambrinus) is an entrance to an underpass. Go down it and you come to a wonderfully small gallery dedicated to the great years of popular song and dance (considered to be the early part of the 20th century). The pink-tiled walls, reminiscent of a Victorian public lavatory, are hung with a lovingly maintained collection of old music-hall programmes and posters, black-and-white photos of the Festa di Piedigrotta and models of La Pulcinella (Naples' original version of Mr Punch). Stereo speakers provide a background of warbling Neapolitan crooners.

The museum is entirely free and provides an interesting glimpse into popular Neapolitan culture.

PALAZZO REALE Map pp248-9

☎ 081 794 40 21; entrance on Piazza Trieste e Trento; admission €4, audioguide €4; 🕒 9am- 8pm Thu-Tue; bus CS to Piazza Trieste e Trento

Facing the grand Piazza del Plebiscito, this magnificent palace was built around 1600. Envisaged as a monument to Spanish glory (Naples was at the time under Spanish rule), it was designed by local architect Domenico Fontana. It wasn't until the mid-19th century, however, that it was finally completed. Construction was finished in 1841 and in 1888 eight statues of the most important kings of Naples were inserted into the façade. Like many buildings in Naples it suffered badly during WWII – just how badly you can see on a series of panels in the royal apartments.

From the courtyard the huge double staircase leads to the royal apartments, which house the **Museo del Palazzo Reale**, a rich collection of furnishings, porcelain, tapestries, statues and paintings. Undoubtedly inferior to the art collection of the Palazzo Reale di Capodimonte or the ancient wonders of the Museo Archeologico Nazionale, it does, however, contain some interesting works.

In Sala (Room) XII, for example, the 16th-century canvas *Gli esattori delle imposte* (The Tax Collectors), by Dutch artist Marinus Claesz Van Roymerswaele, confirms that attitudes to tax collectors have changed little in 500 years. The two tax collectors are depicted as hideous creatures gleefully recording their day's takings in a ledger.

The next room, Sala XIII, used to be Joachim Murat's study during the 19th-century but was used as a snack bar by Allied troops in WWII.

A rotating reading desk made for Maria Carolina and displayed in Sala XXIII is an interesting example of innovative furniture design. Crafted by Giovanni Uldrich at the end of the 18th century, it consists of a desk with a rotating mount from which a series of extended arms stretch out. At the end of each arm is a small shelf onto which you place your book. Once you've finished with one book you simply push the rotating arm upwards and the next book swings into place.

Other more famous attractions include the *Teatrino di Corte* (1768), an opulent private theatre, and, in the *Cappella Reale* (Royal Chapel), a huge 18th-century *presepe* (nativity scene). The figures crowding the nativity scene were made by a series of big-name Neapolitan artists including Giuseppe Sammartino, better known for his *Cristo Velato* in the Cappella Sansevero (see p56).

The palace did at one time boast some impressive hanging gardens. Extending out from Sala IX, they are still officially closed for restoration, although if you want a quick look smile sweetly at the member of staff sitting by the French window. There is also a small but perfectly formed garden to the left of the palace's main ground-floor entrance. Entry to this is free.

Since 1925 the palace has been home to the **Biblioteca Nazionale** (National Library; ☎ 081 40 12 73; 🕒 9am-7.30pm Mon-Fri, 9am-1.30pm Sat), which includes the vast Farnese collection brought to Naples by Charles of Bourbon, with at least 2000 papyruses discovered at Herculaneum and fragments of a 5th-century Coptic Bible. Visitors should bring ID as staff check it as a security measure.

PALAZZO SAN GIACOMO Map ppp244-6

☎ 081 795 11 11; Piazza del Municipio; bus R2 to Piazza del Municipio

This vast edifice is home to Naples' city council. Constructed between 1819 and 1825 by Stefani and Luigi Gasse and named after the adjoining 16th-century **Chiesa San Giacomo degli Spagnoli** (see p70), it was immediately taken over by the Bourbon bureaucrats. Today the bureaucrats are still there, albeit municipal rather than royal, and the building has a rather beleaguered air. Small crowds of extremely important office workers are often seen milling around the entrance shouting into mobile phones.

PIAZZA DEL MUNICIPIO Map pp244-6
Bus R2 to Piazza del Municipio

Dominated by one of Naples' most famous landmarks, Castel Nuovo (Maschio Angioino), Piazza del Municipio is not looking its best at the moment. Like plenty of other central locations, this traffic-heavy square resembles a giant building site as construction work continues on the new metro system.

At the head of the square stands the 19th-century Palazzo San Giacomo to which is attached the Chiesa San Giacomo degli Spagnoli. On the northern flank, the Teatro Mercadante is a theatrical institution in Naples. To the north the Fontana di Nettuno marks the beginning of Via Medina.

PIAZZA DEL PLEBISCITO Map pp248-9
Bus CS to Piazza Trieste e Trento

Until the world's G7 leaders arrived in Naples for their 1994 summit, this vast open space was one of Europe's most impressive car parks. Today, Naples' largest piazza is traffic-free and, if not exactly peaceful, it does at least provide somewhere to sit without having to buy something.

Originally called Largo di Palazzo, it was christened Piazza del Plebiscito following the plebiscite of 21 October 1860, which rubber-stamped the incorporation of the Kingdom of the Two Sicilies into the new Italy. Today it's the venue of traditional New Year's Eve celebrations and regularly hosts concerts and outdoor exhibitions.

Dominating the square, the dramatic **Chiesa di San Francesco di Paola** (see p70) was a later addition to the colonnade of columns that formed the highlight of Joachim Murat's original piazza (1809). The opposite flank is formed by the western wall of the Palazzo Reale, along which stand eight statues of past kings. In the centre of the square, Antonio Canova's equestrian statue depicts the Bourbon king Charles VII, while nearby the statue of Ferdinand I, his son, is by Antonio Calì.

PIAZZA TRIESTE E TRENTO Map pp248-9
Bus CS to Piazza Trieste e Trento

Situated at the southern end of Via Toledo, this elegant and busy square leads through to the much bigger Piazza del Plebiscito. A magnet for tourists, well-to-do Neapolitans, poseurs and police (there's usually at least one police van parked somewhere in the square), its main focus is **Caffè Gambrinus** (p113), Naples' most famous café. To the east lie the Palazzo Reale and the Teatro San Carlo, while head along Via Chiaia to the west for some serious shopping.

TEATRO SAN CARLO Map pp248-9
☎ 081 797 21 11, tour bookings ☎ 081 40 03 00; www.teatrosancarlo.it; Piazza Trieste e Trento, Via San Carlo 98; tours €5; bus R2 to Via San Carlo

One of Naples' more elegant squares, Piazza Trieste e Trento is fronted on the northeastern side by Italy's largest opera house, the sumptuous Teatro San Carlo. Neapolitans proudly boast that it is older than Milan's La Scala, pre-dating its northern rival by 41 years. Inaugurated on 4 December 1737 by King Charles VII, it was severely damaged by a fire in 1816 and rebuilt by Antonio Niccolini, the same architect who a few years before had added the façade. From the outside there are no clues as to the opulence of the red and gold interior, which boasts six levels and perfect acoustics.

Twenty-minute guided tours depart from the San Carlo shop every 20 minutes and are conducted in various languages, including English.

MONTE ECHIA

Rising up behind Piazza del Plebiscito, Monte Echia is the oldest part of Naples. Inhabited in the 7th century BC by Greek traders, it formed the ancient city of Parthenope. Today it's an area of few sites but some remarkable views. The best place from which to enjoy these is the unkempt garden at the top of Via Egiziaca a Pizzofalcone: from Piazza Carolina (behind the columns on the northern side of Piazza del Plebiscito) head up the hill until you reach Via Egiziaca a Pizzofalcone, turn left and carry on all the way to the top of the steep hill. You'll know when you get there.

CHIESA SANTA MARIA DEGLI ANGELI
Map pp248-9
☎ 081 764 49 74; Piazza Santa Maria degli Angeli;
◴ 7.30-11.30am & 5.30-7pm Mon-Sat, 8.30am-1.30pm & 6-7.30pm Sun; bus C22 to Via Monte di Dio

The yellow façade of Santa Maria degli Angeli fronts the small piazza to which the church gives its name. This baroque church was financed by Costanza Doria del Carretto, a noble lady with a deep purse and pious heart, and donated to the priests of the Teatini order.

The church features works by Neapolitan stalwarts Massimo Stanzione and Luca Giordano, although its most obvious attraction is Francesco Grimaldi's huge dome.

LA NUNZIATELLA Map pp248-9

☎ 081 764 15 20; Via Generali Parisi 16; bus C22 to Via Nunziatella

The convent of Nunziatella is home to one of Italy's most prestigious military schools. The Royal Military Academy of the Nunziatella was inaugurated in 1787, some 20 years after the convent's previous occupants, the Jesuits, were kicked out of town. Built in 1588, the convent was donated to the Jesuits by its benefactor, the aristocrat Anna Mendozza Marchesana della Valle, and became an important religious centre in the Renaissance.

Adjacent to the military academy, the church shared the same fate as the convent and is today still part of the military school. Famous for its beautiful 17th-century baroque interior – frescoes by Francescoi de Mura, an altar by Sammartino, the floor by Ferdinando Sanfelice – it is open to the public by appointment only.

VOMERO

Eating pp116–7; Shopping pp142–3; Sleeping pp154-6

Rising 250m above the city centre, Vomero (*vom*-e-ro) is Naples' highest point. Dominated by the stunning Certosa di San Martino and the foreboding Castel Sant'Elmo, it's an area of spectacular views and tree-lined streets, new shops and smart restaurants.

One of Naples' more recent residential districts, it was, until the late 19th century, an area of green fields and aristo-cratic estates; the only way up from the city was via a few paths of steep steps. However, the great urban-renewal projects of the late 1800s put pay to that. The result was an area of upmarket Art Nouveau palazzi, gardens and geometrically ordered streets. Further construction in the post-WWII period added hundreds of cheap and unsightly housing blocks.

Despite the presence of two of Naples' most visible landmarks, Vomero is not an area that's likely to detain you long. True, the views make the trip up worthwhile, the Certosa di San Martino is one of Naples' must-see sites, there's a pleasant park and the tree-lined streets are lively and clean – but it's missing something. It lacks the edge of the city below, and the underlying sense of menace that makes much of Naples so exciting. It's a self-contained place where the successful middle class comes to live, shop and work.

The central hub is Piazza Vanvitelli, a smart square of cafés and swish palazzi. This is where dressed-up teenagers come on a Saturday evening to hang out, flirt, smoke and make plans for the night ahead.

Branching off from the square, pedestrianised Via A Scarlatti is effectively Vomero's high street. A busy shopping strip with trees for shade and benches to sit on, it's where the entire neighbourhood comes to take its afternoon stroll.

To the south, Villa Floridiana is a well-tended park that's home to the Museo Nazionale della Ceramica Duca di Martina, while Castel Sant'Elmo and the Certosa di San Martino both lie to the east of Piazza Vanvitelli.

Naples' three funicular railways all run up to Vomero.

CASTEL SANT'ELMO Map p247

☎ 081 578 40 30; Via Tito Angelini 22; admission €2; ☾ 8.30am-7.30pm Tue-Sat, 9am-6.30pm Sun; metro Vanvitelli, funicular Montesanto to Morghen

Commanding spectacular views across the city and bay, this austere, star-shaped castle is the result of a 16th-century conversion of a 13th-century castle. Originally, however, it was neither a castle nor a fort that topped the tufa rock, but a church.

Dedicated to St Erasmus (from which the name Elmo is derived), a small church stood on the top of Vomero hill for some 400 years before Robert of Anjou decided to turn it into a castle in 1349. It took on its current aspect in 1538 the Spanish viceroy Don Pedro de Toledo had it further fortified.

Impressive though it is, the castle has seen little real military action. The biggest blow it received came in 1587 when a bolt of lightning hit the castle's stock of gunpowder, killing some 150 people. It has, however, seen plenty of prisoners. A long-time jail, its dungeons were used as a military prison until the 1970s.

Nowadays, the castle is mainly used as an exhibition and conference centre. Although you can visit the castle's roof (for the best view in town) most of the castle is closed if there's no exhibition on. Admission times and price vary according to the exhibition.

CERTOSA DI SAN MARTINO Map p247

☎ 081 578 17 69; Largo San Martino 5; admission €6; ⏱ 8.30am-7.30pm Tue-Sun; metro Vanvitelli, funicular Montesanto to Morghen

Barely 100m from the castle stands this stunning Carthusian monastery. Originally built by Charles of Anjou in 1325, it was given a new look in the 17th century by baroque master Cosimo Fanzago. Today it houses the **Museo Nazionale di San Martino** and the valuable collection that the canny Carthusian brothers built up over the centuries.

The monastery's church and the rooms that flank it contain a feast of frescoes and paintings by some of Naples' most important 17th-century artists. In the *pronaos* (a small room flanked by three walls and a row of columns), for example, Micco Spidaro's frescoes of Carthusian persecution seem to defy perspective as figures sit with their legs hanging over nonexistent edges. Elsewhere in the chapel you'll find works by Francesco Solimena, Massimo Stanzione, Giuseppe de Ribera and Battista Caracciolo.

Adjacent to the church, the **Chiostro dei Procuratori** is the smaller of the monastery's two cloisters. A grand corridor on the left leads to the larger **Chiostro Grande** (Great Cloister). Originally designed by Giovanni Antonio Dosio in the late 16th century and later added to by Fanzago, the Great Cloister is a beautiful space of manicured gardens, marble statues and white porticoes. A series of skulls mounted on the balustrade add a sinister touch.

One of the highlights of the museum is the Sezione Presepiale, several rooms devoted to a collection of Neapolitan *presepi* carved in the 18th and 19th centuries. These range from the miniscule – a nativity scene in an ornately decorated eggshell – to the massive. The most famous piece, the Cuciniello *presepe*, covers one wall of what used to be the monastery's kitchen. Angels fly down to a landscape of rock houses and shepherds, all made out of wood, cork, papier-mâché and terracotta.

The Quarto del Priore (Prior's Quarter) in the southern wing houses the bulk of the picture

Travelling by funicular (p208)

collection, as well as one of the museum's most famous pieces, Pietro Bernini's *La Vergine col Bambino e San Giovannino* (Madonna and Child with the Infant John the Baptist).

A pictorial history of Naples is told in the section *Immagini e memoria dell città* (Images and Memories of the City). Here you'll find portraits of historic characters (Don Pedro de Toledo in Room 33, Maria Carolina di Borbone in Room 43); antique maps, including a 35-panel copper map in Room 45; and rooms dedicated to major historical events such as the Revolt of the Masaniello (Room 36) and the plague (Room 37).

MUSEO NAZIONALE DELLA CERAMICA DUCA DI MARTINA Map p247
☎ 081 578 84 18; admission €2.50; ☽ 8.30am-2pm Tue-Sun; metro Vanvitelli, funicular Chiaia to Cimarosa

Situated at the bottom of the Villa Floridiana is the stately home that gives its name to the park. Built in 1817 by Ferdinand I for his second wife, the Duchess of Floridia, today the villa houses the 6000 piece-collection of the Museo Nazionale della Ceramica Duca di Martina.

The extensive collection of European, Chinese and Japanese china, ivory, enamels and Italian majolica was originally created by the Duke of Martina and donated to the city in 1911.

The Oriental collection, including some Chinese Ming (1368–1644) ceramics and Japanese Edo (1615–1867) vases, is displayed in the basement, while upstairs on the ground floor you'll find Renaissance majolica pottery. Continue up to the 1st floor to view European ceramics. These include ornate pieces from the top European porcelain producers.

VILLA FLORIDIANA Map p247
Via Domenico Cimarosa 77; ☽ 9am-1 hr before sunset Tue-Sun; metro Vanvitelli, funicular Chiaia to Cimarosa

A short walk from Piazza Vanvitelli, this public park is a tonic, spreading down the slopes from Via Domenico Cimarosa to Mergellina. The paths wind down the hill, flanked by vegetation with the odd bench here or there. Ball games are technically forbidden on the grass but the ban is routinely ignored and kickabouts are a common sight. However, there's normally a quiet corner to be found for a picnic or to grab forty winks.

LA SANITÀ & CAPODIMONTE

Eating p118; Shopping p143; Sleeping p156; Walking Tours p107–8

Squeezed into the V shape formed by Via Santa Teresa degli Scalzi heading north and Via Foria branching off northeast, La Sanità is an overpopulated area of dirty impoverished streets and crumbling façades. Cheap markets sell garish clothes and scooter repair shops do a thriving business.

It is, however, an area held in considerable affection by many Neapolitans. They'll tell you that La Sanità is where the soul of the genuine Naples still lives on and that Prince Antonio De Curtis, aka Totò, the city's best-loved comedian, was born here. They'll reminisce about Eduardo De Filippo's famous 1961 stage play, and subsequent TV series, *Il sindaco del rione Sanità* (The Mayor of the Sanità Quarter), and they'll tell you about the catacombs.

In fact, for the visitor it's what lies underground rather than what you see on the surface that makes this such an interesting area. Positioned outside the city walls until the 18th century, La Sanità (despite its name, which means 'healthy') was for centuries where the city buried its dead. The network of underground chambers and catacombs that lies beneath the noisy streets relate a grisly history of medieval inhumation. Details of the different burial techniques used on the rich and poor are graphically revealed in the catacombs of San Gaudioso under the Chiesa Santa Maria della Sanità. Further north in Capodimonte, the catacombs of San Gennaro, where the city's patron saint is said to be buried, are famous for their Paleo-Christian frescoes.

It was Charles VII of Bourbon who transformed Capodimonte into what it is today. His project to build a hunting reserve turned what had up until then been a hill of little interest into an area fit for royalty. The green lawns of the Parco di Capodimonte stretch away to the north while in the south, Charles' extravagant hunting lodge, the Palazzo Reale di Capodimonte, houses one of Italy's largest and most spectacular art collections. Here you can admire works by Caravaggio, Titian, Botticelli and Andy Warhol.

ALBERGO DEI POVERI Map pp242-3

Piazza Carlo III; metro Cavour

Dominating the not-very-lovely Piazza Carlo III, the Albergo dei Poveri (Hotel of the Poor) is said to be the largest public building in Europe. If all had gone according to architect Ferdinando Fuga's plans, though, it would have been bigger. His original designs called for a façade of 600m long, with five internal courtyards. When construction came to a halt in 1829, however, he settled for the smaller version that you see today. The façade measures 349m, there are three internal courtyards and the whole edifice covers 103,000 sq metres.

The building was commissioned in 1751 by Charles VII of Bourbon to house the city's poor. Today it is undergoing huge restoration after it was damaged in the earthquake of 1980.

CATACOMBA DI SAN GENNARO Map p250

☎ 081 741 10 71; Via Capodimonte 16; adult/child €5/3; ⏱ guided tours 9am,10am, 11am & noon Tue-Sun; bus 24 to Via Capodimonte

The oldest and most famous of Naples' ancient catacombs, the Catacomba di San Gennaro date to the 2nd century. Originally they belonged to a noble family, but when San Gennaro's body was interred here in the 5th century they became an important destination for Christian pilgrims. Naples' bishops were also buried here until the 11th century.

Spread over two levels, the catacombs house a mix of tombs, corridors and broad vestibules held up by columns and arches. The crumbling walls are decorated with 2nd-century Christian frescoes and 5th-century mosaics.

To get to the catacombs, go through the gates to the left of the Chiesa di Madre di Buon Consiglio; the ticket office is in a small ivy-clad building. Tours (in Italian) last about 45 minutes but only depart if there are more than two people.

CATACOMBA DI SAN SEVERO Map p250

☎ 081 544 13 05; Piazzetta San Severo a Capodimonte 81; ⏱ by appointment only; metro Cavour

San Severo, Naples' first bishop, was buried here in AD 410, under a monastery that he had founded. Nothing remains of the original monastery, as it was abandoned after the saint's bones

Top Five La Sanità & Capodimonte

- Palazzo Reale di Capodimonte (p79)
- Catacomba di San Gennaro (left)
- Chiesa San Giovanni a Carbonara (below)
- Parco di Capodimonte (p80)
- Chiesa Santa Maria della Sanità & Catacomba di San Gaudioso (p78)

were removed to the Chiesa di San Domenico Maggiore in the 9th century. The church that you see today dates to the 15th century. Not a lot remains of the original catacombs either; the small chamber that you can see contains 4th-century frescoes of St Peter and St Paul.

CHIESA DI MADRE DI BUON CONSIGLIO Map p250

☎ 081 741 49 45; Via Capodimonte 13; bus 24 to Via Capodimonte

This imposing church overlooking the busy Via Capodimonte is one of Naples' newest landmarks. Completed in 1960 after 40 years of construction, the Chiesa di Madre di Buon Consiglio is an obvious replica of the Basilica di San Pietro in Rome. Designed by Vincenzo Veccia, it contains several works of art transferred here after the earthquake of 1980; none are likely to excite art buffs.

CHIESA SAN GIOVANNI A CARBONARA Map pp242-3

☎ 081 29 58 73; Via Carbonara 5; ⏱ 9.30am-1pm Mon-Sat; metro Cavour

This wonderful, Gothic religious complex comprises a church, a chapel and a cloister. Unfortunately, the chapel is closed for restoration; fortunately, the church is a treasure trove of superb sculpture.

Standing at 18m the colossal monument to King Ladislas (built in 1428) is just one of a number of works that together comprise one of Naples' most interesting collections of Renaissance sculpture. Other important works include *Crocifisso* (Crucifixion; 1545) by Giorgio Vasari, the early 16th-century *Monumento Miroballo* by Tommaso Malvito and Jacopo dell Pila, and *Cappella Caracciole del Sole* with its majolica-tiled floor and colourful 15th-century frescoes. In this beautiful round chapel you'll find Leonardo da Besozzo's 1433 tomb of Gianni Caracciolo, the ambitious lover of King Ladislas' sister Queen Joan II who was stabbed to death in 1432.

The entrance to the church is by way of a grand flight of stairs designed by Ferdinando

Sanfelice in 1707 as part of a major reconstruction project. The original 14th-century church has undergone numerous renovations, the last after WWII bomb damage.

CHIESA SANTA MARIA DELLA SANITÀ & CATACOMBA DI SAN GAUDIOSO

Map p250

☎ 081 544 13 05; Via della Sanità 124; catacombs adult/child €5/3; church ☾ 8.30am-12.30pm & 5-8pm Mon-Sat, 8.30am-1.30pm Sun, catacombs ☾ guided tours 9.30am, 10.15am, 11am, 11.45am, 12.30pm; metro Cavour

As you look down on La Sanità from the Ponte della Sanità (the Napoleonic bridge that passes over the quarter) you'll see a large tiled dome. This is the Chiesa Santa Maria della Sanità, a much-loved church built in the 17th century and known to many Neapolitans as the Chiesa di San Vincenzo.

The highlight of the church's interior is a semi-circular double stairway that leads up to the raised altar. Underneath, the 5th-century **Cappella di San Gaudioso** marks the entrance to the catacombs.

San Gaudioso, the bishop of Abitina in north Africa, died in Naples in AD 452. It is said that he arrived in Italy by chance – legend has it that he was forced to board an old boat which was then set adrift by a certain King Genserico. He subsequently became a much-venerated saint in Naples.

The catacombs reveal traces of mosaics and frescoes from various periods; the earliest from the 5th century, while later examples are from the 17th and 18th centuries. But it's not so much the art that strikes you as the gruesome history that the catacombs tell.

The damp walls of the catarombs reveal two medieval methods of burying the dead. The first involved burying the corpse in the foetal position in the belief that you should depart this world as you enter it. The second method, and the one favoured by the 17th-century rich, was to build the body into the wall with a fresco outlining the position.

Tours of the catacombs last about an hour and are conducted in Italian.

CIMITERO DELLE FONTANELLE Map p250

☎ 081 29 69 44; Piazza Fontanella alla Sanità 154; metro Museo

Carved into the tufa rock of the Materdei hill, this vast underground cemetery contains the skeletons of some 40,000 Neapolitans. During the cholera epidemics of 1835 and 1974 the

Chiesa Santa Maria della Sanità (left)

city authorities moved the city's dead here in an attempt to control the spread of the disease. At the end of the 19th century it became a cult spot for the worship of the dead. Adherents would adopt a skull and treat it to gifts in the hope of good fortune.

The cemetery is currently closed to the public.

ORTO BOTANICO Map pp242-3

☎ 081 44 97 59; Via Foria 223; ☾ 9am-2pm by appointment only; metro Cavour

Naples' botanical gardens provide a green haven in the middle of traffic hell. It's difficult to believe that the fumes from the gridlocked cars on Via Foria can do the flora much good, but the vegetation seems to flourish.

Founded by Joseph Bonaparte between 1807 and 1819, the gardens belong to Naples university and are consequently only open to the public on request. But it's worth making the request – if for no other reason than to wander the paths in the shade of the tall palm trees and escape the urban chaos outside. For dedicated botanists there's an impressive collection of plants from the major American, African, Asian and Australian deserts, a section given over to arboreal ferns and an ancient citrus orchard.

The white steps leading up to the gardens were designed by Giuliano De Fazio.

OSSERVATORIO DI CAPODIMONTE

Map p250

☎ 081 557 51 11; Salita Moiariello 16; bus 24 to Via Capodimonte

Hidden down a small road opposite the main entrance to the Parco di Capodimonte, Naples' observatory is the oldest in Italy. Founded by King Ferdinand I of Bourbon in 1819 and built according to the designs of astronomers Giuseppe Piazzai and Federico Zuccari, it is a fine example of neoclassical architecture.

On the upper terrace you can admire a fine collection of astronomical instruments and the wonderful views of the sea 150m below you.

At the time of writing visits had been temporarily suspended; at other times they are by appointment only.

PALAZZO REALE DI CAPODIMONTE

Map p250

☎ 081 749 91 11; Parco di Capodimonte; adult/child €7.50/free, adult 2-5pm €6.50; ⏲ 8.30am-7.30pm Tue-Sun; bus 24 to Via Capodimonte

This massive palace took more than a century to build. Designed by architect Antonio Medrano, it was originally intended as a hunting lodge for Charles VII of Bourbon but as construction got underway in 1738 the plans kept on getting grander and grander. The result was the monumental palace that since 1759 has housed the art collection that Charles inherited from his mother Elisabetta Farnese.

The Fatal Wedding Presence

In one of the dank passageways of the Catacomba di San Gaudioso you can just make out the fading image of a couple standing hand in hand, their other hands pressed to their hearts. Not far away a knight is buried.

The story goes that the knight and the girl were greatly in love. Understandably, however, the girl's betrothed wasn't overly happy. In fact, he was so jealous that not even the knight's subsequent death would calm him. Enraged further by his girlfriend's grief, he challenged the dead knight to a duel. Thinking this to be the end of the matter he continued to prepare for his wedding.

On the big day the couple were busy tying the knot when they noticed a mysterious figure arrive, his face covered by a great black hood. As they challenged the apparition, the knight pulled back his cloak to reveal his skeletal form. The bride and groom instantly collapsed to the ground dead, their hearts broken by two massive heart attacks.

Artists and 17th-century travellers came from all over Europe to admire the phenomenal collection which was displayed on the *piano nobile* (noble floor). Visits were abruptly halted, however, during the decade of French rule (1806–15) when the palace became the official residence of Joseph Bonaparte and Joachim Murat.

The history of the museum proper resumes in 1860 when a Galleria d'Arte Moderna (Gallery of Modern Art) was established. Paintings and sculptures by contemporary Neapolitan artists were displayed alongside works taken from former Bourbon residences. In 1957 this became the **Museo Nazionale di Capodimonte** and the Farnese collection, which had previously been transferred to the Palazzo dei Regi Studi (the city university, now the Museo Archeologico Nazionale), was returned to its historic home.

The museum is spread over three floors and 160 rooms. The 1st floor is dominated by the Galleria Farnese and the Appartamento Reale (Royal Apartment); the 2nd floor contains the Galleria delle Arti a Napoli; while the top floor is dedicated to modern art. Before you embark on the museum, consider forking out €4 for an audioguide – the commentary in English and Italian is interesting.

To do the whole museum in one day is simply impossible – you'd need at least two to start getting to grips with the place. For most people, though, a full morning is sufficient for a shortened best-of tour.

First-floor highlights are numerous. In Room 2 you can see family portraits of the Farnese by Raphael and Titian; depictions of Cardinal Alessandro Farnese, later Pope Paul III, show a thin, rather weedy-looking man. Next door in Room 3 the *Crocifissione* (Crucifixion; 1426) by Masaccio is one of the museum's most famous pieces. Botticelli's *Madonna con Bambino e Angeli* (Madonna with Baby and Angels; Room 6), Bellini's *Trasfigurazione* (Transfiguration; Room 8) and Titian's *Danae* (Room 11) are all important pieces, while Pieter Bruegel's disturbing 16th-century canvases make an eerie impression in Room 17.

In the recently opened **Galleria Delle Cose Rare** (Gallery of Rare Objects) you can imagine how the dinner table of Cardinal Alessandro Farnese might have looked. His blue majolica table service has his coat of arms embossed in gold on every piece, while the elaborate centrepiece depicting Diana the huntress can be used as a goblet by taking off the stag's detachable head.

Voracious Collecting, Farnese Style

The Farnese art collection is one of the most important in Italy; and in terms of Renaissance art, that means the world. It was Cardinal Alessandro Farnese who founded the collection. On becoming Pope Paul III in 1534 Farnese began to gathering art treasures for the Vatican, then turned his attention to embellishing the family seat, Palazzo Farnese, in Rome. Through papal influence, the Farnese family monopolised excavations around the city. In 1545 the *Toro Farnese* (Farnese Bull) was discovered near the Terme di Caracalla and installed in the gardens of Palazzo Farnese. It remained there until 1787, when it was moved to Naples' **Museo Archeologico Nazionale** (p66), now the home of other famous Farnese treasures such as *Venere Callipigia* (The Callipygian Venus) and *Ercole* (Hercules).

This particular pope's vow of celibacy didn't prevent him from fathering four children. One of the most interesting paintings at the Palazzo Reale di Capodimonte is an unfinished portrait by Titian of Paul III with his two grandsons – Ottavio, who became the Duke of Parma and Piacenza, and Gran Cardinale Alessandro, who later became a serious collector in his own right. Alessandro continued the collection, commissioning works from Michelangelo, El Greco and other contemporary painters of renown.

The collection was transferred to Capodimonte from the Farnese family's power base in Rome, Parma and Piacenza in 1759. Many paintings were sold off in the 19th century, when the entire remaining collection was transferred to what is now the Museo Archeologico Nazionale. The paintings were returned to Capodimonte in 1957.

The **Appartamento Reale** (Royal Apartment) occupies Rooms 31 to 60. The hugely ornate rooms are full of valuable Capodimonte porcelain, heavy curtains and inlaid marble. The *Salotinno di Porcellana* (Room 51), for example, is a study in tasteless extravagance, boasting more than 3000 pieces of porcelain. It was originally created between 1757 and 1759 for the Palazzo Reale in Portici but was transferred to Capodimonte in 1867.

The 2nd floor is no less rich than the 1st, packed to its elegant rafters with works produced in Naples between the 13th and 18th centuries. The first room you come to, however, is lined with a series of gigantic 16th-century Belgian tapestries depicting episodes from the Battle of Pavia.

Simone Martini's work *San Ludovico di Tolosa* (1317) is brilliantly displayed in Room 66. Considered the museum's finest example of 14th-century art, Martini's golden work portrays the canonisation of Ludovico, brother of King Robert of Anjou.

The piece that many come to Capodimonte to see, *Flagellazione* (Flagellation; 1607–10) hangs in reverential solitude in Room 78, at the end of a long corridor. Caravaggio's dramatic image of Jesus about to be flogged was originally painted for the De Franchis family chapel in the Chiesa di San Domenico Maggiore. And like his other great Neapolitan work *Le sette opere di Misericordia* (The Seven Acts of Mercy; see p63), its intensity and revolutionary depiction of light was to have a huge influence on his contemporaries.

Continue through the 28 rooms that remain on the 2nd floor for works by Ribera,

Giordano, Solimena and Stanzione. If you have any energy left, the small **gallery of modern art** on the 3rd floor is worth a quick look, if nothing else for Andy Warhol's colourful image of Mt esuvius erupting.

But you're not finished yet. On the ground floor, the **Gabinetto Disegni e Stampe** (Drawing and Print Room) contains some 27,000 pieces, including several sketches by Michelangelo and Raphael.

PALAZZO SANFELICE Map p250
Via della Sanità 2; metro Cavour

It's difficult to imagine the architectural impact that this building had in 18th-century Naples. Today in the scruffy streets of La Sanità district, it looks just like any other building. But when Ferdinando Sanfelice built it for his family in 1726 it quickly became a model of avant-garde architecture. The main talking point was the open double-ramped staircase in the second internal courtyard. Sanfelice went on to perfect his hallmark staircase design in various palazzi across the city. A famous example is in the **Palazzo dello Spagnolo** (Map p250; Via Vergini 19).

Neither of these two buildings is technically open to the public but if you ask the porter to let you have a quick look, they'll probably oblige. Porters generally work office hours, so avoid the early afternoon if you want to find someone there.

PARCO DI CAPODIMONTE Map p250
☾ 9am-1hr before sunset; bus 24 to Via Capodimonte
Covering some 130 hectares, the Parco di Capodimonte was designed by Ferdinando

Felice in 1742. Initially a hunting reserve for King Charles VII (hence the wall that surrounds the park), today it is a popular weekend spot for Neapolitans, but you don't need to walk far to avoid the crowds round the Palazzo Reale.

Within the park walls there are five lakes, a wood, and various 18th-century buildings, including the **Palazzo Porcellane**, where porcelain was once produced. The easiest entrance is through the Porta Grande on Via Capodimonte.

PORTA SAN GENNARO Map p250
Via Foria; metro Cavour

This city gate was rebuilt in its current position in the 15th century after the expansion of the city walls. Named after San Gennaro because it marks the beginning of the route up to the Catacomba di San Gennaro, it retains traces of a 17th-century fresco by Mattia Preti. The artist decorated all the major city gates to give thanks for the end of the plague epidemic in 1656.

MERCATO

Eating pp118–9; Shopping pp143–4; Sleeping pp156-7

This part of town is gritty, poor and difficult to like much. It's also Naples' most cosmopolitan area, with a growing Chinese community and a considerable Arabic presence.

At the eastern end of central Naples, the Stazione Centrale is a convenient landmark. To the south the streets lead to Via Nuova Marina and the port, while Corso Umberto I runs southwest from Piazza Garibaldi to Piazza Bovio and the university.

Unpleasant and unavoidable, Piazza Garibaldi is a vast cauldron of cars, buses, dodgy street sellers, cheap electrical shops and budget hotels; it's noisy, smelly and colourful. This is where you'll get offered a brand-new mobile phone at a knockdown price or a designer suit straight off the lorry. It's also a major transport hub: long-distance buses arrive here and the main train station forms the square's eastern flank.

Corso G Garibaldi cuts across the western end of the square. Head south past the intimidating groups of red-eyed, rake-thin young men for Piazza Nolana and the 15th-century city gate, Porta Nolana. Famous for its madcap morning market, this part of town is wonderfully alive during the day and quietly menacing at night. Further west, the medieval Borgo degli Orefici (Goldsmith's Quarter) is still full of jewellery shops.

Today a carpark-cum-open-air shopfloor, Piazza del Mercato has a gory history. As well as being the site of city executions it was here that the plague epidemic broke out in 1656. To its immediate east, Piazza del Carmine is where fisherman Tommaso Aniello sparked off the short but violent Masaniello uprising (see p45). Just on the other side of the 14th-century Porta del Carmine, the traffic thunders down Via Nuova Marina, the seafront road past the port.

The main traffic road in downtown Naples, Corso Umberto I is known as *il Rettifilo* (the straight line) for pretty obvious reasons. Built in 1884, it is today a choking four-lane carriageway lined with cheap shoeshops and sportswear stores. To the north lie the mean streets of Forcella, a poor district that has borne more than its fair share of Camorra violence. Controlled in the 1980s by the much-feared Giuliano brothers, Carmine and Luigi, the area has in recent times seen a resurgence of gangland violence.

BASILICA SANTISSIMA ANNUNZIATA MAGGIORE Map pp244-6

☎ 081 254 26 08; Via dell'Annunziata 34; ☾ 7.30am-noon & 4.30-7.30pm Mon-Sat, 7.30am-1pm Sun; bus R2 to Corso Umberto I

This 14th-century religious complex is as well known for its former orphanage (see boxed text, p91) as it is for its large and bright basilica. Designed and built by Carlo Vanvitelli, son of the better-known Luigi, at the end of the 18th century, the basilica's white and light-grey interior is wonderfully cooling on hot days. It is

also very big – some 44 Corinthian columns line the nave and the dome is 67m high.

To the left of the basilica, a courtyard (closed to the public) adjoins the orphanage.

Transport
Bus R1, R2, R3, 3S, 201, 404 Destra
Metro Line 2 Piazza Garibaldi
Tram 1, 29

Quarters – Mercato

BORGO DEGLI OREFICI Map pp244-6
Bus R2 to Corso Umberto I

South of Corso Umberto I and west of Via Duomo lies the Borgo degli Orefici (Goldsmiths Quarter). Since the 13th century goldsmiths and silversmiths have worked and lived in these cramped streets. Virtually every shop is a jewellers and signs declaring 'Compro Oro' ('I buy gold') are everywhere.

In medieval times the goldsmiths would meet in Piazzetta Orefici to consult and discuss issues with their union bosses, the four members of the Corporation of Goldsmiths' ruling council.

CHIESA DI SAN PIETRO AD ARAM
Map pp244-6

☎ 081 28 64 11; Corso Umberto 1 292; ⏰ 7-11am Mon-Sat, 7am-1pm Sun; bus R2 to Corso Umberto I

Tradition has it that it was on this spot that St Peter converted St Candida and St Asprenus; the latter was Naples' first bishop.

The origins of the church are not clear but restoration work in 1930 revealed the crypt of a Paleo-Christian church and some catacombs. Certainly the original structure was enlarged in the 12th century with the addition of a monastery, the remains of which can be seen in the vestibule, but in its current form the church dates to the 17th century. The baroque interior boasts paintings by Luca Giordano, Andrea Vaccaro and Massimo Stanzione. A more recent addition is the *grotta di Lourdes* (Lourdes grotto), a space dedicated to the famous French shrine.

CHIESA DI SAN PIETRO MARTIRE
Map pp244-6

☎ 081 552 68 55; Piazzetta Bonghi 1; ⏰ 7am-1pm & 5-7pm; bus R2 to Corso Umberto I

Opposite the main university building, this late 14th-century church has an unusual history. Originally commissioned by king Charles II of Anjou as part of a project to clean up the surrounding crime-infested area, it was at the outset a modest Dominican monastery and church. Various enlargements followed,

including the addition of a 16th-century cloister by Giovan Francesco di Palma (also known as Mormando). During the decade of French rule (1806–15) the monks were kicked out and the monastery became a tobacco factory. It remained so until 1978 when, after it had a major revamp, the professors of the faculty of Literature and Philosophy moved in to their new, and current, home.

CHIESA DI SANTA MARIA DEL CARMINE Map pp244-6

☎ 081 20 11 96; Piazza del Carmine; ⏰ 6.30am-12.30pm & 5-7.30pm Mon-Sat, 6.30am-2pm & 5-7.30pm Sun; bus C55 to Corso G Garibaldi

One of the oldest churches in Naples, Chiesa di Santa Maria del Carmine plays an important role in Neapolitan folklore. Originally built at the end of the 12th century, the church was rebuilt in the 13th century thanks to money donated by Elisabetta di Baviera, who was the mother of Conrad (Corradino) of Swabia. She had initially collected the money in order to pay Charles I of Anjou a ransom for her son's life after Conrad tried and failed to depose the king. But the money arrived too late and in 1268 Conrad was beheaded for treason. In her grief Elisabetta gave the money to the church on the condition that the Carmelite brothers said mass every day on behalf of her son. Today you can see a monument to Conrad in the transept.

However, it is the 13th-century Byzantine icon behind the main altar, the *Madonna della Bruna*, that lies at the heart of the church's enduring popularity. Attributed with miraculous powers, the Madonna is celebrated every year on 16 July when huge crowds gather at the church for a spectacular fireworks display. The pyrotechnic show lights up the church's impressive **campanile**, which at 75m is the highest bell tower in Naples. Designed by Giacomo di Conforto and Giovanni Donzelli (who was also known as Fra Nuvolo), it was completed in 1631.

Further myth (and miracle) surrounds a wooden crucifix that hangs in a tabernacle under the church's main arch. According to the faithful, in 1439 a cannonball fired at the church during the war between Alfonso of Aragon and Robert of Anjou penetrated the church wall and headed straight for the crucifix. In the nick of time Jesus ducked and the cannonball sailed harmlessly past.

Top Five Mercato
- Chiesa di Santa Maria del Carmine (right)
- Basilica Santissima Annunziata Maggiore (p81)
- Porta Nolana & Mercato (p91)
- Chiesa di San Pietro ad Aram (above)
- Chiesa Sant'Eligio (opposite)

(Continued on page 91)

1 Shopping, centro storico
(p137) **2** Chiesa del Gesù Nuovo
(p56) **3** Neapolitans playing cards
4 Football fans, Stadio San Paolo
(p133)

O S. PAOLO – NAPOLI

1 Lion statue, Piazza dei Martiri
(p94) 2 Detail, Castel Nuovo (p69)
3 Basilica di Santa Chiara (p55)
4 Interior, Duomo (p60)

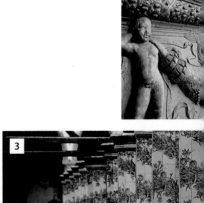

1 Palazzo Reale di Capodimonte
(p79) *2* Piazza del Plebiscito (p73)
3 Castel dell'Ovo (p68)
4 Castel Sant'Elmo (p74)

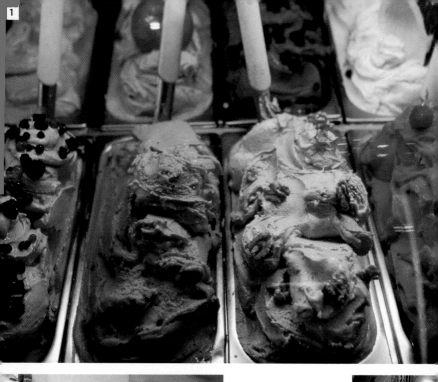

1 *Gelati* 2 *Caffè Gambrinus (p113)*
3 *Pizza margherita (p30)* 4 *White Bar (p129)*

1 *Chocolates, Gay-Odin (p139)*
2 *Designer labels, Via Calabritto (p141)* 3 *Galleria Umberto I (p139)*
4 *Market stalls, La Pignasecca (p144)*

1 Positano (p192) 2 Fishing nets
3 Tempio di Nettuno (p203)
4 Boats in harbour, Salerno (p201)

(Continued from page 82)

History rather than tradition records that it was from this church that the young, illiterate fisherman Tommaso Aniello (aka Masaniello) harangued the mob into rising against the Spanish rulers. Defeated and killed by the Spanish, he is said to be buried in an unmarked tomb in the church.

CHIESA SANT'ELIGIO Map pp244-6

☎ 081 553 84 29; Via Sant'Eligio; ☒ 9am-1pm Mon-Wed, 9am-1pm & 5-6.30pm Thu-Sat, 9.30am-2pm Sun; bus C55 to Corso G Garibaldi

The first Angevin church in Naples, Sant'Eligio suffered heavy bomb damage in WWII. What was left of the baroque interior was subsequently removed by restorers keen to recreate the original Gothic look.

The church was built in 1270 by Charles I of Anjou, although its most noticeable feature, the external clock arch, dates to the 15th century.

Just a few doors down, the **Chiesa San Giovanni a Mare** (Map pp244–6; ☎ 081 26 47 52; Via San Giovanni 8; ☒ 9am-noon) is one of Naples' few remaining examples of Romanesque architecture (c 1050–1200).

PIAZZA BOVIO Map pp244-6

Bus R2 to Corso Umberto I

Piazza Bovio marks the end of the road for Corso Umberto I. Branching off to the south, Via Agostino Depretis leads down to Piazza del Municipio, while Via G Sanfelice runs west towards Via Toledo.

On the northern side of the square stands the important-looking **Palazzo della Borsa** (Stock Exchange). A sand-coloured building guarded by two lions, it was built by Alfredo Guerra in 1895 and is now home to the Banco di Napoli and the Banca di Roma. The square was also home to the Fontana di Nettuno (see p71) until work on the new metro turned the square into a building site and the fountain was moved to Via Medina.

PIAZZA DEL MERCATO Map pp244-6

Bus C55 to Corso G Garibaldi

Charles I of Anjou moved the city market here from Piazza San Gaetano sometime in the 13th century. Considered an important and lively square, it was for centuries the site of public executions, including that of Conrad of Swabia, whose mother paid for the nearby **Chiesa di Santa Maria del Carmine** (see p82) to be rebuilt, and more than 200 ill-fated supporters of the 1799

What's in a Name?

Flick through the Naples telephone directory and you'll notice an awful lot of people are called Esposito. A Neapolitan name, it derives from the Italian word *esposto* (exposed) and was traditionally given to babies abandoned at the orphanage of the Real Casa Santa Annunziata.

At the former **orphanage** (☎ 081 28 90 32; Via dell'Annunziata 34; ☒ 9am-6pm Mon-Sat), which adjoins the Basilica Santissima Annunziata Maggiore, you can still see the **ruota** (wheel) in which the abandoned babies were left. In use up until the 1980s, the wheel was set into the orphanage wall so that desperate parents could leave their baby anonymously. Made out of wood, it consists of a concertinaed drum with a hollow cut into it. The hollow was set facing out onto the street and parents would place the baby in the wheel and turn it. On the inside sat a nun ready to take the baby, wash it in the adjacent basin and record its time and date of entry.

A cold-hearted and cruel system, it did, in fact, save many babies who would otherwise have been left on the streets of Naples.

Parthenopean Republic. These days it is a scruffy combination of car park and shop floor.

Lying the north of the square shines the green-tiled dome of the boarded-up Chiesa di Santa Croce al Mercato, while the car park in the centre doubles up as a football pitch. In the southwest corner you'll find a curious pyramid supported by four weird creatures, each with the body of a lion and the face of a puffy-cheeked young girl.

PORTA NOLANA & MERCATO

Map pp244-6

Via Sopramuro; bus C55 to Corso G Garibaldi

At the head of Via Sopramuro stands the 15th-century Porta Nolana, one of the medieval city gates. Two cylindrical towers, optimistically named Faith and Hope, support an arch decorated with a bas-relief of Ferdinand I of Aragon on horseback.

But you come here not for the architecture but for the most vivacious street market in all of Naples. Street theatre at its very rawest, the market is colourful, noisy and well stocked. Among other things you'll find plastic buckets and spades; fish of every shape and size; pallets of loo paper; Marilyn Manson T-shirts; pirate CDs; fruit, veg, cheese, ham and olives; corn on the cob; lottery tickets; cheap underwear; digital watches and inflatable dolphins.

Università (below)

UNIVERSITÀ Map pp244-6

☎ 081 547 71 11; cnr Corso Umberto 1 & Via Mezzo-cannone; bus R2 to Corso Umberto I

One of the oldest universities in Europe, the University of Naples was founded by King Frederick II of Swabia in 1224, more or less where the current university stands. Following his death in 1250, the university transferred to Salerno until the reign of King Manfred (1254-66). The vast neoclassical edifice that today houses the university's central administration was built between 1887 and 1908.

CHIAIA

Eating pp120–1; Shopping pp144–6; Sleeping pp157-9

Rich, smart and vibrant, Chiaia is where the city's wealthy come to relax. That might mean shopping in the expensive designer boutiques along Via G Filangieri and Via dei Mille, or simply hanging out in fragrant groups in Piazza dei Martiri. After dark it means a meal in one of the areas' many trattorie before adjourning to the trendy bar of the moment.

The area is situated west of Santa Lucia. From Piazza Trieste e Trento, Via Chiaia becomes Via S Caterina as it leads to Chiaia's central square, Piazza dei Martiri. The cobbled streets to the west of this elegant 19th-century piazza are among the liveliest in Naples, particularly after dark when well-dressed drinkers spill out of many bars.

To the south you have to cross the busy Riviera di Chiaia to reach the city's most famous park, the Villa Comunale. Not a park in the sense of green lawns and picnics, it's a long manicured strip of wide paths and palm trees, swings and water sprinklers. In the centre the Stazione Zoologica is Europe's oldest aquarium.

More garden-like is the green area around the 19th-century Villa Pignatelli. The one-time residence of the Rothschild family currently houses the Museo Pignatelli with its eclectic collection of art, a blue room that isn't blue and some royal hunting paraphernalia.

Dividing the Villa Comunale from the sea, Via Francesco Caracciolo follows the bay round to Mergellina. Just west of the aquarium, Viale Anton Dohrn branches off this major thoroughfare and runs into Piazza della Repubblica at the western tip of the Villa Comunale. More a road junction than a piazza, the square's main feature is the monument to *Le quattro giornate napoletane* (the four days of Naples; between 27 and 30 September 1943 popular uprisings helped Allied forces force the Germans from the city).

CHIESA ASCENSIONE Map pp248-9

☎ 081 8141 16 57; Piazzetta Ascensione; ☯ 8-11.30am & 4.30-7.30pm Mon-Sat, 8am-1pm Sun; metro Amedeo

One of the many Cosimo Fanzago–designed churches appearing in Naples, Chiesa Ascensione was constructed on the site of an earlier 14th-century monastery, of which nothing remains. When the baroque building was finished in 1645 the church was renamed the Chiesa ai Santi Michele, Anna e Pietro Celestino but the name met with little popular support and never caught on.

Boasting a couple of Luca Giordano paintings, the church is today a popular choice for weddings.

CHIESA SANTA MARIA IN PORTICO

Map pp248-9

☎ 081 66 92 94; Via Santa Maria in Portico 17; ☯ 8-11am & 4.30-7pm; bus C25 to Riviera di Chiaia

The interior of this 17th-century church is a veritable gallery of baroque art. There are frescoes by Fabrizio Santafede (a good name for a church painter – 'Santafede' means 'holy faith'), Paolo De Matteis, Giovan Battista and Fedele Fischetti. In the sacristy there's a life-size 17th-century *presepe*, while the stuccowork is by Domenico Antonio Vaccaro. The façade is by Arcangelo (another apt name – it means 'archangel') Guglielminelli and not, as was thought for many years, Cosimo Fanzago.

CHIESA SANTA TERESA A CHIAIA

Map pp248-9

Via Vittorio Colonna 22; ☯ 7.30-10.45am Mon-Sat, 7.30am-1.30pm & 5.30-7pm Sun; metro Amedeo

Overlooking Via Colonna, the entrance to the baroque Chiesa Santa Teresa a Chiaia is by the elegant double-ramped staircase that flares up to the main doorway. Although architect Cosimo Fanzago finished work on the church in 1650 it was largely rebuilt after an earthquake in 1688. Characterised by a three-storey façade, it also contains a statue of Santa Teresa on the main altar and several paintings by Luca Giordano.

Top Five Chiaia

- Stazione Zoologica (p94)
- Museo Pignatelli (right)
- Piazza dei Martiri (p94)
- Chiesa Santa Maria in Portico (above)
- Lungomare (above)

Transport

Bus R3, C5, C25, 404 Destra
Metro Line 1 Amedeo
Tram 1

LUNGOMARE Map pp248-9

Bus C25 to Via Partenope

Running the length of Via Partenope and Via Francesco Carrociolo, the *lungomare* (seafront) is a favourite Neapolitan walk. Linking Santa Lucia in the east with Mergellina in the west, the 2.5km seaside stroll is particularly beautiful as the sun sets and the light over the sea takes on an orange hue. With the island of Capri silhouetted on the horizon and Mt Vesuvius looming to the south, the views are fabulous. Sunday morning is another good time as Via Francesco Carrociolo is closed to traffic and becomes a colourful parade of strollers, skaters, scooters and joggers.

In the summer you'll probably see local kids swimming off a tiny wedge of sand near the Monumento a Diaz. It's a local habit and not to be recommended.

MUSEO PIGNATELLI Map pp248-9

☎ 081 761 23 56; Riviera di Chiaia 200; adult/child €2/1; ☯ 9am-2pm Tue-Sun; bus C25 to Riviera di Chiaia

The full title of this museum is quite a mouthful – the Museo Principe Diego Aragona Pignatelli Cortes. If you need directions just ask for the Villa Pignatelli and you'll be right.

Originally commissioned by Ferdinand Acton, a minister at the court of King Ferdinand IV (1759–1825), Villa Pignatelli is a fine example of the Graeco-Roman style that was so popular in early 19th-century Naples. Architect Pietro Valente based his grandiose design on the noble houses of Pompeii, completing construction in 1826. Set in its own beautiful grounds, it was bought by the Rothschild family in 1841 and 20 years later by the Pignatelli prince, to whom the villa and museum owe their name. In 1952 Rosina Pignatelli donated the villa to the state.

You can see photos of the Pignatelli family in the museum, in the Salotto Azzuro (Blue Room), which curiously enough isn't blue. Similarly, La Biblioteca (library) is something of a misnomer as the room lacks any books.

The museum contains a mixed bag of opulent furniture, porcelain, hunting paraphernalia (including a collection of royal whips) and art. Of particular note is the Maissen and Viennese porcelain in the Salotto Verde (Green Room).

The 1st floor's mainly 18th- to 20th-century Neapolitan works are part of the Banco di Napoli's extensive art collection. They include a number of busts as well as paintings.

The adjoining **Museo delle Carrozze** contains a collection of 19th- and 20th-century carriages, but is currently closed for restoration.

PALAZZO CELLAMARE Map pp248-9
Via Chiaia 149; bus C25 to Piazza dei Martiri

On the corner of Via Chiaia and Via G Filangieri stands Palazzo Cellamare. Dating to the 16th century, it was built as the summer residence of Giovan Francesco Carafa, a close friend of the Spanish viceroy Don Pedro de Toledo. Before it was bought some hundred years later by the Prince of Cellamare, Antonio Giudice, it was used as a hospital for victims of the 1656 plague epidemic.

In 1726 it underwent a facelift: La Cappella di Ferdinando Fuga was cleaned up and frescoes were added by Pietro Baidellino, Giacinto Diano and Alessandro and Fedele Fischetti. The décor obviously impressed the Bourbon monarchy which, in 1799, started renting the building. Rather than live there though, they lent it out to favoured artists and intellectuals, including Goethe.

Nowadays the Palazzo Cellamare is a residential block of upmarket flats and is not open to the public.

PIAZZA AMEDEO Map pp248-9
Metro Amedeo

At the top of Via Vittorio Colonna, the Piazza Amedeo is a small busy square of trees and stylish Art Deco palazzi. The metro station sits on the northern side, while curving away to the east the 19th-century Via del Parco Margherita winds its way up to Vomero. It's a popular spot with shoppers returning from a hard day's spending on Via dei Mille.

PIAZZA DEI MARTIRI Map pp248-9
Bus C25 to Piazza dei Martiri

If Chiaia is the drawing room of Naples – as it's sometimes called – then Piazza dei Martiri is the smart coffee table around which people languidly drape themselves. In fact, the square-side café **La Caffettiera** (p121) is a top spot to be seen sporting a laid-back demeanour.

The piazza takes its name from the monument to the martyrs of the 1799 Parthenopean Republic in the centre of the square. Designed by the 19th-century architect Enrico Alvino, the obelisk is supported by four large lions.

On the western flank of the square, at No 58, **Palazzo Partanna** (Map pp248–9) is a neoclassical update of an original 18th-century edifice, while at No 30, **Palazzo Calabritto** (Map pp248–9) is a Luigi Vanvitelli creation.

Culture of a more readable nature is on hand at **Feltrinelli** (p94), Naples' best bookshop, in the northeastern corner of the square.

STAZIONE ZOOLOGICA (AQUARIO) Map pp248-9
☎ 081 583 32 63; www.emmeti.it; Viale Aquario 1; adult/child €1.50/1; ☼ 9am-6pm Mon-Sat, 9.30am-7pm Sun summer, 9am-5pm Mon-Sat, 9am-2pm Sun winter; bus C25 to Riviera di Chiaia

This small but elegantly neoclassical marine research centre can't compete for size with the massive aquarium in Genoa. But what it lacks in size it makes up for in age. Founded in 1872 by German naturalist Anton Dohrn, it is Europe's oldest aquarium and is today considered a research centre of international renown. Its 26 tanks contain some 200 species of marine flora and fauna exclusively from the Bay of Naples, while its biology library is one of the largest of its kind in the world.

VIA CHIAIA Map pp248-9
Bus CS to Piazza Trieste e Trento, bus C25 to Piazza dei Martiri

Linking Piazza Trieste e Trento with Piazza dei Martiri, Via Chiaia is a popular, albeit expensive, shopping street. Built in the 16th century, it follows the line of the natural divide that separates the hills of Pizzofalcone and Mortella. Towards the western end of the street you pass under what looks from below to be a triumphal arch but is, in fact, a bridge built in 1636 to connect the two hills.

Nowadays Via Chiaia is lined with shops, imposing palazzi, a hotel, a theatre, a church and a former brothel. Of the palazzi, it is the **Renaissance Palazzo Cellamare** (p9), a once-royal residence, that is the most famous.

VILLA COMUNALE Map pp248-9
☎ 081 761 11 31; Piazza Vittoria; ☼ 7am-midnight; bus C25 to Riviera di Chiaia

Boasting a bandstand, an aquarium, numerous statues, at least eight fountains and a tennis club, Villa Comunale is Naples' most famous park. Dividing the Riviera di Chiaia from Via Francesco Caracciolo and the sea, it was originally laid out by Carlo Vanvitelli to provide a garden for the Bourbon monarchy. At the time of its inauguration in 1781, it was known as the

Passeggio Reale (Royal Walkway) and for 364 days a year was off-limits to the plebs. Only on 8 September, the day of the **Festa di Piedigrotta** (see p9), was it open to the general public. Nowadays it's open to everyone every day.

The main entrance is at the eastern end in Piazza Vittoria. From here a wide avenue leads down to the bandstand and the Stazione Zoologica. Two famous statues to look out for include the 19th-century monument to Neapolitan philosopher Giambattista Vico (1668–1744) and the *Fontana delle Paperelle*. Named after the ducks that used to swim in the fountain, it was brought in to replace the *Toro Farnese* which, in 1825, was transferred to the **Museo Archeologico Nazionale** (p66).

MERGELLINA & POSILLIPO

Eating p122; Shopping p146; Sleeping pp159-60

The old adage 'See Naples and Die' may have been a warning to avoid Naples – if the cholera doesn't get you the gangsters will. More likely though, it was an expression of admiration – once you've seen Naples everywhere else will seem so dull as to render life meaningless. No-one knows who first coined the phrase, but what is known is that poets and writers used to extol the beauties of Mergellina and Posillipo.

An area of fishermen, Mergellina was lively and atmospheric. To the west, Posillipo was famously unspoiled, with pine woods growing over the rocky slopes and the villas of the rich discreetly built into the landscape. In this last respect Posillipo hasn't changed much: private villas still stand overlooking the sea, hidden from view by the walled gardens that surround them. In many other respects the two areas are not what they were.

At the western end of the seafront, Mergellina is today an important transport hub. Dominating Piazza Piedigrotta, the Art Nouveau train station is both a metro stop and a busy mainline station. Down on the seafront thousands of people set off every day for the islands from Mergellina's hydrofoil terminal, while nearby in Piazza Sannazarro traffic roars through the hideous tunnel that links central Naples with the Fuorigrotta area.

Reminders of Mergellina's fishing past are scarce, although in the marina you will see the odd fishing boat moored between the gleaming yachts and motor cruisers. It is, however, the seafront that is Mergellina's best feature. The lively *gelaterie* (ice-cream parlours) and bars, collectively known as the **Chalets** (Map pp248–9), attract huge crowds, especially in the summer. Just over the road, the **lungomare** (p93) is a famous Neapolitan walk.

Following the bay round to the west, Via Francesco Caracciolo rises to become Via Posillipo, Posillipo's main thoroughfare. The headland that divides the Bay of Naples from the Bay of Pozzuoli, Posillipo is an area of smart restaurants and beautiful views, caves and cliffs. It's an area where people come to walk and teenagers to smooch, where privacy is sought and, with enough money, bought.

For some spectacular views the Parco Virgiliano at the western tip of the cape is the place to head. Here you can look over the bay to Mt Vesuvius or over to the island of Nisida where Brutus is said to have conspired against Julius Caesar. To the north lie the abandoned steelworks of Bagnoli.

Quarters – Mergellina & Posillipo

CHIESA SANTA MARIA DEL PARTO

Map pp248-9

☎ 081 66 46 27; Via Mergellina 21; ✆ 7.30-11am & 5.30-7.30pm Mon-Sat, 8am-12.30pm & 6-7.30pm Sun; metro Mergellina

A Renaissance church, Santa Maria del Parto owes most of its fame to the Neapolitan poet Jacopo Sannazzaro, who is not only buried here but was also the church's founder. Built on land donated to Sannazzaro by King Frederick of Aragon in 1497, the church was completed shortly before the poet died in 1530.

Sannazzaro's tomb is behind the altar. The 1537 creation of Giovanni Angelo Montorsoli, Bartolomeo Ammannati and Francesco del Tadda, features gods, including Apollo, Minerva, Pan and Mars in a depiction of Arcadia.

Transport

Bus R3, 140, 152
Metro Line 2 Mergellina
Funicular Mergellina

Top Five Mergellina & Posillipo

- Parco Virgiliano (right)
- Chiesa Santa Maria di Piedigrotta (below)
- Porticciolo (opposite)
- Grotta di Seiano (below)
- Marechiaro (right)

Villa Pausilypon takes its name from the Greek word *pausilipon* (from which Posillipo is derived) meaning a respite from pain. Its original owner Publio Vedio Pollione left the villa to his friend, the emperor Augustus, when he died in 15 BC.

Both the villa and the tunnel are currently closed indefinitely for restoration.

Also worth noting is Leonardo da Pistoia's painting of *St Michael Vanquishing the Devil*, also known as the *Devil of Mergellina*. Tradition holds that the devil in question was a local lass who'd tried to seduce the unwavering bishop Diomede Carafa.

CHIESA SANTA MARIA DI PIEDIGROTTA Map pp248-9

☎ 081 66 97 61; Piazza Piedigrotta 24; ✆ 7am-noon & 5.30-8pm Mon-Sat, 7am-1.30pm & 5.30-8pm Sun; metro Mergellina

The fishing families of Mergellina had already built a church on this site when, in 1353, the Virgin Mary appeared to a Benedictine monk, a nun and Pietro the Hermit (later to become Pope Celestine V; see Chiesa San Pietro a Maiella on p62) telling them to build her a church. She was taken at her word and the church was consecrated within the year. Since then, and despite numerous makeovers, the church has remained the central focus of the **Festa di Piedigrotta** (p9), celebrated on 8 September.

The first major renovation was in 1452, although it was the 1553 work that was the most significant. Originally, the façade faced the rock, or *grotta*, to which the church owes its name (*piedigrotta* means 'foot of the cave'), but in the 16th century it was reversed to face the city, as it does today. Further work on the façade took place in 1853 when Enrico Alvino added his neoclassical touch.

Inside, it is the 13th-century wooden statue, the *Madonna con Bambino* (Madonna with Baby) that the faithful come to see.

GROTTA DI SEIANO Off Map pp242-3

☎ 081 230 10 30; Discesa Coroglio 36; bus 140 to Via Posillipo

At the bottom of a long, steep and exhausting descent (Discesa Coroglio), the Grotta di Seiano is not, in fact, a cave but a 1st-century tunnel. Linking Villa Pausilypon to Pozzuoli, it was dug out of the tufa rock by Cocceius, the same Roman engineer who built the Crypta Neapolitana. At the time the tunnel was the only link between Pozzuoli and Naples.

MARECHIARO Off Map pp242-3

Via Marechiaro; bus 140 to Via Posillipo

Immortalised in the traditional 19th-century Neapolitan song 'Marechiaro' (Clear Sea) by Salvatore di Giacomo and Francesco Paolo Tosti, Marechiaro is a tiny fishing village. A picturesque place with its own church, the Chiesa di Santa Maria del Faro, it's an ideal spot for a romantic dinner in one of the many good restaurants.

To get here, get off the bus on Via Posillipo and head down Via Marechiaro on the left. It takes about 30 minutes on foot.

PALAZZO DONN'ANNA Off Map pp242-3

Largo Donn'Anna 9; bus 140 to Via Posillipo

The most famous unfinished palazzo in Posillipo, Palazzo Donn'Anna takes its name from Anna Carafa, for whom it was built. Commissioned by the Spanish viceroy of Naples, Ramiro Guzman, as a wedding present for his bride Anna, it was destined to remain incomplete. When Guzman hot-footed it back to Spain in 1644 he left his wife heartbroken in Naples. She died shortly afterwards and Cosimo Fanzago gave up the project. The semi-derelict palazzo is not open to the public.

Not far from Palazzo Donn'Anna are the ruins of Villa Hamilton, the former residence of the British ambassador to the Kingdom of Naples. Sir William Hamilton is remembered less as a diplomat than as a wronged husband – his wife Emma was the long-time mistress of Lord Horatio Nelson.

PARCO VERGILIANO Map pp248-9

☎ 081 66 93 90; Salita dell Grotta 20; ✆ 9am-1hr before sunset Tue-Sun; metro Mergellina

A small landscaped park next to the railway bridge in Mergellina, the Parco Vergiliano (also spelled Virgiliano, but not to be confused with the larger Parco Virgiliano in Posillipo) is where Virgil is buried alongside 19th-century Italian poet Giacomo Leopardi. The subject of much historical speculation, the whereabouts of Virgil's body is a mystery. He died in Brindisi in 19 BC, and tradition has it that his remains were then bought to Naples (see boxed text, p70). Buried in a vault dating to the Augustan age, his tomb lies at the top of an exceedingly steep flight of stairs above the entrance to the *Crypta Neapolitana*. Not a crypt at all but an abandoned road tunnel, the *crypta* was built in the 1st century AD to connect Naples with the Campi Flegrei. At 700m long, it's the world's longest Roman tunnel.

Giacomo Leopardi was for a very long time buried in the Chiesa San Vitale a Fuorigrotta after he died of cholera in 1837. His tomb was placed here in 1939, some nine years after the park had been given a total makeover on the occasion of the 2000th anniversary of the death of Virgil.

PARCO VIRGILIANO Off Map pp242-3
Viale Virgilio; 🕑 9.30am-11.30pm; bus 140 to Via Posillipo

Between 1999 and 2002 the city authorities spent €5 million on smartening up the 9600 sq metres of the Parco Virgiliano. Situated on the westernmost tip of Posillipo, the park offers some of the best views in the whole city. On a clear day and if you have good eyesight you can make out the islands of Capri to the south; Nisida, Procida and Ischia to the southwest; the Bay of Pozzuoli and Bagnoli; to the west; and to the east the Bay of Naples, the Sorrento Peninsula and, of course, Mt Vesuvius.

The park is open 14 hours a day and is a great place to get away from the fumes of the city below. For the kids there are swings and slides, for the adults well-tended paths, benches and a bar or two.

PORTICCIOLO Map pp248-9
Via Francesco Caracciolo; bus 140 to Via Francesco Caracciolo

Once home to the area's fishing fleet, Mergellina's marina now counts more yachts and leisure cruisers than working boats. A picturesque little port at the western end of Via Francesco Caracciolo, it gets very busy on summer evenings as strollers walk along the seafront and the bumper-to-bumper traffic idles past the Chalets.

Bearing no resemblance to anything remotely Alpine, the Chalets are the *gelaterie* and bars that face out to the marina. It's a favourite place for an ice cream; Neapolitans will think nothing of driving down to the Chalets, double-parking and snaffling down a cone before heading off to bar or club.

STAZIONE MERGELLINA Map pp248-9
☎ 081 761 21 02; Piazza Piedigrotta; metro Mergellina

Overlooking Piazza Piedigrotta, Mergellina train station is an impressive example of beaux-arts architecture. A form of neoclassicism, the decorative beaux-arts style takes its name from the Ècole des Beaux-Arts in Paris. Designed by Gaetano Costa in 1925, the station boasts an iron-and-glass structure, huge windows and a series of massive columns. Among the ornate details is a coloured clock held aloft by an eagle and flanked by two figures depicting a resting Mercury.

Just down from the station in Piazza Sannazarro, the 1925 Galleria della Laziale road tunnel cuts through the Posillipo hill to emerge in the Fuorigrotta district.

VILLA ROSEBERY Off Map pp242-3
Via Ferdinando Russo; bus 140 to Via Posillipo

The official Neapolitan residence of the President of the Republic of Italy, the 18th-century Villa Rosebery has a prestigious history. It was used by Luigi of Bourbon in the early 19th century for his trysts with the dancer Amina Boschetti, and it was from here that King Vittorio Emanuele III left Italy in 1946 after the abolition of the monarchy.

The complex consists of three buildings – the Palazzina Borbonica, the Piccolo Foresteria and the Cabina a Mare – surrounded by an extensive estate.

Porticciolo (left)

CAMPI FLEGREI

The Campi Flegrei (Fiery Fields) is a classical term for the volcanic activity that has made this one of the globe's most geologically unstable areas. Predating the city of Naples, the Greek settlements of the Campi Flegrei are the oldest in Italy. Cuma, the first mainland stronghold in the area, was already a thriving city in the 7th century BC when the Greeks founded Parthenope (the area around Pizzofalcone in Naples) in 680 BC. Pozzuoli was founded around 530 BC while Neapolis (where Naples' *centro storico* now stands) sprung up in 470 BC.

Before exploring the area it's worth stopping at the **tourist office** (☎ 081 526 66 39; Piazza G Matteotti 1a; ☺ 9am-3.30pm) in Pozzuoli to pick up a copy of the very useful leaflet *Welcome to the Campi Flegrei*. Also a good idea is the €4 cumulative ticket that covers the Tempio di Serapide, the Solfatara crater and the archaeological sites of Baia and Cuma.

The three main attractions of the Campi Flegrei are Pozzuoli, Baia and Cuma.

POZZUOLI

The unlovely and scruffy port town of Pozzuoli was originally founded by political exiles from the Aegean island of Samos. Initially under Cuman control, it came into its own under the Romans when in 194 BC colonised it and renamed it Puteoli (Little Wells). An important port, it was here that St Paul is said to have landed in AD 61 and also where San Gennaro was beheaded. Its downfall was brought on by *bradeyism* (the slow upward and downward movement of the earth's crust), which left much of the harbour underwater, and the fall of the Roman Empire.

Now a dreary suburb northwest of Naples, Pozzuoli is where Italian film goddess Sophia Loren spent her childhood.

The **tourist office** (above) is beside the Porta Napoli gate, a five-minute walk downhill from the metro station.

ANFITEATRO FLAVIO

☎ 081 526 60 07; Via Terracciano 75; admission €4; ☺ 9am- 1hr before sunset Wed-Mon; Cumana train, metro to Pozzuoli

The third-largest amphitheatre in Italy, the Anfiteatro Flavio could hold over 20,000 spectators and was occasionally flooded for mock naval battles. Wanted by Nero and completed by Vespasian (AD 69–79), it's not in great nick now. The most interesting and best-preserved remains are under the main arena. Here you can wander among the fallen columns and get some idea of the complex mechanics involved in hoisting the caged wild beasts up to their waiting victims. In AD 305 seven Christian martyrs were thrown to the animals by the emperor Diocletian. They survived only to be beheaded later. One of the seven was San Gennaro, the patron saint of Naples.

RIONE TERRA

☎ 848 800 288; Largo Sedile di Porto; admission €3; ☺ 9am-6pm Sat & Sun, guided tours 11am, noon, 4pm & 5pm; Cumana train, metro to Pozzuoli

At the western end of the seafront, the Rione Terra is the oldest part of the Roman city of Puteolis. Within its 2 sq km stood the acropolis and a temple to Augustus. Inhabited up until 1970 when *bradeyism* forced the authorities to evacuate the quarter, it has recently been partially reopened.

Archaeological excavations have revealed considerable sections of the Roman street network and adjoining buildings. You can now walk down the *decumanus maximus* flanked by what are thought to be taverns. Elsewhere you'll find millers' shops complete with intact grindstones and an area that archaeologists think was either a brothel or a small *pensione* (small hotel).

To enter the site you need to book a visit.

SOLFATARA CRATER

☎ 081 526 23 41; Via Solfatara 161; admission €5; ☺ 8.30am-7pm; Circumflegrea train, metro to Pozzuoli

About 2km uphill from the metro station you come to the Solfatara crater. You can catch any city bus heading uphill. A weird, white, hissing volcanic crater, this place is ugly and unnerving. Known to the Romans as the Foro Vulcani (home of the god of fire), its acrid steam, sulphurous waters and mineral-rich mud were famed as a health cure from classical times until the 20th century. At the far end of the crater you can see the **Stufe**, a brick construction in which two ancient grottos were excavated at the end of the 19th century to create two *sudatoria* (sweat rooms). Charmingly christened Purgatory and Hell, the two rooms reach temperatures of up to 90°C.

With the whiff of brimstone in your nostrils, pass beside the pool of glooping mud as steam jets squirt and burp from the ground. The entire crater is a layer of rock supported by the steam pressure beneath.

TEMPIO DI SERAPIDE
Via Serapide; Cumana train, metro to Pozzuoli

Just east of the port, you'll find the *Tempio di Serapide* (Temple of Serapis) in a sunken area in the middle of a piazza. The temple takes its name from a statue of the Egyptian god Serapis, which was found among its ruins in 1750. In fact it is not a temple at all but the *macellum* (town market) with what archaeologists reckon are skilfully designed toilets at either side of the eastern apse. It has been badly damaged over the centuries by *bradeyism*, which raises and lowers the ground level over long periods. The church of **Santa Maria delle Grazie**, some 400m away, is sinking at a rate of about 2cm a year because of this.

BAIA

About 7km west of Pozzuoli, Baia takes its name from Baios, a shipmate of Ulysses who died and was buried here. An upmarket Roman holiday resort, it acquired something of a reputation as a sordid centre of sex and sin. Today much of the ancient town is underwater (*bradeyism* again) and modern development has left what is effectively a built-up, ugly and uninspiring coastal road. It does, however, boast a dramatic castle that is home to the area's best archaeological museum.

Its extensive Roman remains are visible in the Parco Archeologico di Baia above the town or from a glass-bottomed boat some 100m off the shore. At weekends between April and September the **Associazione Aliseo** (☎ 081 526 57 80; tours €7.75) runs boat tours to the underwater sites.

MUSEO ARCHEOLOGICO DEI CAMPI FLEGREI
☎ 081 523 37 97; Via Castello; admission €4;
☻ 9am-1 hr before sunset Tue-Sun; Ferrovia Cumana to Lucrino, Sepsa bus to Baia

Year-round you can see the elaborate *Nymphaeum*, dredged up and reassembled in the small Museo Archeologico dei Campi Flegrei. The museum also displays various Roman finds from the **Rione Terra** (p98) in Pozzuoli.

The vast castle that houses the museum was constructed in the late 15th century by

the house of Aragon as a defence against possible French invasion. Later enlarged by the Spanish viceroy of Naples Don Pedro de Toledo, it served as a military orphanage for most of the 20th century.

PARCO ARCHEOLOGICO DI BAIA
☎ 081 868 75 92; Via Fusaro 35; admission €4;
☻ 9am-1 hr before sunset Tue-Sun; Ferrovia Cumana to Lucrino, Sepsa bus to Baia

This archaeological park preserves the remains of what scholars now think was an imperial Roman palace and not, as previously thought, a temple. Within the 1st-century BC palace complex are a number of impressive thermal baths, including the misnamed Tempio di Mercurio (Temple of Mercury). Sunlight enters this ancient swimming pool through a large dome.

CUMA

The oldest of the three centres is Cuma, or Cumae as it was originally known. The earliest Greek colony on the Italian mainland, it was founded in the 8th century BC by Greek colonists from the island of Euboea. Best known as the home of the oracle Sybil, Cuma is a place that exerted a powerful sway on the ancient imagination. Homer, for example, believed Lago di Averno (Lake Avernus) to be the entrance to Hades, while Virgil wrote of the Sybil in the sixth book of *The Aeneid*.

ACROPOLI DI CUMA
☎ 081 854 30 60; Via Montecuma; €4; ☻ 9am-2 hrs before sunset; bus 12 from Pozzuoli

The centre of the ancient settlement of Cuma was the *acropoli* (acropolis). Situated at the base of the acropolis, the **Tempio di Apollo** (Temple of Apollo) was built on the site where Daedalus is said to have flown into Italy. According

Transport

For Pozzuoli Bus 152; Metro Line 2; Ferrovia Cumana from Montesanto

For Baia Ferrovia Cumana to Lucrino and any Sepsa bus to Biaia

For Cuma Bus 12 from Pozzuoli

Archeobus (☎ 800 00 16 16) A new bus service connected to the Campania artecard promotion (p212). Departures are on the hour between 9am and 7pm from the Tempio di Serapide in Pozzuoli for Baia, Baccoli and Cuma.

Quarters – Campi Flegrei

to Greek mythology, Daedalus and his son Icarus took to the skies to escape King Minos in Crete. En route Icarus flew too close to the sun and plunged to his death as his wax-and-feather wings melted in the heat.

At the top of the acropolis stands the **Tempio di Giove** (Temple of Jupiter). Dating to the 5th century BC it was later converted into a Christian basilica, of which the remains are still visible.

However, it's the **Antro della Sibilla Cumana** (Cave of the Cumaean Sybil) that is the big attraction here. A 130m-long trapezoidal tunnel carved out of the tufa rock leads to the vaulted chamber where the Sybil was said to pass on messages from the god Apollo. Virgil, probably inspired by a visit to the cave himself, writes of Aeneas descending into Hades (from nearby Lago di Averno) after a visit to the Sybil. Less romantic are the recent studies that maintain the tunnel was originally built as part of Cuma's defence system.

ELSEWHERE

In the northwestern suburbs of the city are two of Naples' best-known modern attractions – the Edenlandia amusement park and the **Stadio San Paolo** (p132) football stadium. In the Fuorigrotta area you will also find the huge exhibition space, the **Mostra d'Oltremare** (off Map pp242–3; ☎ 081 725 80 00; Piazzale Tecchio 52; bus 152) built by Mussolini between 1937 and 1940 to celebrate the success of his colonial wars.

On the other side of town, hidden away in the sprawling suburb of Portici is Europe's largest railway museum.

For information on Vesuvius, Pompeii and the Amalfi Coast, see the Bay of Naples & the Amalfi Coast chapter on p163.

CITTÀ DELLA SCIENZA Off Map pp242-3
Science City; ☎ 081 372 37 28; www.cittadella scienza.it in Italian; Via Coroglio 104; adult/child €7/6; ❧ 9am-5pm Tue-Sat, 10am-7pm Sun, 5pm-midnight Fri, Sat & Sun 21 Jun–1 Sep; metro Bagnoli, bus C9/10
Life has returned to the abandoned Bagnoli steelworks in the form of the Città della Scienza. A huge science museum, its high-tech collection of videos, games and computers leads visitors on an interactive exploration of the world around us. Among the themes investigated are natural phenomena, the science behind modern communication and, in the planetarium (€1.50), the night sky.

EDENLANDIA Off Map pp242-3
☎ 081 239 40 90; www.edenlandia.it in Italian; Viale Kennedy 76; adult/child under 1.1m €2/free; ❧ varies, call ahead; Ferrovia Cumana to Edenlandia
In the Fuorigrotta area near the football stadium is Edenlandia, Naples' historic amusement park. It boasts more than 200 attractions, ranging from the traditional Big Dipper and dodgems to the high-tech 3D cinema and flight simulator. The €2 admission covers the cinema, variety show and children's theatre.

MUSEO NAZIONALE FERROVIARIO PIETRARSA Off Map pp242-3
☎ 081 47 20 03; Via Pietrarsa, Portici; admission free; ❧ 9am-1pm Mon-Sat; FS train to Pietrarsa–San Giorgio a Cremano
Southeast out of Naples in the unlovely suburb of Portici is the Museo Nazionale Ferroviario Pietrarsa, Europe's largest railway museum. Housed in a royal factory built by the Bourbon King Ferdinand II in 1840, it covers 36,000 sq metres and tells the fascinating story of the construction of Italy's railway network. The first stretch of Italian rail line was completed between Naples and Portici in 1839.

Walking Tours

Walking Tours

If you know one thing about Naples, it's probably that you don't want to drive here. Ever. Italians will warn you not to take a car into Naples; Neapolitans will tell you (with just the hint of a swagger) that you only need to get used to the road conditions. But unless you're staying for about 18 years you don't have time to get used to anything. The solution is simple – walk.

Even walking is not without its hazards. Scooters shoot past, brushing you as they go, parked cars block the pavements, and no car will ever stop at a pedestrian crossing unless physically forced to do so. The best advice is to cross the road with a local (ideally a nun) between you and the oncoming traffic.

Naples is a big city but it can easily be divided up into manageable areas and explored on foot. The itineraries we describe here will take you through the heart of the city and give you a good overview.

SPACCANAPOLI & THE CENTRO STORICO

This tour takes you through the *centro storico* (historic centre), concentrating on its two main streets, Via San Biagio dei Librai and Via dei Tribunali.

Starting from **Piazza Garibaldi** (p81), head a short way down Corso Umberto I before turning right into Via Ranieri and then left into Via dell'Annunziata. A little way down on your left you'll see the **Basilica Santissima Annunziata Maggiore 1** (p81), famous for its orphanage. It's a sad but moving experience to see the *ruota*, the wooden wheel where babies were once abandoned. Continue down the street and turn right down Via Forcella. After crossing Via Pietro Colletta, follow the street as it veers left and merges into Via Vicaria Vecchia. Where it meets the busy cross street, Via Duomo, stands the **Basilica di San Giorgio Maggiore 2** (p60) on your left and, two blocks northwest up Via Duomo, the **Duomo 3** (p60). Thousands gather at the Duomo in May, September and December to witness San Gennaro's dried blood miraculously liquefy. Over the road from the cathedral is the entrance to the **Chiesa dei Girolamini 4** (p60).

Double back down Via Duomo until you meet Via dei Tribunali. Known to the Romans as the *decumanus maior*, this street runs parallel to the *decumanus inferior*, aka Spaccanapoli, aka Via San Biagio dei Librai. Before heading right into the heart of the *centro storico*, quickly nip left to admire Caravaggio's masterpiece *Le sette opere di Misericordia* (The Seven Acts of Mercy) in the **Pio Monte della Misericordia 5** (p63). Before you retrace your steps to Via Duomo, have a quick look at the baroque **Guglia di San Gennaro 6** (p62) in the small square opposite the church.

After you've crossed Via Duomo make for Piazza San Gaetano, about 150m down on the right. The tiny square where the Roman forum once stood is now dominated by the imposing **Chiesa di San Paolo Maggiore 7** (p61). Tucked away to the side is **Napoli Sotterranea 8** (p53). It is here that you enter Naples' extensive underworld. Some 30m to 40m under the surface, the ancient network of tunnels was originally cut out by the Greeks to extract the tufa rock, but the tunnels were used in WWII as air-raid shelters. Back on the surface, opposite the piazza, is the **Chiesa di San Lorenzo Maggiore 9** (p61). A stark but beautiful Gothic church, it stands atop yet more Roman *scavi* (excavations) and is one of the highlights of the *centro storico*.

It's at this point that you leave Via dei Tribunali and head down **Via San Gregorio Armeno 10** (p59). In December people come from all over Italy to visit the shops in this street. They specialise in the *presepi* (nativity scenes) that no traditional Italian house is without at Christmas. Along this street you'll also find the **Chiesa di San Gregorio Armeno 11** (p59), famous for its extravagant baroque décor and weekly miracle – the blood of Santa Patrizia is said to liquefy here every Tuesday.

Walk Facts

Start Piazza Garibaldi
End Piazza Bellini
Distance 3km
Duration Four hours
Transport Metro Piazza Garibaldi

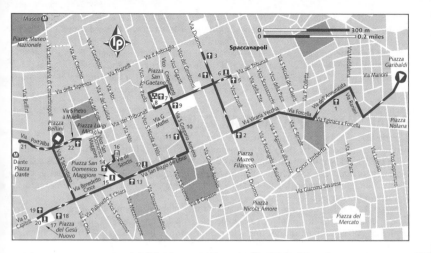

At the end of the road you hit Via San Biagio dei Librai. Turn right and after about 250m you'll pass the **Statua del Nilo 12** (p59) on your right. Less imposing is the altar to footballer Maradona on the wall opposite the statue. Further down on the left, the **Chiesa di Sant'Angelo a Nilo 13** (p57) is entered from the small sidestreet Vico Donnaromita.

The rear of the imposing **Chiesa di San Domenico Maggiore 14** (p57) abuts onto the café-fringed, pedestrianised piazza of the same name. At the heart of the square is the **Guglia di San Domenico 15** (p58), topped by a statue of the good saint himself. The not-to-be-missed **Cappella Sansevero 16** (p56) is just off this square in a lane east of the church. A jewel of a chapel, it's home to the stunning *Cristo Velato* (Veiled Christ), as beautiful a sculpture as any in Naples.

Back on Via San Biagio dei Librai, the road becomes Via Benedetto Croce and continues west to **Piazza del Gesù Nuovo 17** (p58), the scene of much nightly revelry. The lively piazza is flanked by the **Basilica di Santa Chiara 18** (p55) and the **Chiesa del Gesù Nuovo 19** (p56), while in the centre the **Guglia dell'Immacolata 20** (p57) is a study in baroque excess. The majolica-tiled cloisters of Santa Chiara provide one of the few peaceful spots in the *centro storico*, while the adjoining church stands as testament to the skill of Naples' restoration experts after it was almost completely destroyed by WWII bombs.

Students hanging out in Piazza San Domenico Maggiore (p58)

Backtrack from the square to the first intersection and turn left along Via S Sebastiano. At the next intersection on your left a short street leads down to book-lined **Port'Alba 21** (p64), a city gate built in 1625, then to Piazza Dante.

Back on route and ahead of you is **Piazza Bellini** (p63) and, to the right, Piazza Luigi Miraglia, flanked by Naples' conservatory and the **Chiesa San Pietro a Maiella 22** (p62). A great place to rest your weary feet is in one of Piazza Bellini's several cafés. While you're at it you could inspect the remains of the ancient Greek city walls under the square.

ROYAL SITES & SPECTACULAR VIEWS

The royal Santa Lucia district features some of the city's most recognisable landmarks, while Vomero boasts the city's highest point and best views. This tour covers both areas – from the Castel Nuovo on the seafront to the Certosa di San Martino 250m up. But don't worry, you don't have to climb all the way to the top (although there is a long, steep stairway that leads up to the Certosa) – the funicular will haul you up to Vomero in about two minutes.

Piazza del Municipio (p73) is a big, brash place that's Naples in a nutshell. Traffic thunders past, spewing out clouds of black fumes; people crowd the pavements simultaneously eating ice cream, smoking and shouting into mobile phones; tourists traipse past on their way

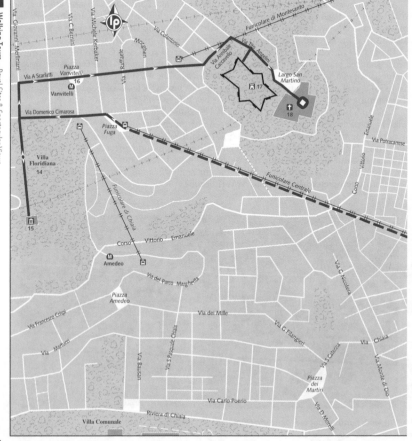

to the ferry port. Overlooking all of this is **Castel Nuovo 1** (p69). Known to Neapolitans as the Maschio Angioino, this sturdy castle dates to the 13th century and now houses a museum. From the castle, cross over the square and turn left towards Via Medina where you'll find the **Fontana di Nettuno 2** (p71), one of Naples' finest baroque fountains. At the head of the piazza stands the **Chiesa San Giacomo degli Spagnoli 3** (p70), where Naples' 16th-century Spanish viceroy Don Pedro di Toledo is buried. Next door the mayor has her office in **Palazzo San Giacomo 4** (p72).

Following Via G Verdi south you emerge onto Via S Carlo and the **Teatro San Carlo 5** (p73). Italy's largest opera house, it predates Milan's La Scala by 41 years. Opposite the theatre is one of four entrances to the **Galleria Umberto I 6** (p71), the 19th-century shopping centre that, like Teatro San Carlo, compares to a similar building in Milan, the Galleria Vittorio Emanuele II. Continuing down Via S Carlo brings you to the massive **Palazzo Reale 7** (p72), home to the national library and some richly furnished royal apartments. The entrance to the royal palace is on **Piazza Trieste e Trento 8** (p73), a magnet for thirsty tourists keen to try the coffee at **Caffè Gambrinus 9** (p113). From the pavement in front of the café, stairs lead down to an unexpected and original gallery, **Napoli nella Raccolta de Mura 10** (p72), dedicated to traditional Neapolitan music and theatre.

Walk Facts

Start Piazza del Municipio
End Certosa di San Martino
Distance 4km (excluding funicular)
Duration Four hours
Transport Bus R2 to Piazza del Municipio & Funicular Centrale Via Toledo to Fuga

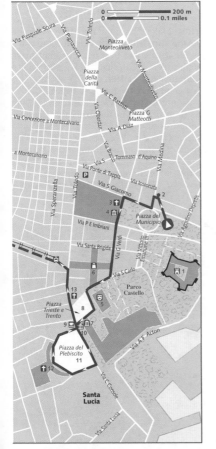

Fuelled with coffee, hop across to the huge **Piazza del Plebiscito 11** (p73) where you'll find Naples' own version of the Roman Pantheon, the **Chiesa di San Francesco di Paola 12** (p70). From here backtrack to Piazza Trieste e Trento, continue past the **Chiesa di San Ferdinando 13** (p70), and about 150m up Via Toledo you will see a funicular station on the left. Jump on any funicular and you'll be headed for Vomero.

When you get out at the top, walk down Via Domenico Cimarosa for **Villa Floridiana 14** (p76), one of the city's rare patches of green and a good spot for a picnic. At the bottom of the park is the **Museo Nazionale della Ceramica Duca di Martina 15** (p76). When you're done with ceramics, exit the park and take Via Giovanni Merliani as far as the first crossroad, Via A Scarlatti. Turn right and follow Vomero's main drag through **Piazza Vanvitelli 16** (p74) as far as it will go. Keep on going straight, up the stairs near the Morghen funicular station, and turn left into Via Colantonio. Turn left again into Via Annibale Caccavello and at the end of the street you'll come out on Via Tito Angelini. Here you'll find **Castel Sant'Elmo 17** (p74) and about 100m further down the road the **Certosa di San Martino 18** (p75). Dating to the 14th century, this stunning monastery houses a fabulous museum and art gallery. And if all that's not enough, just look at the views – they're the best in town.

Walking Tours – Royal Sites & Spectacular Views

A SEAFRONT STROLL

Starting at the Borgo Marinaro and the wonderfully named Castel dell'Ovo (Castle of the Egg), this route leads up to Piazza del Plebiscito, and round Via Chiaia to Piazza dei Martiri. From here you head seawards to pick up Villa Comunale and the *lungomare* (seafront) as it curves around the bay to the Mergellina district. The seafront is a favourite Neapolitan walk that is most enjoyable in the cool of a summer evening.

Start on the island of volcanic rock known to the ancient Greeks as Megaris and to modern Neapolitans as the **Borgo Marinaro** (p68). Naples' oldest castle, **Castel dell'Ovo 1** (p68) has stood here since the 12th century. Returning to the mainland you'll see a row of luxurious hotels across the busy seafront road Via Partenope. Before you cross the road, however, take a second to admire the dramatic **Fontana dell'Immacolatella 2** (p71) a few metres down on your right.

Fontana dell'Immacolatella (p71)

From the fountain cross Via Partenope, turn left and take the second right into Via Santa Lucia. Make your way up this attractive street to the top, turn left, and after about 200m you'll find yourself at **Piazza del Plebiscito 3** (p73). Traverse the square and bear left into Via Chiaia. Cobbled and smart, this historic street cuts through to Via S Caterina and **Piazza dei Martiri 4** (p94), the centre of the upmarket Chiaia district, dominated by a 19th-century obelisk. This is a good place to stop for a coffee.

Continue down Via Calabritto, pausing to shop or look in the expensive designer shops, until you reach Piazza Vittoria and the entrance to **Villa Comunale 5** (p94). This spark of palms, statues and swings is home to Europe's oldest aquarium, the **Stazione Zoologica 6** (p94). For more greenery and some priceless porcelain make for the **Museo Pignatelli 7** (p93), on the inland side of the park.

Walk Facts

Start Borgo Marinaro
End Parco Vergiliano
Distance 5km
Duration Four hours
Transport Bus C25 to Via Partenope

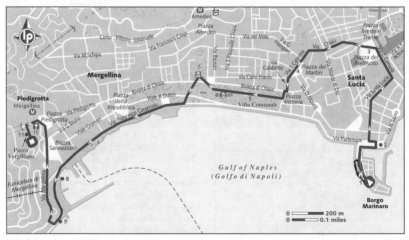

To get back to the *lungomare* (seafront), retrace your steps over the Riviera di Chiaia and Villa Comunale to Via Francesco Caracciolo, the extension of Via Partenope. From here it's a pleasant and relaxing walk around the bay to Mergellina. This stretch of the route has no sites per se but if you look out to sea you'll spot the distinctive shape of Capri in the distance. When you get to Mergellina – you'll know you're there once you pass the **Porticciolo 8** (p97) – make a beeline for the bars and gelaterie (ice-cream parlours) known as the **Chalets 9** (p97). Here you can rest up and either call it a day or, if you've energy left, push on for a short final leg.

If you can tear yourself away from beer and ice cream cross over the main road to pick up Via Mergellina which heads north, becoming Salita Piedigrotta after Piazza Sannazzaro. At the top of the short incline you'll see the **Chiesa Santa Maria di Piedigrotta 10** (p96) on your left and across the road Mergellina train and metro station. At the church, go left, hold your breath as you walk under the railway bridge, and you'll come to the **Parco Vergiliano 11** (p97) on your left. A small but well-tended park, this is where Virgil is said to be buried.

FROM CATACOMBS TO CAPODIMONTE

This tour takes in two museums, three catacombs, a few churches and a park. From the Museo Archeologico Nazionale on Piazza Museo Nazionale, the route explores the La Sanità district and continues up to the Palazzo Reale di Capodimonte before finishing up at the Catacomba di San Gennaro.

You don't need to be an archaeologist to appreciate the collection at **Museo Archeologico Nazionale 1** (p66). Highlights here include the *Toro Farnese* (Farnese Bull) sculpture and the incredible mosaics, many of which once adorned noble houses in Pompeii.

From Piazza Museo Nazionale follow the traffic along Via Foria, passing Piazza Cavour (the grand name for a strip of bald grass) until shortly after the Cavour metro station. Take a left at Via Vergini and enter the Sanità district.

Known as La Sanità (literally 'healthy'), this area of crumbling buildings and impoverished streets was for centuries where the city buried its dead. The network of catacombs that runs underground is the main reason to come here.

At the end of Via Vergini the road forks. Follow the left-hand street, Via Arena della Sanità, which becomes Via della Sanità as it approaches Piazza della Sanità. On the square, **Chiesa Santa Maria della Sanità 2** (p78) is the entrance to the dark and dank **Catacomba di San Gaudioso**. Here you'll find mosaics and frescoes from the 5th century and learn the secrets of medieval inhumation.

Back in the open air and with your back to the church, turn left down Via San Severo a Capodimonte towards the Chiesa di San Severo. Under the 16th-century church lies Naples' first bishop, buried in the **Catacomba di San Severo 3** (p77) in AD 410.

The road, or rather alleyway, now turns north. The Salita Capodimonte rises to the left of Piazzetta San Severo. At the top of the steps, head left and follow the street as it

Walk Facts

Start Piazza Museo Nazionale
End Catacomba di San Gennaro
Distance 3km
Duration Four hours
Transport Metro Cavour

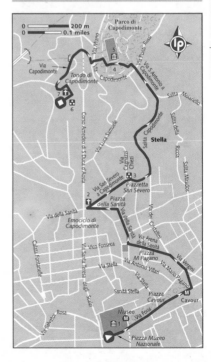

carves its winding way up to Via Capodimonte and, over the road, to the **Parco di Capodimonte 4** (p80). Enter through the gate and follow the path round to the **Palazzo Reale di Capodimonte 5** (p79). This majestic Bourbon palace houses one of Italy's most important art collections. Paintings by artists ranging from Caravaggio to Warhol line some 160 rooms spread over three floors.

To get to the last port of call, the **Catacomba di San Gennaro 6** (p77), you can either walk down Via Capodimonte, or jump on a bus (any going downhill from outside the park gate) for the quick trip down to the catacombs. Get off the bus by the impossible-to-miss **Chiesa di Madre di Buon Consiglio 7** (p77) on the right-hand side. The catacombs are the last resting place of San Gennaro and are known for their Paleo-Christian frescoes and mosaics.

CLIMB THE ANCIENT HILL

Rising behind Piazza del Plebiscito, Monte Echia and the Pizzofalcone district is the oldest inhabited part of Naples. The Greeks founded the city of Parthenope here in the 7th century BC, predating Neapolis (New Town) by some 300 years. Although the short tour outlined here does not include a whole host of must-see sites, it's an atmospheric (and relatively peaceful) walk that offers some fine views. Be warned though that it does involve a fairly steep climb and a hairpin descent.

Walk Facts

Start Piazza Carolina
End Via Santa Lucia
Distance 1.5km
Duration Two hours
Transport Bus CS to Piazza Trieste e Trento

Behind the columns on the northern side of Piazza del Plebiscito, **Piazza Carolina 1** is the starting point for the climb up to Monte Echia. Rising up the hill are two narrow streets – Vico Santo Spirito di Palazzo and Via Gennaro Sorra. Take one of these streets, it doesn't matter which, and head up to **Piazza Santa Maria degli Angeli 2**. A small, undistinguished square,

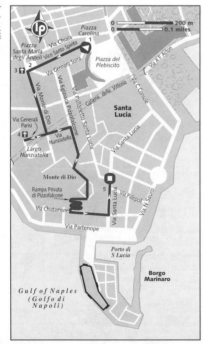

it takes its name from the yellow-fronted **Chiesa Santa Maria degli Angeli 3** (p73). A baroque church, its most impressive feature is its huge dome.

From the square continue upwards along Via Monte di Dio until, on your right, you come to Via Generali Parisi. At the end of this short street is **La Nunziatella 4** (p74), one of Italy's most prestigious military schools.

Backtracking to Via Monte di Dio, continue straight down Via Nunziatella until the first crossing. Turn right up Via Egiziaca Pizzofalcone and head uphill. The street is dark and atmospheric and the climb comfortable. At the top, continue straight up the Salita Echia and carry on until you come to the shabby gardens at the top. From here the views are your reward.

To return to sea level you can either go back the way you've come or follow the path that leads right off the garden terrace. Technically a private road, the Rampa Privata di Pizzofalcone zigzags its steep way down the side of the rock face until it flattens out into Via Chiatamone. As you descend notice the houses carved into the rock. Once you get to the bottom turn left and after a few metres you'll find yourself on **Via Santa Lucia 5** (p68), an ideal place to plonk yourself at a pavement table and order a pizza.

Eating

Eating

A bad eating experience in Naples is rare. Even the snack bar at Stazione Centrale serves very acceptable *panini* (bread rolls), and lemon *granita* (crushed-ice drinks) with fresh mint. Great pride is taken in the cuisine, and many of the *ristorante* (restaurants) have been in the same family for generations. Neapolitans don't believe in drizzle and fusion; the best cuisine here is deliciously simple and traditional, and based on fresh seasonal ingredients. Freezer containers take up very little space at supermarkets and you will rarely hear that heart-plummeting ping of a microwave when eating out.

Although the choice of eateries is vast, the best culinary initiation to the city is pizza, which is said to have been invented in Naples and which bears little resemblance to the piled-high cardboard export. Always go for the *Vera Pizza* sign; this is not a prolific local chain, but a designation awarded to those places that make their pizzas according to traditional methods. The sign shows the distinctive Pulcinella (Punch-like) figure, so famed in Neapolitan folklore.

Aside from the ubiquitous pizzeria, you will see trattoria or *osteria* signs. These are both inexpensive, family-owned restaurants, often with a chalked-up menu outside the door. Don't be put off by simple décor. Neapolitans have their priorities right and believe in spending more money on ingredients and cooking than on decorating the dining room.

Many of the best traditional restaurants are in the *centro storico* (historic centre). For somewhere fancier, push the boat out and head for the old fisherman's quarter of Santa Lucia where some of the finest seafood establishments are located on the waterfront.

Neapolitans love to eat. They like a drink as well, but you won't find the bar culture that exists, for example, in Spain. Cafés are big-time, however, and an integral part of the eating, drinking and social scene. Don't leave town before tasting a *sfogliatella* (flaky pastry filled with ricotta cheese) or having a *gelati* (ice cream); two more culinary delights that the Neapolitans are very good at indeed.

For more information about specific food and drinks, see p30.

Opening Hours

Restaurants usually open for lunch from noon to 3pm and for dinner from 7pm to around 11pm. Many restaurants in the commercial *centro storico* close on Sunday, while others will close on Monday. Roughly half of Naples' restaurants close in August.

Where opening times are listed in reviews, this indicates that they vary from the usual opening times. Where no opening hours appear, assume that the standard hours given above apply.

How Much?

In general, a three-course meal with wine (described in the reviews as a 'full meal') will cost around €14 per person in a pizzeria, €18 in a simple trattoria, up to €40 at a mid-range restaurant and around €60 or more at the city's most exclusive restaurants.

Don't forget to add the additional *coperto* (bread and cover charge) to your restaurant bill; this can range from €1.50 to €3 per person.

If you are euro-economising, go for pizza or a simple pasta dish and make sure you check the drink prices; a beer can easily cost €3 to €4 at fancier restaurants. Also, be wary when ordering fish which has to be weighed; ask for a quote *before* it hits the flame. In this chapter, cheap eats are defined as those where main courses cost €6 or less.

The Best...
- **Sfogliatella** La Sfogliatella (p119)
- **Coffee** Caffè Mexico (p113)
- **Pizza** Da Michele (p118)
- **Pasta** Donna Teresa (p117)
- **Ice Cream** Scimmia (p115)

Booking Tables

Booking a table is generally not possible in a simple trattoria or pizzeria, although it is advisable at mid- to top-range restaurants, especially over the weekend.

Tipping

Always check your bill carefully as it may include a service charge of 10% to 15%, in which case you shouldn't feel obliged to leave an additional amount. Otherwise a tip of between 5% and 10% is appreciated, although Neapolitans often don't bother to leave anything at all.

CENTRO STORICO

This honeycomb of narrow streets and tight piazzas is, unsurprisingly, home to some of the city's most traditional trattorie and pizzerie. A good place to start your culinary exploration is on the corner of Via dei Tribunali and Via San Paolo, with its daily fruit-and-vegetable stalls. Wander down Tribunali in either direction and you will pass neighbourhood bakeries, delicatessens, snack bars and eateries of every description. In short, the *centro storico* is all about *food*.

ANTICA TRATTORÍA DA CARMINE
Map pp244-6   *Trattoria*
☎ 081 29 43 83; Via dei Tribunali 330; full meals around €14; ☽ lunch only; metro Piazza Dante
All the right elements are here: a homely atmosphere, no-nonsense food and attentive old-fashioned service. The menu is limited – often a good sign – and includes a hearty and delicious *penne alla sorrentina* (penne, mozzarella and tomatoes). The walls are papered with black-and-white photos of Naples and its characters (there are plenty). The wine list includes well-priced carafes of house wine.

BELLINI Map pp244-6   *Ristorante*
☎ 081 45 97 74; Via Santa Maria di Costantinopoli 79-80; full meals around €28; ☽ lunch daily, dinner 7.30pm-1am Mon-Sat; metro Piazza Dante
The fish trolley by the entrance will alert you to the house speciality, seafood. Pasta portions are served on a grand scale and the fish is as fresh as the morning catch. Try the vermicelli with

clams and mussels (€9). The candlelit terrace fringed with flowers attracts romantics and a voguish clientele. Bellini's waiters are from the elderly cummerbund school of service, which contributes to the value-for-money vibe.

CAMPAGNOLI Map pp244-6   *Trattoria*
☎ 081 45 90 34; Via dei Tribunali 47; full meals from €12; ☽ lunch only; metro Piazza Dante
Fronted by an *enoteca* (wine bar) with shelves of dusty bottles. In the back is the humble dining room where the elderly owner and his chums play cards in between customers. Come here with a laid-back attitude, as the service and setting are perhaps a tad too kitchen-sink informal. But who cares as long as the food is taken seriously, and there are such winners as *spaghetti alla maccheronata* (fresh tomatoes and lashings of basil, topped with a creamy layer of *pecorino* cheese). Expect long queues at weekends.

IL CAFFÈ ARABO Map pp244-6   *Café*
☎ 081 442 06 07; Piazza Bellini; snacks from €3; ☽ daily; metro Piazza Dante
Shares the same atmosphere as the trendier surrounding bars and cafés, but a glass of wine is half the price and the Middle Eastern nibbles are good value, too. The menu has snacks such as falafel, hummus, *fuul* (a bean-based dip) and kebabs. Heartier fare includes a vegetarian couscous and a brave attempt at curry (more like a vegetable stew). Service can be slow.

INTRA MOENIA Map pp244-6   *Café*
☎ 081 29 07 20; Piazza Bellini 70; snacks from €8; ☽ daily; bus CD to Via Santa Maria di Costantinopoli
Arty, literary, left-leaning with a mixed gay and hetero clientele, Intra Moenia is a great place to pass an hour or two pondering one of Naples' more beautiful piazzas. The food is lightweight and healthy, including sandwiches and a menu page of salad choices (€8). There is reasonable Internet access available, plus a small bookshop. House wine costs €4 a glass.

Top Five Centro Storico

- Bellini (above)
- Lombardi a Santa Chiara (p112)
- Sorbillo (p112)
- Campagnoli (above)
- Vesi (p112)

Eating – Centro Storico

LA CANTINA DELLA SAPIENZA

Map pp244-6   *Trattoria*

☎ 081 45 90 78; Via della Sapienza 40; full meals from €14; metro Cavour

For those preferring pared-down simplicity to culinary acrobatics, the dishes here change according to whatever is in season. This place has a real neighbourhood feel, right down to the strung-up washing outside. Enjoy Neapolitan staples such as *parmigiana di melanzane* (baked aubergine with layers of tomato and parmesan) and the classic *pizza bianco* topped with nothing more than a drizzle of extra virgin olive oil and crunchy sea salt. The house wine is palatable, the desserts reliably good.

LA LOCANDA DEL GRIFO

Map pp244-6   *Ristorante*

☎ 081 442 08 15; Via F del Giudice 14; full meals around €22; metro Piazza Dante

Elegant outdoor terrace under an enormous cream-coloured awning. Dishes are classic, and exquisitely prepared and presented. Start with a plate of *mozzarella e prosciutto* (mozzarella and Parma ham) and end up with one of the dessert thrills, like the perfectly moist *torta caprese*, a cake made with chocolate and hazelnuts. Afterwards, waddle round the corner to one of the classy cafés on Piazza Bellini for a limoncello nightcap.

LOMBARDI A SANTA CHIARA

Map pp244-6   *Ristorante*

☎ 081 552 07 80; Via Benedetto Croce 59; full meals around €25; ⏰ Tue-Sun; metro Piazza Dante

A classy restaurant on this busy shopping street near Basilica di Santa Chiara. Lombardi's air of faded grandeur provides a comfortable setting for classic pizza and Neapolitan dishes with an emphasis on pasta and seafood, often happily combined. Vegetarians have plenty of choice here, especially among the antipasti where courgettes, artichokes and fresh buffalo mozzarella are artfully combined, and there are several salad choices. Justifiably popular, so book ahead or kick-start your appetite with an aperitif at the pretty tiled bar while you wait for a table.

PORT'ALBA

Map pp244-6   *Pizzeria*

☎ 081 45 97 13; Via Port'Alba 18; pizzas from €5; ⏰ Thu-Tue; metro Piazza Dante

An institution in these parts, this perpetually packed-out restaurant (across from Bellini's) has outside seating on one of the city's headiest historical streets. The multilingual menu is vast and, while pizzas are the star turn, the pasta

dishes are pretty good as well. The only letdown here is the staff, who are overkeen for tourist tips, making it uncomfortable to linger.

SORBILLO Map pp244-6   *Pizzeria*

☎ 081 44 66 43; Via dei Tribunali 32; pizzas from €5; metro Piazza Dante

Another popular pizza parlour that vies for the city's No 1 spot. There are now three generations of the Sorbillo family, all in the pizza business in Italy or the US. Again, more has been invested in the *pizzaiola* (pizza maker) than interior finery, which is basic and rustic, with a corner TV permanently switched to the football channel. There's a massive choice ranging from a pizza margherita to the regal seafood special.

Cheap Eats

O SOLE E NAPULE Map pp244-6   *Pizzeria*

☎ 081 93 63 58; Via dei Tribunali 292; pizzas from €2.50; ⏰ daily; metro Piazza Dante

It's small, it's bright and it's shiny white with butcher shop–style tiles; it's so clean you could (almost) eat off the floor. There are 29 different pizzas with regular size starting at €2.50 and *gigante* (large) from €4. You can get *fritture* (deep-fried) bits and pieces here, too, and they're always crisp and fresh thanks to the constant turnover.

VESI Map pp244-6   *Pizzeria*

☎ 081 45 90 34; Via dei Tribunali 338; pizzas €4-7; ⏰ daily; metro Piazza Dante

Not much elbow room at this pizza favourite with its unmistakable smoky, salty smell and long, narrow room crammed with wooden tables. The pizzas are excellent and huge, ranging from the classic *marinara* (seafood) to the elaborate *rustica* (ricotta, mozzarella, parmesan, peppers, oregano and basil). Vesi does a brisk takeaway business, and a creamy tiramisu (€3). It attracts a zippy young crowd.

TOLEDO & QUARTIERI SPAGNOLI

The contrast between the fashionable shopping street of Toledo and the crumbling warren of the Spanish quarter is reflected in the food on offer. At the southern end of Toledo are some of the city's finest *fin de siécle* cafés and restaurants, while west of the shopping strip are the earthier and less expensive establishments, with quick-eat kiosks and family-run trattorie.

ANTICO TRATTORIA DON PEPPINO

Map pp244-6 *Trattoria*

☎ 081 551 28 54; Vico 1 Gravina 7-10; mains from €6; bus CD to Via Monteoliveto

A side-step away from Piazza Monteoliveto, this restaurant has a dining room decorated with a head-bonking array of rustic artefacts, including brass pots, dried corn and ropes of garlic and peppers. More than 20 specialities of the house are here including several risottos, linguine, penne and pasta choices. There are seafood and meat dishes as well; the *carne al ragù* (beef cooked slowly in a rich tomato sauce) is particularly good.

BRANDI

Map pp248-9 *Pizzeria*

☎ 081 41 69 28; Salita S Anna di Palazzo 1; pizzas from €6; bus CS to Piazza Trieste e Trento

Everything about Brandi promises a serious pizza slice above the ordinary, from the linen napkins and snooty bow-tied staff to the multi-lingual flyers that claim this was where the pizza margherita was invented in 1889, in honour of the Italian queen. That said, the pizzas are huge and excellent. Alternatively, hunker down à la carte with pasta, fish and meat choices of high quality (and price).

CAFFÈ GAMBRINUS

Map pp248-9 *Café*

☎ 081 41 75 82; Via Chiaia 1-2; ☼ daily; bus R2 to Piazza Trieste e Trento

A veritable institution, Naples' oldest and most stylish café is popular with artists, politicians and musicians past and present, including Oscar Wilde and Bill Clinton. The interior is suitably grand, with lots of shiny marble, antiques and paintings, plus the odd Grecian-style statue. The outside is well placed for poseur-watching and there are sweet and savoury snacks, plus cocktails and coffees. Don't expect much friendly chat from the waiters unless you're famous or rich.

CAFFÈ MEXICO

Map pp244-6 *Café*

☎ 081 549 93 30; Piazza Dante 86; metro Piazza Dante

After your meal, the freshly roasted coffee in this gem of a shop smells heavenly. Pick up a bag of beans roasted on the premises and treat yourself to a cup of what is arguably the

Caffè Gambrinus (above)

best coffee in the city. Brits suffering from their daily cuppa withdrawal can pick up a box of Twinings here, too.

CHINATOWN Map pp244-6 *Chinese*
☎ 081 552 08 88; Via G Sanfelice 39; mains from €5; bus CS to Via Toledo

The name is as unoriginal as the migraine-inducing interior, complete with its moving-water pictures. But the food is fine and makes a change if you're growing weary of the pizza-and-pasta combo. Few surprises for those used to the international genre of Chinese restaurant, although the vegetarian menu is longer than most. Mainstays include crispy duck with sesame, and sweet-and-sour pork.

CIRO A SANTA BRIGIDA
Map pp244-6 *Ristorante*
☎ 081 552 40 72; Via Santa Brigida 71-74; mains from €15; bus CS to Via Toledo

Fatten your credit card at one of Naples, classiest restaurants with sumptuous old-fashioned service. Don't expect newfangled concoctions. Go ahead and order *pasta e fagioli* (a delicious soupy dish based on fresh pasta and white beans) or any other pasta dish. It's what the place is famous for: typical Naples cuisine at its best accompanied by some of the area's top wines.

D.M L.U.I.S.E. Map pp244-6 *Ristorante*
☎ 081 41 53 67; Via Toledo 266-288; buffet dishes from €4; bus CS to Via Toledo

The palm-fringed terrace here is a prime spot for people-watching at the more elegant end of Via Toledo a few steps away from the funicular station, Centrale. Good for fussy families, with a lavish buffet of delectable-looking fare, including spinach pie, fried pizza, risotto, lasagne and more salad choices than you can shake a carrotstick at. The inside dining room is dingy; weather permitting, eat outside.

KUKAI Map pp248-9 *Sushi*
☎ 081 41 19 05; Via Carlo de Cesare 55-56; sushi from €4; ☽ 7.30pm-1am Tue-Sun; metro Piazza Dante

A real one-off in these parts. The owner is well travelled and authenticity is his thing; even the most savvy sushi fan won't be able to fault the presentation and taste, and the dining room has an appropriate light-wood Zen feel. California rolls, sushi mix, sashimi, temaki… it's all here and freshly prepared each day. There is also a brisk takeaway and delivery service.

LA SFOGLIATELLA MARY
Map pp244-6 *Kiosk*
☎ 081 40 22 18; Galleria Umberto 1, Via Toledo; ☽ Mon 8am-2.30pm, Tue-Sat 8am-8.30pm; bus CS to Via Toledo

Not to be confused with **La Sfogliatella** (p119) in the Mercato district, this is the best place for undecided tastebuds to try *sfogliatelle* as this place sell a mini size for just €0.50. Once initiated, this is the place to stock up with the steady, steaming-hot supply coming out of the oven behind the counter. La Sfogliatella Mary is located at the entrance to a swanky shopping mall on the corner of Via Toledo; expect a queue of hungry shoppers.

LEON D'ORO Map pp244-6 *Trattoria*
☎ 081 549 94 04; Piazza Dante 48; meals around €15; ☽ Tue-Sun; metro Piazza Dante

A typical, gritty Naples trattoria with an excellent position on this grand old square which separates the *centro storico* from Via Toledo's shopping strip. Photos of happy diners cover the walls and the simple food is good value, although the quality varies depending on the dish. The pizza here is not the best in town, but the pasta dishes are reliably good and include such classics as *gnocchi con mozzarella* and *spaghetti alla vongole* (with a clam sauce). This place is best during hot summer evenings when you can enjoy sitting outside on the square.

LO SPACCO Map pp244-6 *Trattoria*
☎ 081 551 02 03; Vico Corrierí 37; mains from €6; bus CS to Via Toledo

In a small street off Santa Brigida, this basic restaurant is hugely popular with locals in the know. The dining room is about as atmospheric as a dentist's waiting room; however, sit outside if you can and choose from the daily chalked-up menu which may include such delights as *penne alla genovesa* (penne with an onion and ham sauce) and a tasty roast meat *arrosto* (€6.20).

PINTAURO Map pp244-6 *Pasticceria*
☎ 081 41 73 39; Via Toledo 275; ☽ Mon-Sat Sep-Jul; funicular Centrale to Augusteo

An exceptionally good selection of Neapolitan sweet treats, including a deliciously light *babà* (rum-soaked sponge) and melt-in-the-mouth biscuits, which are often based on almonds. You can smell the *sfogliatelle*, served fresh from the oven throughout the day, as you approach. Expect to queue – it's worth it.

SCIMMIA Map pp244-6 *Gelateria*
☎ 081 552 02 72; Piazza Carità; ⏱ 7.30am-midnight; metro Montesanto

The oldest, best and biggest of this famous ice creamery. Made on the premises, you can't go wrong with the *stacciatella* (vanilla ice cream with chocolate chunks) or the creamy *zabaglione* (made with eggs and sweet Marsala wine).

Cheap Eats
FRIGGITORIA FIORENZANO
Map pp244-6 *Snacks*
☎ 081 551 27 88; Piazza Montesanto; snacks from €1; metro Montesanto

Unpretentious eatery famed for its Italian-style tempura, including crispy deep-fried aubergines, courgettes and artichokes (in season). Décor is sunny blue and white, and the locality is high on atmosphere, opposite an open-air fruit-and-vegetable market and surrounded by cafés and other eateries, including a pizzeria next door under the same ownership.

MA TU VULIVE 'A PIZZA
Map pp244-6 *Pizzeria*
☎ 081 551 44 90; Via S Maria la Nova 46; mains from €5; bus CS to Via Toledo

To appreciate this popular neighbourhood pizzeria/trattoria, build up an appetite beforehand – groaning plates of pizza or pasta will satisfy those with the heartiest. Other treats include *polpette* (meatballs served in a thick tomato sauce) and an excellent *pescatore* pizza with octopus, shrimps and clams. The crowd runs from chattering mammas to students and crusty old men, giving the place a nice buzz.

SANTA LUCIA

Santa Lucia is home of five-star hotel folk and the restaurants that feed them. The yachts moored are similarly splash-your-cash sized. Overall, the waterfront restaurants are justifiably priced, however, with seductive sea-and-city views, and outstanding food. There are less expensive options, too, and more good choices in the streets around Piazza Plebiscito, Naples' old fishing quarter.

AMOR E FANTASIA Map pp248-9 *Ristorante*
☎ 081 764 70 40; Via Raffaele de Cesare 15-17; mains from €10; bus C25 to Via Partenope

On a lively pedestrian street close to the sea, this restaurant may sound like an S&M club but the only fantasy you can expect here is

its signature dish, *scaloppina fantasy*, a kind of glorified English fry-up with sausage and smoked cheese (instead of chips) that is belly-filling and good. The outside seating has a summer Med feel with its red geraniums and palms, while the galleried upstairs is woody and intimate for when the sun goes down.

BERSAGLIERA Map pp248-9 *Ristorante*
☎ 081 764 60 16; Borgo Marinaro 10-11; meals around €40; ⏱ noon-3.30pm, 7.30pm-midnight Wed-Mon, closed 2 weeks in Jan; bus C25 to Via Partenope

On the port's edge, Bersagliera is a famous restaurant that attracts famous folk. The palatial dining room, with its magnificent carved ceiling, has a photo gallery of star diners including Ingrid Bergman and Sophia Loren. Dating from 1923 and now run by the family's third generation, it has a terrace with fantastic views of the harbour and castle. Whet your palate on the clam and mussel soup, followed by *taglierini* (fine ribbon pasta) with baby octopus, black olives and tomatoes, or risotto with gorgonzola.

CIRO Map pp248-9 *Ristorante*
☎ 081 764 60 06; Borgo Marinaro 29-30; meals around €45; ⏱ Thu-Tue; bus C25 to Via Partenope

Another top favourite here, with its ace location beneath the castle. The long, narrow terrace is generally packed with boat owners and tourists, so get here early. Ciro is a bastion of traditional food; its menu groans with hearty dishes, such as pasta with clams and mussels, and creamy risotto with seafood. The pizzas here have won local awards. Finish off your meal with one of the delicious calorie-loaded desserts; the kiwi tart is a speciality.

LA CANTINELLA Map pp248-9 *Ristorante*
☎ 081 764 86 84; Via Cuma 42; mains from €16; bus C25 to Via Partenope

Arguably Naples' most famous restaurant, with linen-dressed tables and professional service, La Cantinella is famed for its creative approach to classic recipes. The stomach-grumbling menu includes wonderful dishes such as *tagliata di*

Top Five Santa Lucia
- Bersagliera (above)
- Ciro (above)
- La Cantinella (above)
- Napoli-Napoli (p116)
- Da Pietro (p116)

manzon (entrecote and rocket in a spicy aromatic sauce) or *penne con calamaro e cavolo* (penne with squid and white cabbage). Desserts are also a deluxe take on comfort food, and the lengthy and interesting wine list yields some excellent quaffs.

NAPOLI-NAPOLI Map pp248-9   *Trattoria*
☎ 081 764 97 52; Via Santa Lucia 99; mains from €7; ☺ daily; bus C25 to Via Partenope

A fashionable spot with a smart, sleek interior in marine blue and white. Good for those with undecided tastebuds, the buffet changes daily and includes shimmering, colourful dishes such as roasted red and yellow peppers, grilled aubergines, anchovies in vinaigrette and salads featuring seafood, fennel, rocket and shrimp. The à la carte menu includes pasta dishes with innovative sauce ingredients such as chick peas, beans, mussels and aubergine. Maitre'd Attereo is agreeably well rounded and affable.

TAVERNA LUCIANA
Map pp248-9   *Ristorante*
☎ 081 764 26 61; Via Santa Lucia 21; mains from €10; ☺ daily; bus C25 to Via Partenope

Classic Neapolitan cuisine dished up by enthusiastic owners Peppe and Maria. The *menu turistico* (tourist menu) is €15, but you're better off with the more adventurous à la carte choices like *linguine al polpi* (linguine pasta with octopus) or the face-filling *pasta e fagioli* (pasta and beans). Vegetarians are spoilt for choice, with inventive salads and several traditional nonmeat choices such as *fusilli con ricotta* and *gnocchi alla sorrentina* (tomato, mozzarella and parmesan). The terrace is well placed for watching the sophisticated swagger of passers-by, while the downstairs tavern, although gloomy, has live Neapolitan music on the weekends. Before you glad-rag it down here, check whether any large groups are booked.

TRANSATLANTICO Map pp248-9 *Ristorante*
☎ 081 764 88 42; Borgo Marinaro; meals around €45; ☺ daily; bus C25 to Via Partenope

Push the boat out at this recent addition to the Borgo. The vast L-shaped terrace is flanked by expensive speedboats and yachts, and it's fun to watch the wealthy here. That said, the bow-tied service is excellent, and flavour is the key in such dishes as the *antipasti mista di mar* (mixed fried fish) and pasta with tomatoes, crayfish and grilled squid. The varied wine list is reasonably priced for a restaurant of this calibre.

Cheap Eats

DA PEPPINO Map pp248-9   *Trattoria*
☎ 081 764 44 49; Via Solitaria 18; mains from €5; bus C25 to Via Partenope

Tucked up one of those narrow washing-hung streets that looks like it's come straight out of a Fellini film, this trattoria is more family-oriented than romantic. There are simple, wooden tables and a fairly limited choice of pasta and pizza, all of which are, however, truly delicious. Try the classic *pasta al ragù*, with meat and tomato sauce. Go for a beer instead of the house wine, which is better suited for pickling onions.

DA PIETRO Map pp248-9   *Trattoria*
☎ 081 807 10 82; Via Lucilliana 27; mains €6; ☺ Tue-Sun; bus C25 to Via Partenope

Flanked by its grander neighbours, but sharing the same five-star harbour view, Da Pietro is simple and unpretentious, right down to the plastic tablecloths, chalked-up daily menu and mildly harassed staff. Dishes like spaghetti with tomato and basil, and home-made soup, are solid and traditional. There are just a few tables, and as this is one of the very few inexpensive restaurants here, be prepared to wait.

VOMERO

Despite the anonymous, building-block air of its main shopping centre, Vomero has some exceptional trattorie and restaurants. Not surprising really, when you consider the number of shops and offices here. These folk have to eat somewhere and, like true Neapolitans, they prefer mamma-style home cooking to those dismally ubiquitous fast-food chains which are, fortunately, as rare in Naples as finding pineapple on a pizza.

ACUNZO Map p247   *Trattoria*
☎ 081 578 53 62; Via Domenico Cimarosa 64; meals around €14; funicular Centrale to Fuga

A bastion of traditional food with the unmistakable smell of fine cooking and a nice low-key ambience. The pasta is good and

Top Five Vomero
- Acunzo (above)
- Angalo de Paradiso (opposite)
- Caprese (opposite)
- Donna Teresa (opposite)
- La Cantina de Sici (opposite)

the pizza excellent with its crisp-edged base topped with choices such as cherry tomatoes, mozzarella and a pile of fresh rocket leaves. Here is a good example of simple Naples cuisine that has not suffered from the over-complication you sometimes find in the city's pricier places. Jack Lemmon has apparently eaten here.

ANGOLO DE PARADISO Map p247 *Pizzeria*
☎ 081 556 71 46; Via Michele Kerbaker 152; pizzas from €5; funicular Centrale to Fuga
This restaurant has the feeling of days gone by, with its freshly scrubbed basic décor and local clientele. The pizzas are good. If you're having a dilemma making a choice, opt for the palate-blowing pizza *cinque gusti* (five good-sized slices with a variety of meat, fish and cheese toppings). The wine is dangerously cheap.

CAPRESE Map p247 *Trattoria*
☎ 081 55 87 58; Via Luca Giordano 25; mains from €6; funicular Centrale to Fuga
This place has a real Caribbean feel, with outside terraces surrounded by colourful flowerbeds, rubber plants and palm trees, plus a bubbling fountain or two. There's a young team at the helm and the place has a lively vibe. The *ravioli caprese* (spinach-filled ravioli with tomato sauce) comes recommended, while other choices include pizza, salad, pasta and fish dishes.

DONNA TERESA Map p247 *Osteria*
☎ 081 556 70 70; Via Michele Kerbaker 58; meals around €14; funicular Centrale to Fuga
This swing-a-cat-sized dining room has just eight tables and, unusually, a no-smoking policy. It's family run; Mamma Teresa's photo looks on approvingly as diners tuck into exceptionally good Neapolitan food. The menu is limited and changes daily but there are usually a couple of nonpasta dishes, which could include chicken with tomato sauce or meatballs. Hugely popular; you'll be lucky to get a table at lunchtime (and you can't book).

LA CANTINA DI SICI Map p247 *Ristorante*
☎ 081 556 75 20; Via Bernini 17, meals around €25; ☺ daily; funicular Centrale to Fuga
Recently refurbished but still reassuringly rustic, with a beamed ceiling and wooden tables. La Cantina serves excellent Neapolitan dishes made with salutary attention to detail. Among the winners are *tubettoni* pasta with courgettes and shrimp; salmon with wine; and *parmigiano di peperone* (layers of peppers in a white-wine

La Cantina di Sica (left)

sauce with parmesan). The exterior is papered with photos of mildly squiffy-looking diners – a good advertisement for the house wine.

ROSSOPOMODORO Map p247 *Trattoria*
☎ 081 556 81 69; Via Domenico Cimarosa 144; pizzas from €5; funicular Centrale to Fuga
Don't be put off by the wall of Andy Warhol–style framed tomato-tin labels or, more worrying still, the fact that this restaurant is part of a chain with 11 branches, some as far away as Madrid and Rio de Janeiro. The formula works thanks to the pizzas that are in a whole different league from the other fast-food biggies. If you're seriously peckish, try the Cilegina classic of mozzarella, ricotta, salami, tomatoes and mushrooms. There are 12 salad choices and several lush desserts including a tiramisu winner with chantilly cream, raspberries and limoncello.

Cheap Eats

FRIGGITORIA VOMERO Map p247 *Snacks*
☎ 081 578 31 30; Via Domenico Cimarosa 44; snacks from €1; ☺ Mon-Sat; funicular Centrale to Fuga
A popular, friendly spot on a busy corner opposite the funicular and handily placed for stoking up before legging it to the Castel Sant'Elmo. Lunchtime fare concentrates on superb *fritture* including deep-fried aubergines, potatoes and courgette flowers. The house wine is local and very drinkable.

tables. The outside terrace can be a bit noisy; this is a busy road for traffic. The reassuringly brief menu has appetising home-made fare. The special of the day is always a sound bet, otherwise the risottos and seafood spaghetti are good, too. Vegetarians are obligingly catered for.

TORRE DEL PALASCIANO

Map p250   *Ristorante*

☎ 081 45 90 00; Villa Capodimonte Hotel, Via Moiariello 66; meals around €30; ☽ daily; bus 24 to Via Capodimonte

A dress-for-dinner restaurant with such upper-crust cuisine as rabbit with aromatic spices (€13), swordfish in balsamic vinegar and mint (€16), and vegetable risotto with peppers and mozzarella (€8.50). The dining room is fairly ordinary in comparison but the view is pretty, overlooking the gardens with their dazzle of flowerbeds around a central fountain.

LA SANITÀ & CAPODIMONTE

Searching for good restaurants in La Sanità evokes the proverbial needle-in-a-haystack dilemma. They are here of course, mostly tucked into a tangle of backstreets and frequented by locals in the know. The best places tend to be those nudging up to the *centro storico*. If you are visiting Capodimonte, take a picnic or opt for one of the choices below; there ain't a whole lot more.

I GIARDINI DI CAPODIMONTE

Map p250   *Ristorante*

☎ 081 744 51 36; Via Capodimonte 19; mains from €7; ☽ daily; bus 24 to Via Capodimonte

Well placed for a little sustenance, this restaurant is high up above the city at the top of the steep steps leading from the Tondo di Capodimonte. Sadly the view of the town below is blocked by the trees but the terrace is shady and large, and the menu choice is good. The *gnocchetti al limon* (small gnocchi with lemon; €7) comes recommended: it's tangy and delicious. The *risotto al funghi* (risotto with mushrooms) is filling and tasty. Portions are on the small side.

LOMBARDI Map p250   *Ristorante*

☎ 081 45 62 20; Via Foria 12; mains from €8; ☽ daily; bus/metro to Cavour

Effortlessly stylish, with a cool beige-and-white interior and clay pots and fresh flowers on the

MERCATO

It can be sleazy, smelly and litter-strewn (especially at post-market times), but this area has a beguiling vitality that is duly reflected in the many cafés and restaurants. The best choices are in the closely packed streets between Corso G Garibaldi and Corso Umberto 1. Also included in this section are restaurants on (or just off) Piazza Garibaldi. In general, expect gut-filling good rather than fancy food.

AVELLINESE Map pp244-6   *Trattoria*

☎ 081 28 91 64; Via Silvio Spaventa 31-35; mains from €7; ☽ daily; metro Garibaldi

Energy-boosting large servings of pasta, and meat and fish dishes. Go for the latter (unless it's Monday), because there's a fish market around the corner. The service is brisk and businesslike and there's an outdoor terrace. Although, be warned: this is one of Naples' shabbier districts, so don't wave your maps around if you're here after dark.

DA MICHELE Map pp244-6   *Pizzeria*

☎ 081 553 92 04; Via Cesare Sersale 1; pizzas €5-7; bus R2 to Corso Umberto

Probably the most famous pizzeria in Naples but you would never know it (until you taste the pizza); the interior is dingy and old fashioned. Founded in 1870, this place only makes two types of pizzas: margherita (tomatoes, basil and mozzarella) or *marinara* (seafood, tomatoes, garlic and oregano) – and they have had a long time to get things just right. You can't make a booking; just turn up, take a ticket and wait your turn.

FRATELLI LA BUFALA

Map pp244-6 _Ristorante_
☎ 081 551 04 70; Via Medina 18; full meals around €14; ⏰ Mon-Sat, lunch Sun; bus R2 to Piazza del Municipio
A restaurant that takes the buffalo very seriously indeed. Main courses include buffalo steaks, barbecued buffalo with potatoes and buffalo hamburgers. Even the desserts feature the beast, with a _torta de ricotta di bufala al limon_ (ricotta cheesecake with lemon). The dining room is decorated with giant batik prints of (yawn) buffalo. The quality is high, however, and if you are a meat-eater you may want to give this place a try.

GRAN CAFFÈ IMPERIUS Map pp244-6 _Café_
☎ 081 20 60 86; Piazza Garibaldi 24; ⏰ daily; metro Garibaldi
Despite the name, there are few airs and graces about this mildly scuffed but atmospheric café with outside tables and a bar piled high with _panini_ of cheese and tomato, _tramezzini_ (sandwiches), and glistening slices of freshly made pizza. There are a few tables outside on this busy corner, if you don't mind your food getting an extra smoking from the traffic.

IRIS Map pp244-6 _Ristorante_
☎ 081 26 99 88; Piazza Garibaldi 121-25; meals around €15; ⏰ daily; metro Garibaldi
A welcome retreat from traffic-congested Piazza Garibaldi and well sited for train travellers needing some comfortable refuelling. There is a vast outdoor terrace, and a formulaic elegant dining room with tanks of fish and grand-sized ceiling fans. Choose à la carte rather than the overpriced tourist menu. The _risotto rucola e gameretti_ (risotto with rocket and shrimps) will fill you up and leave you happy at just €5.16. An aside here: it's always

a good sign when euros aren't rounded off, as it generally means a fairer conversion from the lira.

LA BRACE Map pp244-6 _Ristorante_
☎ 081 26 12 60; Via Silvio Spaventa 14; full meals around €14; ⏰ Mon-Sat; metro Garibaldi
A no-nonsense eatery with simple wooden tables, providing a welcome bolthole from the mayhem of nearby Piazza Garibaldi and Stazione Centrale. The menu changes but favourite dishes include _penne alla scarpariello_ (pasta with pecorino cheese, fresh tomatoes, basil and a hint of chilli) or the gnocchi served with several different sauces. Seafood is also a speciality. The street can be dodgy; don't dangle any bags.

LA SFOGLIATELLA Map pp244-6 _Pasticceria_
☎ 081 28 56 85; Corso Novara 1; ⏰ daily; metro Garibaldi
It's difficult for even the staunchest dieter to pass by this sumptuous display of cakes, pies and pastries. This historic _pasticceria_ is famous for its _sfogliatelle_ and house specialities: _zeffiro all'arancia_ (orange delicacy), chocolate and rum cakes, and _riccias_ (_millefeuilles_ pastry with an apple-custard filling). Elbow yourself to the front counter; this place is always crammed and buzzing. There's another branch on Piazza San Domenico.

PASTICCERIA CARRATURO

Map pp244-6 _Pasticceria_
☎ 081 554 53 44; Corso G Garibaldi 59; ⏰ daily; metro Garibaldi
A classic with black-bowtied counter staff. The area in front is dominated by a long marble and dark-wood bar where you can find savoury treats, while the back is given over to sweet delights like _babà_ and _zeppole_ (fried dough with custard cream). This place is a hub of neighbourhood activity; you may be in trouble ordering if you don't speak the lingo.

TRIANON Map pp244-6 _Pizzeria_
☎ 081 553 94 26; Via Pietro Colletta 42-46; pizzas from €5; metro Garibaldi
An institution in Neapolitan circles – film director Vittorio de Sica and comic actor Totò were regulars – this historic pizzeria does its city proud. On the dough since 1923, it's still tossing the pizzas with the best of them. On two floors and basic, it is decorated with black-and-white photos of old Naples. Expect queues and Japanese tourists (the word is out).

Eating – Mercato

Top Five Mercato
- **Da Michele** (opposite)
- **Iris** (above)
- **La Brace** (right)
- **La Sfogliatella** (right)
- **Trianon** (right)

A pizzaiolo at work at Trianon (p119)

Cheap Eats

ANTICA GASTRONOMIA FERRIERI

Map pp244-6   *Snacks*

☎ 081 554 01 65; Piazza Garibaldi 82-88; snacks from €3; ☿ daily; metro Garibaldi

Right on bustling Piazza Garibaldi near the metro station, so it's ideally situated to get an early fix of Neapolitan snacking at its best. Try the *pagniottiello*, a cross between a pizza and a bread roll, with delicious fillings like aubergine, tomatoes and fresh ricotta. Smaller appetites can go for the little sandwiches on white bread that taste much better than they look. If you still haven't had your fill, there's a self-service restaurant upstairs.

ORBINATO ANTONIO

Map pp244-6   *Pizzeria*

☎ 081 20 11 21; Via A Poerio 52; pizzas from €4.50; metro Garibaldi

Service can be excruciatingly slow at this popular place, which attracts all sorts, with its vast pavement terrace spread between the shops. No surprises on the menu, except the *pizza fritta* which comes folded and filled to perfection with ricotta, mozzarella, tomato and ham. The *bufalina* pizza with mozzarella and fresh tomatoes is a good example of how just a couple of simple ingredients can outclass piled-high pizzas.

CHIAIA

Another super-concentrated Naples district for anything to do with food or drink (or ice cream). A short high-heeled flounce from the designer shops around Piazza dei Martiri and you can find all the dining choice you could possibly need, ranging from swanky see-and-be-seen cafés to family-

run, rough-edged restaurants serving gems of traditional dishes.

ANTICA OSTERIA DA TONINO

Map pp248-9   *Osteria*

☎ 081 42 15 33; Via Santa Teresa a Chiaia 47; mains from €12; metro Amedeo

Via Santa Teresa a Chiaia is home to several home-cooking restaurants and this is one of the longest established. Fronted by an *enoteca*, there are just a few tables filling the wood-panelled dining room. The portions are generous and it's easy to fill up on the starters, such as *antipasto misto* (mixed antipasto) or *funghi trifolati* (mushrooms with anchovies, garlic and lemon). But leave room for the mains, even if you share; the excellent *pasta al pomodoro* (pasta with tomatoes), for example, is hefty enough for two.

CASTELLO Map pp248-9   *Osteria*

☎ 081 40 04 86; Via Santa Teresa a Chiaia 38; mains from €10; ☿ Mon-Sat Sep-Jul; metro Amedeo

Despite the name, you don't have to shift your credit card into overdraft to eat here; the dishes are delicious, original and well priced. Pasta choice includes *pappardelle* (wide ribbon pasta) with courgette flowers and mussels, and *filetto al castelo* (veal in a creamy courgette sauce). It's hard to fault this place, right down to the friendly owners, red-check tablecloths and home-made desserts. *Zeppola* is the sweet speciality, a deliciously light yet doughy pie filled with custard and fresh berries.

DI BRUNO Map pp248-9   *Ristorante*

☎ 081 251 24 11; Riviera di Chiaia 213-14; mains from €12; ☿ Tue-Sun; bus C25 to Riviera di Chiaia

The name Di Bruno is well known among foodies here. Papa used to run two restaurants, but has now scaled down to one with the next generation helping out. The interior is sparkling white, with panoramic photos of Naples, and candles are lit at night. It's very popular with French tourists, which is probably a good sign. The linguine is made daily and features in the *pasta alla Bruno* signature dish, doused with a rich sauce of mushrooms, courgettes, ham and cream.

DORA Map pp248-9   *Ristorante*

☎ 081 68 05 19; Via Ferdinando Palasciano 30; meals around €45; bus C25 to Riviera di Chiaia

At the top of yet another skinny washing-hung street, the exterior here looks remarkably mundane. In fact, this is one of Naples' most famous restaurants for fish and seafood, and it is always chock full. Breezy blue-and-white tiles, old nautical memorabilia including model boats, and friendly staff equal a convivial atmosphere for tucking into dishes like *frittura di pesce* (fried fish) and exceptional fresh prawns.

LA CAFFETTIERA Map pp248-9   *Café*
☎ 081 764 42 43; Piazza dei Martiri 30; ☯ daily; bus C25 to Piazza dei Martiri

One of Naples' grand cafés that pulls in a mon-eyed crowd taking a break from perusing the designer-store surroundings. The large decked terrace is more appealing than the indoor seating space, which is a bit stuffy with its dark wood, fabric wallpaper and satin tablecloths. Never mind about all that, try the plum cake.

MAKTUB Map pp248-9   *Ristorante*
☎ 081 764 73 37; Vico Satriano 8c; mains from €8; ☯ Tue-Sun, lunch Mon; bus C25 to Riviera di Chiaia

The interior here is modern and arty, with rows of niches displaying identical single roses and the puzzle of a gnarled tree trunk which grows in the centre of the dining room, seemingly nurtured by terracotta tiles. The menu is equally worrying – it's handwritten in small parchment books (where are the splodges of tomato?). For lunch there is light fare such as fettuccini with a choice of sauces and fish curry. At night there's a DJ and candlelit tables, making this a handy pre-clubbing venue for couples.

MEDINA Map pp248-9   *Trattoria*
☎ 081 66 68 77; Riviera di Chiaia 165-68; mains from €8; ☯ Mon-Sat; bus C25 to Riviera di Chiaia

A large modern restaurant better suited for a family blowout than a romantic dinner for two. The dining room has jolly seascape murals, the toilets are space-age modern and there's a gallery dining area upstairs. Easy-on-the-eye waiting staff dish up such classic Neapolitan dishes as *linguine con scampi*, good pizzas and several salad choices. There's a daily menu of specials and a superb ice-cream cake.

TARANTO Map pp248-9   *Café*
☎ 081 40 06 69; Via G Bausan 59-60; snacks from €4; bus C25 to Riviera de Chiaia

Taranto is good for cakes and crepes; the latter are a real delight, traditionally rolled up with chocolate and eaten on the go. If you are here early, pick up a *cornetto con crema* (sweet custard croissant), which is a real morning-coffee treat. If you're looking for a change from pizza and pasta, this street is worth a wander for its

Top Five Chiaia
- **Castello** (opposite)
- **Di Bruno** (opposite)
- **Dora** (opposite)
- **Maktub** (left)
- **Umberto** (below)

(at last count) Mexican, Spanish and Chinese restaurants.

UMBERTO Map pp248-9   *Ristorante*
☎ 081 41 85 55; Via Alabardieri 30-31; full meals €25; bus C25 to Piazza dei Martiri

A smart place with saffron-coloured walls and gilt mirrors. The *menu di degustazione* is good value at €25 and may include dishes such as *pesce all'acqua pazza* (white fish with tomatoes, garlic and parsley). Lighter gourmet delicacies include a roll of pizza stuffed with lettuce, parsley and smoked cheese. The pizzas include a few choices for those poor, deprived Neapolitans who don't like tomato, including the *caponata* with anchovies, artichokes and marinated vegetables. The restaurant has the added surprise of a gluten-free menu.

Cheap Eats
LA FOCACCIA Map pp248-9   *Snacks*
☎ 081 41 22 77; Vico Belledonne a Chiaia 31; focaccias from €1.60; bus C25 to Piazza dei Martiri

The best place in town for fat focaccia squares topped with all the best combos, such as artichokes, tomatoes and mozzarella, or aubergine, *pecorino* cheese and smoked ham. There's a funky young atmosphere with red-panelled walls and shelves of imported beers. Not much space, so large groups should opt for takeaway. Owner Simone speaks good English.

RESTAURANTE DE VIOLA
Map pp248-9   *Ristorante*
☎ 081 658 14 09; Via Santa Maria en Portico; meals €6; metro Amedeo

There's just 10 or so tables in this friendly family restaurant. The daily menu is chalked up outside, with a couple of choices for antipasto and following courses. The portions are huge and the atmosphere is homey and convivial. The best news of all is the price, which in some places in Santa Lucia would barely cover the cost of bread. Don't come here for culinary revelations, just classic local dishes honestly prepared from simple fresh ingredients.

Eating – Chiaia

MERGELLINA & POSILLIPO

These two seaside places get packed out with large noisy families at weekends, especially on Sundays in the summer. As well as having the restaurants listed, Mergellina is ice-cream heaven. To find the best places, just head for those with the longest queues. Posillipo will give you a taste of the Amalfi Coast; the seafood restaurants are comparable in quality to those in Mergellina but generally cheaper.

A LAMPARA Off Map pp242-3   *Ristorante*
☎ 081 575 64 92; Via Discesa Coroglio 79; full meals around €15; bus 140 to Via Posillipo
Run by a charming family and fronted by a narrow terrace overlooking this popular strolling street. If you have ever wondered what bolognese *ought* to taste like, try the *ravioli alla bolognese*; it's delicious. There's a healthy selection of local wines and a highly popular buffet on Sundays in summer; get here early.

AL CICLOPE Off Map pp242-3   *Trattoria*
☎ 081 769 23 40; Via Discesa Coroglio 20, Posillipo; full meals around €18; bus 140 to Via Posillipo
The dining room is in a cave built right into the rock, so it's suitably intimate and atmospheric, albeit a little gloomy. There's the choice of a terrace for sunny days. This place is handily situated for continuing your travels to Capo Posillipo and Marechiaro (the bus stop is right outside). Try the *ravioli al pescatore* (€5), followed by a slice of to-die-for chocolate hazelnut *torta* (cake).

BARBECUE RESTAURANT
Map pp248-9   *Steakhouse*
☎ 081 66 94 53; Via Sannazzaro 5; ☽ daily; meals around €38; metro Mergellina
Grandly located on the lower level of a classic Neapolitan house. The name says it all. Dedicated carnivores can chow down on barbecued buffalo beef, Argentinian steak, Irish beef or *fondue bourguignonne* (minimum two). Other meaty choices include fried steak with a choice of sauces, including green pepper, parmesan and mushrooms. Vegetarians will have to make do with a baked potato and plate of grilled vegetables. Outside dining is in a pretty garden setting, with lofty palm trees and parasols.

CIBUS Map pp248-9   *Ristorante*
☎ 081 68 17 05; Via Francesco Caracciolo; meals around €20; ☽ Tue-Sun; metro Mergellina
This place can't go wrong with its bay views and enthusiastic manager Luigi. The food is pretty good as well, with a spoilt-for-choice menu of pizzas including rocket with tomato and fresh mozzarella, and house favourites like *fusilli* with pesto and fish. There are three terraces, a dining room and a small takeaway counter selling (oh dear) hot dogs and burgers.

REGINELLI Off Map pp242-3   *Ristorante*
☎ 081 575 40 20; Via Posillipo 45; meals around €40; bus 140 to Via Posillipo
High on atmosphere, with an outside terrace and seamless sea views. The menu is a little pricey as befits the filmstar setting but, as always, you can keep the costs down by ordering a pizza. The fish display near the entrance reflects the speciality here, however. Reassuringly, the menu is in Italian only. The raspberry tart is delicious and the limoncello costs a reasonable €2, so order another glass and linger. If you're arriving here by bus, ask the driver to let you off outside Reginelli.

SALVATORE Map pp248-9   *Ristorante*
☎ 081 68 18 17; Via Mergellina 4A; meals around €35; metro Mergellina
Near the water, with a small leafy terrace and an elegant dining room hung with chandeliers and old prints, the emphasis here is on fish and meat. Unusual dishes including *cecinielle* (fried fish patties), a light and tasty *minestre in brodo* (thick noodle broth) and *calamaretti con uva passa* (baby squid with pine nuts and raisins). Owner Tonino is a serious wine buff, so ask for his advice when selecting *vino*.

Cheap Eats

DA PASQUALINA Map pp248-9   *Ristorante*
☎ 081 68 15 24; Piazza Sannazzaro 77-79; mains from €5; ☽ Wed-Mon; metro Mergellina
A slightly scruffy restaurant dating back to 1898, full of happily chomping locals. Soak up the atmosphere by grabbing a table on the piazza. The menu holds few surprises but is good value if you are euro-economising. The pizza is excellent; so is the *frittura*, which includes deep-fried mozzarella, aubergine and potatoes.

Top Five Mergellina & Posillipo
- **A Lampara** (left)
- **Cibus** (left)
- **Reginelli** (above)
- **Salvatore** (above)
- **Da Pasqualina** (above)

Entertainment

Entertainment

To entertain yourself in Naples it's often enough just to park yourself at a streetside table and simply watch the world go by. The gregarious locals are a spectacle in themselves. Certainly Neapolitans take to the streets en masse in the evening and are happy to while away the hours strolling up and down, chatting with each other, smoking and eating *gelati* (ice cream).

The petite piazzas of the *centro storico* (historic centre) are famously lively. Here you'll find all sorts: bands of traveller-punks huddled round a bottle of beer surreptitiously passing joints; swarms of happy students noisily greeting each other; and middle-aged jazz-loving bohemians talking into the small hours over a glass of something chic. Flitting round the edges, tourists of every nationality look on, not quite sure whether to be charmed or nervous. Popular haunts include **Piazza Bellini** (p63), **Piazza Gesù Nuovo** (p58) and **Piazza San Domenico Maggiore** (p58).

For a more elegant *serata* (evening) head for the *lungomare* (seafront) and the Chiaia district. The seafront is a hugely popular parade and at its Mergellina end the Chalets are famous for their spectacular ice-cream creations.

Chiaia is the city's well-to-do fashionable heart. Among the picturesque cobbled streets west of Piazza dei Martiri you'll find a whole host of trattorie, restaurants, bars, clubs and cafés. In contrast with the *centro storico*, people dress up to party in Chiaia and the bars are smart, stylish and more expensive. Many bars and clubs close for a period in high summer (usually July and August) and decamp to nearby beach haunts, which are usually difficult to get to without a car. Fortunately, Neapolitans are universally sociable and are dedicated drivers, often happy to help a foreigner in distress. Needless to say most drivers are young men.

But there's more to enjoying yourself in Naples than bar-hopping and clubbing with the beautiful people. The city's cultural calendar ranges from festivals of street artists and pizza-making to world-class opera. To join the knowledgeable audience at the Teatro San Carlo is a magnificent experience. No stuffy applause here – reactions are rapturous or nothing. There's no such thing as a lukewarm audience in Naples.

Other concerts are held in atmospheric chapels or, between May and September, in various outdoor locations. Each May the city authorities organise Maggio dei Monumenti, a month of concerts and cultural activities in museums and monuments around town, most of which are free. In summer the Amalfi Coast and Bay of Naples islands host a range of festivals, chief of which is the world-famous Festivale Musicale di Ravello (see p200 for details). For more festival dates, see p8.

The monthly *Qui Napoli* (in Italian and English) and local newspapers (in Italian) are the best guides to what's on when, or ask at tourist offices for details.

For background information on many aspects of Naples' arts scene and for more on architecture, see p18.

THEATRE

Naples has a long tradition of theatre. In fact, it was in 16th-century Naples that the *commedia dell'arte* was born. A popular form of streetside theatre, performances featured a cast of stock characters, including the Pulcinella, the white-gowned, black-masked symbol of Naples and forerunner of Mr Punch.

Out of these beginnings grew the city's love affair with the theatre. Some of Naples'

most famous cultural icons are playwrights or actors who started on the city's theatre circuit. Names such as Eduardo De Filippo, Totò and Massimo Troisi hold a special place in the Neapolitan heart.

Today the scene is lively if not as vibrant as it once was. Playwrights such as Roberto De Simone and Enzo Moscato attract large audiences with their modern takes on Neapolitan traditions, while young international artists are encouraged to experiment on the city's smaller stages.

Ticket prices range from about €8 for smaller, experimental theatres to €30 and upwards for big-budget productions at grander venues. To reserve a ticket either contact the theatre direct, or if possible log onto its website. Alternatively, try a ticketing agency such as **Box Office** (Map pp244–6; ☎ 081 551 91 88; Galleria Umberto I 15-16), near Teatro San Carlo. Many hotels can also help with reservations.

BELLINI Map pp244-6

☎ 081 549 96 88; www.teatrobellini.it; Via Conte di Ruvo; tickets from €15; ☽ box office 10am-1.30pm & 4-7pm Tue-Sun; bus CD to Via Santa Maria di Costantinopoli

Regarded by many Neapolitans as the city's most beautiful theatre, the 19th-century Bellini is a picture of classical gold and red. Its repertoire tends to be fairly conservative, with big-budget musicals sharing the stage with works by Shakespeare, Manzoni and Oscar Wilde.

GALLERIA TOLEDO Map pp244-6

☎ 081 42 58 24; www.galleriatoledo.com in Italian; Via Concezione a Montecalvario 34; tickets from €12; ☽ box office 10.30am-7pm Tue-Sat Sep-May; metro Montesanto

Tucked away in the Quartieri Spagnoli district, this theatre-cum-cinema presents a mixed bag of theatrical fare. The emphasis is on modern experimental works by international playwrights, but don't be surprised to see the odd Greek tragedy pop up.

MERCADANTE Map pp244-6

☎ 081 551 33 96; www.caspi.it/mercadante in Italian; Piazza del Municipio 1; tickets from €15; ☽ box office 10.30am-1pm & 5.30-7.30pm Tue-Sun Sep-Apr; bus R2 to Piazza del Municipio

The Mercadante is one of Naples' oldest theatres. Dating to 1779, it has a reputation for staging top-quality productions and regularly plays host to local luminaries Luca de Filippo and Roberto de Simone.

TEATRO NUOVO Map pp244-6

☎ 081 42 59 58; www.nuovoteatronuovo.it in Italian; Via Concezione a Montecalvario 16; tickets about €15; ☽ box office 11am-1.30pm & 4-6.30pm Mon & Thu Jul-Sep; metro Montesanto

Samuel Beckett and controversial Italian director Pier Paolo Pasolini are among the more recognisable names to appear on the Nuovo's

Theatre Festivals

Benvenuta Primavera (☎ 081 247 11 23; ☽ Mar) The city's piazzas and gardens become the backdrop for a series of outdoor performances. Guided tours are also offered.

programme. A modern theatre, it provides a stage for emerging European writers whose works may or may not appeal.

TRIANON Map pp244-6

☎ 081 225 82 85; www.teatrotrianon.it; Piazza Vincenzo Calenda 9; tickets from €8; bus R2 to Corso Umberto I

An old-fashioned music hall catering to tourists and traditionalists, this is the place for a good ol' sing-along. The Trianon orchestra belts out a repertoire of unashamedly sentimental Neapolitan classics, while the jolly audience joins in the chorus. Pre-concert you can visit the small museum dedicated to opera star Enrico Caruso.

DANCE

Although the Teatro San Carlo is better known as the home of Neapolitan opera, it is also home to the oldest dance academy in Italy. Founded in 1812 by the French ruler Joachim Murat, it was re-opened in 1950 after almost a century of inactivity. The San Carlo Ballet Company, under the artistic directorship of Elisabetta Terabust, performs a year-round repertoire of traditional and modern works.

It's rare for international dance companies to venture this far south in Italy, so if you are after cutting-edge international choreography you'll have to head north to Rome, or better still, Milan.

TEATRO SAN CARLO Map pp248-9

☎ 081 797 21 11; www.teatrosancarlo.it; tickets €20-90; ☽ box office 10am-3pm Tue-Sun Oct-May, 10am-4.30pm Mon-Fri Jun-Sep; Via San Carlo 98; bus R2 to Via San Carlo

The inhouse ballet company performs to a consistently high standard. Tickets start at €20 and rise to €90. If you're 26 or under, and can prove it, you qualify for a €15 ticket. In the summer some performances are staged in the courtyard of the Castel Nuovo. For information about the theatre's opera performances, see p130.

CINEMAS

Like all Italians, Neapolitans love going to the cinema. But like many Italian activities it has an etiquette of its own. Firstly, it's primarily a winter activity; many smaller cinemas close in the summer and although open-air projections are popular, most Neapolitans would rather be sporting themselves by the sea. Secondly, the young go to the 10.30pm showing, families and older viewers to the 8pm feature. And thirdly, it's very important as you leave the cinema to stop in the doorway, light a cigarette and start loudly discussing the film.

Nearly all films screened in Italy are dubbed, which means that unless you speak Italian your choices are fairly limited. Most are also screened with an interval which means 10 minutes of frantic comings and goings as viewers nip out for a quick smoke or toilet break, invariably returning after the film has re-started.

Films shown in their original language are indicated in listings by *versione originale* or VO after the title.

Cinema tickets cost between €4.50 and €8. As a general guide screenings begin every two hours from 4.30pm to 10.30pm. Afternoon and early evening screenings are generally cheaper than films shown later in the evening. Check the listings press or daily papers for cinema schedules and ticket prices.

ABADIR Map p247
☎ 081 578 94 47; Via G Paisiello 35; tickets €7.20; metro Collana

For the latest Hollywood releases, the Abadir in Vomero is a popular spot that screens films in their original language on Tuesday night. It's only downfall, however, is that it is some distance from the centre.

CINEMA AMEDEO Map pp248-9
☎ 081 68 02 66; Via Campiglione Martucci 69; tickets €6.70; metro Amedeo

Thursday night is English-language night at this well-known cinema near Piazza Amedeo in Chiaia. Films tend to be of the blockbuster variety.

A Prince, a Pauper and a Goddess

In one of the sexiest screen strips of celluloid history Sophia Loren languidly peels of her simple dress and black silk stockings to reveal her famously fulsome figure. Sitting on the bed in front of her, Marcello Mastroianni can barely control himself, wriggling around like a child on Christmas morning. From the film *Ieri, Oggi, Domani* (Yesterday, Today, Tomorrow; 1963), it's one of Loren's great scenes.

Now, at the age of 70, Sophia Loren (1934–) has made the transformation from screen goddess to national treasure. And although she no longer lives in Naples she often talks about her past. Born poor, Sofia Villani Scicolone (she later changed the spelling of 'Sofia' to 'Sophia') spent her childhood in the slums of Pozzuoli. From all accounts she was a scrawny child – one of her nicknames was The Stick – but she soon developed into a voluptuous beauty and hit the beauty-pageant circuit, a tried-and-tested route to stardom. It bore fruit when she met the film producer who was later to become her husband, Carlo Ponti. Charmed by her looks and ambition, he signed her to a contract and her career never looked back.

The most famous actress to come out of Naples, Sophia Loren was the most internationally successful of a trio of Neapolitan film stars whose combined careers span virtually the entire 20th century.

Antonio de Curtis (1898–1967), aka Totò, was born in the working-class Sanità district. The son of a marquis, he was nonetheless poor and took to the stage early. A consummate performer, he met with considerable success and by the 1930s was travelling the country with his own one-man show. He made his first film in 1937 and went on to appear in more than 100, until his death 30 years later.

A star of the black-and-white screen, Totò has often been compared to Charlie Chaplin. Certainly his physical style compared to Chaplin's, but his humour was pure Neapolitan. His typical role of a down-on-his-luck hustler living on nothing but his wits and guile hit a chord with the Neapolitans, for whom the art of *arrangiarsi* (getting by) is a way of life.

The third of the trio, Massimo Troisi (1953–94) is best known to foreign audiences for his role in *Il Postino* (The Postman). Tragically, the Oscar-winning film was his last and he died of heart disease within 12 hours of the end of filming. Within Italy, the Neapolitan comic was adored for his unique brand of rambling humour. Virtually incomprehensible thanks to a mumbled style of speaking and his use of Neapolitan dialect, Troisi initially came to nationwide fame in a comic trio known as *La Smorfia*. But it's for his later film work that he's best remembered. Ask an Italian for a Troisi moment and chances are they'll think for a minute and then recall the classic scene from the film *Non ci resta che piangere* (Nothing Left to Do But Cry) in which Troisi and Roberto Benigni, having travelled back in time, fail to teach Leonardo da Vinci the classic card game *scopa*.

Film Festivals

Estate a Napoli (www.napolioggi.it in Italian; ☽ Jun-Sep) Open-air screenings occur as part of the summer-long cultural fest.

Artecinema (www.artecinema.com in Italian; ☽ Oct) International festival of documentaries about contemporary art and artists.

Cortocircuito (www.cortocircuito.it in Italian; ☽ Dec) A three-day celebration of audiovisual communication in the form of short films, music videos, adverts, multimedia and the like.

GALLERIA TOLEDO Map pp244-6

☎ 081 42 58 24; www.galleriatoledo.com in Italian; Via Concezione a Montecalvario 34; tickets €6; metro Montesanto

Cinephiles will appreciate the Galleria Toledo. When not in use as a theatre (see p225) it screens anything from American sci-fi classics to seriously obscure European arthouse flicks, often in the film's original language.

DRINKING

Neapolitans are not big drinkers, so the drinking scene does not revolve around large, characterless English- or Irish-style pubs. In fact, it's perfectly possible to enjoy an evening's drinking without going anywhere near a pub. In the *centro storico* many people simply buy a bottle of beer from the nearest bar and hang out on the streets.

The *centro storico* is, however, packed with bars and cafés (which are effectively the same thing as both stay open late and both serve alcohol), with the highest concentration around Via Cisterno dell'Olio, Piazza Bellini, Piazza del Gesù Nuovo and Piazza San Domenico Maggiore. The proximity of the university ensures a lively, unpretentious atmosphere.

In upmarket Chiaia, the pretty cobbled streets west of Piazza dei Martiri conceal an ever-increasing number of clubs and bars, attracting crowds of trendy well-dressed drinkers. The fashionable street of the moment is Vico dei Sospiri.

As a rough guide cafés usually open from about 7am until about 1am. Bars will either open for aperitifs, at around 6pm, or directly for the evening shift at 10pm. Closing is rarely much before 2am or 3am. Where there are no opening hours indicated assume they correspond with these. Also note that many city centre bars close for a month over the summer.

AL BARCADERO Map pp248-9

☎ 333 222 70 23; Banchina Santa Lucia 2; bus C25 to Via Partenope

Turn left down the steps as you walk towards Borgo Marinaro and you'll find Al Barcadero, a lovely unpretentious bar for a beer. Right down by the waterfront you can watch the fishermen come and go in their rowing boats or gaze up at the menacing profile of Mt Vesuvius.

ARET'A'PALM Map pp244-6

☎ 339 848 69 49; Piazza Santa Maria La Nova 14; ☽ 10am-2am Mon-Fri, 6pm-2am Sat & Sun; bus CS to Via Diaz

Billing itself as a wine bar, Aret'a'Palm, is informal and cheerful. The thin, dimly lit interior fills quickly with a fashionable crowd (more grunge than designer) that comes as much for the thumpingly loud world music as for the extensive wine list. The name Aret'a'Palm is a homage to the enormous palm tree in the piazza.

BAR DELL'OVO Map pp248-9

☎ 081 240 53 06; Via Partenope 6; ☽ 8am-6.30pm Mon, 8am-3am Tue-Sun; bus C25 to Via Partenope

A seafront spot to be seen at, the Bar dell'Ovo is the place for an afternoon coffee in the company of label-conscious yuppies. Later on things hot up in the stylish upstairs bar and Arabian-style downstairs lounge as the music kicks in and the beautiful people start to let their hair down.

BAR LAZZARELLA Map pp244-6

☎ 081 551 00 05; Calata Trinità Maggiore 7-8; bus CD to Via Monteoliveto

A small, utterly unpretentious café-cum-bar, this is a favourite watering hole just off Piazza del Gesù Nuovo. Generally packed with students and young drinkers, it's an ideal spot to pick up a bottle of beer and watch the nighttime crowds drift by.

ENOTECA BELLEDONNE Map pp248-9

☎ 081 40 31 62; Vico Belledonne a Chiaia 18; ☽ 9am-2pm & 4.30pm-2am Tue-Sun; bus C25 to Riviera di Chiaia

Welcoming and vibrant, this is *the* place for a glass of wine in Chiaia. A classic brick-walled

Enoteca Belledonne (p127)

enoteca (wine bar) with wooden tables and a good wine list, it heaves in the early evening as the trendy young stop by for a quick glass.

FUSION BAR 66 Map pp248-9
☎ 081 41 50 24; Via Bisignano; bus C25 to Riviera di Chiaia

In the heart of Chiaia, this fashionable bar is popular with a well-dressed 30-plus crowd. The aperitif set swan in around 8pm for an elegantly served nibble and a glass of something cool, spilling out onto the cobbled street outside. DJs entertain with chilled tunes.

KINKY BAR Map pp244-6
☎ 081 552 15 71; Via Cisterna dell'Olio 21; ⊕ Oct–mid-Jun; metro Piazza Dante

Operating from a smoky cellar, this reggae and dub joint attracts an up-for-it, mainly student crowd. It's a popular haunt and overspill often fills the lively street outside. In summer the Kinky crew organises beachside parties and reggae concerts.

LAS TAPAS Map pp244-6
☎ 081 552 21 68; Piazzetta del Nilo 36; ⊕ Wed-Mon; bus CS to Via Duomo

Tucked away in the heart of the *centro storico*, Las Tapas is a colourful little bar overlooking the busy Via San Biagio dei Librai. Although the burnt-red, candle-lit interior is tiny, the street-side tables are an ideal spot for watching the endless circus of tourists, students, punks and their dogs. Confusingly, however, Las Tapas serves no tapas.

LE BAR Map pp248-9
☎ 081 764 57 22; Piazzetta Marinari 18; ⊕ 9.30pm-late daily summer, Sat & Sun winter; bus C25 to Via Partenope

On the Borgo Marinaro, Le Bar is considered by some the coolest bar in Naples. The ethnic-chic black-and-red décor provides the backdrop for a smooth soundtrack of oriental beat, hip-hop and R&B. Tropical cocktails flow freely as the DJ mixes the sounds and the studiously cool check each other out with their shark-like eyes.

Top Five Bars

- **Vibes** (opposite) A buzzing bar with live tunes in an atmospheric square.
- **Enoteca Belledonne** (p127) The wine bar of choice for the chic.
- **Kinky Bar** (left) Beer, reggae and attitude.
- **S'move** (opposite) Colourful décor and well-dressed drinkers.
- **Al Barcadero** (p127) An unpretentious spot to sip by the sea.

Café Culture

Naples, like many Italian cities, is blessed with a thriving café culture. It's not just tourists who flock to big-name cafés – professionals hold ad hoc meetings over a coffee, workmen pop in for a bite to eat and shoppers rest their weary legs.

Many cafés serve an assortment of *dolci* (sweets including Italy's breakfast staple, the *cornetto*), coffee, freshly squeezed orange juice (a *spremuta*) and *panini* (rolls).

The most famous cafés in Naples are **Caffè Gambrinus** (Map pp248–9; ☎ 081 41 75 82; Via Chiaia 1-2; bus R2 to Piazza Trieste e Trento) and **Intra Moenia** (Map pp244–6; ☎ 081 29 07 20; Piazza Bellini 70; bus CD to Via Santa Maria di Costantinopoli). For reviews of these see p113 and p111, respectively.

Another classic café is the **Gran Caffè Cimmino** (Map pp248–9; ☎ 081 41 83 03; Via G Filangieri 12/13; ☽ Mon-Sat; bus R2 to Piazza Trieste e Trento). In the heart of the city's upmarket shopping district, it has an outdoor terrace and uniformed waiters who earn their tips serving a steady stream of designer-clad customers.

LONTANO DA DOVE Map pp244-6

☎ 081 549 43 04; Via Bellini 3; ☽ 10.30am-1pm & 5pm-1am Wed-Sat, 10.30am-1pm & 5-8pm Tue; bus CD to Via Santa Maria di Costantinopoli

This is the ideal place to discuss Baudelaire over an espresso while listening to Chet Baker. In the bohemian Piazza Bellini area, Lontano da Dove is a laid-back literary café that hosts poetry readings and plays jazz.

S'MOVE Map pp248-9

☎ 081 764 58 13; Vico dei Sospiri 10a; ☽ Sep-Jul; bus C25 to Riviera di Chiaia

Pronounced 'smoove', S'move is one of Chiaia's top drinking spots. A perennial favourite with the area's well-dressed young drinkers, it's a friendly place with a colourful modern look that's as good for an early-evening drink as it is for a late dance. The music is generally house or techno.

SUPERFLY Map pp244-6

☎ 347 127 21 78; Via Cisterna dell'Olio 12; ☽ Tue-Sun; metro Piazza Dante

One of a series of bars along Via Cisterna dell'Olio, the Superfly is a cool jazz hangout. A tiny contemporary-style bar – there are only five barstools – it often fills quickly but drinkers happily spill out onto the street. The barman mixes a range of cocktails; his daiquiris are said to be particularly good.

TEMPIO DI BACCIO Map pp244-6

☎ 081 29 43 54; Vico San Domenico Maggiore 1; bus CS to Via Duomo

A pricey wine bar situated in a cellar, Tempio di Baccio boasts innovative décor that combines neon lights, life-size Greek statues, a horse's head and chains. The music is smooth and laid-back and the wine is sold by the bottle (about €20).

TRINITY BAR Map pp244-6

☎ 081 551 45 69; Calata Trinità Maggiore 5; bus CD to Via Monteoliveto

From the outside Trinity Bar looks just like any other café on the block, so why it should draw bigger crowds than anywhere else on busy Piazza del Gesù Nuovo is a mystery. Still, it does, so do as the locals do – grab a bottle of beer, light your fag and hang out.

VIBES Map pp244-6

☎ 081 551 39 84; Largo San Giovanni Maggiore 26/7; ☽ 8am-3am Mon-Fri, 7pm-3am Sat & Sun; bus R2 to Corso Umberto I

A fashionable bar in a picturesque square, Vibes is friendly, trendy and fun. During the day it serves coffee to a stream of students from the nearby university, while at night it transforms itself into a buzzing drinking spot and live-music venue. The metal-grey interior, complete with small dance floor, is usually heaving, but if you're lucky you'll find a seat outside. Music is mainly jazz-orientated.

WHITE BAR Map pp248-9

☎ 081 64 45 82; Vico Satriano 3b; bus C25 to Riviera di Chiaia

A newcomer to the Neapolitan night-life scene, this bar has quickly found approval with the city's cool set. As the name suggests the look is minimalist white, while the atmosphere is decidedly moneyed.

OPERA

Opera and Naples go together like a house on fire. After La Scala in Milan, the Teatro San Carlo is considered Italy's most important opera house and regularly stages world-class performances. Which is just as well, as the Neapolitan audience is hugely demanding. Big-star status is not enough to justify rapturous applause and top singers are expected to justify their reputations. When they do there is no more appreciative audience.

Watching an opera at San Carlo is a memorable experience, especially as tickets are not easy to come by. Most are snapped up by season ticket holders who pay up to €800 for a year's subscription.

The opera season at Teatro San Carlo runs from January to December with a mid-season break in July and August. Tickets are not cheap: reckon on €35 (€15 if you're under 26) for a place in the sixth tier and €90 for a seat in the stalls.

For reservations contact the **Teatro San Carlo Box Office** (Map pp248–9; ☎ 081 797 23 31, 081 797 24 12; www.teatrosancarlo.it; Via San Carlo 98) at the theatre itself or go online.

For current performances check the local press.

TEATRO SAN CARLO Map pp248-9
☎ 081 797 21 11; www.teatrosancarlo.it; Via San Carlo 98; box office 10am-3pm Tue-Sun Oct-May, 10am-4.30pm Mon-Fri Jun-Sep; bus R2 to Via San Carlo

Italy's largest opera house, the opulent Teatro San Carlo is one of the world's premier venues. A six-tier arena in classical gold and red, it can seat up to 1000 people. The year-round programme is largely traditional; works by Wagner, Tchaikovsky and Verdi are reliable crowd-pleasers. The theatre also showcases dance performances; for more information, see p125.

CLUBBING
Neapolitans are enthusiastic clubbers, but most of the big clubs are out of town and are virtually impossible to get to without a car. Those in town tend to be small-scale affairs, often gouged out of the tufa rock that underlies much of the city. Despite this you should find somewhere to suit your tastes – there's everything from seriously expensive, seriously tacky soap-star hangouts to grungy rock caverns and labyrinthine gay discos.

Most places open around 10.30pm or 11pm and continue through to the early hours, although it's worth noting that some places either close up for the summer (usually July to September) or transfer to an out-of-town beach location. Opening hours are only included here when they vary from the norm.

Admission charges vary, but expect to pay anywhere between €5 and €25, which may or may not include a drink.

Clubs are mainly concentrated in the *centro storico* and Chiaia areas.

ARENILE DI BAGNOLI Off Map pp242-3
☎ 081 230 30 50; Via Nuova Bagnoli 10; admission €10; May-Sep; metro Bagnoli

This huge complex near the sea in Bagnoli has several bars and cabanas which regularly host concerts, particularly in the hot summer months when Neapolitan night owls look to the beach for their fun. It's also the venue for the annual **Neapolis Rock Festival** (p132). Without wheels it's a difficult place to get to.

BAR B Map pp244-6
☎ 081 28 76 81; Via Giovanni Manna 14; Thu & Sat; bus CS to Via Duomo

One of Italy's biggest gay saunas (see opposite), Bar B opens its steamy doors to revellers on Thursday and Saturday nights. Boys dance to a mix of Latin American and techno in this labyrinthine pleasure palace.

CHEZ MOI Map pp248-9
☎ 081 40 75 26; Via del Parco Margherita 13; metro Amedeo

For more than 20 year *Napoli per bene* (roughly translated as 'moneyed Naples') has been partying at Chez Moi. A small conventional disco, some distance out of the centre, it continues to attract suits and elegant dresses more than grunge and jeans.

EX-ESS Map pp248-9
☎ 081 246 17 29; Via Martucci 28/30; admission €15; midnight-4am Tue-Sat Oct-May; metro Amedeo

One of Naples' swishest discos, Ex-ess is a favourite playground of the seriously well-heeled.

Things heat up late as the house music urges the beautiful people onto the dance floor.

FREEZER Map pp242-3

☎ 081 750 24 37; Centro Direzionale Isola G6; ☽ Tue-Sun Sep-Jul; metro Garibaldi

A gay favourite, Freezer provides a futuristic and surreal setting for Naples' most extravagant clubbers. Dressed to kill in fabulously concocted costumes of plastic and latex, they match perfectly the industrial Clockwork Orange–style décor of acid-green walls, neon lights and heavy-duty steel. Resident DJs play a mix of up-to-the-minute house and dance.

GOA DISCOBÀ Map pp248-9

☎ 081 41 02 70; Largo Principessa R Pignatelli 217; ☽ 7pm-3am Tue-Sun; bus C25 to Riviera di Chiaia

Famous for its frozen cocktails, Goa is where soap stars and their perma-tanned hangers-on come to let their hair down. It's a dressy place with modern décor and a mainly commercial soundtrack.

LA MELA Map pp248-9

☎ 081 41 02 70; Via dei Mille 40/bis; ☽ Thu-Sat; metro Piazza Dante

Right next door to the British Consulate, this well-known disco is good for a city-centre boogie. Guest DJs spin mainstream sounds and the young dancers are good-looking and up for it. If you like dressing up wait for one of the many theme nights.

LORNA DOONÈ Map pp248-9

☎ 081 254 10 80; Vico Satriano 19; ☽ 7pm-3am Tue-Sun; bus C25 to Riviera di Chiaia

Lorna Doonè is nearly always packed, but on Friday night it's virtually impossible to squeeze in. DJs pump out a selection of chill-out, house and tribal sounds to the hip 25-plus Chiaia crowd.

NEW AGE DISCO Map pp244-6

☎ 081 29 58 08; Via Atri 36; admission €8; ☽ Tue-Sun; metro Piazza Dante

From its cavernous quarters in the *centro storico*, the New Age bangs out everything from '80s-revival music to industrial and techno. A predominantly gay disco, it has a darkroom, and screens films on Friday and Sunday nights.

SLOVENLY RNR BAR Map pp244-6

☎ 081 29 23 72; Vico San Geronimo 24; bus R2 to Corso Umberto I

In a former life this underground cellar was known as Echos Club. It's had a change of name but it's more or less the same scene – heavy metal, indie rock and new talent. A novelty is the bizarre cinema night on Tuesday that features films by such cult directors as Russ Meyer, director of *Faster Pussycat…Kill! Kill!*

UNDERGROUND Map pp244-6

☎ 081 552 75 75; Vico Santa Maria dell'Aiuto 4; ☽ Tue-Sun; bus CS to Via Diaz

Cut into the tufa stone under the *centro storico*, Underground is a favourite disco for Naples'

Entertainment – Clubbing

Gay & Lesbian Naples

The islands off the coast of Naples have been a popular gay destination for hundreds of years. Capri and Ischia, in particular, have established reputations as fertile cruising grounds. On the mainland things are not so open. Naples, like most southern Italian cities, is a conservative place where the traditional role of the family is sustained by the all-seeing Church.

Fortunately Neapolitans rarely leave the last word to the authorities, and although the gay scene is hardly cutting edge, it does exist. There's no particular gay part of town but the tight alleyways of the *centro storico* conceal several good gay spots. It's also becoming increasingly common for straight clubs to host regular gay and lesbian nights. Details are provided in the gay press and through local organisations (see p213). Throughout this chapter gay bars and clubs are included in the main listings.

Some gay venues insist you have an Arci-Gay membership card. These cost €10 and are available from any venue that requests them.

Naples boasts a number of saunas. The most famous are:

Bar B (Map pp244-6; ☎ 081 28 76 81; Via Giovanni Manna 14; admission €12; ☽ 2pm-1am; bus CS to Via Duomo) Bar B claims to be one of Italy's largest gay saunas. On three levels, it advertises two bars, five darkrooms, one Finnish sauna, one Turkish bath and a Jacuzzi.

Blu Angels (Map pp242-3; ☎ 081 562 52 98; Centro Direzionale Isola A7; admission €12; ☽ 3.30pm-midnight; metro Garibaldi) This place is similarly well equipped, with two Finnish saunas, one Turkish bath, a gym and a darkroom.

gay community. Spread out over two levels, it is noted for its fine cocktails and smooth sounds, with local jazz and blues outfits regularly performing on the small stage. There's also a darkroom.

VELVET ZONE Map pp244-6

☎ 347 810 73 28; Via Cisterna dell'Olio 11; admission €10; ☷ mid-Sep–May; metro Piazza Dante

Different night, different sound; you'll hear an eclectic mix of hip-hop, rock, techno, pop and more at the Velvet. There are occasional live gigs but most of the time it's a DJ and one helluva hot dance floor.

MUSIC

Most people associate Naples with opera and corny classics such as the advertisers' favourite 'O Sole Mio'. Although there's some truth in this stereotype, it doesn't tell the whole story. There is, for example, a thriving jazz culture. Most nights of the week it's possible to catch a live concert and big-name jazz stars regularly perform. Fans of classical-music are also well catered for with year-round performances and numerous festivals.

But come to Naples and hope to catch a big rock concert and you'll probably be disappointed. Other than the occasional gig in Piazza del Plebiscito or at the Stadio San Paolo, large international groups rarely make it as far as Naples. Many, in fact, never venture further south than Bologna. The Neapolis Rock Festival, however, is the exception, drawing big-name acts and huge crowds.

Ticket prices range from about €5 to €10 for a jazz gig in a club to €25 for a big stadium concert. In the smaller venues you can usually buy your ticket at the door but for bigger events they are available from the small box office in the CD section of the bookshop Feltrinelli (Map pp248–9; ☎ 081 240 54 11; Piazza dei Martiri) or from an agency such as Box Office (Map pp244-6; ☎ 081 551 91 88; Galleria Umberto I 15-16).

Naples' premier classical-music organisation, Associazione Scarlatti (Map pp248–9; ☎ 081 40 60 11; www.napoli.com/assocscarlatti in Italian; Piazza dei Martiri 58; bus C25 to Riviera di Chiaia), organises an annual programme of chamber-music concerts. Contact the organisation directly for information.

Music Festivals

Neapolis Rock Festival (www.neapolis.it) A huge international rock fest billed as the largest in southern Italy. Every July in Bagnoli.

Rock

NOTTING HILL Map pp244-6

☎ 081 554 08 39; Piazza Dante 88/a; ☷ Oct-May; metro Piazza Dante

A well-known venue for rock and indie gigs, Notting Hill stages Italian and international bands as well as regular turns by local DJs. Housed in a cellar on Piazza Dante, it's a fairly small place which gets very busy, particularly on Saturday night.

PALAPARTENOPE Off Map pp242-3

☎ 081 570 00 08; Via Barbagallo 115; www.palapartenope.it in Italian; bus 152

In the Fuorigrotta zone, west of Mergellina, the Palapartenope is the biggest indoor concert venue in Naples. Although it's a pretty uninspiring arena, it seats over 8000 and stages both Italian and international acts.

STADIO SAN PAOLO Off Map pp242-3

☎ 081 593 23 23; Piazzale Vincenzo Tecchio, Fuorigrotta; bus 152

The massive football stadium sometimes hosts big-name Italian groups. Italian rock god Vasco Rossi sold out here, performing to 80,000 delirious Neapolitan fans.

Jazz

AROUND MIDNIGHT Map p247

☎ 081 558 28 34; Via Bonito 32a; metro Vanvitelli

One of Naples' most famous jazz clubs, Around Midnight has live music six nights out of seven. Concerts are generally mainstream, but the occasional blues band puts on a performance. Some way out of the city centre, this is for true aficionados.

BOURBON STREET Map pp244-6

☎ 328 068 72 21; Via Bellini 3; ☷ Sep-Jun; bus CD to Via Santa Maria di Costantinopoli

A small corner of New Orleans in the centre of Naples. The tunes certainly fit the bill, with American and Italian jazz musicians performing virtually every night to a knowledgeable and appreciative clientele.

MURAT Map pp244-6

☎ 081 544 59 19; Via Bellini 8; ☾ Sep-Jun; bus CD to Via Santa Maria di Costantinopoli

Great cocktails, smooth sounds and a fashionable older crowd make this a laid-back place for a relaxed drink. There are concerts at weekends with local and international artists playing a largely jazz-based repertoire.

OTTO JAZZ CLUB Map p247

☎ 081 552 43 73; Piazzetta Cariati 23; ☾ Sep-Jun; funicular Centrale to Corso Vittorio Emanuele

Up the hill towards Vomero, Otto's is considered by many to be the top jazz joint in town. Over the years it has hosted some of the biggest names in jazz and today still features top-quality concerts by local and international artists. There's also a drinks menu with more than 200 cocktails.

Classical

CAPPELLA DELLA PIETÀ DEI TURCHINI Map p247

☎ 081 40 23 95; www.turchini.it in Italian; Via Santa Caterina da Siena 38; funicular Centrale to Corso Vittorio Emanuele

Home to the Baroque Orchestra Cappella della Pietà dei Turchini, this deconsecrated church is an evocative venue for a classical concert. Works by 17th- and 18th-century Neapolitan composers form the core of the orchestra's repertoire. Tickets for concerts cost about €10.

SPORTS, HEALTH & FITNESS
Watching Sport
FOOTBALL

Despite losing a relegation battle (in the courts, rather than on the playing field; see p134 for more information) from Italy's second division, Naples' football team is the third-most supported in the country. Only northern giants Juventus and Milan can claim more *tifosi* (fans). Big matches attract crowds of up to 80,000 to the San Paolo stadium where the light blues play on alternate Sundays.

The football season runs from September to May with a short mid-season break around Christmas. The cost of a ticket varies depending on the opposition but as a rough guide you can expect to pay around €20 for a place in the *curve* (the stands located behind the goals) and up to €50 for the *tribune* (side stands).

Tickets are available from the stadium, **Stadio San Paolo** (off Map pp242–3; ticket information ☎ 081 593 23 23; Piazzale Vincenzo Tecchio; bus 152) or from the official outlet **Azzurro Service** (Map pp242–3; ☎ 081 593 40 01; Via Galeota 17; bus 152). Both are in the Fuorigrotta district which is west of Mergellina.

For further information on Naples' football team check out www.calcionapoli.it (in Italian).

Football match, Stadio San Paolo (above)

Film Producer Saves the Day

More used to casting the hero than playing one, movie mogul Aurelio De Laurentiis became a saviour to thousands of *tifosi* (fans) when he bought Napoli football club in September 2004. The last act in a long-running saga, the De Laurentiis deal effectively secured the future of professional football in Naples – at least until the next scandal.

In recent years the ups and downs of Napoli would have stretched the imagination of all but the Italian football-following public. A club president imprisoned for selling fake paintings on a cable shopping channel, players being attacked by irate fans, relegation, promotion, relegation again, numerous changes of manager and, finally, bankruptcy.

In August 2004 Napoli SSC (Società Sportiva Calcio) was declared bankrupt. The coffers were empty and no amount of creative accounting could cover the fact. This was a crushing blow as under Italian league rules, to play in the league you have first to pay your subscription fees and Napoli couldn't even afford to pay their bootboys.

But like all good Italian scandals, it ended up in the courts; and like all good dramas it had a cast in place. Head bogeyman Franco Carraro, president of Italy's football federation, came down from Rome to see that the league rules were being followed, mayor Rosa Jervolino and regional president Antonio Bassolino traipsed into court hoping to play on the emotional sensibilities of the judge, while controversial businessman Luciano Gaucci promised fans that he'd sort out everything.

A larger-than-life man who'd made a name for himself as chairman of Perugia and Catania football clubs, Gaucci failed to win public support and the club's receivers didn't buy his proposals. Instead they went for Aurelio De Laurentiis who, for a paltry £20 million (roughly the price of a top international player), was able to acquire Italy's third-most followed football team.

Whether or not Laurentiis will be able to fulfil his promise to have Napoli competing in Europe within five years remains to be seen. To do so the team would have to get out of *Serie* C1 (Italy's third division) pretty sharpish, win promotion from the second division and start playing for one of Italy's top six slots. Still, in the mad world of Italian football you wouldn't bet against it. After all, it wasn't so very long ago that Maradona was leading Napoli to victory in the *scudetto* (national championship) in 1987 and 1990, and in the UEFA Cup in 1989.

TENNIS

Naples is never going to compete with Paris or London as a venue for a grand-slam event. However, every April the **Tennis Club Napoli** (Map pp248–9; ☎ 081 761 46 56; Viale Anton Dohrn; bus C25 to Riviera di Chiaia) hosts the Naples Open tournament. You're unlikely to spot many top-rank players but entrance to the games is free until the final stages. Contact the club directly for tickets.

Outdoor Activities

Running is a popular activity and places to jog include the seafront between Castel dell'Ovo and Mergellina, Villa Comunale and the Parco di Capodimonte.

Serious road runners descend on Naples in March for the city marathon. If you feel you're up to the 42km course you can get further information by calling the organisers on ☎ 081 873 19 5 or logging in at www .napolimarathon.it (in Italian).

Health & Fitness

GYMS

Neapolitans are great gym-goers. For a city-centre workout there are a number of places.

One you could try is **Athenae** (Map pp248–9; ☎ 081 40 73 34; Via dei Mille 16; admission €10; ✆ 8am-10pm Mon-Fri, 9am-6pm Sat, 9am-12.30pm Sun; metro Amedeo) a well-furnished gym offering everything from spinning and step to kick boxing.

SWIMMING

You're unlikely to want to go swimming in the sea in central Naples – the water's not very clean and with so many better options within easy travelling distance the prospect isn't overly appealing. If you're determined to take the plunge head out to Posillipo. A favourite spot there is **La Gaiola** (take bus C27 to Via Posillipo, then, on foot, go left down Discesa Coroglio and left again down Discesa la Gaiola).

In town there are two public swimming pools:

Piscina Collana (off Map p247; ☎ 081 560 19 88; Via Rossini 8, Vomero; adult/child €4/2; ✆ 9.30am-2.30pm & 3.30-9pm Mon-Sat, 9am-4pm Sun Jul-Aug; bus C30 to Via Rossini) A 25m indoor pool with a sunbathing area.

Piscina Scandone (off Map pp242–3; ☎ 081 570 26 36; Via Giochi del Mediteraneo; adult/child under 12 €6/3; ✆ 9am-7pm Jul-Aug; Cumana rail to Edenlandia) In the Fuorigrotta area, this is a 50m indoor pool.

Shopping

Shopping

Neapolitans like to shop almost as much as they like to eat. In this city they can happily combine both; the open-air markets (see p144) are some of the best in Italy, as are the numerous delicatessens and *pasticcerie* (pastry shops).

Food aside, shopping in Naples is a fascinating and fun combination of the old and the new, with the sophisticated strut of the designer boutiques in Chiaia against the dusty, dark shops in the *centro storico* (historic centre). There's diversity, too, in the number of enterprising individuals running small idiosyncratic shops and the overall lack of the anonymous international stores you find in most cities this size. Chains in Naples tend to be family-run and low-key. **Gay-Odin** (p139), a chocolate shop with several branches in town, is a good example of a culinary winner that Neapolitans have, regrettably, kept to themselves.

If you want to minimise the chaos and energy on the streets (not easy in Naples), avoid hitting the main shopping strips on Saturday morning. And for the best bargains and one-of-a-kind deals, stick to the smaller shops rather than department stores.

Aside from all kinds of edible treats, Naples is renowned for its jewellery (particularly cameos and coral), its lemon liqueur limoncello, and for its craft of the crèche: a big-business world of Christmas-crib miniatures that dates back more than 600 years (see p138 for more information).

Shopping Areas

Naples' shopping map is neatly divided between 'upmarket and expensive' and 'cheap and cheerful'. If you're after top-designer threads, have an amble up Chiaia's Via Calabritto: a palm-flanked pedestrian way where you can flash your gold card at Armani and similarly classy retailers. More 'Made in Italy' haute fashion can be found close by in stores on Via dei Mille and Via G Filangieri.

Via Chiaia has mid-priced but smart shops and boutiques, and runs between Piazza dei Martiri and the grand Piazza Trieste e Trento. Heading north from here is Naples main shopping street, well-heeled Via Toledo, with its big-store branches, traditional shops, Italian and international fashion, ice cream and *sfogliatelle* (pastry) stalls.

For atmosphere and original wares, the *centro storico*'s narrow quirky streets are hard to beat with their antique shops, delicatessens and artisan workshops; this is where you buy stock for your Christmas manger (or doll's house). Don't miss it.

Another shop-happy district is Vomero, with its pedestrianised Via A Scarlatti lined with department stores, boutiques and smaller shops. It's a fairly anonymous street, however, where only the presence of a *pasticceria* or two will remind you which country you are in.

If you can take the noise, the smells and the crowds, Naples' markets may be the most memorable shopping experience of all (see p144). There are bargains, too, from the boot-leggers found throughout the centre with their wares displayed on the pavement. Always bargain and be wary of the sometimes-dud DVD and CD copies.

Opening Hours

Shops are usually open from 9am to 1pm and 3.30pm to 7.30pm (in winter) or 4pm to 8pm (in summer) Monday to Saturday, although a small boutique or speciality shop may not open until 10am, and afternoon hours might be shortened. Department stores and larger chains are open from 9.30am to 7.30pm. Many shops throughout the city close in August.

Where opening hours are listed in the reviews below, it indicates that they vary from standard opening times.

Consumer Taxes

A value-added tax of around 19%, known as IVA (*Imposta de Valore Aggiunto*), is slapped onto just about everything you buy. If you are a non-EU resident and spend more than €154.94 on a purchase, you can claim a refund when you leave. See p212 for more information.

After you have made your purchase, make sure that you are given the receipt. By law, the *guardia de finanza* (special financial police) can make a spot check of your purchases outside the shop and if you don't have a receipt, you may be fined.

CENTRO STORICO

BERISIO Map pp244-6 · Books
☎ 081 549 90 90; Via Port 'Alba 28-29; metro Piazza Dante

One of a row of bookshops dealing in scholastic, rare and antique books. A great place to browse as, although they are all written in Italian, many books are beautifully illustrated and cover Naples' history, architecture and culture.

BLUE CHIARA LUCE Map pp244-6 · Clothing
☎ 081 45 18 93; Via dei Tribunali 340; metro Piazza Dante

The name gives little away and the window display also doesn't help much with its classical statuettes draped in material. Peer inside and you see the seamstress hard at work. A man's suit here will cost around €85, dresses less, and there is a selection of material to choose from (or you can bring your own). Favourite garments can be copied – probably the safest option, unless you speak Italian.

CHARCUTERIE Map pp244-6 · Food
☎ 081 551 69 81; Via Benedetto Croce 43; metro Piazza Dante

Despite the cop-out name, this small deli is unabashedly geared to tourists. There are some nifty gift ideas for those hard-to-shop-for friends, including bags of stripy pasta, brilliantly coloured spices and herbs, lemon-flavoured olive oil, macaroons, grappa and chocolate-coated figs. Everything is beautifully packaged and, if you can't find what you want, chances are the near-identical shop next door will have it.

ENOTECA DANTE Map pp244-6 · Wine
☎ 081 549 96 89; Piazza Dante 189-19; metro Piazza Dante

An excellent range of Italian wines spread over two spacious rooms. Despite the obvious emphasis on the local Campanian *vino*, you can also pick up a good Sicilian or Tuscan vintages. Prices are good and, if you're not too fussed about flavour, there's usually a bin of €2 vintage – in bottles and with corks – by the door.

LA GALLERIE BOMBONIERE
Map pp244-6 · Gifts
☎ 081 551 80 95; Via Enrico Pessina; metro Piazza Dante

Perhaps the best place in town for traditional chintzy ceramics, if that's your thing. Every inch of shelving in this massive old shop is piled high with floral-patterned ceramics, along with cameos, fussy decorations and silver. Prices are very reasonable.

LATE E NATURA Map pp244-6 · Food
☎ 081 45 90 69; Via dei Tribunali 44; metro Piazza Dante

A choice small deli with outside racks displaying traditional goodies such as bags of shiny sun-dried peppers and tomatoes, ready-mixed spices for pasta and risotto, all kinds of wonderful pasta shapes, cheese including fresh ricotta and mozzarella, and some health foods such as bulgur wheat, pulses and aromatic teas.

LIMONÉ Map pp244-6 · Gifts
☎ 081 29 94 29; www.limoncellodinapoli.it in Italian; Piazza San Gaetano 72; metro Piazza Dante or Cavour

People travel across town for the organic limoncello, made on the premises using traditional methods which include peeling the lemons by hand. They also make *crema di melone* (melon liqueur), which is equally delicious, despite being the colour and consistency of hair conditioner. The fancy bottles will add class to anyone's kitchen and tastings are available, if you ask nicely.

MECINO Map pp244-6 · Boutique
☎ 081 552 12 04; Piazza San Domenico Maggiore 1-2; metro Piazza Dante

A practical yet stylish range of floaty women's wear in cotton and linen. The colours are cool and earthy, with lots of russet red and olive green. Best buys are the separates, such as perfectly cut waistcoats and trousers which, at €86 a pair, aren't cheap but are made to last, and have that distinct air of Italian chic. A modest range of snazzy accessories is also on sale here.

Craft of the Crèche

On and around Via San Gregorio Armeno in the *centro storico*, shops sell just one thing or, rather, they sell thousands of very little things. This is the strange home of Naples' nativity scenes, or *presepi*, whose origins date back to 1025. The craft didn't reach its golden age until the 18th century under the reign of the crèche-crazed Bourbon monarch Charles III. The *presepi* appealed to Neapolitans because they served both as a demonstration of faith and as a way to flaunt one's riches, no matter how meagre these were.

These days, Italians arrive from all over the country at Christmas time to buy furniture for their crib at home. The tiny objects and figurines range from the sublime to the supremely kitsch. You can buy an exquisite hand-carved Virgin Mary, a tiny roast pig, a baby Jesus with a flashing halo, a dish of pasta, or just marvel at a 25-piece biblical scene complete with electrically pumped running water. The crib-makers have also expanded the genre to include landmarks of Naples, local heroes and contemporary celebrities. Some of the most entertaining *presepi* shops include:

Corcione (Map pp244-6; ☎ 081 29 77 85; Via dei Tribunali 34) This place has some spectacular larger models with water features and dizzy detail. You can duck around and see the workshop out back.

Giuseppe Ferrigno (Map pp244-6; ☎ 081 552 31 48; Via San Gregorio Armeno 8) One of the most famous *presepi* shops. Ferrigno's terracotta figures are sought by collectors worldwide.

L'Arte del Pulcinella (Map pp244-6; ☎ 081 70 88 31; Via dei Tribunali 338) Specialises, rather oddly, in exquisitely carved bunches of red peppers – large and small. Also here are dramatic black masks with red ribbon for a real class act at Carnival time.

Maria Costabile (Map pp244-6; ☎ 081 559 11 86; Via Benedetto Croce 38) It's not just angels, halos and sanctification here; this place sells all kinds of tiny stuff, such as models of animals, furniture and, in particular, food. It's a small, thickly covered display space, so don't swing any handbags around – breakages must be paid for.

OSPEDALE DELLE BAMBOLE

Map pp244-6 *Dolls*
☎ 081 20 30 67; Via San Biagio dei Librai 81; metro Piazza Dante

You may not happen to have a doll that needs urgent medical attention while you are visiting Naples, but this charming doll hospital is still worth a visit. A Neapolitan institution, it's tiny and packed full of dolls and parts of dolls, as well as puppets. There is a definite Pinocchio feel to the place.

ROBERTO COLETTE Map pp244-6 *Art*
☎ 081 442 07 92; Via dei Tribunali 86; metro Piazza Dante

More exquisitely crafted *presepi* (nativity scene) figures (above), as well as fruit, vegetables, tiny loaves of bread and animals. There's also Pierrots, Venetian-style masks and hanging angels to give your home a heavenly feel.

SECRETIELLO Map pp244-6 *Jewellery*
☎ 081 552 30 09; Via San Biagio dei Librai 18; metro Piazza Dante

A quaint stuck-in-a-timewarp shop that sells all description of old silver, including teapots, frames, candlesticks, platters and some wonderfully *Mafioso*-looking heavy silver-link chains. The elderly owner of the tiny shop is always up for giving you a good price on an item.

SOUND CHECK Map pp244-6 *Music*
☎ 081 551 69 40; Via Benedetto Croce 5;
🕑 10am-2pm & 3-7.30pm Mon-Fri, 10am-1.30pm & 4.15-7.30pm Sat; metro Piazza Dante

In the heart of the *centro storico*, this place sells an eclectic range of music, ranging from big-beat boogie-woogie orchestras to Brazilian crooning and North African rhythm. There's an excellent vinyl selection as well. You can also buy concert tickets here and find out what's happening on the Naples music scene.

TATTOO Map pp244-6 *Music*
☎ 081 552 12 51; www.tattoorecords.cjb.net in Italian; Piazzetta del Nilo 15; metro Piazza Dante

Most categories of music are stocked here, although the focus is on hip-hop and soul. While this place carries CDs and tapes, vinyl is the big seller. The owner knows his business and is very obliging if you want to listen before you buy.

TRÉS JOLIE Map pp244-6 *Gifts*
☎ 081 45 18 93; Via dei Tribunali 165; metro Piazza Dante

Folksy and kitsch but fun, this swing-a-cat-size shop sells home-décor items, including teapots, watering cans and lamps, all in painted wood. The owner, Maria, does most of the painting, hence the feminine themes of flowers, butterflies and the like.

TOLEDO & QUARTIERI SPAGNOLI

ANTICHE DELIZIE Map pp244-6   *Food*
☎ 081 551 30 88; Via Pasquale Scura 14; metro Montesanto

Don't come here hungry, because this is one of Naples' most famous delis, and when you step inside you'll understand why. The smells are heavenly, and everything looks irresistibly fresh and delicious. There's a prepared-food section including aubergine antipasti and *caprignetti* (goat's cheese stuffed with herbs), as well as equally appetising pasta dishes. Whole hams hang over the counter, which is crammed with mozzarella and other cheeses, plus salamis and other cold cuts. Local wines are on sale, too, making this the perfect place for a picnic pit-stop (there's a bakery just up the road).

ANTONIO BARBARO Map pp248-9   *Shoes*
☎ 081 42 56 07; Piazza Trieste e Trento; bus CS to Trieste e Trento

Fashionable and funky footwear from designers such as Camper, Adidas, Walsh, Ralph Lauren, Wusho and Paciotti. Nobody likes to wear a pair of shoes for more than a season in this town, which is why there is a spoilt-for-choice number of shoe shops around. This one is larger than most – at the very least, check out the window display.

DOLCE IDEA Map pp244-6   *Food*
☎ 081 420 30 90; Via S Liborio 2; ✆ Sep–mid-Jul; metro Montesanto

These traditional Neapolitan chocolates have won several international awards; judge for yourself by biting into one of their heavenly dark truffles. With their pretty painted lids, the boxes are almost as memorable. Chocolate connoisseurs (or those after a free sample) can make an appointment to visit the workshop; otherwise, read the history of the company (in Italian and English) in a small booklet available at the shop. Failing that, at least drool over the window display.

FAMÁ Map pp244-6   *Accessories*
☎ 081 552 55 67; Via Toledo 9; metro Piazza Dante

In this corner store you'll find a good selection of colourful, hip bags, as well as snap-shut classic leather handbags, wallets and, for the business bod, a range of important-looking briefcases. For a lot less dosh, pick up a nifty straw-and-leather tote (around €10) or a soigné silk-and-sequinned number that costs a little more. You may be able to get the price down if you smile a lot; the congenial staff are open to bargaining.

FUSARO Map pp244-6   *Men's Clothing*
☎ 081 420 70 14; Via Toledo 28; bus CS to Via Toledo

The men's fashions at Fusaro (which has several branches in town) are aimed squarely at the stylish, but corporate 30- and 40-somethings, and are slick and fashionable. There's a constant influx of new designs. The emphasis here is on collar and cuffs with plenty of colour and style choice, plus high-quality shirt materials such as silk, linen and cotton. The prices here are reasonable to expensive.

GALLERIA UMBERTO I
Map pp248-9   *Shopping Centre*
Via San Carlo; ✆ 24hrs; bus R2 to Via San Carlo

A grand Renaissance-style shopping gallery, with a soaring glass-and-steel dome and a giant central mosaic of the Zodiac. Inaugurated in 1890, the arcade was built to replace the whole neighbourhood of Santa Brigida which was wiped out by a cholera epidemic. Not as exclusive as it was in Naples' *belle époque* era, there are still several reputable shops here and a couple of smart cafés. It's popular with locals taking their early evening *passeggiata* (stroll).

GARLIC Map pp244-6   *Boutique*
☎ 081 5524 49 66; Via Toledo 111; metro Piazza Dante

This boutique sells savvy urbanwear, plus spray-on-style tiny T-shirts and funky outfits for clubbing. Draws in a young, image-conscious crowd searching for that distinctive head-turning look. Check out downstairs for the best bargains.

GAY-ODIN Map pp244-6   *Food*
☎ 081 40 00 63; Via Toledo 214; ✆ 9.30am-8pm Mon-Sat, 10am-2pm Sun; metro Piazza Dante

The peculiar name gives little away. No, not a gay bar, but based on a suitably sugary tale. Apparently, master chocolate-maker Isidore Odin fell in love with his assistant Onorina Gay; the rest is delicious history. At last count, there were five branches around town with the one on Via Benedetto Croce dating back to 1894. The chocolates here are delicious, with plenty of palate-pleasing varieties, including a wicked little number with chillies. The packages look like jewel boxes.

INTIMISSIMI Map pp244-6 *Lingerie*
☎ 081 552 55 67; Via Toledo 47-48; metro Piazza Dante

Despite the high-street chain label (there are three branches in Naples alone), Intimissimi is well worth checking out for its classy, reasonably priced undies. There are chic colour mixes, such as deep red and black satin ensembles which will have you – and yours – purring with pleasure.

LA RIGGIOLA NAPOLETANA
Map pp244-6 *Art*
☎ 081 551 80 22; Via Donnalbina 22; bus R2 to Corso Umberto I

Make room in your case for a couple of these exquisite traditional tiles. They are real works of art and worthy of a frame. They are also an original gift idea for those 'too good for just a T-shirt' friends and family back home.

LA RINASCENTE
Map pp244-6 *Department Store*
☎ 081 41 15 11; Via Toledo 340; ☼ 9am-8pm Mon-Fri, 9am-2pm Sat, 10am-9pm Sun; bus CS to Via Toledo

Upmarket shopping at this well-placed store, which has bludgeoned all the local competition to become the best-known department store in the city. Sells a good variety of products, from quality clothes, cosmetics and perfumes to household goods and crockery.

LEONETTI CIRO Map pp244-6 *Toys*
☎ 081 41 27 65; Via Toledo 350-51; metro Piazza Dante

A two-storey traditional toy wonderland, with wooden toys, puzzles and games, plus soft toys, fancy dress, and the standard shelves of pink and plastic for girls, and footballs and model cars for boys. Be prepared, your children will be ever eager to enter but hard to drag away. Luckily there are ice creams for sale nearby to bribe them with.

LIBRERIA INTERNAZIONALE
Map pp244-6 *Books*
☎ 081 41 52 11; Via Toledo 249-250; bus CS to Piazza Trieste Trento

A classic wood-panelled bookshop which has a small selection of books in English, including maps and guidebooks, and a healthy number of Lonely Planet titles. Books here are mostly in Italian, although it's always fun to look at the pictures, especially in those sumptuous Italian cookery books.

MAGLIERIA Map pp244-6 *Boutique*
☎ 081 40 36 49; Via Toledo 291; bus CS to Via Toledo

Step inside this glorious shop, even if you're a fashion misfit – or just want to have a gawp. The interior is gorgeous: all stained glass and carved wood. The women's fashions are appropriately glamorous with a collection that, at the time of writing, included sequin-

La Rinascente (above)

patterned silk dresses in brilliant peacock colours. There are usually more relaxed linen separates for sale as well, and just a few pairs of classy shoes.

NAPOLIMANIA Map pp244-6 *Souvenirs*
☎ 081 41 41 20; Via Toledo 312; bus CS to Via Toledo

A tongue-in-cheek souvenir shop with quirky keyrings, jolly clocks, CDs, kitsch statues, T-shirts and baseball caps emblazoned with witty slogans, and lots more frivolous items that, thanks to the owner's wacky imagination, are not available elsewhere. Sophisticates should stay away.

TERZO MILLENNIO
Map pp244-6 *Health & Beauty*
☎ 081 251 24 22; Via Toledo 320; Tue-Sat; bus CS to Via Toledo

A sophisticated beauty salon for a spot of self-pampering, Terzo Millennio offers acid peeling, massages, sauna, waxing, acne treatment, manicures, pedicures or a simple haircut and blowdry (€11). There is a solarium and the possibility of a whole beauty day that includes most of the above for a mere €73 – not much for a makeover these days.

USED WORLD VINTAGE
Map pp244-6 *Second-Hand Clothing*
Vico Campane 10c; bus CS to Via Toledo

An eye-popping selection of vintage second-hand fashion, including pick-and-mix casual wear, floaty dresses and the occasional designer label. The prices are good, but the presentation is more jumble sale than colour-coordinated racks. The opening times are also erratic and depend on the whim of the owner.

SANTA LUCIA

BOWINKEL Map pp248-9 *Antiques*
☎ 081 764 43 40; Via Santa Lucia 24; bus C25 to Via Partenope

One of two branches of this renowned dealer in vintage prints and photographs, plus a superb selection of period watercolour paintings. If you can't find what you are looking for here, check out the larger branch at **Piazza dei Martiri 24** (☎ 081 764 43 44; bus C25 to Via Partenope). The helpful owner speaks a smattering of English and will arrange shipments abroad.

DE PAOLA Map pp248-9 *Jewellery*
☎ 081 245 11 69; Via Cesario Console 23; bus C25 to Via Partenope

A respected name in the cameo world, this business was started by Vincenzo de Paola about 70 years ago. These days his son Renato is skilfully carrying on the tradition while Vincenzo carries on in the Vomero branch (see p142). As well as the gorgeous, finely carved cameos, de Paola also works in coral to produce a fine display of necklaces, earrings, pendants and bracelets.

INTERFOOD Map pp248-9 *Wine*
☎ 081 764 97 92; Via Santa Lucia 6-8; bus C25 to Via Partenope

You can usually get good gluggable deals here, like three bottles of reasonable wine for just €15. Just off the piazza, this *enoteca* (wine bar) sells mainly wines from Campania, a rising star on the Italian wine scene. Among the more reliable producers, look for *Cantina del Taburno* or *Ocone* or *D'Ambra* for reds, and *Falanghina* or *Coda de Volpe* for whites. Interfood also sells bags of *cantucci* (almond) biscuits, cocktail mixes and fancy jars of liqueur-doused fruit.

VOMERO

DE PAOLA CAMEOS Map p247 *Jewellery*
☎ 081 578 29 10; Via Annibale Caccavello 67;
🕒 9am-2pm Mon-Sat, 9am-noon Sun; funicular
Centrale to Fuga

This is the main de Paola workshop and, if you're after a cameo, an excellent place for choice and quality. There is a splendid range, including traditional designs and colour, and more contemporary and unusual styles. The owner, Vincenzo, speaks good English and there's no pressure to buy.

ELENA MIRO Map p247 *Boutique*
☎ 081 556 99 47; Via Bernini 47-49; funicular Centrale to Fuga

Well established on the fashion scene, Elena Miro has made her name outside the country as well as at home. This is where Naples' elegant, 30-something woman heads when she wants a special-occasion suit or dress. Well cut with very few synthetic materials used, Miro's clothes are reasonably priced for the quality and keep their shape well. There are branches throughout the city.

GALLERIA SCARLATTI
Map p247 *Shopping Centre*
☎ 081 578 86 83; Via A Scarlatti 142; funicular
Centrale to Fuga

A few metres down the hill from Piazza Fuga, this shopping centre looks a bit dated and could do with a lick of paint and some cool designer to do a revamp. It's still worth ducking into, however, with its fashion parade of reasonably priced boutiques, shoe shops and the like.

KUROS Map p247 *Men's Clothing*
☎ 081 578 86 83; Via A Scarlatti 142; funicular
Centrale to Fuga

The place to buy your tailored suit off the peg at a tolerable price. There is a small select showroom and the staff are helpful without being pushy, but you won't get far if you don't speak Italian.

OTTICA BOVA Map p247 *Optician*
☎ 081 578 90 52; Via Gianlorenzo Bernini 38;
funicular Centrale to Fuga

A modest-sized optician with a surprisingly wide selection of frames and sunglasses, the latter including such famous brands as Gucci, Diesel and Burberry. Ottica Bova also sells cameras and film.

OVIESSE Map p247 *Clothing*
☎ 081 556 18 08; Via Michele Kerbaker 22-26;
funicular Centrale to Fuga

Using modern fabrics and bright colours, this store sells mainstream fashion for guys and gals. Snug knit sweaters start at around €10 and there are jackets, jeans, shirts and skirts, as well as a limited range of sportswear.

PETER PAN Map p247 *Children's Clothing*
☎ 081 40 19 54; Via Gianlorenzo Bernini 24; funicular
Centrale to Fuga

Eye-catching basics for tots to teens at comparatively low prices (Italians love to dress their children in designer wear). There are even better reductions at sale time. Always in stock are smocked dresses, dungarees, T-shirts, vests and other separates in a myriad of colours and cuts.

PROMOD Map p247 *Boutique*
☎ 081 229 56 26; Via A Scarlatti 120; funicular
Centrale to Fuga

Avoid Saturday, when this boutique jostles with streetwise hip young things looking for threads. There are often brilliant buys such as dazzling (and unusual) peacock-green and turquoise leather jackets and button-up rainbow knits. Prices are good, whether items are on sale or not.

SPAR Map p247 *Supermarket*
☎ 081 440 34 99; Via Gianlorenzo Bernini; funicular
Centrale to Fuga

A good-sized branch of this well-known international chain. Handy for all those items travellers frequently forget, like toothpaste and soap, as well as basic picnic goodies, breakfast cereals and all the other typical supermarket products. There is also a modest choice of wine, beer and liqueurs.

TOYS Map p247 *Toys*
☎ 081 578 40 10; Via Bernini 17; funicular Centrale
to Fuga

Beside the restaurant **La Cantina di Sica** (p117), this place, with a spacious basement showroom, is heaven for doll collectors. They range from the bald, ugly and lifelike to hand-knitted and colourful. Boys will have to make do with mini-tractors, model cars and the like.

LA SANITÀ & CAPODIMONTE

CASEIFICIO LA BUFALA Map p250 *Food*
☎ 081 564 50 17; Via S Teresa degli Scalzi; ⏱ 9am-1pm & 3.30pm-7.30pm; metro Cavour
Shiny-tiled small deli specialising in buffalo mozzarella. It also sells other cheeses, as well as bags of pasta, jars of sauces and local wine. In fact, everything you need to make a home-cooked Italian meal, aside from the cookery book.

CIAO MARILYN Map p250 *Boutique*
Piazza Cavour 1; metro Cavour
This is the place to pick up your sequinned ballgown in time for next year's season. Despite the incongruous location in this grimy, traffic-choked square, this boutique has a lot of class, as well as a loyal following with its sexy and feminine line of eveningwear.

Clothing Sizes
Measurements approximate only, try before you buy

Women's Clothing

Aus/UK	8	10	12	14	16	18
Europe	36	38	40	42	44	46
Japan	5	7	9	11	13	15
USA	6	8	10	12	14	16

Women's Shoes

Aus/USA	5	6	7	8	9	10
Europe	35	36	37	38	39	40
France only	35	36	38	39	40	42
Japan	22	23	24	25	26	27
UK	3½	4½	5½	6½	7½	8½

Men's Clothing

Aus	92	96	100	104	108	112
Europe	46	48	50	52	54	56
Japan	S		M	M		L
UK/USA	35	36	37	38	39	40

Men's Shirts (Collar Sizes)

Aus/Japan	38	39	40	41	42	43
Europe	38	39	40	41	42	43
UK/USA	15	15½	16	16½	17	17½

Men's Shoes

Aus/UK	7	8	9	10	11	12
Europe	41	42	43	44½	46	47
Japan	26	27	27½	28	29	30
USA	7½	8½	9½	10½	11½	12½

MERCATO
ALBERTO DE FALCO
Map pp244-6 *Collectables*
☎ 081 552 82 45; Corso Umberto I 24; bus R2 Corso Umberto I
Take a trip back in time at this hole in the wall, which is a treasure trove of tarnished old coins and notes from the pre-euro era. Examples of prices are: a 1974 500 lire note for €5, a 1939 one lire note for €12, and a 1900 one lire coin for €36. There are on-the-spot valuations, and according to the experts, prices are fair.

CARPISA Map pp244-6 *Accessories*
☎ 081 563 57 77; Corso Umberto I 342; bus R2 Corso Umberto I
This shop has loads of bags but don't expect any elegant leather numbers – it's anything but. These bags are fun, colourful and cheap, with eye-squinting colours and snazzy designs. There are larger totes as well, which are practical as well as funky. You can pick up something to sling over your shoulder here for as little as €10.

CRYPTON Map pp244-6 *Sportswear*
Corso Umberto I 105; bus R2 Corso Umberto I
Two crammed-full floors of mainly sports attire, although you can pick up a pair of jeans here, too. The layout is haphazard but if you take the time to peruse the racks you can find some excellent threads. Brands include Crypton, Lee, Wrangler and Lonsdale, and there is a limited range of trainers as well.

IL CASEIFICIO MARIGLIANO
Map pp244-6 *Food*
☎ 081 553 51 65; Via Castromediano; metro Garibaldi
A tiny shop just off Piazza Garibaldi (next to Hotel Terminus), specialising in buffalo mozzarella, plus an alluring selection of salamis, olives and cheese. The ricotta *limone torta* (lemon cheesecake) has real made-by-mamma appeal. You can buy it by the slice. This place is way off the tourist trail – it's where the locals go.

LE PULCI Map pp244-6 *Antiques*
Via Santa Maria a Cancello 1; metro Garibaldi
Don't expect anything fancy; this place is more like a mini boot sale disgorging a array of weird stuff and collectables including old phones, keys and postcards. The owner also displays a peculiar penchant for rusty padlocks, ancient keys and old umbrellas. If this turns you on, there are similar places round the corner. Bargaining is part of the fun.

MUSEO APERTO NAPOLI

Map pp244-6   *Souvenirs*

☎ 081 563 60 63; Via Pietro Colletta; metro Garibaldi

Museo Aperto Napoli is a classy souvenir shop that is attached to a privately run tourism office (there's a good pizzeria here, too). Expect to pay a bit more, but at least everything is under one roof – which saves on shoe leather. There are classical-style ceramics, religious figurines, art books, gloves, jewellery, ornaments and original artwork, as well as more knick-knacky stuff.

OTTICA STREVELLA Map pp244-6 *Optician*

☎ 081 20 27 34; Corso Umberto I 213; bus R2 to Corso Umberto I

A full-service optician who offers free eye tests and can sell you prescription glasses from €50, depending on your frame choice. There's also a vast range of sunglasses with big-name brands such as Polo Sport, Gucci, DKNY, Ray-Ban, Ralph Lauren, Cesare Paciotti, Valentino and (of course) Armani. There is also a basic repair service.

PASTIFICIO LA TORRE Map pp244-6 *Food*

☎ 081 553 63 73; Via Sopramuro 30-31; bus R2 to Corso Umberto I

Appropriately located and surrounded by fruit-and-veg stalls in the atmospheric and earthy Mercato district; follow the signs. As the name suggests, this *pastificio* is a bastion of home-made pasta; all the shapes and sizes are here, including gnocchi. No preservatives are used, so don't plan on keeping purchases in the suitcase for too long.

PELLETTERE DE GREGORIO

Map pp244-6   *Suitcases*

☎ 081 26 97 51; Via D Marvasi 10; metro Garibaldi

This is the place to come if you need to buy an extra suitcase to carry all those bottles of limoncello home. Many of the well-known brands are here, including Samsonite and Belsey, as well as cheaper copies for €10 or less.

ZERODODOCI OF BENETTON

Map pp244-6   *Children's Clothing*

☎ 081 26 12 51; Corso Umberto I 215; bus R2 to Corso Umberto I

No real surprises here except that, during the sales, you can get 70% discount on these cheerful snazzy basics for youngsters. Benetton's clothes may be pricey at new-season time but they are very durable and some of the smaller designs are dangerously cute. Be aware that sizes tend to run teenier than elsewhere.

CHIAIA

ANTOINE COIFFEUR Map pp248-9 *Beauty*

☎ 081 41 88 56; Via Chiaia 132; ☯ Fri-Wed; bus CS to Piazza Trieste e Trento

It may not be the most funky or upmarket hairdresser in town but Antoine Coiffeur has all the enthusiasm and attitude you expect from an Italian hairdresser. There is a full range of hair treatments on offer, plus manicures and pedicures. A straightforward cut will cost from €15, a perm from €55 and a simple shampoo is a mere €2.50. This place is popular, so make an appointment.

Market Time

The markets in Naples are challenging, atmospheric and just a tad edgy: hang on to your wallet and beware the digital/video camera scam reported by several readers – in short, you buy an empty box. If you *are* tempted, then insist that you buy the camera that is being demonstrated, rather than one that is pre-packaged. The following markets are the best:

Fiera Antiquaria Napoletana (Map pp248-9; Villa Comunale; ☯ 8am-4pm last Sun of month; bus C25 to Riviera di Chiaia) With an evocative setting by the waterfront, this market has silverware, jewellery, furniture, paintings, prints and wonderful overpriced junk.

La Pignasecca (Map pp244-6; Via Pignasecca & Toledo's surrounding streets; ☯ 8am-1pm; metro Montesanto) Naples' largest, oldest and arguably best market in a bustling downmarket neighbourhood. Sells it all, including fruit and vegetables, CDs, lingerie, kitchenware and live eels.

Mercato dei Fiori (Map pp244-6; Castel Nuovo; ☯ dawn-noon; bus R2 to Piazza del Municipio) Has a colourful flower market.

Porto Nolana (Map pp244-6; Via Porta Nolana; ☯ 8am-6pm; metro Garibaldi) Seems to be constantly spreading, with trestle streets in all the surrounding streets heaving under their wares. Again, it's all here, including lots of fascinating junk, plus food and fish.

CARLA G Map pp248-9 *Boutique*
☎ 081 44 29 86; Via Vittorio Colonna 15E-F; metro Amedeo

Just a few racks of clothes in this season's colours, such as beautifully cut cuffed trousers and jackets, simple tops with sequins, and classic dresses in simple figure-hugging designs. Ignore the snooty shop assistants; these are fabrics you can't help but fondle.

DELIBERTI Map pp248-9 *Shoes*
☎ 081 41 60 64; Via Chiaia 10 ; bus C25 to Piazza dei Martiri

This is the place to replenish your designer-trainer range. Sales are common, and brands include Helmut Lang, Puma, Bikkemberg and Adidas. Keep an eye out for a small, dangerous-looking range of stilettos by Casadei.

EDDY MONETTI Map pp248-9 *Boutique*
☎ 081 40 70 64; Piazzetta Santa Caterina; bus C25 to Piazza dei Martiri

Selling sophisticated women's fashions, Eddy Monetti opened in 1887. The emphasis here is on an exquisite cut, with more jackets, trousers and skirts than dresses. Prices start at about the €250 mark for separates. Monetti is an institution among those wealthy fashion-conscious Neapolitans who are just edging into middle age.

ETHNIC Map pp248-9 *Boutique*
☎ 081 41 39 68; Via dei Mille 83A; metro Amedeo

A boutique that has a dazzling range of hip young clothes in colours such as shocking pink and acid green for the streetwise and for clubbers. Designs are real one-offs and include

skirts, tops and figure-clinging dresses. There are a few funky shoes here, too, including unusual combos like rainbow-coloured rubber thongs with kitten heels.

FELTRINELLI Map pp248-9 *Books*
☎ 081 240 54 11; Piazza dei Martiri; ☯ 10am-10pm Mon-Sat, 10am-2pm Sun; bus C25 to Piazza dei Martiri

A three-storey monster on the corner of the piazza, with a wide range of books spread over all floors. There's a fair-sized English-language section, including novels and some of the latest publications on Neapolitan culture and history. There is also a vast stock of CDs, videos and DVDs. Concert and theatre tickets can be purchased on the 1st floor.

GIALLO NAPOLI Map pp248-9 *Art*
☎ 081 764 06 22; Via Carlo Poerio 114; bus C25 to Piazza dei Martiri

You could do your entire gift shopping in one swoop at this superb ceramics shop. They make it easy with a worldwide shipping service. The craftsmanship is exceptional and sophisticated, with subtle colours and classic designs. Not cheap but the quality is up there. The tiles make great hotplates.

JOSSA Map pp248-9 *Men's Clothing*
☎ 081 39 92 23; Via Carlo Poerio 43; bus C25 to Riviera di Chiaia

Nothing restrained about the ultra-cool men's clothing here: lilac-and-white striped jackets, brilliantly coloured shirts, trousers of various cuts, snappy knitwear and soft leather jackets in rich earthy colours. These are the kinds of clothes guys who drive Ferraris wear to get noticed.

Shopping – Chiaia

Porto Nolana's seafood market (opposite)

LIGHT Map pp248-9 *Jewellery*
☎ 081 40 03 25; Via Chiaia 225; bus C25 to Piazza Trieste e Trento

There's a rare, old-fashioned courtesy about the owners of this small jewellery shop. Expect to be offered a coffee, even if you don't buy. You may be tempted, however. The display cases are crammed with some fine coral and jade pieces, as well as cameos, delicately made pendants, strings of pearls and exquisite silver crosses.

LUISA SPAGNOLI Map pp248-9 *Boutique*
☎ 081 075 45 91; Via Chiaia 200; bus CS to Piazza Trieste e Trento

Fashions come and go, but Luisa Spagnoli rarely wavers from her design vision: pure lines in excellent-quality cotton, wool and silk. The best buys here are the classic suits that keep their shape for years. For a touch of glamour, there are fur stoles, little black numbers and body-fitting satin dresses with retro taffeta petticoats. There are two more branches, on Via Toledo 316 and Via Cimarosa 87/A.

MARINELLA Map pp248-9 *Men's Clothing*
☎ 081 245 11 82; Piazza Vittoria 287; bus C28 to Piazza Vittoria

It has been possible to buy shirts, sweaters, shoes and, most famously, ties in this shop since 1914. Some of Marinella's most loyal customers were Luchino Visconti, Aristotle Onassis, Gabriele d'Annunzio and Gianni Agnelli. You can have a tie made to measure here, or cop out and buy one off the peg.

PASKAL Map pp248-9 *Shoes*
☎ 081 40 94 66; Via dei Mille 83A; metro Amedeo

A fashionable range of casual and classy women's footwear including funky laced trainer-boots by Tommy Hilfiger, strappy sandals by Café Noir, savvy streetwear by Clarks and dressy new designs by Jeiday; something for everyone to step out in.

PISTOLA Map pp248-9 *Boutique*
☎ 081 42 20 58; Via Santa Caterina a Chiaia; bus CS to Piazza dei Martiri

The most famous shop in Naples for gloves. But forget the woolly, made-by-gran style you may be used to; these are made from butter-soft lambskin and kidskin in colours to match every outfit. Specialist shops like this are always fun to check out, even if you don't fancy forking out this much for your mitts.

SEPHORA Map pp248-9 *Perfume*
☎ 081 41 76 54; Via Chiaia 145; bus CS to Piazza del Martiri

Beautifully packaged perfumes, including most of the best-known brands, as well as locally produced traditional scents. If you ask nicely, you can get a few sample squirts.

TABACCHERIA SISIMBRO
Map pp248-9 *Cigars*
☎ 081 40 69 83; Via San Pasquale a Chiaia 74-76; metro Amedeo

Sisimbro is a temple to tobacco, with a wide assortment of cigarettes including the hard-to-find Dunhill, Dupont and Cartier varieties. This is also the place to come for Cuban cigars, which are maintained at optimum temperature in a special humidified walk-in room. The shop also stocks a handsome range of Italian pipes and various smoking accessories, such as cigar cutters, lighters and ashtrays.

VERDEGRANO Map pp248-9 *Homewares*
☎ 081 668 92 34; Via Santa Teresa a Chiaia 24; ☮ 10am-1.30pm & 4.30-7pm Wed-Mon; metro Amedeo

A small classy shop selling fine porcelain pots, vases, plates and decorative items, exquisitely patterned and painted by hand. The prices are reasonable and there are some easy-to-pack smaller pieces. The main drawback here is the lack of choice and space; small children – and the clumsy – should definitely wait outside.

YAMAMAY Map pp248-9 *Boutique*
☎ 081 40 51 93; Via Chiaia 94; bus CS to Piazza dei Martiri

Stylish beachwear aimed at the young and pencil-slim – and proud of it. There are several racks of stringy little numbers to choose from, with plenty of colour and design choice. If you wait until after the beach season, however, you can stock up for next year at half the price.

MERGELLINA & POSILLIPO
L'OASI DELLA NATURA
Map pp248-9 *Food*
☎ 081 761 22 13; Via Jan Palach 31; metro Mergellina

A rare herb and health-food shop with a fairly limited selection of aromatherapy oils, Bach flower essences, incense and vitamins, plus a few healthy munchies like bags of mixed nuts, dried apricots and seeds, fancy jars of organic jams and local organic honey.

Sleeping

Sleeping

Ranging from opulent five-star hotels to beautiful historic palazzi (mansions), small family-run B&Bs and cheerful backpacker hostels, accommodation in Naples is plentiful and full of character.

Many of the best-known budget hotels are situated around Stazione Centrale and Piazza Garibaldi. Although cheap and central, this is not a particularly pleasant place to be and at night it becomes distinctly seedy. All the places we list, however, were clean, safe and reliable at the time of research.

To stay in the heart of historic Naples head for the *centro storico* (historic centre). There are a host of charming places hidden away behind heavy doors, and if you're lucky you could find yourself sleeping in the frescoed bedroom of a 16th-century palazzo. The chaotic atmosphere in the centre is great fun and many of the city's sights are within easy walking distance.

For a more refined feel, Santa Lucia is an expensive area by the sea. Here you'll find the top hotels in town along busy Via Partenope. Further round the seafront, Chiaia is well-to-do and elegant, while Mergellina is handy for popping out to the Bay of Naples islands on a hydrofoil. To really get away from it all, take a funicular up to Vomero with its spectacular views and relatively muted atmosphere.

The accommodation listed in the reviews below has been divided into two categories, mid-range to top end and cheap sleeps. Those places listed as cheap sleeps charge anywhere up to €100 for a double and €50 for a single.

Accommodation Styles

BED & BREAKFAST
A recent trend, B&Bs are becoming increasingly popular in Naples. New places are opening all the time and there are some great places to be found.

The bonus of B&B accommodation is that Italian houses are invariably spotlessly clean. The drawback is that you are staying in someone's home and might be expected to operate within their timetable. However, many of the new B&Bs are run by young Neapolitans who'll happily give you your room key and leave you to get on with it. Rooms in the newer places generally come with an en-suite bathroom.

Naples' **main tourist office** (Map pp248–9; ☎ 081 40 53 11; Piazza dei Martiri 58; ☽ 8.30am-2.30pm Mon-Fri) has a list of B&B operators, or you can try **Rent A Bed** (Map pp248–9; ☎ 081 41 77 21; www.rentabed.com; Vico Sergente Maggiore 16; per night from €31) an agency with an extensive selection of B&Bs and apartments on its books, covering Naples, the Amalfi Coast and the Bay of Naples islands.

HOSTELS
There are several hostels in Naples, but the only *ostello per la gioventù* (youth hostel) affiliated to Hostelling International (HI) is the Ostello Mergellina (see p159).

Here you'll require a valid HI card. You can either get this in your home country or at any HI youth hostel. In the latter case you either pay the full cost of €16 (over 21 years old) or €12 (under 21), or collect a €3 stamp on each of the first six nights you spend in the hostel. With six stamps you are considered a full member.

For HI contact details, see p209.

Accommodation is in segregated dormitories, although many hostels offer doubles or family rooms (at a higher price per person). Hostels usually have a lock-out period between 9am and 3.30pm. Check-in is 6pm to 10.30pm, although some hostels will allow you a morning check-in before they close for the day. Curfew is usually 10.30pm or 11pm in winter and 11.30pm or midnight in summer. It is usually necessary to pay before 9am on the day of your departure, otherwise you could be charged for another night.

HOTELS

Naples has a wide range of hotels catering to all budgets. Prices are generally cheaper here than in the rest of Italy but recent inflation has led to price hikes across the board. It's also worth noting that the star-rating system relates to facilities only, and gives no indication of value, comfort, atmosphere or friendliness.

At the top end, rooms in converted palazzi are often small (albeit luxurious), and there are seldom swimming pools. Hotels generally provide minibar, air-conditioning, TV, fine linen, 24-hour room service and private baths with hairdryers and bathrobes. Facilities are more basic in mid-range places; you won't always find a hairdryer, minibar, room service or even air-conditioning, and the only guarantee at budget places is a bed and a roof.

Breakfast in cheaper accommodation is rarely worth getting up early for so, if you have the option, save a few bob and pop into a bar for a coffee and *cornetto* (croissant) as the locals do.

Check-in & Check-out Times

Hotels usually require you to check out on the day of departure at any time between 10am and noon. Later than this and you run the risk of being charged for a further night. With check-in times, there are no hard-and-fast rules, but if you are going to arrive late in the afternoon or evening it's probably best to mention this when you book your room.

Many hostels will not accept prior reservations for dormitory beds, so arrive after 10am and, then it's first come, first served. Checkout times are often earlier in hostels, typically around 9am.

Price Ranges

It's very difficult to be precise when outlining price ranges as not only do rates fluctuate madly between periods but also between hotels in the same category. However, as an approximate guide, for a double in a one-star hotel you can expect to pay €40 to €90; in a two-star €45 to €115; in a three-star €75 to €180; in a four–star €140 to €300; and in a five-star from €250. A double in a B&B will cost €70 to €150.

Many hotels offer considerable discounts for low-season visits, longer stays or for weekend breaks. Check hotel websites for special deals.

Lone travellers are particularly hard hit, with single rooms often disproportionately expensive compared to double or triple rooms.

While room prices should always be read as a guide rather than the gospel truth, the rates we quote here are the maximum listed price for each place. Unless otherwise stated all rooms include a bathroom.

Reservations

Although not absolutely necessary, it's always a good idea to book ahead. This is particularly true in May when the **Maggio dei Monumenti** (p9) draws huge crowds and in high season (April to mid-June, Christmas and New Year). Many hotels will request a faxed confirmation of your reservation together with a credit-card number as a deposit. However, a request for a credit-card number does not always mean that the hotel will accept payment by plastic, so check in advance. If you don't have a credit card, you'll often be asked to send a money order to cover the first night's stay.

Many hotels now, however, are encouraging guests to book directly over the Internet which saves the hassle of international faxes and money orders.

When booking make sure you ask for a *camera matrimoniale* if you want a double bed. Ask for a *camera doppia* (double room) and you'll get two twin beds.

Longer-Term Rentals

Expect to pay around €500 per month for a studio apartment or a small one-bedroom place in the centre of Naples. On top of the rent there will be bills for electricity (which is quite expensive in Italy) and gas. There is usually also a *condominio* (building maintenance charge) of between €25 and €155 per month depending on the size and location of the apartment. However, for a longer stay a rented flat can often work out cheaper than an extended hotel sojourn.

Useful publications for flat-hunters include *Bric-a-Brac* (€1.90, Monday, Wednesday and Friday) and *Il Mattone* (€1, Saturday). Estate agents specialising in short-term rentals are listed in the telephone directory under *Agenzie immobiliari*. As a rule, they charge a fee of up to one months' rent for their services.

CENTRO STORICO

For a high-voltage shot of pure Naples, you can't beat the *centro storico*. Nowhere in town is more theatrical than the highly charged Spaccanapoli area, where the streets are dark and the pace is frenetic. Accommodation tends to be charming rather than spectacular – think converted palazzi – and rooms are, on the whole, smaller rather than larger.

ALBERGO SANSEVERO Map pp244-6 *Hotel*
☎ 081 21 09 07; www.albergosansevero.it; Via Santa Maria di Costantinopoli 101; d without/with bathroom €75/95; bus CD to Via Santa Maria di Costantinopoli

This hotel (one of four under the same ownership) is excellent value for money. Situated in a historical building overlooking Piazza Bellini, one of Naples' most atmospheric squares, it's decorated with simple, tasteful wicker. The building is protected so the owners can't erect a sign, making it hard to find. Look for the two fine marble pillars flanking the courtyard entrance as you head north from Piazza Bellini. Breakfast is included in the price.

ALBERGO SANSEVERO DEGAS
Map pp244-6   *Hotel*
☎ 081 551 12 76; www.albergosansevero.it; Calata Trinità Maggiore 53; d without/with bathroom €75/95; bus CD to Via Monteoliveto

So named because the building once belonged to French impressionist painter Edgar Degas, this bright and friendly place offers cool and spacious rooms. Enter the courtyard opposite Caffè Novocento and take the lift to the 3rd floor.

The Best...
- Hotel San Francesco Al Monte (p155)
- Parteno (p159)
- Costantinopoli 104 (right)
- B&B Donnaregina (right)
- Portalba 33 (opposite)

B&B COSTANTINOPOLI Map pp244-6   *B&B*
☎ 081 44 49 62, 333 613 59 27; lauramazzella@hotmail.com; Via Santa Maria di Costantinopoli 27; s/d €65/93; bus CD to Via Santa Maria di Costantinopoli

Don't be put off by the dingy staircase; B&B Costantinopoli is a great place to stay. The family of artists who own this large and exuberantly decorated 3rd-floor flat extend a warm Neapolitan welcome and offer two bright and comfortable rooms.

B&B DONNAREGINA Map pp242-3   *B&B*
☎ 081 44 67 99; Via Settembrini 80; d/tr/q €93/120/150; bus CS to Via Duomo

Step through the door into this treasure trove of a flat and you'll never want to leave. Part art-gallery/museum and part family home, there's not an inch of wall that isn't covered by works of art or lined with heaving bookshelves. Even the open-plan kitchen, complete with huge wooden table, is a picture. The four bedrooms are individually decorated and all have an en-suite bathroom and satellite TV. The garrulous artist–owner cooks breakfast himself, enthusiastically giving pride of plate to his organic *pancetta* (bacon).

CARAVAGGIO HOTEL Map pp244-6   *Hotel*
☎ 081 211 00 66; www.caravaggiohotel.it; Piazza Riario Sforza 157; s/d/ste €118/175/230; bus CS to Via Duomo

A stylish mix of 17th-century elegance and modern design, the four-star Caravaggio is both slick and welcoming. Colourful abstract paintings hang opposite stone arches, yellow sofas line 300 year-old brick walls and original wood-beamed ceilings cap comfortable bedrooms. The mod cons are all there, too, and the staff are friendly.

COSTANTINOPOLI 104 Map pp244-6 *Hotel*
☎ 081 557 10 35; www.costantinopoli104.it; Via Santa Maria di Costantinopoli 104; s/d €145/170; bus CD to Via Santa Maria di Costantinopoli; P

A contemporary Art Deco hotel, Costantinopoli 104 is the result of a stylish refurbishing of a

Sleeping – Centro Storico

Costantinopoli 104 (opposite)

19th-century villa. Rooms are decorated with tasteful simplicity – those on the 1st floor open onto a sun terrace, while ground-floor rooms look out onto the inviting swimming pool. Antique furniture and stained-glass windows add to the sense of understated charm.

HOTEL DES ARTISTES Map pp242-3 *Hotel*
☎ 081 44 61 55; www.hoteldesartistesnaples.it; Via Duomo 61; s/d €90/110; bus CS to Via Duomo
Within a stone's throw of the Duomo, this rather old-fashioned hotel – picture heavy wooden furniture, chandeliers and a colour scheme that relies on brown – offers a warm welcome and large, unspectacular rooms.

HOTEL EUROPEO FLOWERS
Map pp244-6 *Hotel*
☎ 081 551 72 54; www.sea-hotels.com; Via Mezzo-cannone 109/c; d €130; bus R2 to Corso Umberto I
Although technically only a one-star hotel, this place's rooms here have more creature comforts than those at many higher rated places. Air-con, electronic blinds and phones in the bathrooms are all the result of a recent makeover that has left everything looking spic and span. Space, however, is tight and rooms are not large.

HOTEL LE ORCHIDEE Map pp244-6 *Hotel*
☎ 081 551 07 21; fax 081 251 40 88; Corso Umberto I 7; d €98; bus R2 to Corso Umberto I
This busy city-centre hotel boasts few frills, but large, functional and clean rooms. It's well positioned for the ferry terminal and within easy walking distance of the *centro storico*. It's situated on the 5th floor, and you'll need a €0.50 coin for the small lift.

HOTEL NEAPOLIS Map pp244-6 *Hotel*
☎ 081 442 08 15; www.hotelneapolis.com; Via Francesco del Giudice 13; s/d €80/120; bus CD to Via Monteoliveto
An unassuming three-star establishment, the Neapolis is a nice laid-back hotel. The staff are personable, and the rooms are cool and spacious, with some boasting fine views up to Naples' highest point in Vomero. All come with a computer on which you can use the hotel's special software to plan your itinerary of the city.

PORTALBA 33 Map pp244-6 *B&B*
☎ 081 549 32 51; www.portalba33.it; Via Port'Alba 33; s/d €120/150; metro Piazza Dante
To do anything as inelegant as sleep in the magazine-spread setting of this ultra-modish

B&B would almost be a crime. A showcase for emerging artists, Portalba 33 boasts an inspired (or deranged) décor that comprises an antique rocking horse, black-net curtains and red roses, fake-fur bedspreads and purple walls. There is even a weights machine for your mid-morning workout. Exciting and fun, it's all a world apart from the more traditional Neapolitan chaos outside.

SOGGIORNO B&B PARADISO

Map pp244-6 *B&B*

☎ 081 442 15 79; www.soggiornoparadiso.it; Vico Purgatorio ad Arco 7; s/d €70/100; bus CS to Via Duomo
Spread out over two floors, this unpretentious B&B offers 10 decent-enough rooms that are comfortable but leave little lasting impression. Situated far enough from busy Via dei Tribunali to be quiet, it is nevertheless well placed for exploring the centre.

SOGGIORNO SANSEVERO

Map pp244-6 *Hotel*

☎ 081 551 57 42; www.albergosansevero.it; Piazza San Domenico Maggiore 9; d without/with bathroom €75/95; bus CD to Via Monteoliveto
Hidden on the 1st floor of an 18th-century palazzo that once belonged to the Prince of Sansevero, this is the third of the stylish Sansevero hotels. You'll find it just around the corner from the Cappella Sansevero on the eastern side of lively – read noisy at night – Piazza San Domenico Maggiore.

Cheap Sleeps

6 SMALL ROOMS Map pp244-6 *Hostel*

☎ 081 790 13 78; www.at6smallrooms.com; Via Diodata Lioy 18; dm €18, s/d per person €25; bus CD to Via Monteoliveto
On the top floor of a venerable old building, this popular hostel is a cheerful choice. Should the lady downstairs be in the mood there's an evening plate of pasta (€3.50), otherwise you can use the kitchen stove. They only accept same-day phone reservations.

ALBERGO DUOMO Map pp244-6 *Hotel*

☎ 081 26 59 88; hotelduomo@libero.it; Via Duomo 228; s/d €40/65; bus CS to Via Duomo
As the name suggests, this is situated less than 100m from the cathedral. The jaunty pink rooms are comfortable and airy, if a little anonymous. But the price is right and you'd do well to book ahead as rooms go quickly.

HOSTEL OF THE SUN Map pp244-6 *Hostel*

☎ 081 420 63 93; www.hostelnapoli.com; Via Melisurgo 15; dm €18, s/d without bathroom €45/50, d with bathroom €70; bus C55 to Via Depretis
Handy for the ferry terminal, this private hostel has quickly established itself as a backpacker favourite thanks to its ultra-helpful young crew. There is a kitchen, no curfew and access to the Internet costs €1.50 for 30 minutes.

HOTEL BELLINI Map pp244-6 *Hotel*

☎ 081 45 69 96; fax 081 29 22 56; Vico San Paolo 44; s/d €55/80; bus CS to Via Duomo
Tucked away in the heart of Spaccanapoli, this small hotel is full of faded Neapolitan charm. The rooms are decorated in a style that's so fashion-free that it's almost trendy, but not quite. A perennial choice for travellers of all ages, it oozes character and what the owner can't tell you about the city isn't worth knowing.

HOTEL COLLEGE EUROPEO

Map pp244-6 *Hotel*

☎ 081 551 72 54; www.sea-hotels.it; Via Mezzocannone 109/c; s/d €62/93; bus R2 to Corso Umberto I
Sister hotel of the slightly more expensive Europeo Flowers, the College offers salmon-pink rooms that are pretty good value for money, if a little small. A favourite with young visitors, it's smack bang in the middle of student country.

HOTEL PIGNATELLI Map pp244-6 *Hotel*

☎ 081 648 49 50; www.hotelpignatellinapoli.com in Italian; Via San Giovanni Maggiore Pignatelli 16; s/d €45/90; bus R2 to Corso Umberto I
Stay at this new hotel in a restored 15th-century noble house and you won't believe your bill. It's incredibly good value. The rooms, which wouldn't look out of place in a three-star pad, are smart and spacious with some boasting original 15th-century wood-beamed ceilings. Breakfast is even included in the price.

LA LOCANDA DELL'ARTE & VICTORIA HOUSE Map pp244-6 *B&B*

☎ 081 564 46 40; www.casaearte.it in Italian; Via Enrico Pessina 66; s/d €70/90; bus CD to Via Enrico Pessina
Run by the same friendly folk, these two B&B options are in the same building overlooking trendy Via Bellini. Rooms in both come with all the requisite comforts, although those in La Locanda are a bit more modern than the larger Victoria rooms. Breakfast is served in the downstairs restaurant.

TOLEDO & QUARTIERI SPAGNOLI

Dividing the Quartieri Spagnoli from the *centro storico*, Via Toledo is Naples' main shopping strip. To the west the Quartieri Spagnoli is notorious for its poverty and crime. Its reputation has, however, been exaggerated and all the hotels we recommend were friendly, comfortable and safe at the time of research.

In this section are you will find everything from expensive hotels in charmless grey concrete blocks to beautifully restored convents.

ALBERGO NAPOLIT'AMO

Map pp244-6   *Hotel*

☎ 081 497 71 10; albergonapolitamo@virgilio.it; Via San Tommaso d'Aquino 15; s/d €75/115; bus R2 to Via Medina

Just off the frenetic Via Toledo, this bright and breezy three-star place is friendly and informal. The lime greens, yellows and blues combine with the wicker and bamboo furniture to give it a relaxed sunny demeanour. From the breakfast room there are some lovely views over Piazza del Municipio.

GRAND HOTEL ORIENTE

Map pp244-6   *Hotel*

☎ 081 551 21 33; www.oriente.it; Via A Diaz 44; s/d €180/310; bus CS to Via Diaz; Ⓟ

A fairly charmless hotel catering to aircrews and the business trade, the Oriente is nevertheless smack-bang in the centre of town and offers all the creature comforts you would expect from a four-star hotel. It's always worth checking out for special weekend rates as you can get some good deals.

HOTEL CONVENTO Map pp244-6   *Hotel*

☎ 081 40 39 77; www.hotelilconvento.com; Via Speranzella 137/a; s/d €145/180; bus CS to Via Toledo

Taking its name from the neighbouring convent, the Hotel Convento is an excellent option in an area that is not really known for its warm-hearted hospitality. The elegantly simple rooms combine cream colours and dark woods with the odd patch of original 16th-century brickwork. Cough up €180 and you can bag a room with a private roof garden. Two rooms here are equipped for disabled travellers.

HOTEL TOLEDO Map pp244-6   *Hotel*

☎ 081 40 68 71; www.hoteltoledo.com; Via Concezione a Montecalvario 15; s/d €85/180; bus CS to Via Toledo; Ⓟ

The Hotel Toledo is a rather smart little hotel snugly situated in an old three-storey building. The smallish rooms have terracotta tiles and mod cons and, although a little on the dark side, are comfortable. There's also a roof-top terrace for breakfast.

NAPOLIT'AMO Map pp244-6   *Hotel*

☎ 081 552 36 26; www.napolitamo.it; Via Toledo 148; s €65-75, d €80-105; bus CS to Via Toledo

Escape from the hordes outside and live like the nobility once did at Napolit'amo in the grand 16th-century Palazzo Tocco di Montemiletto. Retaining much of the atmosphere of its former glory days, it boasts magnificent 18th-century mirrors, high ceilings and plenty of natural light. A highly recommended palatial hideaway.

SANSEVERO D'ANGRI Map pp244-6   *Hotel*

☎ 081 21 09 07; www.albergosansevero.it; Piazza VII Settembre 28; d/ste €110/150; bus CS to Via Toledo

Staying here is like actually sleeping in a genuine palace – not surprising given that Vanvitelli, the original architect, also designed the royal palace at Caserta. Some of the huge rooms have interesting frescoes, the parquet is genuine 17th century and Garibaldi was an early guest.

Cheap Sleeps

TOLEDO 205 Map pp244-6   *Apartment*

☎ 081 410 70 77; www.toledo205.it; Via Toledo 205; apt per person €23; bus CS to Via Toledo

Overlooking Galleria Umberto I are two mini-apartments, one for five people and one for four. Neither is luxurious, or even particularly smart, but both are clean and the communal terrace is a definite plus. Ideal for a group of friends who want somewhere cheap and central.

SANTA LUCIA

This is where the super rich come to stay – in the luxury hotels on the seafront. There are, however, a number of less expensive options, many of which boast fantastic views over the Bay of Naples. As a general rule you'll pay slightly more for a room with a sea view.

Sleeping – Toledo & Quartieri Spagnoli

B&B SANTA LUCIA Map pp248-9 *B&B*
☎ 081 245 74 83; www.borgosantalucia.net; Via Santa Lucia 90; d €140; bus C25 to Via Partenope
A spanking new B&B with six sparkling white-tiled rooms. There's not much in the way of character – the reception area resembles an upmarket health clinic – but the rooms are a good size and the location's great, not 50m from the seafront.

GRAND HOTEL SANTA LUCIA
Map pp248-9 *Hotel*
☎ 081 764 06 66; www.santalucia.it in Italian; Via Partenope 46; s/d €235/390; bus C25 to Via Partenope
Five-star elegance and discreet service are the hallmarks of this long-standing hotel. Dating back to 1906, it owes much of its Art Nouveau look to celebrated architect Giovan Battista Comencini. Rooms incorporate all the mod cons with impeccable taste and there is even a nonsmoking floor – something rare in Italy.

GRAND HOTEL VESUVIO
Map pp248-9 *Hotel*
☎ 081 764 00 44; www.vesuvio.it; Via Partenope 45; s/d €370/400; bus C25 to Via Partenope; **P**
The choice of US Presidents – Bill Clinton stayed here during the 1994 G7 summit – the Vesuvio is a Neapolitan landmark. From the explosion of greenery that greets guests to the famed rooftop restaurant, the dedication to luxury is total. Rooms are opulent and the service is never less than top class.

HOTEL EXCELSIOR Map pp248-9 *Hotel*
☎ 081 764 01 11; www.excelsior.it; Via Partenope 48; s/d €270/330; bus C25 to Via Partenope
The third of three luxury hotels lining the sea-front opposite Borgo Marinaro, the Excelsior offers style on a grand scale – massive marble columns, sparkling crystal chandeliers and rooms as large as medium-sized apartments. But as spectacular as the interiors are, it's the views of Mt Vesuvius and Capri that really take the breath away.

HOTEL MIRAMARE Map pp248-9 *Hotel*
☎ 081 764 75 89; www.hotelmiramare.com; Via Nasario Sauro 24; s/d €190/237; bus C25 to Via Partenope
Built in 1914, this Art Nouveau villa now houses a charming seafront hotel. Slightly scruffy around the edges and featuring an alarming black-and-gold ostrich in the foyer, this place oozes the sort of character that only age can confer. The 3rd-floor roof garden is a delight, with flowers, hammocks and sea views.

HOTEL REX Map pp248-9 *Hotel*
☎ 081 764 93 89; www.hotel-rex.it; Via Palepoli 12; d €125; bus C25 to Via Partenope
Just a little bit back from the seafront, the Rex is a welcoming and relaxed three-star pad. The good-sized rooms come with balconies and understated décor and because there's no dining room, breakfast has to be brought up to you. Shame.

Cheap Sleeps

B&B I 34 TURCHI Map pp248-9 *B&B*
☎ 081 764 71 36; www.i34turchi.it; Via Marino Turchi 34; d €100; bus C25 to Via Partenope
More than just a room, you get a small self-contained apartment at this homely B&B. It's divided from the family home, and you get your own key so you're free to come and go as you please. The flat has a small double room on a mezzanine floor and a sofa-bed in the main living area. In the low season the flat-rate price for singles and doubles is €40 per person.

PENSIONE ASTORIA Map pp248-9 *Hotel*
☎ 081 764 99 03; Via Santa Lucia 90; s/d without bathroom €26/50; bus C25 to Via Partenope
In an area that's full of five-star palaces, Pensione Astoria defiantly flies the flag for the budget traveller. Cheap, cheerful and clean, this friendly place has 23 rooms, all of which come with a washbasin, bidet and a TV. The only downside is that rooms overlooking Via Santa Lucia are far from quiet. Also, expect the occasional yap from the owner's territorial Yorkshire terriers.

VOMERO

Vomero is an area apart. More subdued than the city spread out below it, it's largely residential and has few attractions per se. However, the views are magnificent and as a place to get away from the hustle and bustle of the city below it's ideal. Reflecting the genteel atmosphere, accommodation tends to the top end.

GRAND HOTEL PARKER'S
Map pp248-9 *Hotel*
☎ 081 761 24 74; www.grandhotelparkers.com; Corso Vittorio Emanuele I 35; s/d €225/260; bus C28 to Via Tasso; **P**
Named after British marine biologist George Parker Bidder, who owned the hotel from 1889

Hotel San Francesco al Monte (below)

to 1908, Parker's is a stately old pile. Classically decorated with imposing antique furniture and gilt-framed paintings, it offers all the five-star comforts without ever losing its air of genteel calm. The views over the Bay of Naples are wonderful.

HOTEL BELVEDERE Map p247 Hotel
☎ 081 578 81 69; fax 081 578 54 17; Via Tito Angelini 51-59; s/d €100/120; funicular Centrale to Fuga

No other hotel in Naples can offer such a magnificent panorama. Right beside the Certosa di San Martino, the aptly named Hotel Belvedere stands at Naples' highest point. Rooms are fine albeit anonymous, but service can be a bit brusque.

HOTEL BRITANNIQUE Map pp248-9 Hotel
☎ 081 761 41 45; Corso Vittorio Emanuele I 133; s/d €99/158; bus C28 to Via Tasso; P

Just down the road from Parker's, the Britannique presents itself as a haven of British upper-class elegance. The public areas are slightly tatty, there are plenty of floral fabrics and the feel is distinctly old-fashioned. But you can't fault the hotel's lush garden overlooking the sea as a place to escape the vulgar stresses of modern life.

HOTEL SAN FRANCESCO AL MONTE
Map p247 Hotel
☎ 081 423 91 11; www.hotelsanfrancesco.it; Corso Vittorio Emanuele I 328; s/d €240/270; funicular Centrale to Corso Vittorio Emanuele

Housed in a 16th-century monastery, this hotel is a magnificent place to stay. The monks' cells have been converted into stylish rooms, the ancient cloisters house an open-air bar and the barrel-vaulted corridors are cool and atmospheric. There's also a swimming pool.

Cheap Sleeps
HOTEL CRISPI Map pp248-9 Hotel
☎ 081 66 80 48; www.hotelcrispi.it; Via Francesco Crispi 104; s/d €55/90; metro Amedeo

The ivy-clad exterior promises great things which, unfortunately, the gloomy interior fails to provide. Rooms are basic, clean and cheap(ish) and the service is far from a selling point. Still, for the area it's a bargain.

PENSIONE MARGHERITA Map p247 Hotel
☎ 081 556 70 44; Via Domenico Cimarosa 29; s/d €37/65; funicular Centrale to Fuga

This place, just a few doors from the funicular station in Vomero, has views over Capri and

Sorrento. The welcome is motherly, and the large no-frills rooms are simple, airy and clean.

LA SANITÀ & CAPODIMONTE

Some way north of the city centre, there are few hotels in La Sanità and Capodimonte. Of the two we list, the first is near the Museo Archeologico Nazionale, while the second is a short hop to the city ring road.

HOTEL DEL REAL ORTO BOTANICO

Map pp242-3   *Hotel*

☎ 081 442 15 28; Via Foria 192; s/d €78/130; metro Cavour

Bang opposite the botanical gardens and fronting busy Via Foria, this decent three-star hotel is surprisingly quiet. The super-strength double glazing keeps out most of the traffic noise and although the modern rooms leave little impression, they are all a good size and comfortably furnished.

HOTEL VILLA CAPODIMONTE

Map p250   *Hotel*

☎ 081 45 90 00; www.villacapodimonte.it; Via Moiariello; s/d €149/201; bus 24 to Via Capodimonte

On top of Capodimonte hill to the north of the city, this is a modern hotel that's geared towards the business market. But if you want to escape the frenetic city centre it has peaceful rooms with parquet flooring and mod cons, a sauna and a lovely garden. If you're without a car, however, be warned that getting here on public transport is something of a trial.

MERCATO

This is where to find the majority of the city's budget accommodation. In and around Piazza Garibaldi and the Stazione Centrale there are any number of cheap hotels. All those we list were clean and reliable at the time of writing, but be warned that the area is bedlam during the day and unpleasantly dodgy at night.

HOTEL IDEAL Map pp244-6   *Hotel*

☎ 081 26 92 37; www.albergoideal.it; Piazza Garibaldi 99; s/d €60/90; metro Garibaldi

Nobody in their right mind would claim that Piazza Garibaldi is an ideal holiday destination, but it is central and it is cheap. Hotel Ideal is a good-value three-star place on the square. The interior gloss has rather faded and the atmosphere is hectic with high turnover, but the rooms all come with air-con and TV, and the staff are helpful.

HOTEL LUNA ROSSA Map pp244-6   *Hotel*

☎ 081 554 87 52; www.hotellunarossa.it; Via G Pica 20/22; s/d €60/95; metro Garibaldi

Tucked away in a sidestreet near Piazza Garibaldi, the Luna Rossa is a bright, light place run by the daughter of a Neapolitan musician. Each room is named after a Neapolitan song, the lyrics of which are framed in the room itself. Decorated in various hues of pink, the rooms are fine and the bathrooms are large.

HOTEL NUOVO REBECCHINO

Map pp244-6   *Hotel*

☎ 081 553 53 27; www.nuovorebecchino.it; Corso G Garibaldi 356; s/d €105/160; metro Garibaldi; P

After more than 100 years as a hotel the name Nuovo (new) might seem a little out of date, but the Rebecchino is still going strong. The large rooms are surprisingly characterless and decorated with uninspiring floral wallpaper and faux-antique furniture. Parking is available for €14 to €22 per night and the staff will help arrange out-of-town excursions.

HOTEL PRATI Map pp242-3   *Hotel*

☎ 081 26 88 98; www.hotelprati.it; Via C Rosaroll 4; s/d €120/137, full meals €20-25; metro Garibaldi

An inviting three-star hotel in an unattractive area, the friendly Hotel Prati boasts a roof-top restaurant and rooms with all the regular creature comforts. It is a decent middle-of-the-road option either as a hotel or dining venue.

HOTEL SUITE ESEDRA Map pp244-6   *Hotel*

☎ 081 553 70 87; www.sea-hotels.com; Via Cantani 12; s/d €145/180; bus R2 to Corso Umberto I

The Esedra stands tall on a tiny square just off Corso Umberto I half way between the train station and the *centro storico*. The snug rooms are decorated with Neapolitan paintings and you might even find a porthole or two in your bathroom. You can cool off after a hard day's sightseeing with a dip in the hotel pool.

HOTEL VERGILIUS Map pp244-6 _Hotel_

☎ 081 26 97 66; hotelvergilius@hotmail.com; Via G Pica 2-14; s/d €124/145; metro Garibaldi

The wrought ironwork, stained-glass windows and hanging flower baskets provide the Hotel Vergilius with a grand exterior. Inside, it's the size of the rooms that's the best feature; they're particularly welcome in such a tightly packed neighbourhood. The staff are friendly in a blunt Neapolitan way, so don't expect much small talk.

STARHOTEL TERMINUS

Map pp244-6 _Hotel_

☎ 081 779 31 11; www.starhotels.com; Piazza Garibaldi 91; s/d €159/239; metro Garibaldi

The Terminus is large, efficient and impersonal. Like modern business hotels everywhere it makes up for its lack of charm by providing a huge list of services, including satellite TV, fast Internet access, a gym full of weight machines and a shuttle service to and from the airport. After dark the area around the entrance is known as a gay cruising spot.

Cheap Sleeps

HOTEL CASANOVA Map pp242-3 _Hotel_

☎ 081 26 82 87; www.hotelcasanova.com; Corso G Garibaldi 333; s/d without bathroom €28/46, with bathroom €35/56; metro Garibaldi

With a name like a brothel this is, in fact, a charming family hotel with a flowery roof terrace and excellent-value rooms. Use the safer Corso G Garibaldi entrance rather than the main one located on Via Venezia.

HOTEL GALLO Map pp244-6 _Hotel_

☎ 081 20 05 12; fax 081 20 18 49; Via Silvio Spaventa 11; s/d €65/90; metro Garibaldi

This is a bustling little no-nonsense hotel on a street striking south from Piazza Garibaldi. Rooms are functional, clean and tidy, in sharp contrast to the surrounding streets.

HOTEL GINEVRA Map pp242-3 _Hotel_

☎ 081 28 32 10; www.hotelginevra.it; Via Genova 116; s without bathroom €30, d €60-75; metro Garibaldi

This long-time travellers' favourite remains a solid choice with basic rooms and a cheerful atmosphere. The exuberant owners have also opened a slightly pricier option on the same floor with the great name **Ginevra 2** (Via Genova 116; d €75), where rooms are plusher.

HOTEL NETTUNO Map pp244-6 _Hotel_

☎ 081 551 01 93; www.albergonettuno.com; Via Sedile di Porto 9; s/d €50/80; bus R2 to Corso Umberto I

Hotel Nettuno is a solid one-star choice. The featureless rooms are modern and well equipped and the staff efficient and courteous. The only real negative is the noise from the neighbouring buildings that can, and often does, continue well into the night.

HOSTEL PENSIONE MANCINI

Map pp244-6 _Hostel_

☎ 081 553 67 31; www.hostelpensionemancini.com; Via Mancini 33; dm €18, s/d/tr/q €45/55/80/100; metro Garibaldi

Space is tight at this welcoming place, so the rooms can become something of a squeeze, but the atmosphere makes it a pleasant haven from the market outside. Cheaper rooms are also available without a private bathroom.

HOTEL SPERANZA Map pp242-3 _Hotel_

☎ 081 26 92 86; www.hotelsperanza.it in Italian; Via Palermo 31; s/d €40/50; metro Garibaldi

Come here expecting airs and graces and you'll be disappointed, but if you want a clean, modest room in a no-frills family-run pension you'll do all right. All rooms have a TV and all but four have a bathroom.

HOTEL ZARA Map pp242-3 _Hotel_

☎ 081 28 71 25; hotelzar@tin.it; 2nd fl, Via Firenze 81; s/d €50/62; metro Garibaldi

Run by the same family as the **Casanova** (left), this place has attentive service and simple, unpretentious rooms. The book exchange is a welcome source of English reading material.

CHIAIA

Upmarket and vibrant Chiaia is a smart patchwork of cobbled streets and seafront boulevards. People dress up here and the feel is one of glossy money out to play. Not surprisingly, budget accommodation is thin on the ground. Your best bets for cheaper sleeps are the two excellent B&Bs.

B&B CAPPELLA VECCHIA 11

Map pp248-9 _B&B_

☎ 081 240 51 17; www.cappellavecchia11.it; Vico S M a Cappella Vecchia 11; s/d €70/100; bus C25 to Piazza dei Martiri

Run by a super-helpful young couple, this great B&B is a wonderfully laid-back place to stay.

Sleeping – Chiaia

Parteno (opposite)

The modern décor mixes minimalism with bold dashes of colour and pop art to give a breezy upbeat feel. There are six rooms, each done up differently, and a spacious communal area where breakfast is served. Another nice touch is the 24-hour free Internet.

CHIAJA HOTEL DE CHARME
Map pp248-9   *Hotel*
☎ 081 41 55 55; www.hotelchiaia.it in Italian; Via Chiaia 216; s/d/superior €95/140/160; bus CS to Piazza Trieste e Trento
Next door to the noble townhouse that is now the refined and elegant Chiaja Hotel de Charme there was until quite recently a discreet establishment that also catered to paying clients. But the premises are no longer a brothel; instead they are being incorporated into the hotel to provide an extra six rooms. All rooms are individually decorated, many with their original furnishings, while those overlooking Via Chiaia come with a Jacuzzi.

HOTEL MAJESTIC Map pp248-9   *Hotel*
☎ 081 41 65 00; www.majestic.it; Largo Vasto a Chiaia 68; s/d €160/200; bus C25 to Riviera di Chiaia
Situated right in the heart of trendy Chiaia, the Hotel Majestic wins no prizes for character but offers plenty of four-star services. For example, parents can enjoy a night off from the kids thanks to the inhouse baby-sitting service. Some rooms are also equipped for disabled travellers.

HOTEL PINTO-STOREY Map pp248-9   *Hotel*
☎ 081 68 12 60; www.pintostorey.it; 4-5th fl, Via Campiglione Martucci 72; s/d €96/155; metro Amedeo
The rooms here are furnished with period pieces and the beds spread with linen sheets at this laid-back, some might say quite sleepy, three-star hotel. The location is great being within easy walking distance of Naples' smartest shopping strips and Chiaia's lively cobbled streets. Air-con is available for an extra €11 a night.

LE FONTANE DEL MARE
Map pp248-9   *Hotel*
☎ 081 764 34 70; Via Niccolò Tommaseo 14; d without/with bathroom €75/100; bus C25 to Via Partenope
Make sure you've got €0.10 for the lift otherwise you'll be walking up five floors of stairs. Once you get to the top you'll find a modest hotel that offers some of the cheapest views in the neighbourhood. In fact, if you're lucky you'll bag yourself a room which has its bed

positioned so that you need only open your eyes to admire the wonderful panorama. The rooms are a little frayed around the edges, and the welcome can be quite gruff rather than effusive, but the place compensates with loads of character. For a room without a view you'll pay €10 less.

PARTENO Map pp248-9 *Hotel*
☎ 081 245 20 95; www.parteno.it in Italian; Via Partenope 1; d €160; bus C25 to Via Partenope

Discretion and style are the bywords for this intimate and elegant hotel. Hidden in a seafront building, its six rooms, each named after a flower, are exquisitely decorated with period furniture and colourful bouquets. Guests wanting to stretch their legs can use a nearby gym and sauna.

Cheap Sleeps
B&B MORELLI Map pp248-9 *B&B*
☎ 081 245 22 91; www.bbmorelli49.it in Italian; Via Domenico Morelli 49; s/d €65/95; bus C25 to Riviera di Chiaia

Fans of cinema memorabilia and pop culture may appreciate the atmosphere at this B&B, with posters advertising Fellini classics and Almodovar films sharing wall space with Madonna and various other screen icons. The four homely rooms are all decorated with skill and humour, mixing classical Florentine floor tiles with colourful plastic lamps and knick-knacks galore. Great fun.

PENSIONE RUGGIERO Map pp248-9 *Hotel*
☎ 081 66 35 36; hotelrug@libero.it; 3rd fl, Via Campiglione Martucci 72; s/d €70/90; metro Amedeo

As you enter the grand old building near the Amedeo metro station, you'll need a sharp pair of eyes to spot the lift hidden in the corner, which is the entrance to Pensione Ruggiero. The rooms here are bright and inviting and the owners extend a warm welcome.

MERGELLINA & POSILLIPO
On and around the lively seafront in Mergellina there are a number of good mid-range hotels. The youth hostel is a 10-minute walk from the sea, just behind the traffic-choked Piazza Piedigrotta. Mergellina is well connected to the city centre and ideal for an early morning hydrofoil out to one of the Bay islands (see the Bay of Naples & Amalfi Coast chapter on p163 for more on these).

HOTEL AUSONIA Map pp248-9 *Hotel*
☎ 081 68 22 78; hotelausonia@interfree.it; Via Francesco Caracciolo 11; s/d €90/120; bus 140 to Via Francesco Caracciolo

Opposite Mergellina marina, the Ausonia is a welcoming modest hotel. The good-sized rooms all carry a nautical theme with portholes and seafaring paraphernalia liberally scattered around the place. The owner is friendly, and the rates are very reasonable for somewhere so near the sea. Only a couple of rooms have sea views but, surprisingly, you pay no extra for them.

HOTEL CANADA Map pp248-9 *Hotel*
☎ 081 68 20 18; www.sea-hotels.com; Via Mergellina 43; s/d €105/155; metro Mergellina

Ideally situated so that you can enjoy the buzzing seafront activity, the Canada begrudgingly offers eight old-style rooms with tall double doors and heavy wooden blinds. Generally on the small side, some rooms have views but these are noisier than the quieter (and slightly cheaper) back rooms.

HOTEL MERGELLINA Map pp248-9 *Hotel*
☎ 081 248 21 42; www.hotelmergellina.it; Via Giordano Bruno 113; s/d €80/110; metro Mergellina

Recently opened on the busy Via Giordano Bruno, this hotel is a small friendly place. The eight rooms are spacious and simply decorated with antique-style furniture and uncluttered white walls. Noise from the street can be a problem though. Breakfast is included in the price.

HOTEL PARADISO Map pp248-9 *Hotel*
☎ 081 247 51 11; www.hotelparadisonapoli.it; Via Catullo 11; s/d €115/199; funicular Mergellina to S Gioacchino

Some way above the city centre, but your efforts getting up here are amply rewarded. Not only are the views over the Bay of Naples to Mt Vesuvius sensational but the staff are courteous, service is efficient and most of the well-furnished rooms come with a balcony. Expect to pay slightly less for a room without a view.

Cheap Sleeps
OSTELLO MERGELLINA
Map pp242-3 *Hostel*
☎ 081 761 23 46; fax 081 761 23 91; Salita della Grotta 23; dm/d per person €14/16; metro Mergellina

This HI hostel is a reliable choice, although it gets busy in peak periods and some readers have complained that the entrance can be seedy after dark. Laundry facilities are a plus but the 12.30am curfew less so. There's a maximum stay of three nights in July and August. Breakfast is included in the price.

ELSEWHERE

The nearest camp site to Naples is in Pozzuoli – ask at the tourist office for details – and there are a number of reasonably priced hotels and *pensioni* (guesthouses) there, too.

HOTEL TERME PUTEOLANE

Off Map pp242-3 *Hotel*

☎ 081 526 13 03; termeputeolane@tiscalinet.it; Corso Umberto I 195; s/d €52/75; ferrovia Cumana to Pozzuoli

Exuding an air of times past, this grand old hotel in Pozzuoli is frequented as much for its sulphurous airs and thermal treatments as for its large and airy rooms. Between April and December you can complete a course of 12 thermal baths for €103, while it costs €155 to wallow in glorious gloopy mud.

Bay of Naples & the Amalfi Coast

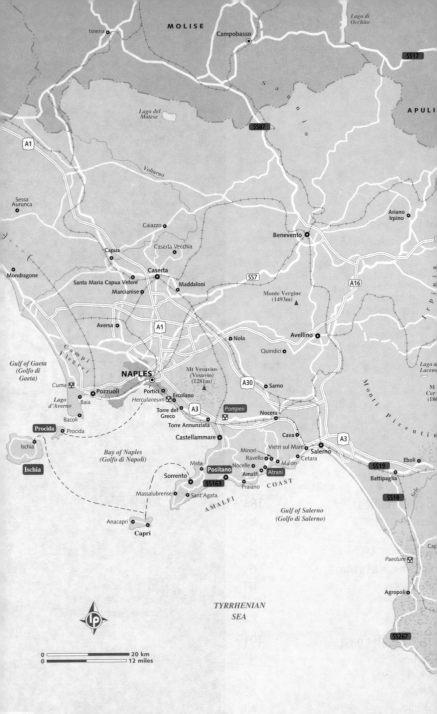

Bay of Naples
& the Amalfi Coast

There are plenty of colourful superlatives to describe Naples. However, the one unalterable fact is that it's a big city and, for many people, no matter how compelling a big city is, there comes a point when you just have to escape for a breather. In most cities this size, an hour's travel would land you firmly in the suburbs. The great thing about Naples' position is the choice of places close by – in the Bay of Naples and along the Amalfi Coast – and the different take on southern Italy you are rewarded with as a result. Among the few constant factors within the whole area are the sense of history and the extraordinary high quality of the food while, on the downside, the places covered in this chapter tend to be more expensive than in Naples.

Enchanting to look at but an ever-present threat, the volcano of Vesuvius (p181) is the heady backdrop to the Bay of Naples, with Pompeii (p181) its ancient (and potential) victim. One of the most popular excursions from the city, Pompeii is a remarkably intact excavated city, complete with houses, shops, public baths and a brothel. For a double dose of ancient history, hop off the train again on your way back to Naples and visit Herculaneum (p179), another fascinatingly well-preserved Vesuvius victim. Further afield, Paestum (p203) also beckons the curious, with its huge Greek temples.

Beyond Pompeii, overlooking the Bay of Naples, lies Sorrento (p186), which manages to retain an elegant working-town feel despite the annual invasion of holidaying Brits.

Out to sea, the Bay's islands vividly reflect the extremities of this region. The stunning island of Procida (p176), just 45 minutes away from Naples by hydrofoil, is tiny, tranquil and unspoiled; locals here still earn their living from the sea. Next stop over the waves is Ischia (p171), a lot bigger and busier, but still retaining an intrinsically Mediterranean-island atmosphere with its vineyards, lemon trees and the added plus of curative mineral springs. And then there is Capri (p164), the Bay's most fashionable and popular island, with its film-star reputation, designer shops and super-luxury hotels.

Back on the mainland, the Amalfi Coast is all about drama. Not so long ago, you could only reach the resorts here by boat. Today there is a winding road and plenty of buses, so you can let someone else be driven around the bend by this snake of a route. The coastal mountains plunge into the sea in a stunning vertical landscape of precipitous crags, forests and resort towns. One such town is Positano (p192), which spills down the hillside in a theatrical shower of pastel-coloured houses.

Amalfi (p195) itself has a weighty history of maritime power and commerce; today, its revenue comes mainly from the tourists disgorged daily from the ferries to idle around the Piazza del Duomo, wander the medieval streets and visit the extraordinary cathedral.

Perched above the Amalfi Coast is the pretty (and heritage-listed) Ravello (p199), most famed for its Wagnerian connection and grandiose villas. Finally there is Salerno (p201), which has suffered on the popularity stakes from its proximity to so many jewels in the Amalfi coastal crown. Yet Salerno has an unhurried orderly charm, an interesting tangle of medieval streets and a welcome lack of limoncello (lemon liqueur) souvenir shops.

BAY OF NAPLES

The Bay of Naples has a tantalising choice of islands and resorts which all have their own very separate identities. Unlike so many bland Mediterranean resorts the islands in the Bay of Naples arose from a geological cataclysm with the eruption of the now dormant volcano Epomeo on Ischia. As if this wasn't sufficiently explosive, an earthquake followed which splintered the mainland around Naples resulting in Ischia and Procida to break away. This was later followed by a good-sized chunk of land breaking away from the Sorrento peninsula leaving in its wake the jagged, dramatic cliffs of the Amalfi Coast and rewarding us, today, with the island of Capri.

CAPRI

Capri, as well as being a legendary idyll, is probably the most mispronounced name in Italy. Unlike the Ford car, the stress is on the first syllable (*ca*-pri), not the second.

A day-tripper's paradise, Capri is heavily geared to tourism, with up to 5000 visitors a day stepping off the ferries in summer. It's also a confirmed spot on the Mediterranean celebrity circuit, which means prices are high. Explore beyond the effortlessly cool cafés and designer boutiques, however, and Capri retains the unspoiled island charm with grand villas, overgrown vegetable plots, sun-bleached peeling stucco and banks of brilliantly coloured bougainvillea. All of this overlooks deep blue water that laps unseen into mysterious grottoes and secluded coves.

The best time to visit Capri is spring or autumn, once the summer crowds have ebbed away.

History

Already inhabited in the Palaeolithic age, the single limestone block of the island of Capri was subsequently occupied by the Greeks. The Romans also had taste; Emperor Augustus made the island his private playground and Tiberius retired there in AD 27. Augustus is believed to have founded the world's first palaeontological museum in the Villa Augustus, to house Stone Age artefacts and fossils unearthed by his workers.

Tiberius, a victim of Tacitus' pen, has gone down in history as having been something of a fiend on the island, although there is little evidence to back the lurid claims concerning the emperor's sexual shenanigans. The mud stuck, however, and until modern times his name has been equated with evil by the islanders. When the Swedish doctor Axel Munthe first began picking about the Roman ruins on the island in the early 20th century and built his villa on the site of a Tiberian palace, locals would observe that it was all *'roba di Tiberio'* – Tiberius' stuff.

Later, the island belonged to the Republic of Amalfi, then the Kingdom of Naples. During the Napoleonic Wars, it changed hands several times between the French and the English.

Throughout history, the people of Capri and Anacapri have been at loggerheads and are always ready to trot out their respective patron saints to ward off the *malocchio* (evil eye) of their rivals.

Orientation

About 5km from the mainland at its nearest point, Capri is a mere 6km long and 2.7km wide. As you approach, there's a great camera shot of the town of Capri with the dramatic slopes of Monte Solaro (589m) to the west, hiding the village of Anacapri.

All hydrofoils and ferries arrive at Marina Grande, a chaotic and shabby place with little evidence of the glitz that awaits you up the hill. This is the island's transport hub: buses connect the port with the towns of Capri and Anacapri, and a funicular railway links the marina with Capri town. Otherwise, jump in a taxi; there will be plenty meeting the boat, or follow Via Marina Grande by foot for a twisting 2.25km puff-you-out climb. Turn left (east) at the junction with Via Roma for the centre of Capri town or right (west) for Via Provinciale di Anacapri, which eventually becomes Via G Orlandi as it reaches Anacapri.

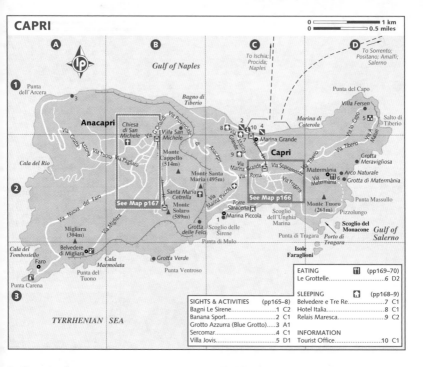

CAPRI

Gulf of Naples	
To Ischia; Procida; Naples	To Sorrento; Positano; Amalfi; Salerno
Punta dell'Arcera	Punta del Capo
Bagno di Tiberio	Villa Fersen
Anacapri	Marina di Caterola	Salto di Tiberio
Chiesa di San Michele	Villa San Michele	Marina Grande
Monte Cappello (514m)	Capri	Grotta Meravigliosa
Monte Santa Maria (495m)	Matermània	Arco Naturale
	Grotta di Matermània
Cala del Rio	Santa Maria Cetrella	
See Map p167	Monte Solaro (589m)	Monte Tuoro (261m)	Punta Massullo
Torre Saracena	Pizzolungo
Migliara (304m)	Marina Piccola	Scoglio dell'Unghia Marina	Scoglio del Monacone	Gulf of Salerno
Grotta delle Felci	Scoglio delle Sirene	Punta di Tragara	Porto di Tragara
Belvedere di Migliara	Punta di Mulo	Isole Faraglioni
Cala del Tombosiello	Cala Marmolata	Grotta Verde	Punta Ventroso	
Faro	Punta del Tuono	
Punta Carena		
TYRRHENIAN SEA		

EATING	(pp169–70)	
Le Grottelle	6	D2

SLEEPING	(pp168–9)	
Belvedere e Tre Re	7	C1
Hotel Italia	8	C1
Relais Maresca	9	C2

INFORMATION		
Tourist Office	10	C1

SIGHTS & ACTIVITIES	(pp165–8)	
Bagni Le Sirene	1	C2
Banana Sport	2	C1
Grotta Azzurra (Blue Grotto)	3	A1
Sercomar	4	C1
Villa Jovis	5	D1

Information

EMERGENCY

Police station (Map p166; ☎ 081 837 42 11; Via Roma 70, Capri)

INTERNET ACCESS

Capri Internet Point (Map p167; ☎ 081 837 32 83; Via de Tommaso 1, Anacapri; per hr €4) This place also has international newspapers and some English books for sale.

INTERNET RESOURCES

Anacapri (www.anacapri-life.com)

Capri Island (www.capri.net)

Capri Tourism (www.capritourism.com)

MEDICAL SERVICES

Hospital (☎ 081 838 11 11; Marina Piccola 2)

POST

Anacapri post office (Map p167; ☎ 081 837 10 15; Via de Tommaso 8)

Capri Town post office (Map p166; ☎ 081 978 52 11; Via Roma 50)

TELEPHONE

Telephone office (Map p166; ☎ 081 837 54 88; Piazza Umberto 1, Capri)

TOURIST INFORMATION

Each office can provide a free stylised map of the island and a more detailed one (€0.80) that also has town plans of Capri and Anacapri. For hotel listings and other useful information, ask for a copy of the free brochures *Capri È* and *Guida Agli Alberghi*.

Anacapri tourist office (Map p167; ☎ 081 837 15 24; Via G Orlandi 59; ☼ 8.30am-8.30pm Jun-Sep, 9am-3pm Mon-Sat Oct-Dec & Mar-May)

Capri Town Tourist Office (Map p166; ☎ 081 837 06 86; Piazza Umberto I; ☼ 8.30am-8.30pm Jun-Sep, 9am-1pm & 3.30-6.45pm Mon-Sat Oct-May)

Marina Grande Tourist Office (Map p165; ☎ 081 837 06 34; ☼ 8.30am-8.30pm Jun-Sep, 9am-1pm & 3.30-6.45pm Mon-Sat Oct-May)

Sights
CAPRI TOWN

In the high season, the centre of Capri is full of the stylish and the rich, ranging from

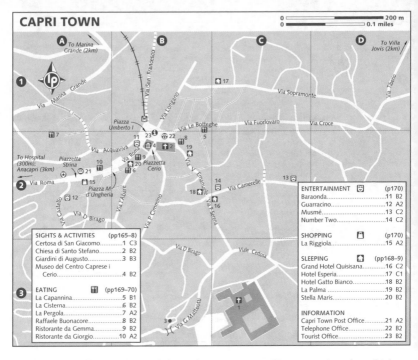

CAPRI TOWN

0 ——— 200 m
0 ——— 0.1 miles

SIGHTS & ACTIVITIES	(pp165–8)
Certosa di San Giacomo	1 C3
Chiesa di Santo Stefano	2 B2
Giardini di Augusto	3 B3
Museo del Centro Caprese i Cerio	4 B2

EATING	🍴 (pp169–70)
La Capannina	5 B1
La Cisterna	6 B2
La Pergola	7 A2
Raffaele Buonacore	8 B2
Ristorante da Gemma	9 B2
Ristorante da Giorgio	10 A2

ENTERTAINMENT	🎭 (p170)
Baraonda	11 B2
Guarracino	12 A2
Musmé	13 C2
Number Two	14 C2

SHOPPING	🛍 (p170)
La Riggiola	15 A2

SLEEPING	🏠 (pp168–9)
Grand Hotel Quisisana	16 C2
Hotel Esperia	17 C1
Hotel Gatto Bianco	18 B2
La Palma	19 B2
Stella Maris	20 B2

INFORMATION	
Capri Town Post Office	21 A2
Telephone Office	22 B2
Tourist Office	23 B2

waif-thin trendy teens to Gucci-clad grandmothers with a chihuahua in their handbags. The best place to people-watch is from one of the cafés on Piazza Umberto I (better known as the Piazzetta); stick to a single drink unless you plan on re-mortgaging your house. When you feel like a little exercise, check out the 17th-century **Chiesa di Santo Stefano** (🕐 8am-8pm) on the same square. Note the pair of languidly reclining patricians in the chapel to the south of the main altar that seem to mirror some of the roués in the cafés outside. There is well-preserved Roman tiling in the northern chapel. Beside it is a reliquary with a saintly bone that apparently saved Capri from the plague in the 19th century.

Head down Via D Birago or Via V Emanuele for **Certosa di San Giacomo** (Map p166; 🕿 081 837 62 18; Viale Certosa; admission free; 🕐 9am-2pm Tue-Sat, 9am-1pm Sun), a 14th-century Carthusian monastery built over one of Tiberius' villas with a Baroque tower, cloisters and some fairly forgettable 17th-century paintings. The nearby colourful **Giardini di Augusto** (Gardens of Augustus; Map p166; 🕐 dawn-dusk daily) were founded by the caesar Augustus. The view from here is breathtaking, looking out to sea over the

Isole Faraglioni limestone pinnacles, which are apparently home to a rare blue lizard.

The **Museo del Centro Caprese i Cerio** (Map p166; 🕿 081 837 66 81; Piazzetta Cerio 5; admission €2.60; 🕐 10am-1pm Tue, Wed, Fri & Sat, 3-7pm Thu) has a library of books and journals about the island (mostly in Italian, but there are a few in English), and a collection of Neolithic and Palaeolithic fossils found locally.

VILLA JOVIS & AROUND

East of the town centre, a comfortable hour-long walk along Via Tiberio leads to the one-time residence of Emperor Tiberius, **Villa Jovis** (Jupiter's Villa; Map p165; 🕿 081 837 06 34; Via Tiberio; admission €2; 🕐 9am-1hr before sunset), also known as the Palazzo di Tiberio. The largest and best preserved of the island's Roman villas was a vast pleasure complex that pandered to the emperor's saucy desires, and included imperial quarters and extensive bathing areas set in dense gardens and woodland.

The stairway behind the villa leads to **Salto di Tiberio** (Tiberius' Leap; Map p165), a cliff from where, says the story, Tiberius had out-of-favour subjects hurled into the sea.

A short jaunt from here down Via Tiberio and Via Matermània and you arrive at the **Arco Naturale**, a rock arch formed by the pounding sea. The doubling back to the first crossroads, you can turn left to drop down a long series of steps and follow the path south, then west, back into town, enjoying good views of Punta di Tragara and Isole Faraglioni on the way.

ANACAPRI & AROUND

Many visitors are lured to **Villa San Michele** (Map p167; ☎ 081 837 14 01; Viale Axel Munthe; admission €5; ☺ 9am-6pm May-Sep, 10.30am-3.30pm Nov-Feb, 9.30am-4.30pm Mar, 9.30am-5pm Apr & Oct) by the words of its most famous inhabitant, Swedish doctor Axel Munthe. The eclectic house he built on the ruined site of a Roman villa is immortalised in his book *The Story of San Michele* (1929; see p27). A compassionate soul, he also built bird sanctuaries on the island and provided refuge for stray dogs. The villa, a short walk north of Piazza Vittoria, houses Roman sculptures from the period of Tiberius' rule. The pathway behind offers superb views over Capri. The (often closed) stairway of 800 steps leading from the town down to the sea was the only link between Anacapri and the rest of the island until the mountain road was built in the 1950s; this helps to explain the historic rift between the two towns.

From Piazza Vittoria, you can take a **chair lift** (lift €6; ☺ 9.30am-sunset Mar-Oct, 10.30am-3pm Nov-Feb) to the top of **Monte Solaro** where, on a (rare) clear day, you can see for miles around. From Anacapri a bus runs every 20 minutes in summer and 40 minutes in winter to **Faro**, less crowded and boasting one of Italy's tallest lighthouses. The trip takes 10 minutes.

GROTTA AZZURRA

Capri's craggy coast is studded with more than a dozen sea caves, most of them accessible and spectacular but none as famous as the **Grotta Azzurra** (Blue Grotto; Map p165; admission €4; ☺ 9am-1hr before sunset). Don't dismiss it as just another overblown tourist attraction; the mysterious iridescent blue light here is magic.

Two Germans, writer Augustus Kopisch and painter Ernst Fries, are credited with discovering the Blue Grotto in 1826. Further research, however, revealed that Emperor Tiberius had built a quay here around AD 30, complete with a *nymphaeum* (shrine to the water nymph). Unfortunately the marble nymphs are now reclining on dry land in an Italian church somewhere. You can still see the carved Roman landing stage, however, discovered towards the rear of the cave.

At some time, geologists believe, the cave sank to its present depth, about 15m to 20m below sea level, blocking every opening except the 1.3m-high entrance. The refraction of sunlight through the water, and its reflection off the white sandy bottom, creates the vivid blue effect that gives the grotto its name.

Boats leave from Marina Grande and a return trip will cost €16.30, comprising return motorboat to the cave (€8), rowing boat into the cave itself (€4.30) and admission fee (€4); allow a good hour. You only

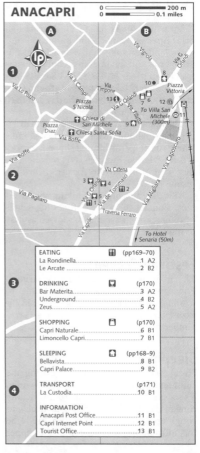

Bay of Naples – Capri

167

save a little money and lose a lot of time by catching a bus from Anacapri or Capri since you still have to pay for the rowing boat and admission fee. The singing 'captains' are included in the price, so don't feel any obligation if they push for a tip.

The grotto is closed if the sea is too choppy so, before embarking, check that it's open at the Marina Grande tourist office, about 25m from the motorboat ticket booth.

It's possible to swim into the grotto before 9am and after 5pm, but it's not advisable as, aside from the unpredictability of the sea currents, you may receive a nasty bump on the head from a rowing-boat oar.

Activities

Capri is obviously ideal for water sports. For scuba-diving, contact Sercomar (Map p165; ☎ 081 837 87 81; www.caprisub.com; Via Colombo 64, Marina Grande). Bagni Le Sirene (Map p165; ☎ 081 837 69 70; Marina Piccola) hires out canoes and motorised dinghies, and can take you water-skiing. For sailboards and catamarans, contact Banana Sport (Map p165; ☎ 081 837 51 88; Via Marina Grande 12). Expect to pay around €200 for a motorised dinghy for the day and €110 for a three-dive package.

The main places to swim are Bagno di Tiberio, a small inlet west of Marina Grande, where the emperor himself dipped; a rocky area at Marina Piccola; at Faro; and further west of the Grotto Azzurra below the restaurants.

There are also plenty of hiking opportunities. Contact the tourist offices for details of routes, which are mostly classed as easy to moderate.

Festivals & Events

The main secular festival is the Gruppo Folkloristico Capresi which runs from 1 to 6 January. Local folk groups perform in Piazza Diaz, Anacapri, and in Capri's Piazza Umberto I.

Sleeping

Hotel space is at a premium during the summer and many places close in winter. There are few really cheap rooms at any time of the year; however, if you are able to cough up a few extra euros, there are some magnificent options in the middle to upper price range, including a couple of Italy's most luxurious hotels.

Camping is forbidden and offenders are either prosecuted or 'asked' to relocate to a hotel. You might want to inquire at the tourist offices about renting a room in a private home.

MARINA GRANDE

Belvedere e Tre Re (Map p165; ☎ 081 837 03 45; www.belvedere-tre-re.com; Via Marina Grande 238; s/d €100/130; ⌘ Apr-Nov; Ⓟ) Five minutes' walk from the port, this hotel has a rather bare, old-fashioned feel and could do with an update (tossing out the plastic flowers would be a start). On the plus side, the rooms are large with views of the beach and there's a sun-bronzing terrace on the top floor.

Hotel Italia (Map p165; ☎ 081 837 06 02; fax 081 837 03 78; Via Marina Grande 204; s/d with breakfast €90/100; ⌘ Apr-Nov) This third-generation hotel has a homely feel, with a *nonna* (grandma) around and a hallway of family knick-knacks. The rooms have high ceilings and a spare-room feel, all with old-fashioned wardrobes and beds. There are lovely shady gardens and use of the pool at the hotel across the street. The only drawback is the dining room, which looks like an institutional canteen.

Relais Maresca (Map p165; ☎ 081 837 96 19; www.relaismaresca.it; Via V Emanuele 32; d with breakfast €200; ⌘ Mar-Dec) A good choice in Marina Grande, this hotel has recently had a total revamp. Run by an affable, multilingual Dutch manager, each floor has a different 'colour of Capri' (turquoise, blue, yellow) twinned with striking traditional-style tiles. The 4th-floor flower-filled terrace has sea views and there's an Internet station (plus slippers and robe) for guests.

CAPRI

Grand Hotel Quisisana (Map p166; ☎ 081 837 07 88; www.quisi.com; Via Camerelle 2; s/d with breakfast from €280/330; ⌘ year-round) Capri's most prestigious address, a few espadrille steps from the Piazzetta. Prices listed are street-facing and cheapest; you can pay up to €800 a night for a duplex suite. The rooms are suitably palatial and gorgeous, with subtle classy colours and seating areas. Many overlook the Quisisana compound of pools, subtropical gardens, restaurants and bars. There's a fitness centre and spa, in case you get bored with playing idle rich.

Hotel Esperia (Map p166; ☎ 081 837 02 62; fax 081 837 09 33; Via Sopramonte 41; s/d with breakfast €140/170; ☻ Apr-Oct) The peeling façade, handsome columns and giant urns help lend an air of faded elegance to this 19th-century former wealthy private home. The rooms are large with modern furniture, a floral theme and good-sized terraces with sea views. There's also a small restaurant.

Hotel Gatto Bianco (Map p166; ☎ 081 837 51 43; www.gattobianco-capri.com; Via V Emanuele 32; s/d with breakfast €150/215; ☻ Apr-Nov) Gay-friendly hotel with sunny blue-and-yellow tilework, pretty rooms with balconies and a downstairs bar. There's an elegant patio garden filled with flowers and the location is ace, a few steps away from the centre.

La Palma (Map p166; ☎ 081 837 01 33; www.lapalma-capri.com; Via V Emanuele 39; s/d with breakfast €165/251; ☻ Apr-May) Dating from 1822 this hotel has stunning rooms, with frescoes and sea views.

Stella Maris (Map p166; ☎ 081 837 04 52; fax 081 837 86 62; Via Roma 27; s/d €60/95; ☻ year-round) A dowdy small hotel, this place would be considered overpriced anywhere else (and you pay extra for air-con and breakfast), but its central position is what you're paying for, just off the classy Piazzetta. The rooms are dinky-sized and basic with bathrooms and TVs. The current owner's son speaks some English and is a bit more welcoming than weary old dad.

ANACAPRI

Capri Palace (Map p167; ☎ 081 978 01 11; Via Capodimonte 2b; s/d with breakfast from €230/290; ☻ year-round; **P**) Overlooking the Bay of Naples, this recently renovated luxury hotel is a real special-occasion place. Built on the site of one of Tiberius' summer palaces, its star-studded guest list includes Liz Hurley, Naomi Campbell and Harrison Ford. The interior is classic Mediterranean, and some rooms have their own terraced garden and private pool. Lavish facilities include a health and water-therapy spa, tennis courts, billiard room, piano bar and private yacht for excursions. The constant piped classical music could irritate those seeking peace and quiet.

Hotel Bellavista (Map p167; ☎ 081 837 14 63; www.bellavistacapri.com; Via G Orlandi 10;

s/d €90/164; ☻ Apr-Oct) A grande dame among hotels here – over a hundred years old. The rooms are large and have love-'em-or-hate-'em 1960s-style tile floors with enormous leaf or flower patterns. There are tennis courts, a pool, and a large formal restaurant with wonderful views.

Hotel Senaria (off Map p167; ☎ 081 837 12 23; www.senaria.it; Via Follicara 6; s/d with breakfast €120/160; ☻ Apr-Nov) This small whitewashed hotel is decorated in a sparse but elegant Mediterranean style, with lots of terracotta and cream paint. The tasteful watercolours of local artist Giovanni Tessitore feature throughout and all rooms have their own terrace and fridge. The ringing of the church bells next door may prevent lie-ins on Sunday mornings.

Eating

Unlike most popular resorts, it's hard to find a bad restaurant here but then, this *is* Italy, plus Capri has long catered to the more discerning and moneyed tourist. The island's culinary gift to the world is *insalata caprese*, a salad of fresh tomato, basil and mozzarella bathed in olive oil. Look out for *caprese* cheese, a cross between mozzarella and ricotta, and *ravioli caprese*, ravioli stuffed with ricotta and herbs.

Many restaurants, like the hotels, close over winter.

La Capannina (Map p166; ☎ 081 837 07 32; Via Le Botteghe 12, Capri; meals around €46; ☻ mid-Mar–Oct) One of the most established, expensive and acclaimed traditional restaurants on the island.

La Cisterna (Map p166; ☎ 081 837 56 20; Via M Serafina 5, Capri; meals around €22; ☻ Mar-Jan) The kitsch artwork on the walls somehow adds to the unpretentiousness of this trattoria, family-run for many generations. Solid traditional dishes like pasta with beans, and veal cutlet braised in lemon feature. Rumbling tummies won't go hungry; the portions are huge. No smoking.

La Pergola (Map p166; ☎ 081 837 74 12; Via Traversa Lo Palazzo 2, Capri; meals around €22; ☻ Thu-Tue Nov-Sep) Owner Giancarlo is also the chef – always a good sign. The food is excellent and innovative, with dishes such as green ravioli in a lemon and cream sauce (€7); the lemons are grown right here. There's a vine-shaded terrace with town and sea views. Hard to find; persevere and follow the signs.

La Rondinella (Map p167; ☎ 081 837 12 23) Via G Orlandi 295, Anacapri; meals around €20; ☒ year-round) Family-run for 50 years; apparently Graham Greene was a fan of La Rondinella. A 10-minute walk from the centre, this place has a relaxed rural feel. There's a tempting antipasti buffet, and the salads are generous and good. Chef Michele's *linguine alla ciammura* is a delicious original dish with a creamy white sauce of anchovies, garlic and parsley.

Le Arcate (Map p167; ☎ 081 837 33 25; Via de Tommaso 24, Anacapri; meals around €25; ☒ year-round) This restaurant has a large covered terrace area with hanging baskets of ivy, sunny yellow tablecloths and terracotta tiles. The discerning reception folk at Capri Palace eat here. Pizzas and pasta dishes are the speciality, the latter including tasty tagliatelle with shrimp and lemon sauce (€9.50). It's open all year for the locals, another good sign.

Le Grottelle (Map p165; ☎ 081 837 57 19; Via Arco Naturale 13; meals around €25; ☒ Apr-Oct) For a touch of grotto dining, Le Grottelle is the place. Tucked inside a couple of small caves 200m before the Arco Naturale (p166), the menu offers no surprises but this place is high on atmosphere, and the dishes are simple and tasty. The dishes include grilled fish, chicken and rabbit.

Raffaele Buonacore (Map p166; ☎ 081 837 78 26; Via Vittorio Emanuele 35, Capri; ☒ Mar-Oct) Does fantastic takeaway pizzas, frittatas (€3.50), waffles and ice cream.

Ristorante da Gemma (Map p166; ☎ 081 837 04 61; Via M Serafina 6, Capri; meals around €30; ☒ Tue-Sun Mar-Dec) There are a couple of oddities on the menu (like the marmalade omelette) at this famous Capri restaurant papered with photographs of diner celebrities such as John Lennon and Graham Greene. One of Capri's originals, it opened 55 years ago and is now run by Gemma's granddaughter. There's an intimate trattoria feel with hanging plants and appealing clutter about the place. The menu comprises mostly pasta and pizza dishes which are good, if unexceptional.

Ristorante da Giorgio (Map p166; ☎ 081 837 08 98; Via Roma 34, Capri; meals around €20; ☒ Wed-Mon Mar-Dec) A low-key restaurant considering the amazing panoramic sea view. If you get tired of all that blue, you can watch sports in the bar. The *ravioli caprese* (€7.50) is both recommended and reasonably priced.

Entertainment
CAPRI

The scene in Capri tends to be expensive and can be surprisingly tacky. Your best bet is to revamp your hip weekend wardrobe and hang out in the central piazzas. Alternatively you can take refuge in one of the numerous bars. Guarracino (Map p166; ☎ 081 837 05 14; Via Castello 7; ☒ 8pm-4am) is among the more pleasant spots for a drink.

To shake a leg or two, try the clubs Musmé (Map p166; ☎ 081 837 60 11; Via Camerelle 61b); Number Two (Map p166; ☎ 081 837 70 78; Via Camerelle 1), a short stroll down the street and a favourite of VIPs including Naomi Campbell; or Baraonda (Map p166; Via Roma 6).

ANACAPRI

Sit in one of the cafés on Piazza A Diaz or shoot pool at Bar Materita (Map p167; Via G Orlandi 140). For nightlife, the clubs Zeus (Map p167; ☎ 081 837 11 69; Via G Orlandi 103; ☒ 10pm-5am), with its commercial music and famous faces, and Underground (Map p167; Via G Orlandi 259), playing dance music and cabaret, might get your blood rushing. Typical cover charges hover around €20 (they accept credit cards).

Shopping

Ceramics and everything lemony are the big sellers. Shops abound but always make sure to check the quality of products. On the lemon front, the island is famous for its perfume and limoncello. The former smells like lemons and the latter tastes like sweet lemon vodka.

Capri Naturale (Map p167; ☎ 081 837 47 19; Via Capodimonte 15, Anacapri) The fashions here are made in whisper-thin linen in delphinium blue or dip-dyed lavender and natural colours. Locally produced and fairly priced.

La Riggiola (Map p166; ☎ 081 837 74 32; Via Roma 67B, Capri) Colourful selection of tiles, both new and antique, with some dating back to the 19th century.

Limoncello Capri (Map p167; ☎ 081 837 29 27; Via Capodimonte 27, Anacapri) Producing some 70,000 bottles of the lemony tipple annually, this place claims to be the birthplace of limoncello. Apparently, the grandmother of current owner Vivica made the tot as an after-dinner treat for the guests in her hotel, some 100 years ago.

Getting There & Away

See p206 and p190 for details of year-round ferries and hydrofoils from different points in Italy and from Sorrento, respectively. In summer there's also a service from Capri to Salerno (hydrofoil €14.50), Positano (hydrofoil €14) and Amalfi (hydrofoil €14.50).

Getting Around

There is no vehicle-hire service on the island and few roads are wide enough for a car. Between March and October you can only bring a vehicle to the island if it's either registered outside Italy or hired at an international airport – but there is really no need as buses are regular and taxis are plentiful.

The best way to get around is by **Sippic bus** (☎ 081 837 04 20). A ticket costs €1.30 on the main routes between Marina Grande (departing from just west of the pier), Capri, Anacapri, Grotta Azzurra and Faro. You can buy an all-day ticket for €6.70, which is valid from 6am to 4am May to September, 6am to midnight October to April. A cable car links Marina Grande with Capri. It is swifter than the bus and also costs €1.30.

You can rent a scooter from **La Custodia** (Map p167; ☎ 081 837 58 63; Via G Orlandi; per 2hrs €30), which is next to the petrol station in Anacapri.

From Marina Grande, a taxi ride costs around €15 to Capri and about €20 to Anacapri; from Capri to Anacapri costs about €10. For a taxi in and around Capri call ☎ 081 837 05 43 and if you are in Anacapri ☎ 081 837 11 75.

ISCHIA

The volcanic outcrop of Ischia is the most developed and largest of the islands in the Bay of Naples. It is an odd combination of bland thermal-spa hotels, filled with elderly Germans, and spectacular scenery, with forests, vineyards and picturesque small towns. Ischia only attracts a fraction of the ice cream–eating, cappuccino-swilling day-trippers that head for Capri daily from Naples in the summer. Perhaps someone should tell them that the beaches are a lot better here.

Ischia's main centres are the busy towns of Ischia and Ischia Porto, Casamicciola Terme, Forio and Lacco Ameno. The last two towns are the most attractive with good beaches and restaurants, and a jolly atmosphere. Other good spots include picturesque Ischia Ponte, Serrara Fontana, Barano d'Ischia and Sant'Angelo. Sant'Angelo is, in addition, tranquil; no cars are allowed in town.

History

Ischia was one of the first Greek colonies in the 8th century and an important stop on the trade route from Greece to northern Italy. The Greeks called the 47-sq-km island Pithekoussai after the *pithos* (pottery clay) found there. In 1301 there was a vast eruption of the now-extinct Monte Epomeo volcano, forcing the inhabitants to flee to the mainland where they remained for four years.

The Spanish took Ischia, along with Naples, in 1495 and controlled the island until the 18th century when France was in brief occupation followed by the British. There were fierce battles, including the bombardment of the Castello Aragonese, the scars of which are still in evidence today. Like so many of these islands during the 19th century, Ischia was a political prison.

Orientation

Ferries dock at Ischia Porto, the main tourist centre. It's about a 2km walk from the pier to Ischia Ponte, which has the atmosphere of an upmarket Naples neighbourhood, its narrow streets lined with all variety of shops, restaurants and cafés.

Information

Bay Watch (☎ 081 333 10 96; Via Iasolino 37) Can assist with finding accommodation and arranging tours.

Ischia Online (www.ischiaonline.it) This Internet resource is considerably more useful than the tourist office.

Tourist office (☎ 081 507 42 31; Via Iasolino, Banchina Porto Salvo; ☼ 9am-2pm & 3-8pm Mon-Sat) Has a free brochure listing hotels on the island. Walkers should pick up the *Lizard Trails* booklet, which lists four short walks and includes maps and level of difficulty.

Sights & Activities

In Ischia Ponte you'll find the **Castello Aragonese** (☎ 081 99 28 34; admission €8; ☼ 9.30am-7pm). Within this castle complex, joined to the mainland by a causeway, are a 14th-century cathedral, several smaller churches and a weapons museum.

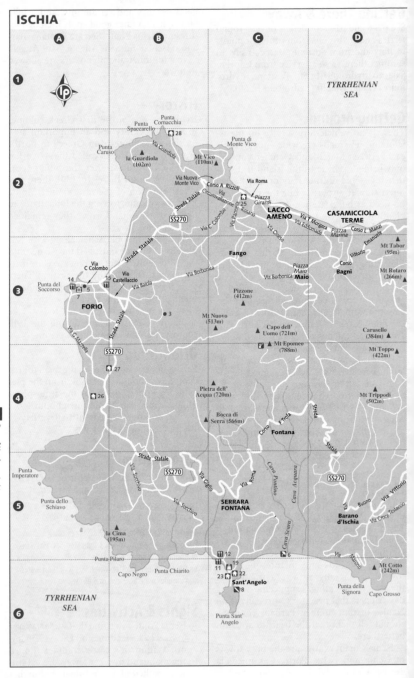

ISCHIA

A · **B** · **C** · **D**

1

*TYRRHENIAN
SEA*

Punta
Spaccarello
Punta
Cornacchia
Via Guardiola
28

Punta di
Monte Vico

Punta
Caruso
la Guardiola
(102m)
Mt Vico
(110m)

2

Via Nuova
Monte Vico
Corso A. Rizzoli
Via Roma
Via
Rosano
Piazza
Girardi
25
Via T Morgera
Piazza
Marina
**LACCO
AMENO**
**CASAMICCIOLA
TERME**
Strada Statale
Circumvallazione
Via Eddomade
Corso L. Manzi
SS270
Via Coreo
Via C. Colombo
Via Palmitella
Corso
Vittorio
Emanuele
Mt Tabor
(95m)

Via
C Colombo
Via
Castellaccio
14
15
5
7
Punta del
Soccorso
FORIO
Via Borbonica
Fango
Via Borbonica
Piazza
Maio
Maio
Corso
Bagni
Mt Rotaro
(266m)

3

Via Baiola
3
Pizzone
(412m)
Mt Nuovo
(513m)
Capo dell'
Uomo (721m)
Mt Epomeo
(788m)
Carusello
(384m)
Mt Toppo
(422m)
Strada Statale
SS270
27

Via C Mazzella
26
Pietra dell'
Acqua (720m)
Mt Trippodi
(502m)

4

Bocca di
Serra (566m)
Corso F Trofa
Fontana
Strada
Statale

Punta
Imperatore
Strada Statale
SS270
Via Succhivo
Via Giglio
Via Roma
Cava Pontino
Cava Acquara
Cava Scura
SS270
Via Buono
Via Vittorio

5

Punta dello
Schiavo
Via Succhivo
**SERRARA
FONTANA**
**Barano
d'Ischia**
Via Croce Tedaccio

la Cima
(195m)
Punta Piloro
12
11
19
23
22
6
Sant'Angelo
8
Via Maronti
Mt Cotto
(242m)
Via Buono

Capo Negro
Punta Chiarito
Punta della
Signora
Capo Grosso

6

*TYRRHENIAN
SEA*
Punta Sant'
Angelo

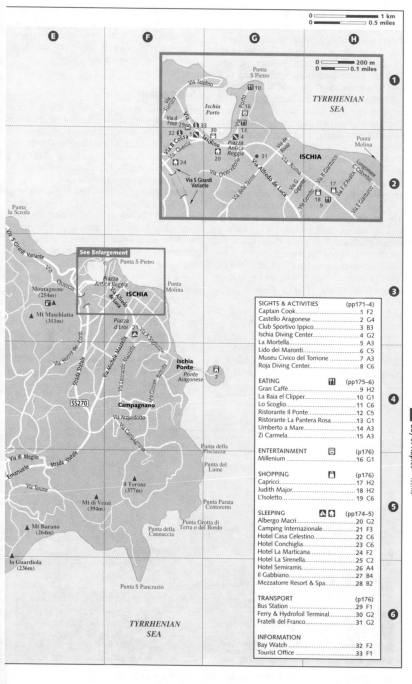

SIGHTS & ACTIVITIES (pp171–4)
Captain Cook.....................................1 F2
Castello Aragonese 2 G4
Club Sportivo Ippico.......................3 B3
Ischia Diving Center........................4 G2
La Mortella.......................................5 A3
Lido dei Maronti..............................6 C5
Museu Civico del Torrione 7 A3
Roja Diving Center..........................8 C6

EATING 🍴 (pp175–6)
Gran Caffè..9 H2
La Baia el Clipper..........................10 G1
Lo Scoglio......................................11 C6
Ristorante Il Ponte........................12 C5
Ristorante La Pantera Rosa............13 G1
Umberto a Mare.............................14 A3
Zi Carmela.....................................15 A3

ENTERTAINMENT 🎭 (p176)
Millenium..16 G1

SHOPPING 🛍 (p176)
Capricci...17 H2
Judith Major...................................18 H2
L'Isoletto..19 C6

SLEEPING 🏠🏠 (pp174–5)
Albergo Macrí................................20 G2
Camping Internazionale.................21 F3
Hotel Casa Celestino......................22 C6
Hotel Conchiglia............................23 C6
Hotel La Marticana........................24 F2
Hotel La Sirenella..........................25 C2
Hotel Semiramis.............................26 A4
Il Gabbiano....................................27 B4
Mezzatorre Resort & Spa...............28 B2

TRANSPORT (p176)
Bus Station 29 F1
Ferry & Hydrofoil Terminal............30 G2
Fratelli del Franco..........................31 G2

INFORMATION
Bay Watch.......................................32 F2
Tourist Office.................................33 F1

Bay of Naples – Ischia

In Forio, the **Museu Civico del Torrione** (☎ 081 33 21 26; admission €2; ☼ 9.30am-12.30pm) dates from the 14th century and is the former jail. These days it is an attractive gallery exhibiting the works of Italian painter Giovanni Maltese. Keen gardeners, and indeed anyone who loves plants, should visit **La Mortella** (☎ 081 98 62 20; Via F Calese 35, Forio; €8; ☼ 9am-7pm Tue, Thu, Sat & Sun Apr-Nov). Designed by Russell Page, the garden at La Mortella was inspired by the Moorish gardens of Granada's Alhambra in Spain. More than 1000 rare and exotic plants from all over the world thrive here, in one of Italy's finest landscaped gardens. The 20,000-sq-m gardens were established by the late British composter Sir William Walton and his wife, who made La Mortella their home in 1949. You can drink Fortnum & Mason's tea in the café and every summer there is a series of concerts held in the gardens

A fairly strenuous uphill walk from the village of Fontana brings you to the top of **Monte Epomeo** (788m), the island's highest point, with superb views of the Bay of Naples.

Among Ischia's better beaches is Lido dei Maronti, south of Barano. If you're interested in scuba diving, **Captain Cook** (☎ 335 636 26 30) and **Ischia Diving Center** (☎ 081 98 50 08) are both in Ischia's port, while **Roja Diving Center** (☎ 338 762 01 45) is based in Sant'Angelo; all have equipment for hire and run courses. A single dive will typically cost from €30.

You can leap on the saddle at **Club Sportivo Ippico** (☎ 081 90 85 18; Via Mario D'Ambra, Forio). Guided treks vary in cost depending on the number of riders, but start from around €24 for two hours.

Sleeping

Most hotels close in winter and prices normally drop considerably at those that do stay open. Prices quoted here are for the high season. In addition to the hotels listed below, there are the spa hotels, most of which only take half- or full-board bookings. The tourist office can supply you with a list.

Albergo Macrí (☎ /fax 081 99 26 03; Via Iasolino 96, Ischia Porto; s/d €40/75; ☼ year-round; ℗) Down a blind alley near the main port, this place has recently been brightened up by a paint-over. The rooms have light-coloured fabrics, cool tilework and bamboo-and-pine furnishings; some have terraces. Go for a room on the top floor for the best views. There's a small downstairs bar serving proper Italian espresso.

Camping Internazionale (☎ 081 99 14 49; fax 081 99 14 72; Via Foschini; per person/tent/car €9/10/8; ☼ Apr-Sep) Not far from Ischia Porto, this camp site is handy for the ferry terminal, and is in a shady spot with plenty of mature trees. There are also bungalow options from €25.

Hotel Casa Celestino (☎ 081 99 92 13; www .casacelestino.it; Via Chiaia di Rosa; Sant'

A ferry heads past the Castel dell'Ovo (p68) on its way to Ischia (p171)

Angelo; s/d €90/160; ⏰ Jan-Oct) On the pedestrian walkway down to the headland, this hotel complements the setting perfectly with lashings of brilliant blue paint. Rooms are sparsely furnished and enlarged by the spacious balconies with sun loungers. There's also a good, unfussy restaurant across the way.

Hotel Conchiglia (☎ 081 99 92 70; Via Chiaia delle Rose; s/d with breakfast €40/80; ⏰ year-round) An excellent price for this Sant'Angelo location. The rooms are old-fashioned with loads of character – just like owner Gennaro, who met his American wife when she arrived here after a Lonely Planet recommendation. There are balconies, fans and interesting paintings. The restaurant is recommended, as well.

Hotel La Marticana (☎ 081 99 32 30; www .lamarticana.it; Via Quercia 48-50, Ischia Port; d with breakfast €112; ⏰ May-Oct; P) A short suitcase trundle from the ferry, this small hotel has a friendly homy feel and there's a well-established garden with grape vines, tomato plants and a barbecue (available for guests). Rooms are small but well equipped with fridges, TVs and hairdryers. The breakfast buffet is more generous than most.

Hotel La Sirenella (☎ 081 99 47 43; www.lasi renella.net; Corso Angelo Rizzoli 41, Lacco Ameno; s/d with breakfast €62/124; ⏰ Apr-Oct) A family-owned hotel, recently done up with classy good taste. You can practically roll out of bed onto the beach here and most of the rooms have large balconies with lovely sea-and-sand views. The bright décor in primary colours gives the place a sunny Mediterranean feel.

Hotel Semiramis (☎ 081 90 75 11; www.hotel semiramisischia.com; Spiaggia di Citara, Forio; d with breakfast €100; ⏰ Apr-Oct; P) This newish hotel has a tropical-oasis feel with its central pool surrounded by palms. Rooms are large and beautifully tiled in the traditional yellow-and-turquoise pattern. Run by friendly Giovanni and his German wife, the garden is glorious with fig trees, vineyards and distant sea views.

Il Gabbiano (☎ /fax 081 90 94 22; SS Forio-Panza 162, Forio; r with breakfast €16; ⏰ Apr-Oct) This hostel is one of the best around. Near to the beach, it has bedrooms sleeping two, four or six. Monastically basic, the rooms are, nevertheless, spotlessly clean and all have small balconies with five-star sea views. There's also a pool.

Mezzatorre Resort & Spa (☎ 081 98 61 11; www .mezzatorre.it; Via Mezzatorre 23, Forio; d from €290; ⏰ mid-Apr–Oct; P) Surrounded by a 7-acre park, this resort oozes luxury with all the modern facilities, like spa and tennis courts, in a tranquil country-castle setting. The sitting rooms and some guest rooms are located in a 15th-century defensive tower (one of just six on the island). Rooms are decorated in earthy colours, some have private garden and Jacuzzi. Check out the infinity pool above the beach for the ultimate film-star setting. If funds are short, just have a long, slow drink in the adjacent bar.

Eating

Gran Caffè (☎ 081 199 16 49; Corso Vittoria Colonna, Ischia Porto; ⏰ year-round) At the smarter end of the port, this wood-panelled traditional café has been treating customers to delicious cakes, pastries, coffees and cocktails for over a hundred years.

La Baia el Clipper (☎ 081 333 42 09; Via Porto 116, Ischia Porto; meals around €40; ⏰ Jan-Oct) Romantic setting for locked-eyes-over-cocktails time, located at the entrance to the port. Now run by the second generation, it has today's catch proudly displayed at the entrance. Indulge in your dress-code daydreams and dress-up – it's that kind of place. The waiters are friendly, the service slick.

Lo Scoglio (☎ 081 99 95 29; Via Cava Ruffano 58, Sant'Angelo; meals around €28; ⏰ Apr–mid-Nov & mid-Dec–31 Dec) Dramatically located jutting out over the sea beside a pretty beach cove, this is a great place for sunsets and seafood. Mussel soup, grilled bass and butterfly noodles with salmon are examples of the fishy fare on the menu. The service is brisk and efficient. Sunday lunchtime is a popular weekly event.

Ristorante Il Ponte (☎ 081 90 42 55; Via Chiaia Delle Rose 89, Sant'Angelo; pizza from €3.50; ⏰ Apr-Oct) A casual, inexpensive restaurant just up from the car park with a vine-covered terrace. You don't have to pay exorbitant prices for dishes here; the pizzas are good, if unexceptional, and the salads are large and varied. Popular with the sun-bronzed boys and babes from the beach across the street.

Ristorante La Pantera Rosa (☎ 081 99 24 83; Riva Destra, Ischia Porto; mains around €6; ⏰ Apr-Nov) Good choices and prices for those suffering from black-tie burnout at this cheery, terraced restaurant on the port's smart suppertime strip. The menu has all the traditional pasta and pizza choices, plus meat dishes such as veal with wine (€9), which comes warmly recommended.

Umberto a Mare (☎ 081 99 71 71; Via Soccorso 1, Forio; mains from €15; ☽ Mar-Dec) In the shadow of the Spanish mission–style Soccorso church, this place has the choice of café-bar for light snacks, or more formal restaurant where the menu changes according to season. A set four-course menu costs €59 or go à la carte with rich just-like-mamma pasta dishes such as penne with lobster and asparagus.

Zi Carmela (☎ 081 99 84 23; Via Schioppa 27, Forio; meals around €20; ☽ Apr-Oct) Frequented by locals, who come here for seafood dishes such as the *fritturina e pezzogne* (a local white fish baked with potatoes and herbs in the wood-fired pizza oven). Dining space is gaily decorated with copper pans, ceramic mugs and strings of garlic and chillies. Undecided tastebuds can go for the €25 four-course set menu.

Entertainment

Millenium (☎ 081 333 11 96; Riva Destra, Ischia Porto; ☽ year-round) One of several bars along this swanky yacht-facing stretch. This bar has a nice moody atmosphere and salsa classes in the summer.

Shopping

Ischia's busiest shopping districts are around the main port on Via Roma and in the web of narrow streets leading to Ischia Ponte.

Capricci (☎ 081 98 20 63; Via Roma 37) Fabulous beachwear and lingerie by Versace, Moschino, Parah and Roberto Cavalli. Expect high quality and matching prices for looking this good in your undies and on the beach.

Judith Major (☎ 081 98 32 95; Via Roma 40) Sells all kinds of cool leatherwear but it's the shoes and, still more, the boots that are the star turn. Prada and Alberto Guardiani are just a couple of the flash names behind the designs here – so be ready to spend.

L'Isoletto (☎ 081 99 93 74; Via Chiaia delle Rose 36, Sant'Angelo) A kaleidoscope of colour in this deli-style gift shop just up the road from the harbour. It's unabashedly tourist-oriented but all the fancy bottles are here, including limoncello, pickles and jams, plus spices, pasta and ropes of brilliant red peppers. The showroom is packed solid; there's got to be something you want.

Getting There & Away

See p206 for details of year-round ferries and hydrofoils. You can catch ferries direct to Capri (€12) and Procida (€3) from Ischia, as well as to Naples and the Amalfi Coast.

Getting Around

The main bus station is in Ischia Porto. There are two principal lines: the CS (Circolo Sinistro, or Left Circle) which circles the island anti-clockwise and the CD line (Circolo Destro, or Right Circle), which travels in a clockwise direction, passing through each town and leaving every 30 minutes. Buses pass near all hotels and camp sites. A single ticket, valid for 90 minutes, costs €1.20, while an all day, multi-use ticket is €4. Taxis and micro-taxis (scooter-engined three-wheelers) are also available.

You can do this small island a favour by not bringing your car. If you want to hire a car or scooter for a day, there are plenty of rental firms. In addition to hiring out cars (from €32 per day) and mopeds (€25 to €35), **Fratelli del Franco** (☎ 081 99 13 34; Via A De Luca 133, Ischia Ponte) also has mountain bikes (around €10 per day). You can't take a rented vehicle off the island.

PROCIDA

The pastel pinks, whites and yellows of Procida's tiny cubic houses cluttered along the waterfront are an evocative first introduction to the island. Exploring further does little to detract from that first image. Procida, not surprisingly, has often been used as the celluloid image of Mediterranean paradise. The international hit *Il Postino* was partly filmed here, as were parts of the sinister tale of *The Talented Mr Ripley*.

Procida is the smallest of the main islands in the Bay of Naples and, even in the height of summer, doesn't attract the numbers of tourists welcomed by its more famous neighbours. Nightlife hasn't caught on here yet, either. Procida is an island for those seeking to escape the crowds.

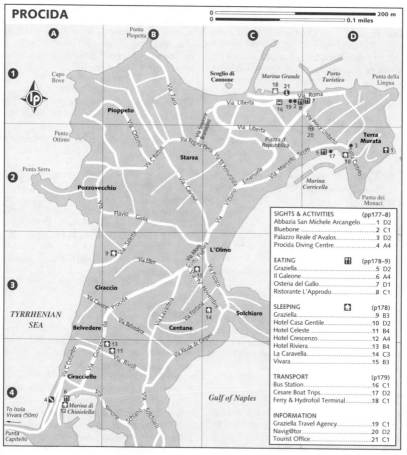

PROCIDA

0 ———————————————————— 200 m
0 ———————————————————— 0.1 miles

SIGHTS & ACTIVITIES	(pp177–8)
Abbazia San Michele Arcangelo	1 D2
Bluebone	2 C1
Palazzo Reale d'Avalos	3 D2
Procida Diving Centre	4 A4

EATING 🍴	(pp178–9)
Graziella	5 D2
Il Galeone	6 A4
Osteria del Gallo	7 D2
Ristorante L'Approdo	8 C1

SLEEPING 🏠	(p178)
Graziella	9 B3
Hotel Casa Gentile	10 D2
Hotel Celeste	11 B4
Hotel Crescenzo	12 A4
Hotel Riviera	13 B4
La Caravella	14 C3
Vivara	15 B3

TRANSPORT	(p179)
Bus Station	16 C1
Cesare Boat Trips	17 D2
Ferry & Hydrofoil Terminal	18 C1

INFORMATION	
Graziella Travel Agency	19 C1
Navig@tor	20 D2
Tourist Office	21 C1

Orientation & Information

Marina Grande is the hop-on, hop-off point for ferries and hydrofoils, and forms most of the tourist showcase. Procida's **tourist office** (☎ 081 810 19 68; www.procida.net; Marina Grande; 🕙 9.30am-1pm & 3.30-6pm Mon-Sat May-Sep, 9.30am-1pm Mon-Sat Oct-Apr) is next to the Caremar ticket office. However, infinitely more useful is the nearby **Graziella Travel Agency** (☎ 081 896 91 91; www.isoladiprocida.it; Via Roma 117) which can help out with accommodation, boat trips and has a much better free map available. Surf the Net at **Navig@tor** (☎ 081 896 05 70; Via Principe Umberto 33; per 1hr €4; 🕙 9.30am-1pm & 3.30-9pm Mon-Sat), which is a five-minute walk from the Marina.

Sights & Activities

The best way to explore the island is on foot – it's only about 4 sq km – or by bike. However, the island's narrow roads can be clogged with cars; one of the island's few drawbacks.

The 16th-century **Palazzo Reale d'Avalos**, recently used as a prison, dominates the island but is now all but abandoned. More interesting is the **Abbazia San Michele Arcangelo** (☎ 081 896 76 12; Via Terra Murata 89; admission €2; 🕙 9.45am-12.45pm year-round, plus 3-5.30pm May-Oct), about a 1km uphill walk from Marina Grande. Within the complex are a church, a small museum with some arresting paintings, and a honeycomb of catacombs.

Procida is home to a fascinating **nature reserve** on the tiny satellite island of Vivara.

177

Linked to Procida by a bridge, at the time of research it was closed indefinitely for infrastructure work. Check at the tourist office for an update.

The **Procida Diving Centre** (☎ 081 896 83 85; www.vacanzeaprocida.it/framediving01 -uk.htm; Via Cristoforo Colombo 6) runs diving courses and hires out equipment. Budget €32 for a single dive, €60 for a full-day dive.

In Marina Corricella, ask for Cesare who runs **boat trips** (per 2½ hrs €20) and half-day trips in a galleon for €90 (minimum 25 people). You can charter a yacht from **Bluebone** (☎ 081 896 95 94; www.isoladiprocida.it /bluebone; Via Roma 117) for around €550 per person, per week.

Festivals & Events

On Good Friday there's a colourful procession of the Misteri. A wooden statue of Christ and the *Madonna Addolorata*, along with life-size tableaux of plaster and papier-mâché illustrating events leading to Christ's crucifixion, are carted across the island. Men dress in blue tunics with white hoods while many of the young girls dress as the Madonna. Good Friday and Easter celebrations are part of Settimana Santa (Easter Week).

Sleeping

Hotel Casa Gentile (☎ 081 896 75 75; Via Marina Corricella 88; d with breakfast €90, meals around €25; ☺ Apr-Oct) It's hard to miss this shocking-pink cubic hotel in desperate need of a sun-bleaching. Rooms have cool tile-and-green modular-style furniture with fans and TVs. There's a large communal terrace overlooking the picturesque harbour, boat service to the nearby beach and a decent seafood restaurant.

Hotel Celeste (☎ 081 896 74 88; www.hotel celeste.it; Via Rivoli 6, Marina di Chiaiolella; d €72; ☺ Apr-Sep) In a quiet residential area overlooking orange groves, the German-run Hotel Celeste is open-plan and ecofriendly, and features the first solar panels on the island. Rooms are bright and functional, and there's a home-style garden, solarium and terraces.

Hotel Crescenzo (☎ 081 896 72 55; www.hotel crescenzo.it; Via Marina di Chiaiolella 33; s/d with breakfast €70/93, meals around €30; ☺ year-round) Just 10 rooms; choose

between a view of the bay or a balcony. Overlooking the yachts moored in the marina, the décor is suitably nautical in blue and white. This hotel is fronted by a restaurant, generally bursting with a loud, good-natured local crowd.

Hotel Riviera (☎ /fax 081 896 71 97; Via G da Procida 36, Marina di Chiaiolella; s/d with breakfast €48/65; ☺ Apr-Oct) This hotel is quite a hike up the hill from the marina but you're rewarded with birdsong, and rural peace and quiet. The rooms are modern and fairly characterless but they're a bargain at the price.

Camp sites are dotted around the island and are open from April to October. Typical prices are €8 per site plus €8 per person. On the eastern side of the island, try **Vivara** (☎ 081 896 92 42; Via IV Novembre) or, on the same road, **La Caravella** (☎ 081 810 18 38; Via IV Novembre). Near the better beaches of Ciraccio on the western side is **Graziella** (☎ 081 896 77 47; Via Salette 15), which has an attractive large leafy site.

Eating

Despite the prime waterfront location, restaurants near the port and the island's harbours are generally well priced and good, with an emphasis on seafood.

Graziella (☎ 081 896 74 79; Via Marina Corricella 14; mains around €6; ☺ Apr-Oct) To be frank, any restaurant along this unpretentious marina will equal a memorable dining experience with its bay view, piles of fishing nets, sleek cats and backdrop of marshmallow-coloured houses. The menu here includes sandwiches and burgers, as well as a spicy *penne alla siciliana* (pasta with a spicy tomato and chilli sauce) and grilled chicken with sweet-chilli sauce.

Il Galeone (☎ 081 896 96 22; Via Marina di Chiaiolella; meals around €25; ☺ year-round) A large wooden-decked restaurant that's a seagull swoop from the harbour. Il Galeone has a large, if predictable, menu of fresh off-the-boat *frutti di mare* (seafood) served with spaghetti, risotto or grilled as a main course. Try the *pesce all'acqua pazza* (fresh fish cooked with tomatoes, garlic and parsley).

Osteria del Gallo (☎ 081 810 19 19; Via Roma, Marina Grande; meals around €20; ☺ year-round) The kitchen at Osteria del Gallo turns out no-nonsense *antipasti di mare* (seafood antipasti; €9) and fish dishes.

The owner Matteo has the ruddy reassuring look of a well-seasoned fisherman and will give you a good welcome.

Ristorante L'Approdo (☎ 081 896 99 30; Via Roma 76, Marina Grande; meals around €25; ☺ Apr-Oct) Serves pizza plus magnificent and reasonably priced seafood. Try the grilled cuttlefish, which really does melt in the mouth, or push the boat out with one of the lobster dishes.

Getting There & Around

Procida is linked by boat and hydrofoil to Ischia (€2.50, 15 minutes), Pozzuoli and Naples (see p206 for more details). There is a limited bus service (€0.80), with four lines radiating from Marina Grande. Bus No L1 connects the port and Via Marina di Chiaiolella. The small, open micro-taxis can be hired for two to three hours for about €35, depending on your bargaining prowess. Contact **Graziella Travel Agency** (☎ 081 896 91 91; www.isoladiprocida.it; Via Roma 117) for information on bicycle hire.

HERCULANEUM & ERCOLANO

Today Ercolano is a truly grim Neapolitan suburb 12km southeast of the city proper. Classical Herculaneum, by contrast, was a peaceful fishing and port town of about 4000 and something of a resort for wealthy Romans and Campanians.

History

The fate of Herculaneum paralleled that of nearby Pompeii. Destroyed by an earthquake in AD 63, it was completely submerged in the AD 79 eruption of Mt Vesuvius. Herculaneum is much closer to the volcano, so it drowned in a sea of mud that essentially fossilised the city. This meant that even delicate items, such as furniture and clothing, were discovered remarkably well preserved. Tragically the inhabitants didn't fare so well; thousands of people tried to escape by boat but were suffocated by the volcano's poisonous gases.

The town was rediscovered in 1709 and amateur excavations were carried out intermittently until 1874, with many finds being carted off to Naples to decorate the houses of the well-to-do or to end up in museums. Serious archaeological work began again in 1927.

Intriguingly, much of the city is still buried under the modern suburb, (a good excuse to knock it down, perhaps). Excavation does continue today, albeit slowly.

Orientation & Information

Get off the train here dutifully clutching your cut-price double-whammy Pompeii-Herculaneum entrance ticket and you're in for a shock. Unlike Pompeii, there are no souvenir stands or cold-water kiosks here to greet you, just urban squalor and a curious lack of signs directing you to the site.

Resist the urge to turn around and climb back on the train. Instead, head for the main street, Via IV Novembre, which leads from the train station, at the town's eastern edge, to Piazza Scavi and the main ticket office for the excavations – an easy, if dreary, 600m walk.

At the **tourist office** (☎ /fax 081 788 12 43; Via IV Novembre 82; ☺ 9am-2pm Mon-Sat) you can pick up a brochure with an inadequate map of the ruined city, and very little else.

On sale at the bookshop beside the exit point at Herculaneum there is the useful guidebook in an English translation: *Pompeii, Herculaneum & Vesuvius* (€7.25), published by Edizioni Kina. It is also available at larger bookshops in the region.

The Ruins

At the **ruins** (☎ 081 739 09 63; admission €10, combined ticket incl Pompeii & 3 minor sites €18; ☺ 8.30am-7.30pm Apr-Oct, 8.30am-5pm Nov-Mar) be prepared for some of the houses to be closed, although an attendant may be around to open them; don't feel obliged to tip.

Similarly, beside the main entrance and ticket office you may be gently assailed by guides – if you do take one on, make sure both of you understand what kind of fee is expected at the end.

Follow the path running above and around the site, then descend through a short tunnel to emerge beside the **Terme Suburbane** (Suburban Baths) in the site's southernmost corner. These baths make a great introduction to the site with their deep pools, stucco friezes and bas-reliefs looking down upon marble seats and floors.

The site is divided into 11 *insulae* (islands) carved up in a classic Roman grid pattern.

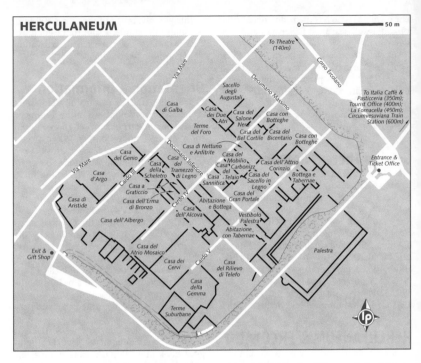

HERCULANEUM

0 _____ 50 m

To Theatre (140m)

Cono Ercolano

Via Mare

Decumano Massimo

Sacello degli Augustali

Casa di Galba

Casa dei Due Atri

Casa del Salone Nero

Casa con Botteghe

To Italia Caffè & Pasticceria (350m); Tourist Office (400m); La Fornacella (450m); Circumvesuviana Train Station (600m)

Terme del Foro

Casa del Bel Cortile

Casa del Bicentario

Casa con Botteghe

Casa di Nettuno e Anfitrite

Decumano Inferiore

Via Mare

Casa del Genio

Casa della Scheletro

Casa del Tramezzo di Legno

Casa del Mobilio Carbonizz

Casa dell'Attrio Corinzio

Entrance & Ticket Office

Casa d'Argo

Cardo III

Casa a Graticcio

Casa del Telaio

Casa Sannitica

Bottega e Tabernae

Casa di Aristide

Casa dell'Erma di Bronzo

Cardo IV

Casa dell'Alcova

Casa del Sacello in Legno

Casa del Gran Portale

Casa dell'Albergo

Abitazione e Bottega

Vestibolo Palestra

Exit & Gift Shop

Casa del Atrio Mosaico

Cardo V

Abitazione con Tabernae

Palestra

Casa dei Cervi

Casa del Rilievo di Telefo

Casa della Gemma

Terme Suburbane

LP

The two main streets, Decumano Massimo and Decumano Inferiore, are crossed by Cardos III, IV and V.

The **Casa d'Argo** (Argus House) is a well-preserved example of a Roman noble family's house, complete with a porticoed garden and *triclinium* (dining area).

The most extraordinary mosaic to have survived intact is in the *nymphaeum* (fountain and baths) of **Casa di Nettuno e Anfitrite** (House of Neptune and Amphitrite; Cardo IV). The warm colours in which the two deities are depicted hint at how lavish the interior of other well-to-do households must have been. For more fine mosaics, make your way to another of the city's public baths, **Terme del Foro** (Forum Baths), with its separate sections for men and women. The floor mosaics in the latter are in pristine condition. While women passed from the *apodyterium* (changing rooms; note the finely executed naked figure of Triton adorning the mosaic floor) through the *tepidarium* (warm room) to the *caldarium* (steam bath), men had the added bracing option of the *frigidarium* – a cold bath. You can still see the benches where bathers sat and the wall shelves for clothing.

Casa del Atrio Mosaico (House of the Mosaic Atrium; Cardo IV), an impressive mansion, also has extensive floor mosaics, although time and nature have left the floor buckled and uneven.

Behind it, and accessible from Cardo V, **Casa dei Cervi** (House of the Deer) is probably the most imposing of the nobles' dwellings. The two-storey villa, built around a central courtyard, contains murals and still-life paintings. In the courtyard is a diminutive pair of marble deer assailed by dogs and an engaging statue of a drunken Hercules peeing.

Casa del Gran Portale (cnr Decumano Inferiore & Cardo V) is named after the elegant brick Corinthian columns that flank its main entrance. Inside are some well-preserved wall paintings.

Sacello degli Augustali, in its time a school, retains a pair of lively, well-preserved murals.

Off the main street is **Casa del Bicentenario** (Bicentenary House; Decumano Massimo), so named because it was excavated 200 years after digging at Herculaneum first began. A crucifix found in an upstairs room is evidence that there might have been Christians in the town before AD 79.

Northwest of the ruins are the remains of a **theatre** (Corso Ercolano), dating from the Augustan period.

Sleeping & Eating

It's unlikely that you will wish to spend the night here, especially as it is an easy rail journey from Naples or Sorrento. If you feel the need, however, check at the tourist office, which can supply you with a list of local accommodation. There are a few restaurants where you can enjoy a meal or snack before legging it back on the train.

Italia Caffè & Pasticceria (☎ 081 732 14 99; Corso Italia 17) A fairly humble café with far-from-humble cakes; pick up a bag-full for your journey.

La Fornacella (☎ 081 777 48 61; Via IV Novembre 90-92; buffet from €3.50) There's a good buffet at La Fornacella, with dishes like *polpi all'insalata* (octopus salad), *pollo alla cacciatora* (chicken baked with tomatoes and paprika) and fresh grilled vegetables. If you really want to fill up fast, grab a couple of wedges of fried spaghetti with tomato – it's a lot nicer than it sounds.

Getting There & Away

By far the easiest way to get from central Naples or Sorrento to Ercolano (and also to Pompeii, which many visitors cover in the same day) is by the Circumvesuviana train (p208). A return ticket to Naples costs €3.50. By car take the A3 from Naples, exit at Ercolano Portico and follow the signs to car parks near the site's entrance.

MT VESUVIUS

This legendary volcano dominates the landscape, looming ominously over Naples and its environs. Although not as active as Mt Etna in Sicily, Vesuvius (Vesuvio; 1281m) is anything but extinct and scientists consider more eruptions a sure thing. After the last blow in 1944, its plume of smoke, long a reminder of the peril, disappeared. This may have eased the minds of some, but for those living in the shadow of Vesuvius (as about three million people do) the question is not if, but when.

Vesuvius' name is probably derived from the Greek *besubios* or *besbios*, meaning 'fire'. The volcano erupted with such ferocity on 24 August AD 79 that it all but destroyed the towns of Pompeii and Herculaneum, and

pushed the coastline out several kilometres. Subsequent years have witnessed regular displays of the mountain's wrath, the more destructive being those of 1631, 1794 (when the town of Torre del Greco was destroyed), 1906 and, most recently, 1944.

Trasporti Vesuviani (☎ 081 559 31 73) buses run from Ercolano train station to Vesuvius car park (€3.10 return); buy your ticket on the bus. There's then a 1.5km walk (allow 30 to 45 minutes) to the summit area (admission €6) and the rim of the crater. **Vesuviani Mobilità** (☎ 081 963 44 20) buses run from Pompeii (with several pick-up points in front of the amphitheatre) or Ercolano train station to Vesuvius car park (€3 one way, buy your ticket on the bus). Buses depart from Ercolano train station at 9.30am, 10.30am, 11.50am, 12.50pm and 1.50pm. They return at 11.35am, 1pm, 1.55pm, 3pm and 4.10pm. All services leave Pompeii 30 minutes earlier. Be warned, however, that when weather conditions are bad they shut the summit path and suspend bus departures. By car, exit the A3 at Ercolano Portico and follow signs for Parco Nazionale de Vesuvio. A licensed taxi from Ercolano should cost about €31 for four people.

Watch out for a couple of scams. Readers have reported independent bus owners in Ercolano lying about public transport times and charging ludicrous sums to get you up and down. And the little old couple who thrust walking sticks at visitors to help them on the push to the summit aren't doing it for charity, as they will make very clear when you descend.

Pack a sweater since it can be chilly up top, even in summer. Sunglasses are useful against the swirling ash, and trainers or walking shoes are more practical than sandals or flip-flops (thongs).

On the winding route up to the crest, check out the **Museo dell'Osservatorio Vesuviano** (Museum of the Vesuvian Observatory; ☎ 081 610 84 83; www.ov.ingv.it in Italian; admission free; ⏰ 10am-2pm Sat & Sun), which tells the history of 2000 years of Vesuvius-watching.

POMPEII

The victim of the world's most famous volcano disaster, Pompeii is Italy's top tourist attraction. About 2.3 million people pile in every year, making the magnificent ruins seem as crowded as the ancient streets must once have been. Ever since Pliny the Younger described the eruption of Vesuvius in AD 79, the city has been the stuff of books, scholarly and frivolous, and a perfect subject for the big screen. It offers the richest insight into the daily life of the Romans. Most of Pompeii is open to the public and requires at least three or four hours to visit.

Less than 1km down the road from the ruins, the pleasant modern town of Pompeii boasts a second big crowd-puller: the Santuario della Madonna del Rosario (Sanctuary of Our Lady of the Rosary), a place famous for its miracles that attracts pilgrims from all over Italy.

History

The eruption of Vesuvius wasn't the first disaster to strike the Roman port of Pompeii. In AD 63 it was devastated by an earthquake. Following a rapid rebuild, it was just beginning to get back into swing when lightning struck for the second time. On 24 August AD 79 Vesuvius blew its top, burying the city under a layer of *lapilli* (burning fragments of pumice stone) and killing some 2000 of the city's 20,000 inhabitants.

This, some might suggest, was a tragically appropriate destiny for a town that had been founded on prehistoric lava from the very same Vesuvius. The origins of Pompeii are uncertain but it seems likely that it was founded in the 7th century BC by the Campanian Oscans. Over the next seven centuries, the city fell to the Greeks and the Samnites before becoming a Roman colony in 80 BC.

After its catastrophic demise some 160 years later, the city gradually receded from the public eye until 1594 when the architect Domenico Fontana stumbled across the ruins while digging a canal. However, short of recording the discovery, he took no further action.

Exploration proper finally began in 1748 under the king of Naples, Charles III of Bourbon, and continued systematically into the 19th century. Giuseppe Fiorelli, who worked for the Italian government from 1858, is credited with most of the major discoveries.

Most of the ancient city has now been unearthed but work continues and new finds are still being made. In 2000, for example, roadworks on the nearby A3 revealed a whole frescoed leisure area.

Today, many of the more spectacular mosaics and murals sit in the **Museo Archeologico Nazionale** (p66) in Naples and other museums around the world. This is an unfortunate byproduct of overtourism and underfunding, which have been eroding the original 66-hectare site. To counter this, hopes are resting on inclusion to Unesco's World Heritage List and a law giving the site-management company commercial autonomy.

Orientation

The Circumvesuviana drops you off at the Pompeii–Scavi–Villa dei Misteri station, beside the Porta Marina entrance. By car, signs and energetic touts direct you from the A3 to the *scavi* (excavations) and car parks. There are camp sites, hotels and restaurants in the vicinity, although the choice is better in the adjacent modern town of Pompeii.

Information

First Aid post (Piazza Immacolata)

Pompeii Online (www.pompei.it)

Police booth (Piazza Esedra)

Post office (Piazza Esedra)

Tourist office Porta Marina (☎ 081 850 72 55; Piazza Porta Marina Inferiore 12; ☯ 8am-3.30pm Mon-Sat Oct-May, 8am-6pm Jun-Sep); Pompeii town (☎ 081 850 72 55; Via Sacra 1; ☯ as above)

Sights & Activities
THE RUINS

Nowadays the Porta Marina is the principle entrance to the ruins (☎ 081 857 53 47; www .pompeiisites.org; admission €10, combined ticket incl Herculaneum & 3 minor sites €18; ☯ 8.30am-7.30pm Apr-Oct – last entry 6pm, 8.30am-5pm Nov-Mar – last entry 3.30pm). Audioguides (€6.50) are available, but a good guidebook available from the gift shop at the site is still a useful tool since it's easy to miss some of the more important sites.

The original town was encircled by a wall punctuated by towers and eight gates. Entering by the southwestern sea gate, **Porta Marina**, which was considerably closer to the water before the eruption, you pass on the right the **Tempio di Venere** (Temple of Venus). Originally one of the town's most lavish temples, its position made it the target of repeated pillaging, leaving it in the abandoned state you see today.

Further along Via Marina, on the left, you pass the striking **Tempio di Apollo** (Temple of Apollo), the oldest of Pompeii's religious buildings, to enter the **foro** (forum), the centre of the city's life. South of this, opposite Tempio di Apollo, is the **basilica**, the city's law courts and exchange. Dating back to the 2nd century BC, it was one of Pompeii's greatest buildings. Among the fenced-off ruins to the left as you enter are some delightfully gruesome body casts.

The forum, which incidentally was closed to cart traffic, is surrounded by the **Tempio di Giove** (Temple of Jupiter), one of whose two flanking triumphal arches remains, the **market**, where you can see the remains of a series of shop fronts, and the **Edificio di Eumachia**, which features an imposing marble doorway.

Continue down Via Marina, which becomes Via dell'Abbondanza after the Edificio, until you reach Via dei Teatri on the right. This leads to the **Foro Triangolare** and the city's theatre district. To your left is the entrance to **Teatro Grande**, originally built in the 2nd century AD and capable of seating 5000 spectators. Adjoining it is the more recent **Teatro Piccolo**, also known as the Odeion. The **Caserma dei Gladiatori** (Gladiators' Barracks), behind the theatres, is surrounded by a portico of about 70 columns.

From the pre-Roman **Tempio di Iside** (Temple of Isis), rebuilt after the AD 63 earthquake and dedicated to the Egyptian goddess, turn left back to Via dell'Abbondanza, which intersects with Via Stabiana. **Terme Stabiane** is a 2nd-century BC bath complex complete with *frigidarium* (cold room), *apodyterium*

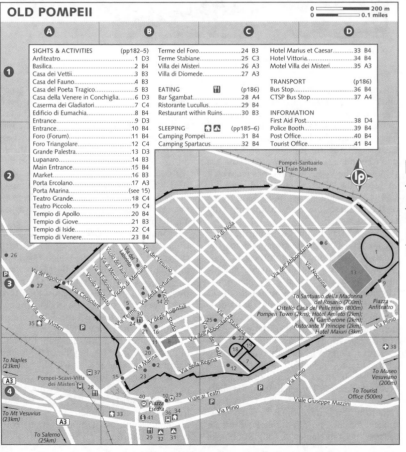

OLD POMPEII

0 — 200 m
0 — 0.1 miles

Bay of Naples – Pompeii

Pompeii (p181)

(changing room), *tepidarium* (warm room) and *caldarium* (hot room). In some you can still see the original tiling and murals, as well as some **erotic frescoes** (see p20). Several body casts are also located here.

Towards the northeastern end of Via dell'Abbondanza, **Casa della Venere in Conchiglia** (House of the Venus Marina) has recovered well from the WWII bomb that damaged it in 1943. Its highlight is the striking fresco of the goddess lounging in an unusually large conch shell.

Hidden away in the green northeastern corner of the city lies the grassy **anfiteatro**, the oldest known Roman amphitheatre. Built in 70 BC, it was at one time capable of holding up to 20,000 bloodthirsty spectators. The nearby **Grande Palestra** is an athletics field with an impressive portico and, at its centre, the remains of a swimming pool. It was here that the young men of the emperor's youth associations worked out.

Return along Via dell'Abbondanza and turn right into Via Stabiana (which becomes Via del Vesuvio) to see some of Pompeii's grandest houses. Turn left into Via della Fortuna to meet, on your right, **Casa del Fauno** (House of the Faun), which featured magnificent mosaics, now in the **Museo Archeologico Nazionale** (p66) in Naples. A couple of blocks further along Via della Fortuna is **Casa del Poeta Tragico** (House of the Tragic Poet), with some decent mosaics still *in situ*. Nearby **Casa dei Vettii** (Vicolo di Mercurio) sports some well-preserved paintings and statues. Across the road from Casa del Fauno, along Vicolo Storto, is the **Lupanaro**, Pompeii's top brothel with murals indicating the services on offer. And what better place for the young rakes to wash away their sins than the **Terme del Foro** (Forum Baths), a short walk away on Via Terme.

From the Terme del Foro you can continue to the end of Via Terme and turn right into Via Consolare, which takes you out of the town through Porta Ercolano at Pompeii's northwestern edge. Once past the gate, you pass **Villa di Diomede**, then turn right and you'll come to **Villa dei Misteri**, one of the most complete structures left standing in Pompeii. The Dionysiac Frieze, the most important fresco still on site, spans the walls of the large dining room. One of the largest paintings from the ancient world, it depicts the initiation of a bride-to-be into the cult of Dionysus, the Greek god of wine.

Museo Vesuviano (☎ 081 8 50 72 55; Via Bartolomeo 12; admission free; ☽ 8am-2pm Mon-Sat), southeast of the excavations, contains an interesting array of artefacts.

SANTUARIO DELLA MADONNA DEL ROSARIO

Dominating modern Pompeii's centre, the **Sanctuary of Our Lady of the Rosary** (☎ 081 857 71 11; Piazza Bartolo Longo; ✆ 6.30am-2pm & 3-6.30pm) was consecrated in 1891, some 15 years after the miracle that guaranteed its fame. In 1876 a young girl was cured of epilepsy after praying in front of the painting, *Virgin of the Rosary with Child*, above the main altar. News rapidly spread and to this day the painting is the subject of popular devotion.

The Santuario is flanked by a freestanding 80m **campanile** (bell tower; ☎ 081 850 70 00; ✆ 9am-1pm & 3-5pm).

Tours

The tourist offices warn against the dozens of unauthorised guides who swoop on tourists, charging exorbitant prices for brief and generally inaccurate tours. Authorised guides wear identification tags and belong to one of four cooperatives:

Cast (☎ 081 856 42 21)

Casting (☎ 081 850 07 49)

Gata (☎ 081 861 56 61)

Promo Touring (☎ 081 850 88 55)

The official price for one of these two-hour tours, whether you're alone, a couple or in a group of up to 25, is €94. Be wary of pickpockets if visiting out-of-the-way ruins unless you're in a group.

Weekly night **tours** (☎ 347 346 03 46; www .pompei-internazionale.it; tours €24; ✆ Thu 9.30pm Jul-Sep) are available in English. The tours last an hour and are accompanied by video projections, light shows and surround sound.

Sleeping

Pompeii is best visited on a day trip from Naples, Sorrento or Salerno, as once the excavations close, there's nothing to do and the area around the site becomes decidedly seedy. All the places mentioned here are open year-round.

Camping Pompei (☎ 081 862 28 82; www .campingpompei.com; Via Plinio 113; per person/tent/car €5/6/6, d €56, bungalow per person from €35) Next to Spartacus (see following), this has similar facilities and is also well established. In fact, the two camp sites are very similar, so take your pick of the best, shady site between the two.

Camping Spartacus (☎ 081 862 40 78; www .campingspartacus.it; Via Plinio 117; per person/tent/car €6/3/2, bungalow for 2 people from €60) The first camp site to open here 25 years ago, therefore greener than some, with towering eucalyptus and pine trees bordered by oleander bushes. Situated 200m from the main entrance to the excavations, the cabins are simple, but comfortable, and there are plenty of creature comforts, including Internet access, supermarket, bar and a pizzeria.

Hotel Amleto (☎ 081 836 10 04; www.hotel amleto.it; Via B Longo 10; d with breakfast €130) Elegant themed rooms in the new town with magnificent trompe l'oeil, antiques and chandeliers.

Hotel Maiuri (☎ 081 856 27 16; www.maiuri .it; Via Acquasalsa 20; s/d with breakfast €70/80) In a leafy residential area around 3km from the archaeological zone. It's a fair walk to the new town as well, so this hotel only really suits those with wheels. The owner is an architect, hence the double-take burgundy-and-turquoise exterior. Thankfully the rooms are calmer, decorated in executive, modern style with cool grey tiles, light wood and dark-blue fabrics. Go for one with a terrace view of Vesuvius and cross your fingers that it doesn't blow.

Hotel Marius et Caesar (☎ 081 536 34 98; www .mecpompei.com; Via Plinio 42-54; s/d with breakfast €60/80) The closest hotel to the main Pompeii site, the prison-like exterior belies the interior, starting with the glossy marble reception. Rooms are bright and modern, and there's a small communal terrace for catching the sun's rays.

Hotel Vittoria (☎ 081 536 90 16; www.pom peihotelvittoria.com; Piazza Porta Marina Inferiore 2; s/d with breakfast €50/90) Hotel Vittoria sits 200m from the Porta Marina entrance to the ruins. Recently refurbished, it successfully combines the *fin de siècle* grandeur of the public areas with up-to-date comforts, like showers and baths, and the toe-curling cosy feel of plush carpeting throughout.

Motel Villa dei Misteri (☎ 081 861 35 93; www .villadeimisteri.it; Via Villa dei Misteri 11; d €75) There are two types of room here: the motel-style room around the pool (good if you have kids) and those in the main building. There's a mildly scuffed air about the whole place, but the price is excellent given the location, the air-con and, above all (in summer), the pool.

Ostello Casa del Pellegrino (☎ /fax 081 850 86 44; Via Duca D'Aosta 4; dm with breakfast €14) Situated a stone's throw from the Santuario in a low-rise ex-convent just off Pompeii town's main square, this HI youth hostel has good, basic facilities in rooms or dormitories for five or six people.

Eating

There's a **restaurant** (Via di Mercurio; pasta from €6) within the ruins which has a reasonable daily buffet. Otherwise, there are plenty of places outside the gates and in modern Pompeii.

Al Gamberone (☎ 081 850 68 14; Via Piave 36; mains from €8; ☽ Wed-Mon) Located near Pompeii's main church in an elegant part of town, this restaurant has plenty of pasta choices, plus good seafood dishes including brandy-doused prawns. Sit under lemon and orange trees in the summer.

Bar Sgambat (☎ 081 861 09 66; Via Villa dei Misteri; snacks from €2.50; ☽ year-round) Has good *scarole* (pies) stuffed with spinach, onions and tomatoes to go.

Ristorante Il Principe (☎ 081 850 55 66; Piazza B Longo; meal about €55; ☽ daily Apr-Oct, Tue-Sat & lunch Mon Nov-Mar) One of Pompeii's classiest restaurants, where white-smocked waiters dish up traditional Campania dishes. Try the pasta and beans with mussels or *salmone e pesce spada affumicato con rucola* (smoked salmon and swordfish with rocket).

Ristorante Lucullus (☎ 081 861 30 55; Via Plinio 129; mains from €7; ☽ Wed-Mon year-round) Set back from the street down a long oleander-fringed drive, there are shady palms, Roman statues and several friendly cats. Specials here include *fettuccine alla boscaiola* (flat noodles with a sauce of tomatoes, mushrooms and peas) and a vast mix-and-match *contorni* (stuffed vegetables) choice.

Getting There & Away
BUS

SITA (☎ 081 552 21 76) operates regular bus services between Naples and Pompeii, while **CSTP** (☎ 089 48 70 01) runs buses from Salerno. **Marozzi** (☎ 089 87 10 09; www.marozzivt.it in Italian) offers services between Pompeii and Rome; prices vary so call or check the website.

SITA buses depart from in front of the post office outside Porta Marina, while CTSP and Marozzi buses leave from in front of Hotel Vittoria.

CAR & MOTORCYCLE
Take the A3 from Naples, a trip of about 23km, otherwise you could spend hours weaving through narrow streets and traffic snarls. Use the Pompeii exit and follow signs to Pompeii Scavi. Car parks are clearly marked and vigorously touted.

TRAIN
From Naples, take the Circumvesuviana train (€2.30) for Sorrento and get off at Pompeii–Scavi–Villa dei Misteri station.

SORRENTO
An unashamed resort town, Sorrento is still a civilised old town. Even the souvenirs are a cut above the normal overpriced tat, with plenty of fine old shops selling ceramics, lacework and inlaid-wood items. The main drawback is the lack of a proper beach; the town straddles the cliffs that look over the water to Naples and Mt Vesuvius. According to Greek legend, the sirens, mythical provocateurs of pure voice and dodgy intent, lurked in these parts. Sailors of antiquity were powerless to resist the beautiful song of these maidens-cum-monsters who would lure them and their ships to their doom. Homer's Ulysses escaped their deadly lure by having his oarsmen plug their ears with wax and by strapping himself to the mast of his ship so he could listern as he sailed past.

Less dangerous now, Sorrento is packed to the gills in high summer, predominantly with British and German holidaymakers. However, even in August, there is still just enough southern Italian charm to make a stay here enjoyable, and it makes a handy base for Capri (15 minutes away) and the Amalfi Coast.

Orientation
Piazza Tasso, bisected by Sorrento's main street, Corso Italia, is the centre of town, having supplanted Piazza Angelina Lauro as its nucleus. It's about a 300m walk northwest of the train station, along Corso Italia;

arriving at Marina Piccola, where ferries and hydrofoils dock, walk south along Via Marina Piccola then climb about 200 steps to reach the piazza. Corso Italia becomes the SS145 on the way east to Naples and, heading west, it changes its name to Via Capo.

Information

EMERGENCY

Police station (☎ 081 807 53 11; Corso Italia 236)

INTERNET ACCESS

Sorrento Info (☎ 081 807 40 00; Via Tasso 19; per 30 mins €3; ☼ 10am-1.30pm & 4-8pm Mon-Sat Nov-Apr, 10am-1.30pm & 5-10.30pm Mon-Sat May-Oct)

INTERNET RESOURCES

Sorrento Tourism (www.sorrentotourism.it) Also has an accommodation-booking service and provides good city maps.

MEDICAL SERVICES

Hospital (☎ 081 533 11 11; Corso Italia 1)

MONEY

Acampora Travel (☎ 081 878 48 00; Piazza Angelina Lauro 12) Represents American Express.

Deutsche Bank (Piazza Angelina Lauro 22-29) Has an ATM.

POST

Post office (☎ 081 878 14 95; Corso Italia 210; ☼ 8am-6.30pm Mon-Fri, 8am-12.30pm Sat)

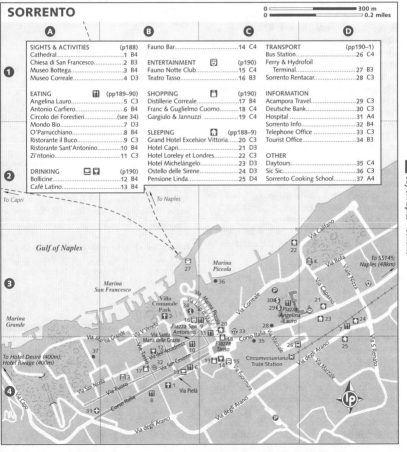

SORRENTO

0 — 300 m
0 — 0.2 miles

SIGHTS & ACTIVITIES	(p188)
Cathedral	1 B4
Chiesa di San Francesco	2 B3
Museo Bottega	3 B4
Museo Correale	4 D3

EATING	(pp189–90)
Angelina Lauro	5 C3
Antonio Carfiero	6 B4
Circolo dei Forestieri	(see 34)
Mondo Bio	7 D3
O'Parrucchiano	8 B4
Ristorante il Buco	9 C3
Ristorante Sant'Antonino	10 B4
Zi'ntonio	11 C3

DRINKING	(p190)
Bollicine	12 B4
Café Latino	13 B4

Fauno Bar	14 C4

ENTERTAINMENT	(p190)
Fauno Notte Club	15 C4
Teatro Tasso	16 B3

SHOPPING	(p190)
Distillerie Correale	17 B4
Franc & Guglielmo Cuomo	18 C4
Gargiulo & Jannuzzi	19 C4

SLEEPING	(pp188–9)
Grand Hotel Excelsior Vittoria	20 C3
Hotel Capri	21 D3
Hotel Loreley et Londres	22 D3
Hotel Michelángelo	23 D3
Ostello delle Sirene	24 D3
Pensione Linda	25 D4

TRANSPORT	(pp190–1)
Bus Station	26 C4
Ferry & Hydrofoil Terminal	27 B3
Sorrento Rentacar	28 C3

INFORMATION	
Acampora Travel	29 C3
Deutsche Bank	30 C3
Hospital	31 A4
Sorrento Info	32 B4
Telephone Office	33 C3
Tourist Office	34 B3

OTHER	
Daytours	35 C4
Sic Sic	36 C3
Sorrento Cooking School	37 A4

To Capri
To Naples

Gulf of Naples

Marina Piccola

Marina San Francesco

Villa Comunale Park

Marina Grande

To Hotel Desiré (400m);
Hotel Rivage (400m)

Piazza San Antonino

Piazza Tasso

Corso Italia

Circumvesuviana Train Station

Via degli Aranci

Via Capo

Via Fuoro

Via San Nicola

Corso Italia

Via Pietà

To SS145;
Naples (48km)

Via Califano

Via Rota

Viale Nizza

Via Capasso

Piazza Angelina Lauro

Via Marziale

Via S Renato

Via degli Aranci

Bay of Naples – Sorrento

187

TOURIST INFORMATION

Tourist office (☎ 081 807 40 33; Via Luigi De Maio 35; ⚓ 8.45am-6.15pm Mon-Sat, 8.45am-12.45pm Sun Jul-Aug) In the Circolo dei Forestieri (Foreigners' Club), it provides the excellent information magazine, *Surrentum*.

Sights & Activities

The gleaming white façade of Sorrento's **cathedral** (Corso Italia; ⚓ 7.30am-noon & 4.30-8.30pm) gives no hint of the exuberance housed within. There's a particularly striking crucifixion above the main altar. The triple-tiered bell tower rests on an archway into which three classical columns and a number of other fragments have been set.

Within the 18th-century Palazzo Correale, which has some interesting murals, is the **Museo Correale** (☎ 081 878 18 46; Via Correale; admission €6; ⚓ 9am-2pm Wed-Mon), containing a small collection of 17th- and 18th-century Neapolitan art and an assortment of Greek and Roman artefacts. The gardens offer views of the bay and steps lead down to the shore. More art plus stunning 19th-century marquetry furniture can be enjoyed at the newer **Museo Bottega** (☎ 081 878 12 03; Via San Nicolà 28; admission €8; ⚓ 10am-1pm & 3pm-6.30pm Mon-Sat) with its suitably gorgeous setting of an 18th-century palace with frescoed vaults and hand-painted wallpaper.

Views up and down the coast from **Villa Comunale Park** are breathtaking, and equally impressive from the gardens of the beautiful, if modest, cloister of **Chiesa di San Francesco** (⚓ 8am-1pm & 2-8pm), by the entrance to the park.

Stroll along Corso Italia, which is closed to traffic in the centre between 10am and 1pm and 7pm to 7am, and through the narrow streets of the old town. At the time of writing, the town council was set to introduce a fee of €1 for cars or mopeds entering the centre; whether this happens remains to be seen.

If you're after a beach, head for **Marina Grande**, a 700m walk west from Piazza Tasso, which has small strips of sand. The jetties nearby sport ubiquitous umbrellas and deck chairs, which cost up to €15 a day. **Bagni Regina Giovanna**, a 2km walk west along Via Capo (or take the bus for Massalubrense),

is more picturesque, set among the ruins of the Roman villa Pollio Felix. To the east is a small beach at Marinella. See p188 for boat-hiring information.

Courses

Three-hour cooking classes, followed by lunch or dinner with wines and champagne, are offered by the **Sorrento Cooking School** (☎ 081 878 32 55; www.sorrentocookingschool.com; Viale Dei Pini 52) for €120.

Tours

Sic Sic (☎ 081 807 22 83; Marina Piccola; ⚓ May-Oct) hires out a variety of boats (starting at about €20 an hour) and organises boat cruises.

Daytours (☎ 081 878 19 84; Corso Italia) offers tours to the Amalfi Coast and Bay of Naples including to Capri (€52), Pompeii (€36) and Positano (€28).

Festivals & Events

The Sorrento Film Festival, regarded as the most important in the country for Italian-produced cinema, is held annually, usually in November.

The city's patron saint, Sant'Antonio, is remembered on 5 February each year with processions and huge markets. The saint is credited with having saved Sorrento during WWII when Salerno and Naples were heavily bombed.

The Settimana Santa Easter processions are famous throughout Italy. There are two main processions: the first takes place at midnight on the Thursday preceding Good Friday with robed and hooded penitents in white; the second major procession occurs on Good Friday itself when those taking part wear black robes and hoods to commemorate the death of Christ.

Sleeping

Most accommodation is in the town centre or clustered along Via Capo, the coastal road west of the centre. To reach this area, catch a SITA bus for Sant'Agata or Massalubrense from the train station. Book early for the summer season.

Grand Hotel Excelsior Vittoria (☎ 081 807 10 44; www.exvitt.it; Piazza Tasso 34; s/d from €235/270; ⚓ year-round) The grand dame of Sorrento, this gracious old hotel sits aloof in its extensive, carefully tended gardens, once the site of a villa belonging to Emperor Augustus. The guest book reads like a *Who's Who*, with Pavarotti, Wagner, Goethe, Sophia Loren and British royalty to name just a few of the entries. It offers the luxury of a bygone age at 21st-century prices.

Hotel Capri (☎ 081 878 12 51; www.albergocapri.it; Corso Italia 212; s/d with breakfast €90/140; ⏳ Mar-Oct) Just across from the Hotel Michelàngelo (below), and elegantly decorated with antique lemon-and-blue tiles and a profusion of plants and flowers. This hotel is better placed for shopping than sand in between the toes.

Hotel Désiré (☎ /fax 081 878 15 63; Via Capo 31b; s/d with breakfast €60/90; ⏳ Mar-Dec) Overlooking the sea, this relaxed hotel has tastefully decorated sunny rooms, TV lounge, panoramic roof terrace and its very own lift down to the rocky beach. The rates are very competitive for all these creature comforts, and the hotel is well sited for both the shops and the sea.

Hotel Loreley et Londres (☎ 081 807 31 87; fax 081 532 90 01; Via Califano 12; d with bathroom €95; ⏳ Mar-Nov) A grand old building looking directly onto Mt Vesuvius, this hotel occupies one of the best sites in town. The interior is faded and floral, with a slight institutional feel. There is a vast terrace bar/restaurant overlooking the sea – perfect for sipping a cocktail at sunset.

Hotel Michelàngelo (☎ 081 878 12 51; www.michelangelohotel.it; Corso Italia 275; d with breakfast €192; ⏳ Apr-Oct) A shiny modern hotel with marble and terracotta floors, decent artwork, a pool and elegant spacious rooms. The whole place has a warm Mediterranean feel and the hotel is well placed for shopping and the beach.

Hotel Rivage (☎ 081 878 18 73; www.hotelrivage.com; Via Capo 11; s/d €88/95; ⏳ Mar-Oct) A low-rise modern hotel just beyond the shops and close to the beach. You can sunlounge on the roof terrace, and there's an OK bar and restaurant. The rooms are beige and bland but all have terraces. This place has a slight tour-group feel but is well placed and priced.

Ostello delle Sirene (☎ /fax 081 877 13 71; Via degli Aranci 160; dm with breakfast €16; ⏳ year-round) This private hostel is a cheap bet for a dorm bed but, for a single or double room, you can do a lot better elsewhere. There are a couple of Internet terminals and snacks are available.

Pensione Linda (☎ /fax 081 878 29 16; Via degli Aranci 125; s/d €50/75; ⏳ year-round) The suburban setting may be mildly off-putting but it's only a short stroll into town. Rooms are clean and reasonably sized, and some have balconies. The modern bathrooms have excellent water pressure, a definite plus in these parts.

Eating

Angelina Lauro (☎ 081 807 40 97; Piazza Angelina Lauro 39-40; buffet dishes from €3; ⏳ daily Jul-Aug, Wed-Mon Sep-Jun) Metal chairs, bright lights but a brilliant buffet with pasta dishes for €3. Alternatively, go mad and order three courses, plus drink, for just €12. The outside terrace with TV is equally low on the atmosphere stakes, but you come here for the reliably good and filling food.

Antonio Carfiero (☎ 081 807 32 52; Corso Italia 142; ⏳ year-round) Papered with photos of Italian celebs who have dropped by, plus the occasional American soap star. The ice creams here are exceptional and all made on the premises. There's even a variety for vegans, including violet or jasmine, made without milk.

Circolo dei Forestieri (Foreigners' Club; ☎ 081 877 32 63; Via Luigi de Maio 35; meals around €20; ⏳ Mar-Nov) A home-away-from-home for expats, Circolo dei Forestieri enjoys one of Sorrento's most spectacular views. The food is only so-so but good for those who are suffering from potato withdrawal (they come fried or baked). Alternatively, just sip a drink and enjoy the view, while showing off your Italian vocab.

Mondo Bio (☎ 081 807 56 94; Via Degli Aranci 146; snacks from €3; ⏳ 10am-3pm Mon-Sat year-round) There's just a few tables at this organic-vegetarian shop and restaurant. Tofu burgers, seitan steaks and lots of healthy alternatives to pizza and pasta, especially for nondairy folk.

O'Parrucchiano (☎ 081 878 13 21; Corso Italia 67; meals around €20; ⏳ Thu-Tue year-round) The narrow entrance to this place does little to prepare you for the massive greenhouse setting within. Dating back to 1868 and still in the same family, this place claims to have invented cannelloni, so go for this (rather than the 'fried peasant and pork sausages' which is also on the menu!). Traditional grub in general and well priced, considering the seriously heady setting.

Ristorante il Buco (☎ 081 878 23 54; Rampa Marina Piccola 5; meals around €40; ✪ Feb-Dec) A former wine cellar once used by monks, there is nothing monastic about the cuisine here which is extravagant and innovative. Highlights include dishes such as ravioli in a fish, pumpkin and pepper sauce. Outside, the stone archway is one of the city's four main gates that led into ancient Sorrento.

Ristorante Sant'Antonino (☎ 081 877 12 00; Via Santa Maria delle Grazie 6; pizzas from €4.60, meals around €20; ✪ Dec-Oct) Owner Luigi is married to an English woman, which helps explain the diverse menu (and the choice of frozen or fresh chips). There are 12 salads, risottos, savoury crepes, pizza and pasta dishes, plus three reasonably priced set menus. Lovely country-cute setting with tables surrounded by greenery and lemon trees.

Zi 'ntonio (☎ 081 878 16 23; Via Luigi De Maio 11; meals around €20; ✪ year-round) There's traditional Italian atmosphere in this low-lit restaurant with its tiled pictures and dizzy ceiling studded with ceramic plates. The menu includes a whole heap of rice dishes, including risotto with lobster or with wild mushrooms. There is also a daily buffet with a 20-plus choice of gorgeous-looking dishes.

Drinking

As well as the inevitable blarney-theme pubs, Sorrento also has some appealing Mediterranean-style bars and, particularly in the main piazzas, some classic meet-and-greet cafés.

Bollicine (☎ 081 878 46 16; Via dell' Accademia 9) You can sample Campanian and other wines by the glass at this snug wine-buffs' bar. Nibble on the local specialities, cheeses or cold meats.

Café Latino (☎ 081 878 37 18; Via Pietà 12; ✪ 10am-2am Apr-Sep) Come here to sip a Mary Pickford (rum, pineapple, grenadino and maraschina) and enjoy a little locked-eyes-over-cocktail time with your mate. It's a lovely garden setting under orange and lemon limes.

Fauno Bar (☎ 081 878 11 35; Piazza Tasso; ✪ Dec-Oct) More a classic café than a bar, with a vast outside terrace well served by black-aproned waiters. A bit pricey (cocktails cost €8) but always packed out with locals, so there's lots to look at.

Entertainment

Outdoor concerts are held during the summer months in the cloisters of Chiesa di San Francesco.

Fauno Notte Club (☎ 081 878 10 21; www .faunonotte.it; Piazza Tasso 1) A fierce competitor to the Teatro, with same start time and theme. Described as 'a fantastic journey through history, legends and folklore', the word is that it is loud and jolly.

Teatro Tasso (☎ 081 807 55 25; www.teatro tasso.com; Piazza San Antonino) If you trill to *The Sound of Music*, you might enjoy *Sorrento Musical* (€21), which plays here at 9.30pm Monday to Saturday from March to October. It's a potpourri of Neapolitan songs, including a sing-along with 'O Sole Mio' and 'Trona a Sorrento', plus many other less overworked Neapolitan numbers.

Shopping

Shoppers will enjoy browsing the squeeze-by pedestrian alleys north of Corso Italia and west of Piazza Tasso, which are lined with all kinds of shops.

Distillerie Correale (☎ 081 877 46 22; Via Tasso 20) You can have a free slug of limoncello here; it's sold in a variety of pretty bottles. This shop also sells other larder favourites such as pickled mushrooms and artichokes, fancy olive oils and classy jams.

Franc & Guglielmo Cuomo (☎ 081 878 11 37; Piazza Tasso 32) A marquetry shop with its workshop right in the showroom, this shop is run by a young craft-skilled couple. The music boxes are exquisite to look at, although the corny tunes may drive you spare.

Gargiulo & Jannuzzi (☎ 081 878 10 41; Viale Enrico Caruso 1) Dating from 1863 this old-fashioned shop is a classic. Elderly shop assistants will guide you through the three-floor haven where locally made crafts are beautifully displayed, and include embroidered lace, pottery and marquetry items. Shipping can be arranged.

Getting There & Away

SITA buses serve the Amalfi Coast and Sant'Agata, leaving from outside the Circumvesuviana train station. Buy tickets at the station bar or from shops bearing the blue SITA sign. At least 12 buses a day run between Sorrento and Amalfi (€2.40), looping around Positano (€1.30); more than 10 buses also run to Ravello (€1).

Circumvesuviana trains run every half-hour between Sorrento and Naples (€3.20), via Pompeii (€1.80) and Ercolano (€1.80).

Linee Marittime Partenopee (☎ 081 807 18 12) runs up to 10 hydrofoils daily to Capri (€19 return, 20 minutes) and at least six to Naples (€15 return, 35 minutes), while **Caremar** (☎ 081 807 30 77) has three fast-ferry sailings daily to Capri (€11.60 return, 25 minutes). All depart from the port at Marina Piccola, where you can buy your tickets.

Getting Around

Bus Line C runs from Piazza Tasso to the port at Marina Piccola. Tickets (€1 for 90 minutes) are available at tobacconists, bars and newsagencies.

Sorrento Rentacar (☎ 081 878 13 86; Corso Italia 210a) is one of several rental companies hiring out scooters (€38) and cars (from €60 a day).

For a taxi call ☎ 081 878 22 04.

THE AMALFI COAST

One of the most breathtaking coastlines in Europe, the Amalfi Coast (Costiera Amalfitana) stretches 50km east from Sorrento to Salerno. In summer the coast is jam-packed with wealthy tourists, prices are inflated and finding a room is next to impossible; you're much better off coming during spring and autumn. The Amalfi Coast all but shuts down in winter with very few restaurants and hotels remaining open.

When planning your itinerary, you may find www.amalfiscoast.com a useful source.

WALKING

In the hills, dozens of small paths and stairways connect the coastal towns with mountainside villages. Useful information can be found in Lonely Planet's *Walking in Italy,* which has a chapter featuring the best walks around the Amalfi Coast and Sorrento peninsula. *Landscapes of Sorrento and the Amalfi Coast* by Julian Tippett has clear descriptions of over 60 mainly short walks in the area, and *Strade e Sentieri* (€6.50; in Italian only) is a worthwhile general guide. The most reliable map to walk by is the Club Alpino Italiano's *Monti Lattari, Peninsola Sorrentina, Costiera Amalfitana: Carta dei Sentieri* (€8) at 1:30,000 scale.

GETTING THERE & AWAY
Boat

Companies including **Metró Del Mar** (☎ 19 944 66 44; www.metrodelmare.com) operate only in summer with hydrofoils between Sorrento, Amalfi, Positano and Capri.

Bus

SITA (☎ 081 552 21 76) operates a service along the SS163 between Sorrento and Salerno with buses leaving around every hour. Buses also connect Rome and the Amalfi Coast, terminating in Salerno.

Car & Motorcycle

The coastal road is magnificent – to a passenger. To drive it can be something of a white-knuckle ride, as bus-drivers nonchalantly career their way round hairpin bends, jauntily tooting at every turn.

From Naples take the A3, then just after Pompeii branch off for Castellammare and follow signs for Sorrento. At Meta you can continue to Sorrento or, if your destination is further east, bypass the town by taking a short-cut over the hills, saving yourself a good 30 minutes. To join the coastal road from Salerno, follow signs for Vietri sul Mare or Amalfi.

Train

From Naples you can either take the Circumvesuviana to Sorrento or a Trenitalia train to Salerno, then continue along the Amalfi Coast, either eastwards or westwards, by SITA bus or by ferry.

POSITANO

Positano is, arguably, the most picturesque and photographed of the coastal towns. What is not in question, however, is that you'll need a sturdy set of knees, for where most towns have streets, Positano has steps. Lots of them. The town is chock-a-block with expensive boutiques and steeply stacked houses whose pastel colours of peach, pink, terracotta and white lend it a slightly theatrical feel. The summer-season artists add to the faintly surreal feel, cramming up the beach entrance with their paintboxes and easels, but painting twee postcard-style scenes rather than what they actually see.

Look closely and Positano is reassuringly real, however, with crumbling stucco, streaked paintwork and even, on occasion, a faint whiff of drains. John Steinbeck visited Positano in 1953 and wrote in an article for *Harper's Bazaar*: 'Positano bites deep. It is a dream place that isn't quite real when you are there and becomes beckoningly real after you have gone.' There certainly is something special about the place and this is reflected, predictably, in the prices which tend to be higher here than elsewhere on the coast.

Orientation

Positano is split in two by a cliff bearing the Torre Trasita (tower). West of this is the smaller Spiaggia del Fornillo beach area and the less expensive side of town; east is Spiaggia Grande, backing up to the town centre.

Navigating is easy, if steep. Via G Marconi, part of the SS163 Amalfitana, forms a huge horseshoe around and above the town, which cascades down to the sea. From it, one-way Viale Pasitea makes a second, lower loop, ribboning off Via G Marconi from the west towards the town centre then climbing back up as Via Cristoforo Colombo to rejoin Via G Marconi and the SS163.

Information

Banca dei Paschi di Siena (Via dei Mulini) Has an ATM.

Banco di Napoli (Via dei Mulini) Also with ATM.

Police station (☎ 089 87 50 11; cnr Via G Marconi & Viale Pasitea)

Post office (cnr Via G Marconi & Viale Pasitea)

Tourist office (☎ 089 87 50 67; Via del Saracino 4; ◷ 8am-2pm & 3.30-8pm Mon-Sat year-round, 3.30-8pm Jul & Aug) At the foot of the Chiesa di Santa Maria Assunta steps.

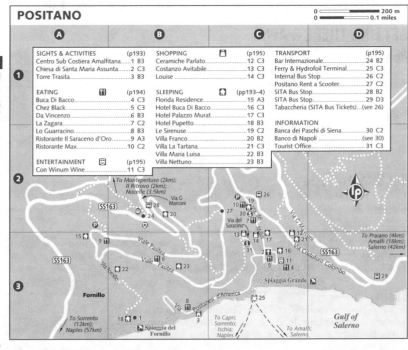

POSITANO

| 0 | 200 m |
| 0 | 0.1 miles |

| SIGHTS & ACTIVITIES | (p193) |
| Centro Sub Costiera Amalfitana......1 B3 |
| Chiesa di Santa Maria Assunta......2 C3 |
| Torre Trasita......3 B3 |

| EATING | (p194) |
| Buca Di Bacco......4 C3 |
| Chez Black......5 C3 |
| Da Vincenzo......6 B3 |
| La Zagara......7 C2 |
| Lo Guarracino......8 B3 |
| Ristorante Il Saraceno d'Oro......9 A3 |
| Ristorante Max......10 C2 |

| ENTERTAINMENT | (p195) |
| Con Winum Wine......11 C3 |

| SHOPPING | (p195) |
| Ceramiche Parlato......12 C3 |
| Costanzo Avitabile......13 C3 |
| Louise......14 C3 |

| SLEEPING | (pp193–4) |
| Florida Residence......15 A3 |
| Hotel Buca Di Bacco......16 C3 |
| Hotel Palazzo Murat......17 C3 |
| Hotel Pupetto......18 B3 |
| Le Sirenuse......19 C3 |
| Villa Franco......20 B2 |
| Villa La Tartana......21 C3 |
| Villa Maria Luisa......22 B3 |
| Villa Nettuno......23 B3 |

| TRANSPORT | (p195) |
| Bar Internazionale......24 B2 |
| Ferry & Hydrofoil Terminal......25 C3 |
| Internal Bus Stop......26 C2 |
| Positano Rent a Scooter......27 C2 |
| SITA Bus Stop......28 B2 |
| SITA Bus Stop......29 D3 |
| Tabaccheria (SITA Bus Tickets)......(see 26) |

| INFORMATION | |
| Banca dei Paschi di Siena......30 C2 |
| Banco di Napoli ......(see 30) |
| Tourist Office......31 C3 |

To Montepertuso (2km);
Il Ritrovo (2km);
Nocelle (3.5km)

Via G Marconi

Via del Saracino

To Praiano (4km);
Amalfi (18km);
Salerno (42km)

Viale Pasitea

Via Cristoforo Colombo

Fornillo

Spiaggia Grande

Via Positano d'America

To Sorrento
(12km);
Naples (57km)

Spiaggia del
Fornillo

To Capri;
Sorrento;
Ischia;
Naples

To Amalfi;
Salerno

*Gulf of
Salerno*

Sights & Activities

Positano's most famous, and pretty much only, sight is the **Chiesa di Santa Maria Assunta** (Piazza Flavio Gioia; ☺ 8am-noon & 3.30-7pm daily), its ceramic dome gleaming under the sun. Inside, regular classical lines are broken by pillars topped with gilded Ionic capitals, while winged cherubs peek from above every arch. Above the main altar of the church is the 13th-century Byzantine Black Madonna and Child.

With the church done, it's time to head for the nearby beach. Hiring a chair and umbrella on the fenced-off areas of the beaches costs around €15 per day but the crowded public areas are free. Boating isn't cheap, either. On Spiaggia Grande, expect to pay about €12 an hour for a rowing boat or €22 for a small motorboat (cheaper rates are offered for half- or full-day rental).

For diving enthusiasts, **Centro Sub Costiera Amalfitana** (☎ 089 81 21 48) operates from Spiaggia del Fornillo.

Lovers of classical music may want to coincide their visit with Positano's **Summer Music**, an annual international chamber-music festival held at the end of August or early September.

If you're a keen walker and reasonably fit, set aside a day for the classic **Sentiero degli Dei** (Path of the Gods; five to 5½ hours). It follows the steep, well-defined paths linking Positano and Praiano, from where you can catch a bus back along the coastal road.

For staggering views with much less effort, stroll the Via Positanesi d'America, the cliffside path that links the two beaches. Reward yourself with a cold drink on the terrace of **Hotel Pupetto** (right).

Sleeping

Positano has plenty of hotels, particularly in the pricier categories. Cheaper accommodation is more limited and usually booked well in advance for summer. Ask at the tourist office about rooms or apartments in private houses.

Florida Residence (☎ /fax 089 87 58 01; Viale Pasitea 171; s/d €75/95; ☺ Apr-Oct; **P**) A lot of perks for the price, including parking, air-con and even a small free-standing pool – more to get wet than for swimming laps. The clean and tidy rooms are fairly forgettable but the same-price apartments are a superb deal, with cooker and fridge which could save you serious euros on dining out.

Hotel Buca Di Bacco (☎ 089 87 57 31; www .bucadibacco.it; Via Rampa Teglia 4; s/d with breakfast €170/210; ☺ Apr-Nov) A 1960's hotel with gorgeous original yellow-and-turquoise tiles in the reception and public areas. Sometimes a stunning lobby can mean anticlimactic rooms – not here. These are luxurious and large, with smart stripy bed linen and good-sized terraces that overlook the domed church and beach.

Hotel Palazzo Murat (☎ 089 87 51 77; www .palazzomurat.it; Via Dei Mulini 23; s/d with breakfast from €205/290; ☺ year-round) An 18th-century palace with a palatial arched entrance lined with palms and giant urns. There are just five rooms in the original part of the building and 26 in the newer bit. The décor in both is exquisite, with antiques, original oil paintings and plenty of glossy marble. The gardens are pretty as a picture with banana trees, bottle-brush, Japanese maple and pine trees.

Hotel Pupetto (☎ 089 87 50 87; www.hotel pupetto.it; Via Fornillo 37; s/d with breakfast €90/160; ☺ Mar-Dec; **P**) Right beside the Spiaggia del Fornillo, all its rooms have sea views and the price includes breakfast. Rooms have dizzily tiled floors offset by lashings of white paint and bed linen. There's a downstairs nautical-theme bar and a Pupetto restaurant on the beach. Go for a room in the front and you can almost tumble out of bed onto the beach.

Le Sirenuse (☎ 089 87 50 66; www.sirenuse .it; Via Cristoforo Colombo 30; d with breakfast from €380; ☺ year-round; **P**) This extraordinary hotel was formerly the private home of the Marchesi Sersale who evidently had impeccable good taste and an eye for art. The result is a luxurious lived-in atmosphere with antiques, original oil paintings, framed Italian fans, giant clay pots and handmade Vietri tiles. There are 60 rooms and suites overlooking the bay, steps down to the sandy beach and a brand-new fitness centre, pool and spa.

Villa Franco (☎ 089 87 56 55; www.villa francahotel.it; Viale Pasitea 318; d with breakfast €190; ☺ Apr-Nov) An immaculate boutique hotel with a sparkling blue-and-white Mediterranean feel. The rooftop pool has some of the best views in town. The rooms are small but chic, with tiled frescoes, balconies and more good views. There's a small downstairs bar, plus gym, if you need any more exercise than walking down and up the steps to the beach.

Villa La Tartana (☎ 089 81 21 93; www.villa latartana.it; Via Vicolo Vito Savino 6-8; d with breakfast €150; ☺ Apr-Sep) A former apartment block, the main disadvantage here is the lack of a lift although, at these prices, you'll probably get your cases lugged up for you. Go for a room on the 3rd floor with huge verandas overlooking the beach. There are bright floral-design tiles, pretty floral bed heads and bathrooms decorated in earthy tones with full-size bath, plus shower.

Villa Maria Luisa (☎ 089 87 50 23; www.pen sionemarialuisa.com; Via Fornillo 42; s/d with bathroom €40/65; ☺ Mar-Nov) A lovely little hotel, the Maria Luisa has quirky old-fashioned rooms. It's well worth paying the €5 extra for a private terrace as there are magnificent views of the bay. The owner Carlo speaks several languages and is very friendly – so are the three cats.

Villa Nettuno (☎ 089 87 54 01; www.villa nettunopositano.it; Viale Pasitea 208; s/d €70/80; ☺ year-round) It's worth tackling the last few steps to find this charming hotel hidden among the foliage. Go for one of the rooms in the 300-year-old part of the building with the frescoed wardrobes and private communal terrace. Other rooms are still good value and have more modern bathrooms, but the cheap furniture is a letdown and the new tiling is seriously naff.

Eating

Most restaurants are overpriced and many close over winter, making a brief reappearance for Christmas and New Year.

Buca Di Bacco (☎ 089 811 461 Viale Del Brigantino 35-37; snacks from €3, mains from €6) The most popular snack bar and restaurant in town, this place covers most tastebuds and budgets. You can pick up an inexpensive well-stuffed *panino* (bread roll) or sweet pastry here, or enjoy pricier sit-down service at the La Pergola restaurant with a menu including risottos, seafood and good-sized salads.

Chez Black (☎ 089 87 50 36; Via del Brigantino 19; meals around €30) A favourite for the old-time trendies who have been coming here since the '60s. Overlooks the main beach with a terrace where you can indulge in seafood dishes like *spaghetti a la Black* cooked in cuttlefish ink or, for a blowout, the mixed seafood grill. This is also a great place to sit over a drink and pick up a few fashion tips from the passers-by.

Da Vincenzo (☎ 089 87 51 28; Viale Pasitea 172-178; meals about €24; ☺ Mar-Oct) Family-run since 1959, the ebullient father-and-son duo wait tables with gusto, while wife Marcela does her creative bit in the kitchen. There's a limited menu that changes every three days according to what is freshest in the market. House specials include *panzarotti* (small fried pastry squares with mozzarella and ham) and *peperoni ripieni* (red peppers stuffed with olives and cheese).

Il Ritrovo (☎ 089 87 54 53; Via Montepertuso 77, Montepertuso; meals about €22; ☺ Thu-Tue) High up in the hills, this trattoria is decorated with tomatoes and, unsurprisingly, they show up frequently on the menu. Owner Salvatore was a construction worker until his love of food led to this culinary success story about eight years ago. The terrace is lovely with lofty sea views.

La Zagara (☎ 089 87 59 64; Via dei Mulini 6) Has overpriced snacks for sweet-tooths and savoury-lovers, but when you're sitting on the terrace in the shade of lemon trees, the prices don't seem to matter so much. Waiters know how to play to the tourists, with their red-check shirts and smiles (except for the poor sod collecting money at the toilets).

Lo Guarracino (☎ 089 87 57 94; Via Positanesi d'America; meals from €30; ☺ Mar-Dec) Here you pay for location. On the cliffside path connecting Positano's two beaches, the panorama overlooking a small beach is unfettered by niggly little eyesores like houses or cars. The food is straightforward, with dishes such as grilled prawns (€20) and *penne all'arrabbiata* (pasta with a spicy tomato and chilli sauce; €7.50), plus more pasta, and pizzas. There are just a few tables, so book ahead if you can.

Ristorante Il Saraceno d'Oro (☎ 089 81 20 50; Viale Pasitea 254; pizzas around €6, meals €24; ☺ Mar-Oct) This highly popular eatery scores well on all counts – food, service, price and décor; the complimentary end-of-meal glass of limoncello is a nice touch. The pizzas are excellent, the profiteroles sublime – try them in chocolate sauce or in lemon cream.

Ristorante Max (☎ 089 87 50 56; Via dei Mulini 22; meals around €38; ☺ Mar-Nov) Smock-and-beret types will love the setting here; the dining room is within an art gallery, with paintings ranging from renaissance style to modern impressionist. There are set menus and specials of the day like ravioli with clams and asparagus, and zucchini flowers stuffed with ricotta and salmon.

Entertainment

Con Winum Wine & Bar (☎ 089 81 14 61; Via Rampa Teglia 12; ☯ 8am-3am Apr-Oct) A snazzy wine bar, art gallery and Internet café with live jazz on Friday and Saturday during the summer. Con Winum attracts boatloads of snappily dressed Italians. The wine list is not to be quaffed at, with its long list including a Mondavi Rothschild: a snip at €550 a bottle.

Shopping

Positano is boutique-mad but, after a while, you may glaze over at the sameness of the fashions here. The humble lemon also enjoys star status again; not just in limoncello and lemon-infused candles, but blazoned across tea towels, aprons and pottery.

Ceramiche Parlato (☎ 089 87 50 97; Via G Marconi 138) Family-run for three generations, the ceramics here reflect the calibre of the hotels across the way, so expect high prices and quality for a discerning clientele.

Costanzo Avitabile (☎ 089 87 53 66; Piazza Amerigo Vespucci 15) One of several handmade shoe shops in town. This one will make you a pair of leather sandals while you wait.

Louise (☎ 089 87 51 92; Via Dei Mulini 22) The window display here will stop you in your tracks; a riot of brilliant floral-patterned dresses, shirts, skirts and scarves. These distinctive fashions have been designed and made here for 40 years under the watchful eye of Louise; the epitome of Positano elegance, she's in the shop most days.

Getting There & Around

To take a SITA bus (services to Amalfi, Sorrento and towns in between) at the top (northern end) of Viale Pasitea, buy your ticket at Bar Internazionale, just opposite the stop. For the easternmost bus stop, get the bus in town from in front of the tobacconist at the bottom of Via Cristoforo Colombo. If you forget, you're in for a long descent and climb back up.

Positano is a snakes-and-ladders town. If your knees can take a steep ascent or drop, there are dozens of narrow alleys and stairways that make walking relatively easy and joyously traffic-free. Otherwise, a small orange bus follows the lower ring road every half-hour, passing along Viale Pasitea, Via

Detour: Nocelle

This tiny, still relatively isolated mountain village (450m) lies east of Positano. It's accessible by road or, more interestingly, by a short walking track from the end of Positano's Via Mons S Clinque. Before heading back, have lunch at **Trattoria Santa Croce** and enjoy the panoramic views from its terrace. In summer the place is open for both lunch and dinner; at other times of the year, it's best to phone and check in advance. Buses link Nocelle and Positano, via Montepertuso, running roughly every half-hour in summer.

Cristoforo Colombo and Via G Marconi. Stops are clearly marked and you buy your ticket (€0.80) on board. It passes by both SITA bus stops.

Between Easter and October, ferries link Positano with Capri, Naples and other towns along the Amalfi Coast.

Positano Rent a Scooter (☎ 089 812 20 77; Viale Pasitea 99; per day €45) rents out scooters.

AMALFI

It is astonishing to think that pretty little Amalfi was once such an important place: a maritime superpower with a population of more than 70,000. The latter fact is particularly hard to get one's head around, as Amalfi is in a tight little cove and clearly too small for that many people. The explanation is chilling – most of the old city, and its populace, simply slid into the sea during the 1343 earthquake.

Today, although the resident population numbers no more than around 5000 people, the numbers swell significantly during the summer, when camera-slung tourists pour in by the coachload. Most head straight for Amalfi's main Piazza del Duomo, overlooked by one of the most stunning cathedrals in southern Italy.

Take an easy stroll eastwards to neighbouring Atrani with its picturesque tangle of whitewashed alleys, arches and humble, yet handsome, piazza. There's an attractive small beach here, as well.

Orientation

Most of Amalfi's hotels and restaurants are around Piazza Duomo or along Via Lorenzo d'Amalfi and its continuation, Via Capuano, which snakes north from the cathedral.

Information

Altra Costiera (☎ 089 873 60 82; www.altracostiera .com; Via Lorenzo D'Amalfi 34) Provides Internet access and accommodation referral, and arranges walking and other tours.

Deutsche Bank (Corso Repubbliche Marinare) Next door to the tourist office; has an ATM.

Post office (Corso Repubbliche Marinare) Next door to the tourist office.

Tourist Office (☎ 089 87 24 67; Piazza Flavio Gioia 3; 🕙 8.30am-1.30pm & 3-5.15pm Mon-Fri, 8.30am-12.30pm Sat) Has little useful information but there's some pretty brochures.

Sights & Activities

The **Sant'Andrea cathedral** (☎ 089 87 10 59; Piazza del Duomo; 🕙 9am-7pm Apr-Jun, 9am-9pm Jul-Sep, 9.30am-5.15pm Oct & Mar, 10am-1pm & 2.30-4.30pm Nov-Feb) makes an imposing sight at the top of its sweeping flight of stairs. The cathedral dates in part from the early 10th century and the striking stripy façade has been rebuilt twice, most recently at the end of the 19th century. Although the building is a hybrid, the Arabic-Norman style of Sicily predominates, particularly in the two-tone masonry and the bell tower. The interior is mainly baroque and the altar features some fine statues together with 12th- and 13th-century mosaics.

The adjoining 13th-century **Chiostro del Paradiso** (admission €2.50; 🕙 9.30am-7pm Jun-Oct, 9.30am-5.15pm Nov-May) was built in Arabic style to house the tombs of prominent citizens.

The small, one-room **Museo Civico** (☎ 089 87 10 66; Piazza Municipio; admission free; 🕙 8.30am-1pm Mon-Fri), behind Corso Republicche Marinare in the town hall building, contains the Tavole Amalfitane, an ancient manuscript draft of Amalfi's maritime code, and other historical documents. Ask at the window halfway up the entry stairs for a guide sheet in English. The former republic's restored **Arsenale** (Via Matteo Camera; admission free; 🕙 9am-8pm Easter-Sep) is the only shipbuilding depot of its kind in Italy.

Up in Valle dei Mulini, an easy walk from town, is **Il Museo della Carta** (Paper Museum; ☎ 0328 318 86 26; Via delle Cartiere; admission €3.10; 🕙 10am-6pm), set up in a paper mill dating from the 13th century.

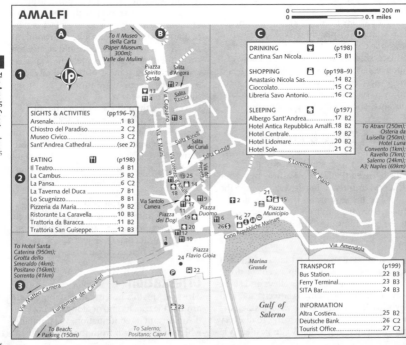

AMALFI

0 — 200 m
0 — 0.1 miles

To Il Museo
della Carta
(Paper Museum,
300m);
Valle dei Mulini

Piazza
Spirito
Santo

Salita
d'Angora

| DRINKING | 🖪 | (p198) |
| Cantina San Nicola | | 13 B1 |

SHOPPING	🛍	(pp198–9)
Anastasio Nicola Sas		14 B2
Cioccolato		15 C2
Libreria Savo Antonio		16 C2

SLEEPING	🛏	(p197)
Albergo Sant'Andrea		17 B2
Hotel Antica Repubblica Amalfi		18 B2
Hotel Centrale		19 B2
Hotel Lidomare		20 B2
Hotel Sole		21 C2

SIGHTS & ACTIVITIES	(pp196–7)
Arsenale	1 B3
Chiostro del Paradiso	2 C2
Museo Civico	3 C2
Sant'Andrea Cathedral	(see 2)

EATING	🍴	(p198)
Il Teatro		4 B1
La Cambus		5 B2
La Pansa		6 C2
La Taverna del Duca		7 B1
Lo Scugnizzo		8 B1
Pizzeria da Maria		9 B2
Ristorante La Caravella		10 B3
Trattoria da Baracca		11 B3
Trattoria San Guiseppe		12 B3

To Hotel Santa
Caterina (950m);
Grotta dello
Smeraldo (4km);
Positano (16km);
Sorrento (41km)

Via Capuano
Salita Rascica
Via E Marini
Salita Bonelli
Salita dei Curiali
Salita Castald
Via Lorenzo D'Amalfi
Via Santolo Camera
Piazza dei Dogi
Piazza Duomo
S Lorenzo del Piano
Corso Repubbliche Marinare
Piazza Municipio
Piazza Flavio Gioia

To Atrani (250m);
Osteria da
Luisella (250m);
Hotel Luna
Convento (1km);
Ravello (7km);
Salerno (24km);
A3; Naples (69km)

Via Matteo Camera
Lungomare dei Cavalieri

Marina
Grande

Gulf of
Salerno

Via Amendola

TRANSPORT	(p199)
Bus Station	22 B3
Ferry Terminal	23 B3
SITA Bar	24 B3

INFORMATION	
Altra Costiera	25 B2
Deutsche Bank	26 C2
Tourist Office	27 C2

To Beach;
Parking (150m)

To Salerno;
Positano; Capri

The ceramics shops that you will see mostly clustered around Piazza Duomo reflect Amalfi's traditional promotion of this craft.

In Conca dei Marini, about 4km along the coast towards Positano, is **Grotta dello Smeraldo** (admission €5; ⏱ 9am-7pm Mar-Oct, 9am-4pm Nov-Feb), a grotto so named for the emerald colour of its sandy floor. SITA buses pass by but it's more fun to take one of the boats that run frequently from Amalfi in season (€5 return; allow 1½ hours). At the grotto, as at the Marina Grande area and Spiaggia Santa Croce, you can hire motorboats for around €24.

The paths and stairways that thread the hills behind Amalfi and up to Ravello make for grand walking. For useful guidebooks, see p191.

Festivals & Events

On 24 December and 6 January, skin-divers make their traditional pilgrimage to the ceramic crib in Grotta dello Smeraldo.

The Regatta of the Four Ancient Maritime Republics, which rotates between Amalfi, Venice, Pisa and Genoa, is held on the first Sunday in June. Amalfi's turn comes round again in 2005 and 2009.

Sleeping

Amalfi does not have the wealth of hotels of nearby Positano as it attracts mainly day-trippers; and they are almost all in the mid-to-upper price bracket. For more accommodation choices, check at the tourist office.

Albergo Sant'Andrea (☎ 089 87 11 45; Via Santolo Camera; s/d €45/75; ⏱ Mar-Oct) Situated about as close to the cathedral as possible, without attending confession, rooms here are fairly underwhelming but the price is right for this bang-in-the-centre location. The on-site restaurant is handy for sudden hunger pangs.

Hotel Antica Repubblica Amalfi (☎ 089 873 63 10; www.starnet.it/anticarepubblica; Vico Dei Pastai 2; s/d with breakfast €90/135; ⏱ year-round) A hotel that has recently invested in an interior makeover. Warm terracotta tiles are tastefully twinned with traditional Amalfi squares of blue, yellow and apple green, and all rooms have a deft strip of stencilling. Breakfast is served on the panoramic rooftop terrace.

Hotel Centrale (☎ 089 87 26 08; www.hotel centraleamalfi.it; Largo Piccolomini 1; s/d €120/135; ⏱ year-round) There are striking views of the cathedral, from this exquisite boutique hotel which has recently benefited from a total spruce-up. The bright green and blue timework gives the place a vibrant fresh look, while the balconies allow you to discreetly people-watch couples out for a romantic Piazza stroll, bless 'em.

Hotel Lidomare (☎ 089 87 13 32; www.lido mare.it; Largo Duchi Piccolomini 9; s/d with breakfast €50/110; ⏱ year-round) It's like stepping into an ancestral home at this lovely family-run hotel. The spacious rooms have a real air of gentility, with their appealingly haphazard décor, old-fashioned tiles and some fine old antiques. Some rooms have Jacuzzi bathrooms and sea views.

Hotel Luna Convento (☎ 089 87 10 02; www .lunahotel.it; Via Pantaleone Comite 33; s/d €190/210; ⏱ year-round) This former convent was founded by St Francis in 1222 and has been a hotel for some 170 years. Rooms in the original building are in the former monks' cells but there's nothing pokey about the bright tiles and white decoration, with balconies and seamless sea views. The newer wing is equally beguiling, with religious frescoes over the bed (to stop any misbehaving). There are two restaurants and a sea-level swimming pool.

Hotel Santa Caterina (☎ 089 87 10 12; www .hotelsantacaterina.it; Strada Amalfitana 9; d from €350; ⏱ Mar-Oct) Lounge by the saltwater pool, work out in the gym or simply enjoy one of the loveliest gardens in southern Italy at one of its top hotels. Located just outside the town, it sits on a cliff-top commanding fabulous sea views from all the rooms. There's even a Romeo and Juliet suite for honeymooners. There's a private beach, pool and fitness centre, and a celebrity guest list that includes former First Lady Hilary Clinton.

Hotel Sole (☎ 089 87 11 47; Largo Della Zecca 2; s/d with breakfast €90/120; ⏱ Mar-Oct) A welcoming and bright hotel with modern rooms. Located just off a pretty small piazza from where a covered passageway takes you to the Piazza del Duomo. The hotel is next to an Irish-themed watering hole that can get high-spirited on Saturday.

Eating

Il Teatro (☎ 089 87 24 73; Via Herculano Marini 19; mains around €6; ☺ Wed-Mon Feb-Dec) Solid home-style restaurant with filling rather than refined food. Il Teatro is usually packed out with local families and young people. The wide ribbon-style *scialatielli* pasta is made daily. Vegetarians can fill up fast with a choice of several dishes, including *scialatiella* with tomato and aubergines. Fisheterians can fork out just €5 for the mussels, served with lemon, tomatoes or wine.

La Cambus (☎ 089 87 31 44; Via Lorenzo D'Amalfi 57; snacks from €2; ☺ year-round) A small cheerful café and snack bar where they won't act snooty if you order a cappuccino after 11am, with bruschettes and sandwiches at bargain-bucket prices. This is a favourite hang-out for the Brits-abroad set.

La Pansa (☎ 089 87 10 65; Piazza Duomo 40; ☺ Wed-Mon year-round) An elegant café on the main piazza, it has been in the Pansa family for five generations. Choose from a selection of died-and-gone-to-heaven cakes and pastries.

La Taverna del Duca (☎ 089 87 27 55; Piazza Spirito Santo 26; meals around €35; ☺ Fri-Wed year-round) This place has a fishy reputation with lobster and seafood specials, like *felicelli* pasta with scampi and prawns. Tucked into the corner of a small piazza away from the centre, the dark woody interior is lined with dusty wine bottles and paintings. There are a few tables out on the square.

Osteria da Luisella (☎ 089 87 10 87; Piazza Umberto, Atrani; meals around €20; ☺ 10am-3am Thu-Tue year-round) Charismatic owner Franco has recently opened this winebar/restaurant and Internet café in its prime piazza setting. The menu is traditional and changes according to the season but usually includes big pasta dishes such as *caporalessa*, a delicious baked concoction with aubergines, tomatoes and cheese, or ravioli stuffed with provola cheese and *rucola* (rocket). There is a lengthy wine list, as well.

Pizzeria da Maria (☎ 089 87 18 80; Via Lorenzo D'Amalfi 16; pizzas €6, meals around €25; ☺ Dec-Oct) Attracts a dedicated crowd ranging from off-the-yacht Neapolitans to local taxi drivers. Head chef Enzo is suitably flamboyant and will explain the dishes to you in rapid Italian. Not the place for a quiet meal; there's a permanent pianist as well. The food is good and traditional, the portions huge.

Ristorante La Caravella (☎ 089 87 10 29; Via Matteo Camera 12; meals around €45; ☺ Wed-Mon Jan–mid-Nov) A Michelin-star restaurant where traditional Amalfi recipes are given a nouvelle zap. The creamy interior attracts a discreet, classy crowd here for such lush dishes as black ravioli with cuttlefish and scampi. Poor famished souls can go for the €65 six-course set menu. There's a head-spinning 15,000-bottle wine cellar here, too.

Trattoria da Baracca (☎ 089 87 12 85; Piazza dei Dogi; meals around €20, tourist menu €15.50; ☺ Thu-Tue Feb-Oct) Seafood restaurant where the genial waiters seem to genuinely enjoy their job, rather than merely angling for a tip. There are stripy blue awnings, fishing-boat murals and a fish soup that is reckoned to be very good indeed.

Trattoria San Giuseppe (☎ 089 87 26 40; Salita Ruggiero II 4; pizzas from €5, mains around €6; ☺ Fri-Wed year-round) Earthy, atmospheric restaurant hidden away under an arch in Amalfi's labyrinthine alleyways. Outside tables may be scented by the smell of antique drains. If so, head inside where the tables are cooled by fans. Some say the pizza here is the best in town. There is a no-fuss pasta choice as well.

Drinking

Cantina San Nicola (☎ 089 830 45 59; Salita Marino Sebaste 8; ☺ Mon-Sat) Atmospheric bar down an ancient sidestreet with a tastefully decorated rustic cavelike space. There are wine tastings on Monday and Thursday at 6pm during the summer (July to September).

Shopping

The centre of Amalfi is overloaded with shops, most of which are geared towards tourists, so be sure to compare prices.

Anastasio Nicola Sas (☎ 089 87 10 07; Via Lorenzo D'Amalfi 32) Deli and gift shop with a wonderland of gourmet goodies, including cheese, coffee, chocolates, pasta, limoncello and preserves.

Cioccolato (☎ 089 87 32 91; Piazza Municipio 12) A couple of doors down from Sole Hotel, this enticing and elegant chocolate shop makes all its sweet treats direct on the premises.

Libreria Savo Antonio (☎ 089 87 11 80; Via Repubbliche Marinare 17; ☺ 7am-11pm)

A piled-high bookshop and newsagent with English-language choices for both books and papers.

Getting There & Away

SITA buses run from Piazza Flavio Gioia to Sorrento (€2.40, more than 12 daily) via Positano (€1.30) and also to Salerno (€1.80, at least hourly) and Naples (€3.10, eight daily, various routes). You can buy tickets and check out current schedules at SITA Bar (Piazza Flavio Gioia).

Between Easter and mid-September there are daily ferry sailings to Salerno (€4), Naples (€9), Positano (€5) and the islands of Capri (€11) and Ischia (€16.50).

RAVELLO

Ravello is a small stylish town that is largely pedestrianised, unabashedly heritaged and extremely touristy during the summer. That said, the views, even by local standards, are spectacular. A former playground of Jackie Kennedy and current home to Gore Vidal, Ravello sits like a natural balcony overhanging Amalfi and the nearby towns of Minori and Maiori. The 7km drive from Amalfi up the Valle del Dragone passes through the soaring mountains and deep ravines that characterise the area.

Ravello's tourist office (☎ 089 85 70 96; www.ravellotime.it; Piazza Duomo 10; ☉ 9am-8pm Mon-Sat Jun-Sep, 9am-6pm Oct-May) has a colour pamphlet, *Ravello The City of Music*, that's packed with information and suggested walking itineraries around the town.

Sights & Activities

The cathedral (Piazza Duomo; ☉ 8.30-1pm & 3-8pm) dates from the 11th century and features an impressive marble pulpit with six lions crouched at its base. The museum (admission €2) is located in the crypt and contains religious artefacts.

Overlooking the piazza is Villa Rufolo. Its last resident in 1880 was the German composer Wagner, who wrote the third act of *Parsifal* here. The villa was built in the 13th century for the wealthy Rufolos and was home to several popes, as well as to Charles I of Anjou. The villa's gardens (☎ 089 851 76 57; admission €5; ☉ 9am-6pm) were created in 1853 by green-fingered Scot Neville

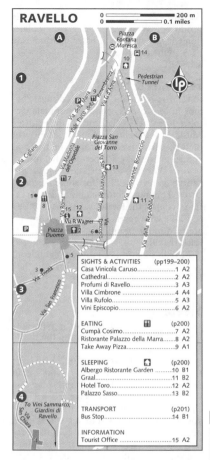

Reid and are the inspirational setting for the town's impressive programme of classical music. With stunning views of the Bay of Naples, they are packed with exotic colours, artistically crumbling towers and luxurious blooms.

Some way east of Piazza Duomo is the early-20th-century Villa Cimbrone (☎ 089 85 80 72; admission €5; ☉ 9am-6pm), set in magnificent gardens and now a hotel. Worth the admission price just for the views, Villa Cimbrone is said to have been used by Greta Garbo as a hideaway.

You can also visit the town's vineyards: the small Casa Vinicola Caruso (Via della Marra), Vini Episcopio (Hotel Palumbo, Via Toro) and Vini Sammarco (Via Nazionale). If you prefer a touch of the hard stuff, visit Giardini di Ravello beside Vini Sammarco, or Profumi di Ravello (Via Trinità), where limoncello is produced. Whatever tickles your palate, don't forget that it's a hairy, hairpin ride back to the coast.

Festivals & Events

Ravello's programme of classical music begins in March and continues until late October. It reaches its crescendo in the Festivale Musicale di Ravello, held in the second half of July, when international orchestras and special guests play a repertoire that always features Wagner. Tickets start at €20 and can go as high as €130 for some performances. For more information and reservations, contact the **Ravello Concert Society** (☎ 089 85 81 49; www.ravelloarts.org). The concerts are held in the beautiful gardens of the **Villa Rufolo** (p199).

Ravello's patron saint, San Pantaleon, is recalled with fun and fireworks in late July.

Sleeping

Book well ahead for summer – especially if you're planning a visit during the music festival in July.

Albergo Ristorante Garden (☎ 089 85 72 26; www.hotelgardenravello.it; Via Boccaccio 4; d with breakfast €105; ☿ mid-Mar–late Oct) This welcoming hotel has faded a little since Jackie Kennedy passed by with her young family in tow, but it's still a good option for a place to stay. Some bathrooms have baths as well as showers. The rooms are on the small side but are compensated for by the private terraces with sea views. There's also a pool. If you arrive by bus, you'll also save on lugging your bags around, as it's right by the stop. The terrace restaurant has one of the best situations in town; apparently Gore Vidal is a regular.

Graal (☎ 089 85 72 22; www.hotelgraal .it; Via della Repubblica 8; s/d with breakfast €59/98; ☿ year-round) Although the public areas could do with updating, the rooms are tastefully decorated with plenty of sun-and-sea colours reflecting the nice balcony views. There are good-sized bathrooms and it is no smoking. The downstairs restaurant has a good reputation in town.

Palazzo Sasso (☎ 089 81 81 81; www.palazzo sasso.com; Via San Giovanni del Oro 28; d with breakfast from €260; ☿ Mar-Oct) A stunning pale-pink 12th-century palace

that became a hotel in 1880, providing refuge for Wagner and, later, Ingrid Bergman. After many decades of closure, the hotel re-opened in 1997 and has been creatively refurbished with brushes of colour from the Moorish palette, coupled with tasteful antiques. There are 44 rooms and suites, most with Jacuzzis and astonishingly beautiful views, and a pool.

Hotel Toro (☎ /fax 089 85 72 11; www.hotel toro.it; Via Wagner 3; s/d with breakfast €74/105; ☿ Easter-Nov) Just off central Piazza Duomo, Hotel Toro is a tasteful place where your only problem might be the clang of the cathedral bells disturbing your beauty sleep. The rooms have terracotta or light marble tiles and cream furnishings; not desperately imaginative but soothing on a hot day. In summertime, the grassy, walled garden is a delightful place in which to sip your sundowner.

Villa San Michele (☎ 089 87 22 37; Castiglione di Ravello 3; d with breakfast €140; ☿ Mar-Dec) Very pretty hotel on the road up to town with blue shutters, colourful gardens and sea views.

Eating

Cumpà Cosimo (☎ 089 85 71 56; Via Roma 44-6; meals around €30; ☿ year-round) It's very much a family affair at this intimate, almost self-sufficient place. Meat comes fresh from the family butcher's shop, vegetables and fruit are homegrown, and even the house wine is homebrew. Owner Netta is smiley and welcoming, and will happily explain the menu in her best English. Dishes include rabbit with tomatoes, penne with hot peppers and tomatoes, and grilled crayfish.

Ristorante Palazzo della Marra (☎ 089 85 83 02; Via della Marra 7; meals €35-40; ☿ Wed-Mon Apr-Sep) Splash out and you may possibly enjoy the best meal of your trip here. The food is a snip above the competition, both in quality and price, and you can't really fault the 12th-century building for style. Dishes include smoked duck with fennel cream, beef fillet in thyme and, to round it off, tiramisu with cream of pistachio.

Take Away Pizza (☎ 089 85 76 05; 41 Viale Parco della Rimembranza; ☿ year-round) If you're pushed for time or counting coins there are 36 pizza choices to select from, with pizzas costing from €2.50.

Getting There & Away

SITA operates about 15 buses daily between Ravello and Amalfi (€1, 25 minutes). If you're arriving by car, turn left (north) about 2km east of Amalfi. Vehicles are not permitted in Ravello's town centre but there's plenty of space available in supervised car parks on the perimeter.

SALERNO

Salerno may seem like a bland big city after all those oh-so-pretty Amalfi towns but the place has a charming, if gritty, individuality, with a tumbledown medieval quarter and pleasant seafront promenade. One of southern Italy's many victims of earth tremors and landslides, it was also left in tatters by the heavy fighting that followed the 1943 landings of the American 5th Army, just to the south of the city. It is an important transport junction and makes an excellent base for exploring the Amalfi Coast to the west, and Paestum (see p203) and the Costiera Cilentana to the southeast.

Originally an Etruscan and later a Roman colony, Salerno flourished with the arrival of the Normans in the 11th century. Robert Guiscard made it the capital of his dukedom in 1076 and, under his patronage, the Scuola Medica Salernitana was renowned as one of medieval Europe's greatest medical institutes.

Orientation

Salerno's train station is on Piazza Vittorio Veneto, situated at the eastern end of town. Most intercity buses stop here and there are a number of hotels nearby. Salerno's main shopping strip, Corso Vittorio Emanuele, leads off northwest to the medieval main part of town; this street is car-free. Running parallel to Corso Vittorio Emanuele is Corso Garibaldi, which becomes Via Roma as it heads out of the city for the Amalfi Coast. Tree-lined Lungomare Trieste, on the waterfront, changes its name to Lungomare Marconi at the massive Piazza della Concordia on its way out of town, southeast towards Paestum.

Information
EMERGENCY
Police station (☎ 089 66 31 11; Via de Carrare)

INTERNET ACCESS
Interlanguage Point (☎ 089 275 35 81; 1st fl, Corso Vittorio Emanuele 14; per 30 mins €2; ☒ 9am-1pm & 3.30-9pm Mon-Sat)

Mail Box (Via Diaz 19; per 25 mins €1.50; ☒ 9am-1.30pm & 5.30-8pm Mon-Sat)

INTERNET RESOURCES
Salerno City (www.salernocity.com in Italian)

Salerno Memo (www.salernomemo.com in Italian)

MEDICAL SERVICES
Ospedale Ruggi D'Aragona (hospital; ☎ 089 67 11 11; Via San Leonardo)

MONEY
There's a Banca Nazionale del Lavoro ATM at the train station. You'll find several banks with ATMs on Corso Vittorio Emanuele.

POST
Post office (Corso Garibaldi 203)

TOURIST INFORMATION
Tourist office (☎ 089 23 14 32; Piazza Vittorio Veneto; ☒ 9am-2pm & 3-8pm Mon-Sat)

Sights
CATHEDRAL
The city's cathedral (☎ 089 23 13 87; Piazza Alfano; ☒ 10am-6pm), built by the Normans under Robert Guiscard in the 11th century and remodelled in the 18th century, sustained severe damage in the 1980 earthquake. It's dedicated to San Matteo (St Matthew), whose remains were reputedly brought to the city in 954 and buried in the crypt. With its 28 Greek columns, most of them plundered from Paestum, it has a decidedly classical air.

Cappella delle Crociate (Chapel of the Crusades), so named because crusader's weapons were once blessed here, has the body of the 11th-century pope Gregory VII interred under the altar.

Next door on the northern side of the cathedral is Museo Diocesano (☎ 089 23 91 26; Largo del Plebiscito 12; admission free; ☒ 9am-6pm), which has a modest collection of artworks including items from the Norman period and a few fragments of Lombard sculpture.

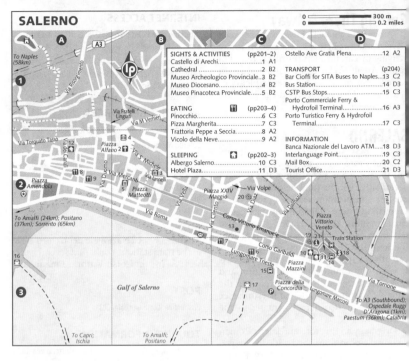

SALERNO

| 0 | 300 m |
| 0 | 0.2 miles |

SIGHTS & ACTIVITIES (pp201–2)
Castello di Arechi....................1 A1
Cathedral 2 B2
Museo Archeologico Provinciale..3 B2
Museo Diocesano.....................4 B2
Museo Pinacoteca Provinciale.....5 B2

EATING 🍴 (pp203–4)
Pinocchio.................................6 C3
Pizza Margherita.......................7 C3
Trattoria Peppe a Seccia............8 A2
Vicolo della Neve.....................9 A2

SLEEPING 🛏 (pp202–3)
Albergo Salerno.......................10 C3
Hotel Plaza.............................11 D3

Ostello Ave Gratia Plena................12 A2

TRANSPORT (p204)
Bar Cioffi for SITA Buses to Naples...13 C2
Bus Station.............................14 D3
CSTP Bus Stops.........................15 C3
Porto Commerciale Ferry &
    Hydrofoil Terminal................16 A3
Porto Turistico Ferry & Hydrofoil
    Terminal.............................17 C3

INFORMATION
Banca Nazionale del Lavoro ATM.....18 D3
Interlanguage Point....................19 C3
Mail Box.................................20 C2
Tourist Office...........................21 D3

CASTELLO DI ARECHI

A steep walk to **Castello di Arechi** (☎ 089 22 72 37; Via Benedetto Croce; admission free; ☼ 7am-noon & 4-7.30pm) along Via Risorgimento is rewarded with good views, if you can ignore the industrial sprawl beneath you. Arechi II, the Lombard duke of Benevento, built the castle over a Byzantine fort. Last renovated by the Spanish in the 16th century, its slow decline has been arrested by modern restoration.

MUSEUMS

The **Museo Archeologico Provinciale** (☎ 089 23 11 35; Via San Benedetto 28; admission free; ☼ 9am-8pm Mon-Sat) contains archaeological finds from around the region, including some particularly fine classical pieces.

Deep in the heart of the medieval quarter, the small **Museo Pinacoteca Provinciale** (☎ 089 258 30 73; Via Mercanti 63; admission free; ☼ 8am-2pm & 3-8pm Tue-Sat, 9am-1pm Sun, 1-8pm Mon) houses an interesting art collection dating from the Renaissance right up to the first half of the 19th century. There are some fine canvases by local boy Andrea Sabatini da Salerno and an assortment of works by foreign artists living in the area.

Sleeping

Albergo Salerno (☎ 089 22 42 11; www.albergo salerno.com; 5th fl, Via G Vicinanza 42; s/d €55/60; ☼ year-round) This place looks discouraging from the outside but the rooms are fine sized with high ceilings, TVs, and fans or air-con. There's a light and cheery sitting area, adjacent to the lobby, and a small bar for coffee or beer.

Hotel Plaza (☎ /fax 089 22 44 77; www.pla zasalerno.it; Piazza Vittorio Veneto 42; s/d €63/95; ☼ year-round) This hotel has gone through three generations and, finally, the current owner is doing something (although possibly not quite enough) about the drab brown-and-cream colour scheme. The bathrooms have sparkling turquoise and white tiles but the brand-new carpets are still brown. The location is good, though, and there's a lift. The back rooms have terraces with station and city views, with mountains in the distance beyond.

Ostello Ave Gratia Plena (☎ 089 79 02 51; fax 089 40 57 92; Via dei Canali; dm with breakfast €14, d B&B per person €15.50; ☼ year-round) This highly recommended HI hostel is light, airy and pristine. It's in a former 16th-century convent and you can look directly down into the adjacent church through windows where the nuns used to follow mass, thus avoiding all eye contact with men.

Eating

There are restaurants throughout the city and the medieval quarter is a good place to head for, as well. It's a lively area full of trattorie and bars, ideal for food followed by a spot of people-watching.

Pinocchio (☎ 089 22 99 64; Via Lungomare Trieste 56-582; meals around €20; ☾ Sat-Thu year-round) Frequented by locals in the know, this restaurant is clean but comfortably informal. Boxes of wine are stacked in the corner, while the decoration is a kid's-room clutter of Pinocchio murals (and mobiles). The big old wooden table in the centre of the room is piled with papers where, with much concentration, your bill

will be totted up. Rodolf and Paula are the second generation running the place. There are no specials, as such, but the *scaloppine al funghi limone o vino* (veal and mushrooms with a lemon or wine sauce) is especially good.

Pizza Margherita (☎ 089 22 88 80; Corso Garibaldi 201; pizzas and mains from €5; ☾ year-round) Don't be put off by the modern streamlined look to this place; the food inspires utter devotion in its regulars and it's always packed. There's a lavish lunch buffet where you can fill up happy, for as little as €4. The devil's tumble dryer, otherwise known as a microwave, is never used here, so be prepared to wait.

Trattoria Peppe a Seccia (☎ 089 22 05 18; Via Antica Corte 5; meals around €15; ☾ year-round) There's a great southern Italian atmosphere here with the tables sprawled out into this tiny medieval piazza, surrounded by equally ancient houses hung with modern multicoloured washing. Choices are

Majestic Paestum

One of the enduring images of southern Italy is that of three Greek temples standing in fields of wild red poppies. The trio are among the best-preserved monuments of Magna Graecia, as the Greeks called their colonies in southern Italy and Sicily.

Paestum, or Poseidonia as the city was originally called (in honour of Poseidon, the Greek god of the sea), was founded in the 6th century BC by Greek settlers and fell under Roman control in 273 BC, becoming an important trading port. The town was hit by the successive blows of the retreat of the Roman Empire, periodic outbreaks of malaria, and savage raids by the Saracens, and was gradually and understandably abandoned. Its temples were rediscovered in the late 18th century by road-builders – who proceeded to plough their way right through the ruins. However, the road did little to alter the state of the surrounding area, which remained full of malarial swamps teeming with snakes and scorpions, until well into the 20th century.

Such days are long past and Paestum is these days a Unesco World Heritage Site, easily covered on foot.

The first temple you meet on entering the site from the northern end, near the tourist office, is the 6th-century-BC **Tempio di Cerere** (Temple of Ceres). The smallest of the three temples, it served for a time as a Christian church.

As you head south you can pick out the basic outline of the large rectangular forum, heart of the ancient city. Among the partially standing buildings are the vast domestic housing area, an Italic temple, the Greek theatre, **Bouleuterion** (where the Roman senate met) and, further south, the amphitheatre – through which that infamous road was ploughed.

Tempio di Nettuno (Temple of Neptune), dating from about 450 BC, is the largest and best preserved of the three temples; only parts of its inside walls and roof are missing. Almost next door, the so-called **basilica** (in fact, a temple to the goddess Hera) is Paestum's oldest surviving monument. Dating from the middle of the 6th century BC and with nine columns across and 18 along the sides, it's indeed a majestic building. Just to its east you can, with a touch of imagination, make out remains of the temple's sacrificial altar.

In its time, the city was ringed by an impressive 4.7km of walls, subsequently built and rebuilt by both Lucanians and Romans. The most intact section is south of the ruins themselves.

Just east of the site, the museum houses a collection of much-weathered metopes (bas-relief friezes), including 33 of the original 36 from **Tempio di Argive Hera** (Temple of Argive Hera), 9km north of Paestum, of which virtually nothing else remains.

To reach Paestum catch one of the hourly buses from Salerno's Piazza della Concordia or, if you are driving, take the A3 highway from Salerno and exit at Battipaglia.

pizza, pasta and gnocchi and, as this place attracts mainly locals, you can bet the standard is high.

Vicolo della Neve (☎ 089 22 57 05; Vicolo della Neve 24; meals around €20; ☽ dinner Thu-Tue year-round) You might well have to queue to get a table at this Salerno institution. The owners have been in the restaurant business for about five centuries so they've had plenty of time to perfect the traditional fare they dish out so efficiently.

Entertainment

There are numerous bars and pubs along Via Roma, as well as dotted throughout the medieval quarter. Join the locals in their *passeggiata* (evening stroll) and see where they stop off for a drink; it's probably the best recommendation you could have.

Getting There & Away

BOAT

Ferries run from Salerno's Porto Turistico to Positano and Amalfi from April through October, while departures for Capri and Ischia leave from Porto Commerciale. Hydrofoils to these destinations also run in summer. Contact the tourist office for more information and current schedules.

BUS

Most **SITA buses** (☎ 089 40 51 45) set out from Piazza Vittorio Veneto, beside the train station. Those that follow the Amalfi Coast leave about every hour. The exception is the Naples service, which departs every 25 minutes from outside **Bar Cioffi** (Corso Garibaldi 134), where you buy your ticket.

CSTP (☎ 089 48 70 01) operates bus Nos 4 and 50 to Pompeii from Piazza Vittorio Veneto. For Paestum and other towns along the southern coast take bus No 34 from Piazza della Concordia.

Buonotourist runs an express weekday service to Rome's Fiumicino airport, departing from the train station (one way €25). The bus also passes by the EUR-Fermi Metropolitana stop in Rome. However, if central Rome (rather than the airport) is your destination, it probably makes more sense to take the train, which costs €25 return.

CAR & MOTORCYCLE

Salerno is on the A3 between Naples and Reggio di Calabria, which is toll-free from Salerno southwards.

TRAIN

Salerno is the major stop between Rome (€20), Naples (€2.90) and Reggio di Calabria (€28.60), and is served by all types of trains – a schedule can be picked up at the tourist office. It also has good train links with inland towns and the Adriatic coast.

Getting Around

Walking is the most sensible option if you're staying in the heart of Salerno. Bus No 41 runs from the train station to the cathedral.

Directory

Directory

TRANSPORT

AIR

Airlines
Airlines with flights to and from Naples include:

Air France (in Italy ☎ 848 88 44 66; www.airfrance.it in Italian) Flies daily to Paris.

Alitalia (in Italy ☎ 081 709 33 33, international flights ☎ 848 86 56 42; www.alitalia.it in Italian) Internal flights and international connections via Rome and Milan.

British Airways (in Italy ☎ 848 81 22 66; www.ba.com) Flies daily to London Gatwick.

British Midland (in UK ☎ 0870 607 05 55; www.flybmi .com) Regular services to Edinburgh, Glasgow and Manchester.

Easyjet (in UK ☎ 0870 607 65 43; www.easyjet.com) Regular services to London Stansted and Gatwick; reduced in low season.

Airports
Capodichino airport (NAP; ☎ 081 789 62 59; www.gesac.it), about 8km northeast of the city centre, is southern Italy's main airport, linking Naples with most Italian and several major European cities.

Travelling to and from the airport there are two main possibilities: **ANM** (☎ 800 63 95 25) bus No 3S (€1, 30 minutes, every 15 minutes) from Piazza Garibaldi, or the **Alibus** (Map pp243–2; ☎ 081 53 11 705) airport bus (€3, 20 minutes, half-hourly) from Piazza del Municipio.

A taxi ride will set you back about €19 – always make sure the meter is switched on. There is a series of set taxi fares to and from the airport. These are: hotels by the sea €19, Mergellina hydrofoil terminal €19, and Stazione Centrale €12.50.

BICYCLE
Cycling is a dangerous option in Naples – a city where all road rules are seemingly ignored. Not only is there a real fear of knocking over an elderly nun or mother pushing a pram (no-one takes any heed of pedestrian crossings here), but most drivers speed, chat on their mobile phones and ignore traffic lights. Also, bicycle and motorcycle theft is rife.

Bicycle hire is costly in Naples (from €20 per day), so if you are staying for some time and are deadset on taking to the saddle, it may be cheaper to actually buy one. Taking your bicycle to the Amalfi Coast is also a fraught option: think blind corners and sheer, precipitous drops.

BOAT
Ferries and hydrofoils leave for Capri, Sorrento, Ischia, Procida and Forio from Molo Beverello in front of the Castel Nuovo.

Longer-distance ferries for Palermo, Cagliari, Milazzo, the Aeolian Islands (Isole Eolie) and Tunisia leave from the **Stazione Marittima** (Map pp244–6), which is next to Molo Beverello.

Alilauro and SNAV also operate hydrofoils to the islands of Ischia, Procida and Capri from Mergellina.

The monthly publication *Qui Napoli* lists current timetables for Bay of Naples services.

Tickets for shorter journeys can be bought at the ticket booths on Molo Beverello and at Mergellina. For longer journeys try the offices of the ferry companies or at a travel agent.

Following is a list of ferry and hydrofoil routes and the destinations they service. The ferry companies all have ticket booths and/or offices at Stazione Marittima. The fares, unless otherwise stated, are for a one-way high-season, deck-class single. The fare for a return journey isn't a significant reduction in price. Note that ferry and hydrofoil services are affected by sea conditions which frequently lead to last-minute cancellations. Services during the winter months may also be reduced according to lack of demand.

Alilauro (☎ 081 761 10 04; www.alilauro.it in Italian) Operates hydrofoils to Ischia (€13.20, eight daily) and Forio (€14.20, five daily).

Caremar (☎ 081 551 38 82; www.caremar.it in Italian) Serves Capri (ferry/hydrofoil €5.60/10.50, 13 daily), Ischia (€5.60/10.50) and Procida (€4.50/7.60, 12 daily).

Linee Lauro (☎ 081 551 33 52; www.lineelauro.it in Italian) Linked with the Med Mar Group, it has ferries to Ischia (€7, three daily) and a year-round service at least weekly to Tunis (deck class €90–130, *poltrona* or airline-style seat €80–135; bed in shared cabin €90–170). It also has direct runs to and from Sardinia and Corsica in summer. Fares for both destinations are €38–75 for deck class and €50–95 for a bed in a shared cabin.

Metró del Mare (☎ 199 44 66 44; www.metrodelmare .com in Italian) Runs a summer-only daily service to and from Amalfi (€9), Positano (€8) and Sorrento (€4).

Navigazione Libera del Golfo (NLG; ☎ 081 552 07 63; www.navlib.it in Italian) Runs hydrofoils to and from Capri (€12, four daily) year-round, and ferries to and from Amalfi (€10, three daily in summer only).

Siremar (☎ 081 580 03 40; www.siremar.it in Italian) Part of the Tirrenia group, Siremar operates boats to the Aeolian Islands and Milazzo (€50). The service occurs up to six times a week in summer, dropping by 50% in the low season.

SNAV (☎ 081 761 23 48; www.snavali.com) Runs hydrofoils to Capri (€12, five daily), Procida (€9, four daily) and Ischia (€12, four daily). In summer there are daily services to the Aeolian Islands. SNAV also operates Sicilia Jet (€58–82), which foams down the coast to Palermo daily mid-April to September.

Tirrenia (☎ 081 317 29 99; www.tirrenia.it) Has a weekly boat to and from Cagliari (deck class €26–35, shared cabin €40–54) and one to and from Palermo (deck class €34–45, shared cabin €36–45). The service increases to twice weekly in summer. From Palermo and Cagliari there are connections to Tunisia, directly or via Trapani (Sicily).

BUS

Most city **ANM buses** (☎ 081 700 11 11; www .anm.it in Italian) operating in the central area depart from and terminate in Piazza Garibaldi. The Italian bus system can be hard to crack – to locate your stop you'll probably need to ask at the **ANM information kiosk** (Map pp244–6) in the centre of the square.

There are four frequent routes (R1, R2, R3 and R4) that connect to other less frequent buses running out of the city centre. Useful bus services include:

Bus 140 Santa Lucia to Posillipo via Mergellina.

Bus C25 Piazza Amedeo to Piazza Bovio via Castel dell'Ovo and Piazza del Municipio.

Bus CD Piazza Garibaldi to Piazza del Municipio along Via Benedetto Croce and Via Monteoliveto.

No 137R From Piazza Dante north to Capodimonte and then back to Piazza Dante.

No 201 From Stazione Centrale to the Museo Archeologico Nazionale and on to Piazza del Municipio and Via San Carlo.

No 24 From the Parco Castello and Piazza Trieste e Trento along Via Toledo and Via Roma to Capodimonte.

No 3S From Piazza del Municipio along Corso Umberto 1 to Piazza Garibaldi and on to the airport.

No 404 Destra A night bus operating from midnight to 5am (hourly departures) from Stazione Centrale through the city centre to the Riviera di Chiaia and on to Pozzuoli, before returning to Stazione Centrale.

R1 From Piazza Medaglie D'Oro to Piazza Carità, Piazza Dante and Piazza Bovio.

R2 From Stazione Centrale, along Corso Umberto I, to Piazza Bovio, Piazza del Municipio and Piazza Trento e Trieste.

R3 From Mergellina along the Riviera di Chiaia to Piazza del Municipio, Piazza Bovio, Piazza Dante and Piazza Carità.

R4 From San Giovanni to Piazza Vittoria via Piazza del Municipio and Via Nuova Marina.

Buses for Italian and some European cities also leave from Piazza Garibaldi. Check destinations carefully or ask at the information kiosk in the centre of the piazza, as there are no signs.

Maco (☎ 080 310 51 85) has buses to Bari (€20, three hours). **Miccolis** (☎ 099 735 37 54) runs to Taranto (€14.25, four hours), Lecce (€24, 5½ hours) and Brindisi (€21.50, five hours), while **CLP** (☎ 081 531 17 07) serves Foggia (€9.50, two hours), Perugia (€28, 3¾ hours) and Assisi (€30, 4¾ hours). Routes for these services vary from season to season, and between weekdays and weekends. Your best bet is to call the bus offices directly.

You can buy tickets and catch **SITA** (☎ 081 552 21 76; www.sita-on-line.it in Italian) buses either from Stazione Marittima or from Via G Ferraris, near Stazione Centrale; you can also buy tickets at **Bar Clizia** (Corso Arnaldo Lucci 173).

Within the Campania region, SITA runs buses to Pompeii (€2.30, 40 minutes) and several other towns on the Amalfi Coast, and Salerno (by motorway) around eight times a day. Casting wider, it also links Naples

---

Public Transport in Naples

You can buy 'UnicoNapoli' tickets at stations, ANM booths and tobacconists. A ticket costs €1 and is valid for 90 minutes of unlimited travel by bus, tram, metro, funicular, Ferrovia Cumana or Circumflegrea. A daily ticket is good value at €3; a weekly ticket costs €9. These tickets are not valid to Pompeii or Ercolano on the Circumvesuviana train line.

with Bari (€20, three hours) and operates a service to Germany, including Dortmund (€110) via Munich (€88), Stuttgart (€88), Frankfurt (€97) and Düsseldorf (€110.50). You can connect from this service to Berlin (€118) and Hamburg (€118).

CAR & MOTORCYCLE

The constant honk of impatient motorists, the blue lights of ambulances and police cars flashing, a car constantly 10cm from your rear end, one-way streets and traffic lights that nobody observes – forget driving in town unless you have a death wish. Park your car at one of the several car parks, most of which are staffed, and walk around the city centre.

In addition to the anarchic driving, car theft is a major problem in Naples.

Both **Avis** (Map pp244–6; ☎ 081 761 13 65; www.avis.com; Corso Arnaldo Lucci 203) and **Hertz** (Map pp244–6; ☎ 081 20 62 28; www.hertz.com; Piazza Garibaldi 91b) have offices at the airport and near Stazione Centrale, as well as at the addresses listed above. You can also try the national company **Maggiore** (Map pp243–2; ☎ 081 552 19 00), which has branches at both the station and the airport. An economy car (eg a Twingo) will cost around €72 a day and €200 for three days.

You can rent a moped in Naples, but it is not recommended due to the high incidence of theft.

Naples is on the major north–south Autostrada del Sole, numbered A1 (north to Rome and Milan) and A3 (south to Salerno and Reggio di Calabria). The A30 skirts Naples to the northeast, while the A16 heads northeast to Bari.

When approaching the city, the motorways meet the Tangenziale di Napoli, which is the major ring road around the city. The ring road hugs the city's northern fringe, meeting the A1 for Rome and the A2 to Capodichino airport in the east, and continuing towards Campi Flegrei and Pozzuoli in the west.

FUNICULAR

Three of Naples' four funicular railways connect the centre with Vomero:

Funicolare Centrale Ascends from Via Toledo to Piazza Fuga.

Funicolare di Chiaia Travels from Via del Parco Margherita to Via Domenico Cimarosa.

Funicolare di Montesanto This line is temporarily closed; it climbs from Piazza Montesanto to Via Raffaele Morghen.

The fourth, Funicolare di Mergellina, connects the waterfront at Via Mergellina with Via Manzoni. Giranapoli tickets are valid for one trip only on the funicular railways.

METRO

The *Metropolitana* (Underground) is, in fact, mostly above ground.

Line 1 Runs north from Piazza Dante stopping at Museo (for Piazza Cavour and Line 2), Materdei, Salvator Rosa, Cilea, Piazza Vanvitelli, Piazza Medaglie D'Oro and seven stops beyond.

Line 2 Runs from Gianturco, just east of Stazione Centrale, with stops at Piazza Garibaldi (for Stazione Centrale), Piazza Cavour, Montesanto, Piazza Amedeo, Mergellina, Piazza Leopardi, Campi Flegrei, Cavalleggeri d'Aosta, Bagnoli and Pozzuoli.

TAXI

Official taxis are white, metered and bear the Naples symbol, the Pulcinella (with his distinctive white cone-shaped hat and long hooked nose), on their front doors. They generally ignore kerbside arm-wavers. There are taxi stands at most of the city's main piazzas or you can call one of the five taxi cooperatives including **Napoli** (☎ 081 556 44 44) or **Consortaxi** (☎ 081 552 52 52). There's also a baffling range of additional charges: €2.60 flag fee, €1.60 extra on Sundays and holidays, €2.10 more between 10pm and 7am, €1.60 for a radio taxi, €2.60 for an airport run, €0.50 per piece of luggage in the boot (trunk) and €1.60 for transporting a small animal (so leave the gerbil at home). Because of traffic delays, even a short trip may end up costing more than you anticipated.

Some taxi drivers may try to tell you that the meter's kaput. However, you can (and should) insist that they switch it on.

TRAIN

The national rail company, **Trenitalia** (☎ 89 20 21; www.trenitalia.com) has a comprehensive network throughout the country, and also operates long-distance trains throughout Europe. For example, you can catch a train from Naples to London, Paris and Madrid. Check schedules and prices via the excellent English-language website.

Naples is the rail hub for the south of Italy. For information, call ☎ 89 20 21. The city is served by *regionale* (regional), *diretto* (direct), Intercity and the superfast Eurostar trains. They arrive and depart from **Stazione Centrale** (Map pp243–2; ☎ 081 554 31 88) or **Stazione Garibaldi** (Map pp243–2; on the lower level). There are up to 30 trains daily to and from Rome.

The Ferrovia Cumana and the **Circumflegrea** (☎ 800 00 16 16), based at **Stazione Cumana di Montesanto** (Map pp244–6) on Piazza Montesanto, 500m southwest of Piazza Dante, operate services to Pozzuoli (€1.50, every 22 minutes) and Cuma (€1.50, 40 minutes, six per day).

The **Circumvesuviana** (Map pp244–6; ☎ 081 772 24 44; Corso G Garibaldi), about 400m southwest of Stazione Centrale (take the underpass from Stazione Centrale), operates trains to Sorrento via Ercolano, Pompeii and other towns along the coast. There are about 40 trains daily running between 5am and 10.30pm, with reduced services on Sunday. A ticket to Pompeii costs €2.30.

TRAMS

The following trams may be useful:

Tram No 1 Operates from east of Stazione Centrale, through Piazza Garibaldi, the city centre and along the waterfront to Piazza Vittoria.

Tram No 29 Travels from Piazza Garibaldi to the city centre along Corso G Garibaldi.

PRACTICALITIES

ACCOMMODATION

Accommodation in Naples ranges from the sublime to the ridiculous with prices to match. Hotels and *pensioni* (guesthouses) make up the bulk of accommodation. although there is a huge gulf between the luxury of top-end hotels and the limited pokey and pricey budget options.

In this book, accommodation is listed in alphabetical order; mid-range and more expensive options have been combined. These listings are followed by Cheap Sleeps, where establishments are €100 or lower for a double room in Naples or Capri (where there are virtually no cheap hotels). All prices quoted are for high season (Easter, summer and Christmas); prices can plummet considerably at other times of the year. To make a

reservation, hotels usually require confirmation by fax or letter as well as a deposit. See p148 for more information.

Booking Services

For general information on accommodation, the local tourist office is your best bet; see p220 for details. Alternatively, the following sections include specific information on local accommodation agencies within the various categories.

AGRITURISMO & B&BS

Holidays on working farms, or *agriturismo*, are not as well organised in southern Italy as in Tuscany or Umbria (where they flourish). Tourist offices should be able to help out with local operators. For detailed information on all *agriturismo* facilities available in and around Naples contact **Agriturist Campania** (Map pp243–2; ☎ 081 28 52 43; www.agriturismo .it in Italian; Corso Arnaldo Lucci 137).

Another increasingly popular option in Italy is the B&B. Options in this category include everything from restored farmhouses, city palazzi (mansions) and seaside bungalows to rooms in family houses. Tariffs cover a wide price range, typically in the €70 to €150 bracket. For more information contact **Bed & Breakfast Italia** (☎ 06 68 78 618; www.bbitalia .it in Italian; Palazzo Sforza Cesarini, Corso Vittorio Emanuele II 282, 00186 Rome). In Naples, **Rent A Bed** (Map pp248–9; ☎ 081 41 77 21; www.rentabed.com; Vico Sergente Maggiore 16) can advise on apartment and B&B accommodation.

HOSTELS

Ostelli per la gioventù (youth hostels) are run by the Associazione Italiana Alberghi per la Gioventù (AIG), which is affiliated with **Hostelling International** (HI; www.iyhf.org). A valid HI card is required in all associated youth hostels in Italy.

The national head office of **AIG** (☎ 06 487 11 52; www.ostellionline.org; Via Cavour 44, Rome) can supply a booklet which lists accredited youth hostels in Italy. Nightly rates vary from €10 to €20, which often includes breakfast.

Rental

Finding rental accommodation in Naples on your own can be difficult and time consuming – there are rental agencies that will assist, for a fee. Rental rates are higher for short-term leases and it is usually necessary to pay a deposit (generally one month in advance).

In major resort areas, such as Capri, Amalfi and Positano, the tourist offices have lists of local apartments and villas for rent. Most offices will be more than cooperative if you telephone beforehand for information on how to book an apartment.

The following websites deal in villa and/or apartment rentals:

- www.apartmentservice.com
- www.indiv-travellers.com
- www.cvtravel.net
- www.villas-in-italy-rentals.com
- www.vacanzaitalia.com

People wanting to rent a villa in the countryside can seek information from specialist travel agencies such as the following:

Cuendet & Cie Spa (☎ 0577 57 63 30; www.cuendet .com; Strada di Strove 17, 53035 Monteriggioni, Siena) One of the major companies in Italy with villas in the Amalfi Coast. In the UK you can order Cuendet's catalogues and make reservations by calling ☎ 0800 085 77 32. In the USA Cuendet bookings are handled by **Rentals in Italy** (☎ 805 987 52 78; 1742 Calle Corva, Camarillo, CA 93010).

Cottages & Castles (☎ 61 3 9853 11 42; www.cottages andcastles.com.au; 11 Laver St, Kew, Victoria 3101) Australia's version of Cuendet & Cie Spa with a portfolio of properties throughout Italy.

Parker Company (☎ 781-596 82 82; www.theparker company.com; Seaport Landing, 152 Lynnway, Lynn, MA 01902) This leading US provider of villa rentals has a huge portfolio ranging from apartments to farmhouses and castles throughout Italy. It also organises adventure and cookery courses, and has an associated service, **Actividayz** (www.actividayz.com), where travellers can book trips over 100 days online (from US$55 to $95).

Tuscany Now (☎ 020 7684 88 84; www.tuscanynow .com; International House, 10-18 Vestry St, London N1 7RE) Established 11 years ago with only three Tuscan villas, this company has now grown to one of the world's largest with high-quality villas throughout Italy, including the Amalfi Coast.

BUSINESS

In general, the consulate section of your embassy should be able to provide you with lists of lawyers, interpreters and translators in Naples, as well as providing you with general advice about conducting business in Italy.

Business Hours

Generally shops open from 9am to 1pm and 3.30pm to 7.30pm (or 4pm to 8pm) Monday to Saturday. They may close on Saturday or Thursday afternoon and on Monday morning. In Naples most department stores and supermarkets now have continuous opening hours from 9am to 7.30pm Monday to Saturday. Some even open from 9am to 1pm on Sunday.

Banks tend to open from 8.30am to 1.30pm and 2.45 to 4.30pm Monday to Friday. They are closed at weekends but it is always possible to find a *cambio* (exchange office) open in Naples and in major tourist areas.

Major post offices are open from 8.30am to 5pm or 6pm Monday to Friday and also 8.30am to 1pm on Saturday. All post offices close two hours earlier than normal on the last business day of each month (not including Saturday).

Farmacie (pharmacies) are open from 9am to 12.30pm and 3.30pm to 7.30pm. They are always closed on Sunday and usually on Saturday afternoon but are required to display a list of *farmacie* in the area that are open.

Bars (in the Italian sense these are coffee-and-sandwich places) and cafés generally open from 8am to 8pm, although some stay open after 8pm and turn into pub-style drinking-and-meeting places. Clubs and discos might open around 10pm but often there'll be no-one there until midnight at least. Restaurants open from noon to 3pm and 7.30pm to 11pm (later in summer). Restaurants and bars are required to close for one day each week with the day varying between establishments.

Opening hours for museums, galleries and archaeological sites vary, although there is a trend towards continuous opening from 9.30am to 7pm; many are closed on Monday, however. Increasingly, the major national museums and galleries remain open until 10pm during the summer.

CHILDREN

Italians love children but there are few special amenities for them. Always make a point of asking staff at tourist offices if they · know of any special family activities and for suggestions about hotels that cater for kids. Discounts are available for children (usually aged under 12 but sometimes based on the child's height) on public transport and for admission to sites.

Book accommodation in advance to avoid any inconvenience, and when travelling by train make sure to reserve seats to avoid finding yourselves standing up for the entire journey. You can hire car seats for infants and children from most car-rental firms, but you should always book them in advance.

You can buy baby formula in powder or liquid form, as well as sterilising solutions such as Milton, at *farmacie*. Disposable nappies (diapers) are widely available at supermarkets, *farmacie* and sometimes in larger *cartolerie* (stores selling paper goods). A pack of around 30 disposable nappies costs about €10. Fresh cow's milk is sold in cartons in bars that have a '*latteria*' sign and in supermarkets. If it is essential that you have milk, carry an emergency carton of UHT milk since bars usually close at 8pm. In many out-of-the-way areas in Campania, the locals use only UHT milk.

Baby-Sitting

Overall, forget it! Although a few top hotels may be able to arrange baby-sitting, children here are generally included in all facets of family life and are carted around just about everywhere, except the swishest restaurants, or left with doting relatives.

Sights & Activities

Successful travel with children can require a special effort. Don't try to overdo things, and make sure activities include the kids – older children could help with the planning of these. Try to think of things that will capture their imagination, like a visit to **Pompeii** (p181) or Capri's **Grotto Azzurra** (Blue Grotto; p167).

For more ideas on how to keep children entertained in Naples, see p62, read Lonely Planet's *Travel with Children*, or check out the websites www.travelwithyourkids.com and www.familytravelnetwork.com.

CLIMATE

The south of Italy has a Mediterranean climate. Summers are long, hot and dry and can easily soar to an enervating 35°C, although it is generally cooler on the Amalfi Coast and islands in the Bay of Naples. Winter temperatures tend to be quite moderate, averaging around 10°C. Spring and early autumn are the best seasons to visit

as temperatures are mild, but still warm. From December to March, you can expect plenty of rain. See p8 for more guidelines on the best times to visit.

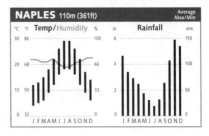

COURSES

Holiday courses are a booming section of the Italian tourist industry and they cover everything – painting, art, sculpture, wine, food, photography, scuba diving and even hang-gliding!

Cooking

Many people come to Italy just for the food so it is hardly surprising that cookery courses are among the most popular courses available. Course cost around €1400 a week – not including accommodation. The useful website www.italycookingschools.com can help you evaluate hundreds of possibilities, including some in Naples, for free.

Language

Language courses are run by private schools and universities throughout the country and are a great way to learn Italian, while also enjoying the opportunity to live in an Italian city or town. Courses cost around €400 for 60 hours a week, not including accommodation.

The Istituto Italiano di Cultura (IIC), with branches worldwide, is a government-sponsored organisation aimed at promoting Italian culture and language. This is a good place to start your search for places to study in Italy. Try the IIC's websites:

Australia (in Melbourne www.iicmelau.org, in Sydney www.iicsyd.org)

Canada (www.iicto-ca.org/istituto.htm)

France (www.iicparis.org in French or Italian)

UK (www.italcultur.org.uk)

USA (www.italcultusa.org)

CUSTOMS

There is no limit on the amount of euros that can be brought into the country. Goods brought in and exported within the EU incur no additional taxes, provided duty has been paid somewhere within the EU and the goods are for personal consumption.

Duty-free sales within the EU no longer exist. Visitors coming into Italy from non-EU countries can import the following duty free: 1L of spirits, 2L wine, 60mL perfume, 250mL eau de toilette, 200 cigarettes and other goods up to a total of €175.50; anything over this limit must be declared on arrival and the appropriate duty paid. On leaving the EU, non-EU citizens can re-claim any Value Added Tax (VAT) on all purchases equal to or over €154.94.

DISABLED TRAVELLERS

Italy is not an easy country for disabled travellers and getting around can be a problem for the wheelchair bound. Even a short journey in Naples or a town on the Amalfi Coast can become a major expedition if cobblestoned streets have to be negotiated. Although many buildings have lifts, they are not always wide enough to accommodate a wheelchair.

The **Italian State Tourist Board** (www.enit.it; p228) in your country may be able to provide advice on Italian associations for the disabled and information on what help is available. It may also carry a small brochure, *Services for Disabled Passengers*, published by the Italian railways company, Ferrovie dello Stato (FS), which details facilities at stations and on trains.

The following organisations provide services for disabled travellers:

Accessible Italy (☎ 011 309 63 63; www.accessibleitaly .com; Piazza Pitagora 9, 10137 Turin) A private company which specialises in holiday services for the disabled, ranging from tours to the hiring of adapted transport.

Associazione Italiana Assistenza Spastici (☎ 02 550 17 564; www.vacanzedisabili.it/ in Italian; Via S Barnaba 29, Milan) Operates an information service for disabled travellers called the Sportello Vacanze Disabili.

Consorzio Cooperative Integrate (COIN; ☎ 06 712 90 11; www.coinsociale.it) Based in Rome, COIN is the best reference point for disabled travellers in Italy. It is happy to share its contacts throughout Italy.

La Viaggeria (☎ 06 7158 29 45; Via Lemonia 161, 00174 Rome).

DISCOUNT CARDS

At museums, never hesitate to ask if there are discounts for students, young people, children, families or the elderly. When sightseeing and where possible always try to buy a *biglietto cumulativo*, a ticket that allows admission to a number of associated sights for less than the combined cost of separate admission fees.

Senior Cards

Senior citizens are often entitled to public-transport discounts but usually only for monthly passes (not daily or weekly tickets); the minimum qualifying age is 65 years.

For rail travel on the FS, seniors (over 60) can get a 20% reduction on full fares by purchasing an annual seniors' pass called the Carta Argento (€21). You can purchase these at major train stations.

Student & Youth Cards

Free admission to galleries and sites is available to under 18s. Discounts (usually half the normal fee) are available to EU citizens aged between 18 and 25 (you will need to produce proof of your age). An ISIC (International Student Identity Card) is no longer sufficient at many tourist sites as prices are based on age so a passport, driving licence or Euro<26 (www.euro26.org) card is preferable. An ISIC card will still, however, prove useful for cheap flights and theatre and cinema discounts; similar cards are available to

---

Cumulative Tickets

To make the best of your time and money in Naples (and indeed the entire Campania region) an excellent investment is the **Campania artecard** (☎ 800 600 601; www.campaniartecard.it in Italian). A cumulative ticket that covers museum admission and transport, it comes in various forms. In Naples a three-day ticket (€13) gives free admission to two participating sites, a 50% discount on others and free transport in Naples and the Campi Flegrei. Other options range from €25 to €28 and cover sites as far afield as Pompeii and Paestum. The tickets can be bought at train stations, newsagents, participating museums, via the Internet or through the call centre.

It's worth noting that in most museums the ticket office closes an hour before the stated closing time of the museum.

teachers (ITIC). For nonstudent travellers who are under 25, there is the **International Youth Travel Card** (IYTC; www.istc.org) which offers the same benefits.

Student cards are issued by student unions, hostelling organisations and some youth travel agencies. In Rome, the office of the Centro Turistico Studentesco e Giovanile (CTS) will issue ISIC, ITIC and Euro<26 cards. In Naples the **CTS** (Map pp244–6; ☎ 081 552 79 60; www.cts.it in Italian; Via Mezzocannone) has an office at the university that can issue the card.

ELECTRICITY

Most electricity wiring here works on 220V. Two-pin adapter plugs can be bought at electrical shops.

EMBASSIES & CONSULATES

For foreign embassies and consulates not listed here, look under 'Ambasciate' or 'Consolati' in the telephone directory. Alternatively, tourist offices generally have a list.

France (Map pp248-9; ☎ 081 59 80 711; Via Francesco Crispi 86, 80122)

Germany (Map pp248-9; ☎ 081 61 33 93; Via Francesco Crispi 69, 80121)

Netherlands (Map pp243-2; ☎ 081 551 30 03; Via Agostino Depretis 114, 80133)

UK (Map pp248-9; ☎ 081 66 33 20; Via Francesco Crispi 122, 80121)

USA (Map pp248-9; ☎ 081 583 81 11; Piazza della Repubblica, 80122)

EMERGENCY

To report a stolen car, call ☎ 081 794 14 35. At Naples' **main police station** (Map pp244–6; ☎ 081 794 11 11; Via Medina 75) there is an office for foreigners.

Ambulance	☎ 118
Coastguard	☎ 1530
Fire	☎ 115
Police	☎ 112/113

GAY & LESBIAN TRAVELLERS

Homosexuality is legal in Italy and well tolerated in major cities, such as Naples. However, overt displays of affection by homosexual couples could attract a negative response in the more rural parts of the south and in smaller towns on the Amalfi Coast. The legal age of consent is 16.

Gay clubs can be tracked down through local gay organisations or publications such as *Pride*, a national monthly magazine, and *AUT*, published by Circolo Mario Mieli in Rome; both are available at gay and lesbian organisations and bookshops. Also see the boxed text on p131.

The largest gay organisation in Naples is a branch of the national **Arcigay-Circola Antinoo** (Map pp244–6; ☎ 081 55 28 815; www.arcigay.it; Vico San Geronimo 17-20) which organises special events, including films and poetry readings, and can provide information on gay bars, clubs and special gay-orientated events in Naples.

The *Spartacus International Gay Guide* (US$32.95; available in bookshops worldwide) also lists gay venues all over Italy, or you could try the useful website www .gay.it/guida (in Italian) for gay bars and hotels.

HOLIDAYS

Most Italians take their annual holiday in August, which means that many businesses and shops close for at least a part of that month. The *Settimana Santa* (Easter Week) is another busy holiday period for Italians. Beware of school-holiday periods (especially Easter) when large groups of children noisily prowl the cultural sights. See p8 for special events and festivals in the city.

Public Holidays

Individual towns also have their own public holidays to celebrate the feasts of patron saints.

New Year's Day 1 January

Epiphany 6 January

Easter Monday March/April

Liberation Day 25 April

Labour Day 1 May

Republic Day 2 June

Feast of the Assumption 15 August

All Saints' Day 1 November

Feast of the Immaculate Conception 8 December

Christmas Day 25 December

Feast of Santo Stefano 26 December

INTERNET ACCESS

The following Internet cafés will get you online in Naples. Also refer to the individual town sections in the Bay of Naples & Amalfi Coast chapter for Internet access in those areas.

Internet bar (Map pp244-6; ☎ 081 29 52 37; Piazza Bellini 74; per 1hr €3; ⏰ 9-2am Mon-Sat, 8pm-2am Sun)

Multimedia (☎ 081 551 47 08; Via San Giovanni Maggiore Pignatelli 34; per 1hr €1.50; ⏰ 9.30am-9.30pm)

You will find lots more Internet cafés throughout Naples; prices hover around €3 per hour. Check out www.netcafeguide.com for an up-to-date list.

If you plan to carry your notebook or palmtop computer with you, remember that the power-supply voltage in the Italy may vary from that at home, risking damage to your equipment. The best investment is a universal AC adaptor for your appliance, which will enable you to plug it in anywhere.

Also, your PC-card modem may not work once you leave your home country. The safest option is to buy a reputable 'global' modem before you leave home, or buy a local PC-card modem if you're spending an extended time in Italy. Keep in mind that the telephone socket may be different, so ensure that you have at least a US RJ-11 telephone adaptor that works with your modem. You can almost always find an adaptor that will convert from RJ-11 to the local variety. For more information on travelling with a portable computer, see www.teleadapt.com.

If you access your Internet email account at home through a smaller ISP or your office or school network, your best option is either to open an account with a global ISP, or to rely on Internet cafés to collect your mail.

If you do intend to use Internet cafés, you'll need to carry three pieces of information: your incoming (POP or IMAP) mail-server name, your account name and your password. Your ISP or network supervisor will be able to give you these.

LEGAL MATTERS

For many Italians, finding ways to get around the law (any law) is a way of life. Few people pay attention to speed limits, and most motorcyclists and many drivers don't stop at red lights. No-one bats an eyelid about littering or dogs pooping in the middle of the pavement, even though many municipal governments have introduced laws against these things. But these are minor transgressions when measured up against the country's organised crime, the extraordinary levels of tax evasion and the corruption in government and business.

The average tourist will only have a brush with the law if they are robbed by a bag-snatcher or pickpocket.

Drink & Drugs

Although Italy's drug laws are relatively lenient, drugs are seriously frowned upon, in part due to the massive heroin problem (most notable in Naples and the poorer south) created by the Mafia's lucrative business. Although a 'few' grams of cannabis or marijuana are permissible for personal use, there is no law stating how much a few grams is. It is better to avoid the risks altogether; if you're caught the police can hold you for as long as it takes them to analyse your case. If the police decide that you are a dealer you could end up in prison.

The legal limit for a driver's blood-alcohol reading is 0.05% and random breath tests do occur.

Police

If you run into trouble in Naples, you are likely to end up dealing with either the state police known as the *polizia statale*, or the *carabinieri* (military police).

The *polizia* are a civil force, take their orders from the Ministry of the Interior, and deal generally with thefts, visa extensions and permissions. They wear powder-blue trousers with a fuchsia stripe and a navy-blue jacket; their headquarters are called the *questura*.

The *carabinieri*, on the other hand, are more concerned with civil obedience. They deal with general crime, public order and drug enforcement, and are therefore more visible on the street. They wear a black uniform with a red stripe and drive dark-blue cars, also with a red stripe. Their police station is called a *caserma* (barracks), which reflects their military status.

Other police include the *vigili urbani*, who are basically traffic police. You will have to deal with them if you get a parking ticket or your car is towed away. The *guardia di finanza* are responsible for fighting tax evasion and drug smuggling. The *guardia forestale* or *corpo forestale* are responsible for enforcing laws concerning forests and the environment in general.

See p213 for police and other emergency numbers.

Your Rights

Italy still has some antiterrorism laws on its books that could make your life very difficult if you happen to be detained by the police – for any alleged offence. You can be held for 48 hours without a magistrate being informed and you can be interrogated without the presence of a lawyer. It is difficult to obtain bail and legally you can be held for up to three years without being brought to trial.

MAPS

The city maps at the back of this book (see p241), combined with tourist-office maps, are generally adequate for visitors to Naples. More detailed maps are available in Italy at good bookshops such as **Feltrinelli** (p145). Excellent city plans and maps are published by de Agostini, Touring Club Italiano (TCI) and Michelin.

MEDICAL SERVICES

Ambulance (☎ 118, 081 752 06 96)

Guardia Medica (doctor; ☺ 24hrs) Phone numbers are found in the listings guide *Qui Napoli*.

Ospedale Loreto-Mare (hospital; Map pp243-2; ☎ 081 254 27 01; Via Amerigo Vespucci)

MONEY

On 1 January 2002 the euro became the currency of cash transactions in all of Italy and throughout the EU (except for three foot-draggers: Denmark, Sweden and the UK). The euro is divided into 100 cents. Coin denominations are one, two, five, 10, 20 and 50 cents, €1 and €2. The notes are €5, €10, €20, €50, €100, €200 and €500.

Exchange rates are given on the inside front cover of this book.

ATMs

Along with debit cards, credit cards can also be used in a *bancomat* (ATM) displaying the appropriate sign or (if you don't

have a PIN) to obtain cash advances over the counter in many banks – Visa and MasterCard are among the most widely recognised. Check what charges you will incur with your bank.

It is possible to use your own ATM debit card in machines throughout Italy to obtain money from your own bank account. This is without doubt the simplest way to handle your money while travelling.

If an ATM rejects your card, don't despair. Try a few more ATMs displaying your card's logo before assuming the problem lies with your card – Italian ATMs are known to be notoriously fickle.

Changing Money

You can change money in banks, at the post office or in a *cambio* (exchange office). Banks are generally the most reliable and tend to offer the best rates. Commission fluctuates and depends on whether you are changing cash or cheques.

While the post office charges a flat rate of €0.60 per cash transaction, banks charge at least €1.55 or more. Travellers cheques attract higher fees. Exchange booths often advertise 'no commission' but the rate of exchange is usually inferior.

Credit Cards

Credit (and debit) cards are the simplest way to organise your holiday funds. Using cards you can get money after hours and on weekends and the exchange rate is better than that offered for travellers cheques or cash exchanges.

Major credit cards, such as Visa, MasterCard, Eurocard, Cirrus and Eurocheques, are accepted throughout the south of Italy. They can be used in many supermarkets, hotels and restaurants (although *pensioni*, smaller trattorie and pizzerie still tend to accept cash only).

If your credit card is lost, stolen or swallowed by an ATM, you can telephone toll free to have an immediate stop put on its use. For MasterCard the number in Italy is ☎ 800 87 08 66, or make a reverse-charges call to St Louis in the USA on ☎ 314-275 66 90. For Visa, phone ☎ 800 81 90 14 in Italy.

American Express is also widely accepted throughout the city (although it is not as recognised as Visa or MasterCard). American

Express's full-service offices will issue new cards, usually within 24 hours, if yours has been lost or stolen. Some American Express offices have ATMs that you can use to obtain cash advances if you've made the necessary arrangements prior to travel.

The toll-free emergency number to report a lost or stolen American Express card varies according to where the card was issued. Check with American Express in your country or contact American Express in Rome on ☎ 06 722 82; it has a 24-hour cardholders' service.

Receipts

Laws aimed at tightening controls on the payment of taxes in Italy mean that the onus is on the buyer to ask for and retain receipts for all goods and services – this applies to everything. Although it rarely happens, you could be asked by an officer of the *guardia di finanza* to produce a receipt immediately after you leave a shop. If you don't have it, you may be obliged to pay a fine of up to €155.

Travellers Cheques

These are a safe way to carry money and are easily cashed at banks and exchange offices, although they are becoming less popular. Always keep the bank receipt listing the cheque numbers separate from the cheques themselves, and keep a list of the numbers of those you have already cashed – this will reduce problems in the event of loss or theft. Check the conditions applying to such circumstances before buying the cheques.

If you buy your travellers cheques in euros, you should not be charged commission when cashing them. Most hard currencies are widely accepted, although you may have occasional trouble with the New Zealand dollar.

Travellers using the better-known travellers cheques (such as Visa, American Express and Thomas Cook) will have little trouble in Italy. If you lose your American Express cheques, call the toll-free 24-hour number on ☎ 800 872 000. For Thomas Cook or MasterCard cheques call ☎ 800 872 050 and for Visa cheques call ☎ 800 874 155.

Take along your passport as identification when cashing in travellers cheques.

NEWSPAPERS & MAGAZINES

Naples' major daily newspaper is *Il Mattino*, although the national *La Repubblica* also has a Neapolitan section. If you are a sports fan (and can read Italian), *Tuttosport* will keep you happy for hours. Foreign newspapers are available, generally one or two days late, at the larger city kiosks and, more commonly, at nearby tourist resorts. The same applies to English or foreign-language magazines.

PHARMACIES

Italian pharmacists are generally well clued up on minor ailments, so check out a pharmacy first (with the help of your dictionary if you need to), unless you are seriously unwell.

Farmacia Cannone (Map p247; ☎ 081 556 72 61; Via A Scarlatti 75; ☯ 9am-midnight; funicular Centrale to Fuga) is part of a national group; its main plus is that it opens daily until midnight. This branch also stocks a range of homeopathic remedies and publishes (in Italian) its own magazine full of helpful health tips.

Officina Profumo Farmaceutica di Santa Maria Novella (Map pp248–9; ☎ 081 40 71 76; Via Santa Caterina a Chiaia 20; bus CS to Piazza dei Martiri), founded by the Dominican Fathers in 1221, reflects the long past and slow-moving world of old-fashioned weighing scales, rows of carefully labelled glass bottles and mysterious ointments made with fragrant herbs. Not a lot has changed, with shelves of natural medicines, floral-scented soaps and aromatherapy oils. Nothing is tested on animals.

PHOTOGRAPHY

If you're using a digital camera check that you have enough memory to store your snaps – two 128 MB cards will probably be enough. If you do run out of memory space your best bet is to burn your photos onto a CD. Increasing numbers of processing labs now offer this service.

To download your pics at an Internet café you'll need a USB cable and a card reader. Some places provide a USB on request but be warned that many of the bigger chain cafés don't let you plug your gear into their computers, meaning that it's back to plan A – the CD.

POST

Italy's postal system is notoriously unreliable. The most efficient service to use is *posta prioritaria* (priority mail).

Francobolli (stamps) are available at post offices and authorised tobacconists (look for the official *tabacchi* sign: a big 'T', usually depicted as white on black). Since letters often need to be weighed, what you get at the tobacconist's for international airmail will occasionally be an approximation of the proper rate, as most tobacconists do not have weighing scales. Tobacconists keep regular shop hours (see p210). If you have urgent mail it can be sent by *posta-celere* (also known as CAI Post), the Italian post office's courier service.

Information about postal services and rates can be obtained on ☎ 800 22 26 66 or online at www.poste.it in Italian.

Receiving Mail

Poste restante (general delivery) is known as *fermo posta* in Italy. Letters marked thus will be held at the counter of the same name in the main post office in the relevant town. Poste restante mail to Naples, for example, should be addressed as follows:

First Name FAMILY NAME,
Fermo Posta,
80100 Napoli,
Italy

You will need to pick up your letters in person and you must present your passport as ID.

If you have an American Express card or travellers cheques you can use the free client mail-holding service at American Express offices. You can obtain a list of these from any American Express office. Take your passport when you go to pick up mail.

RADIO

The state-owned stations RAI-I (89.3 and 94.1 MHzFM stereo and 1332 KHz AM), RAI-2 (91.3 and 96.1 MHzFM stereo and 846 KHz AM) and RAI-3 (93.3 and 98.1 MHz FM) all play light music and have hourly news bulletins.

There are no English-language radio stations, unless you bring your shortwave along.

SAFETY

Naples has a certain reputation and, although you're unlikely to encounter Mafia shootouts, petty crime can be a problem. However the situation is certainly improving, due in part to the sheer number of police on the streets. For some tips on how to reduce the risk of being a victim of petty crime, see p218. Be especially vigilant for moped bandits grabbing at your handbag and pickpockets on crowded transport.

Car and motorcycle theft is also rife, so think twice before bringing a vehicle into town.

Travellers should be careful about walking alone in the streets at night, particularly near Stazione Centrale and Piazza Dante. Never venture into the dark sidestreets at night unless you are in a group. The area west of Via Toledo and as far north as Piazza Carità, although safe enough during daylight hours, can be threatening after dark.

Annoyances

It requires a lot of patience to deal with the Italian concept of service. What for Italians is simply a way of everyday life can be horrifying for foreign visitors. Anyone in a uniform or behind a counter (including police officers, waiters and shop assistants) is likely to regard you with imperious contempt. Long queues are the norm in banks, post offices and any government offices. It pays to remain calm and patient. Aggressive, demanding and angry customers stand virtually no chance of getting what they want.

Pollution

Noise and air pollution are problems in Naples, caused mainly by the heavy traffic. In summer there are periodic pollution alerts, where the elderly, children and people who have respiratory problems are warned to stay indoors. If you fit into one of these categories, keep yourself informed through the tourist office or your hotel.

Racism

As with nearly all European countries there has been a disturbing rise in racism in southern Italy. For decades Italy was one of the world's largest exporters of immigrants around the world but now it has become the first port of call for a huge influx of refugees from the Balkans, Eastern Europe and North Africa. For such a homogenous society with one of the lowest birthrates in Europe the sudden influx has been traumatic and there are now an estimated half million *clandestini* (illegal immigrants) in the country. Travellers should be aware of this and, if subjected to any racial discrimination, you should report it to your embassy immediately.

Theft

Pickpockets and bag-snatchers operate in most large towns in Italy and are particularly active in Naples. The best way to avoid being robbed is to wear a moneybelt under your clothing. Keep all important items such as money, passport, other necessary documents and tickets in your moneybelt at all times and wear bags or cameras slung across the body.

You should also watch out for groups of dishevelled-looking women and children asking for money. Their favourite haunts are major train stations, tourist sites and in shopping areas. If you have been targeted by a group take evasive action (such as crossing the street) or shout '*Va via!*' (Go away!) in a loud voice. You should also be cautious of sudden friendships, particularly if your newfound *amico* or *amica* wants to sell you something.

Parked cars are also prime targets for thieves, particularly those that have foreign numberplates or display rental-company stickers. Try not to leave anything in the car if you can help it and certainly don't do this overnight. Car theft is a serious problem in Naples. It is a good idea to leave your car in a supervised car park. Throughout Italy, particularly in the south, service stations along the motorways are a haunt of thieves. If possible park where you can keep an eye on your car.

Some Italians practise a more insidious form of theft: short-changing. If you are new to euros, take the time to acquaint yourself with the denominations. When paying keep an eye on the bills you hand over and then count your change.

In case of theft or loss, always report the incident to the police within 24 hours and ask for a statement, otherwise your travel-insurance company won't pay out.

Traffic

Naples' traffic can at best be described as chaotic and at worst downright dangerous for the unprepared tourist. Drivers are not keen to stop for pedestrians, even at pedestrian crossings, and are more likely to swerve. Italians simply step off the footpath and walk through the (swerving) traffic with determination. It is a practice that seems to work, so if you feel uncertain about crossing a busy road, wait for the next Italian. (Better still, wait for a nun or priest to cross the road – most Italians seem to 'stop for God'.)

In many cities, roads that appear to be for one-way traffic sometimes have lanes for buses travelling in the opposite direction – always look both ways before stepping onto the road.

TAXES & REFUNDS

A value-added tax of around 19%, known as IVA (Imposta di Valore Aggiunto), is slapped on to just about everything in Italy. If you are a non-EU resident and you spend more than €154.94 on a purchase, you can claim a refund when you leave. The refund only applies to purchases from affiliated retail outlets which display a 'Tax Free for Tourists' sign. You have to complete a form at the point of sale, then get it stamped by Italian customs as you leave. At major airports you can then get an immediate cash refund; otherwise it will be refunded to your credit card. For information, pick up a pamphlet on the scheme from participating stores.

TELEPHONE
Domestic Calls

Rates, particularly for long-distance calls, are among the highest in Europe. The cheapest time for domestic calls is from 11pm to 8am and all of Sunday. A local call from a public phone will cost €0.10 for three to six minutes, depending on the time of day you call. Peak call times are 8am to 6.30pm Monday to Friday and 8am to 1pm on Saturday. Rates for long-distance calls within Italy depend on the time of day and the distance involved. At the worst, one minute will cost about €0.20 in peak periods.

Telephone area codes all begin with '0' and consist of up to four digits. The area code is followed by a number of anything from four to eight digits. Area codes, including the '0', are an integral part of all telephone numbers in Italy. Mobile-phone numbers begin with a three-digit prefix such as 330. Toll-free (free-phone) numbers are known as *numeri verdi* and usually start with 800. National call rate numbers start with 848 or 199.

For directory inquiries dial ☎ 12.

International Calls

If you need to call overseas, beware of the cost – calls to most European countries cost about €0.50 per minute, and it's closer to €1 from a public phone. Travellers from countries that offer direct-dialling services paid for at home-country rates (such as AT&T in the USA and Telstra in Australia) should think seriously about taking advantage of them. The number to call for international directory inquiries is ☎ 176.

Direct international calls can easily be made from public telephones by using a prepaid phonecard. Off-peak times are between 11pm and 8am and all of Sunday. Dial ☎ 00 to get out of Italy, then the relevant country and area codes, followed by the telephone number. Italy's country code is ☎ 39.

To make a reverse charges (collect) international call from a public telephone, dial ☎ 170. For European countries dial ☎ 15. All operators speak English.

It's easier, and often cheaper, to use the country direct service in your country – you dial the number and request a reverse charges call through the operator in your country. Numbers for this service include:

Australia (Optus/Telstra)	☎ 172 11 61/172 10 61
Canada	☎ 172 10 01
France	☎ 172 00 33
New Zealand	☎ 172 10 64

Mobile Phones

Italy has one of the highest levels of mobile-phone penetration in Europe, and there are several companies through which you can get a temporary or prepaid account if you already own a GSM, dual- or tri-band cellular phone. You will usually need your passport to open an account.

Both TIM (Telecom Italia Mobile) and Omnitel offer *prepagato* (prepaid) accounts for GSM phones (frequency 900 MHz), where you can buy a SIM card for either

network which gives you a predetermined amount of calls. You can then top up the account as required. There are TIM and Omnitel retail outlets in virtually every Italian town. Calls on these plans cost around €0.10 per minute.

The dual-band operator Wind works on frequencies of 900mHz and 1800mHz and also offers prepaid accounts. You don't pay for Wind's SIM card but calls are more expensive than Telecom and Omnitel – around €0.25 per minute for the first three minutes, then €0.10 per minute. There are Wind retail outlets in most Italian towns.

Always check with your mobile service provider in your home country to ascertain whether your handset allows use of another SIM card.

Phonecards

The state-run Telecom Italia is the largest telecommunications organisation in Italy and its orange public payphones are liberally scattered about the country. The most common accept only *carte/schede telefoniche* (telephone cards), although you will still find plenty that accept cards and coins. Some cardphones accept credit cards.

Telecom payphones can be found on the streets, in train stations and in some stores as well as in Telecom offices. Where these offices are staffed, it is possible to make international calls and pay at the desk afterwards. You can buy phonecards (usually a fixed euro rate of €5, €10 and €20) at post offices, tobacconists and newsstands. You must break the top left-hand corner of the card before you can use it. You need to be aware that phonecards have an expiry date, usually 31 December or 30 June depending on when you purchase the card.

Public phones operated by the private telecommunications companies Infostrada and Albacom can be found in airports and stations. These phones accept Infostrada or Albacom phonecards (available from post offices, tobacconists and newspaper stands). The rates are slightly cheaper than Telecom's for long-distance and international calls.

There are cut-price call centres all over Italy. These are run by various companies and the rates are lower than Telecom payphones for international calls. You simply place your call from a private booth inside the centre and pay for it when you've finished.

TELEVISION

Italian TV consists largely of variety shows, dubbed (and feeble) American sitcoms and various dubious soaps. Mid-range to expensive hotels will generally provide a satellite TV service which, at the very minimum, will pick up CNN, BBC World and a couple of music video channels.

TIME

Italy is one hour ahead of GMT. Daylight-saving time, when clocks are moved forward one hour, starts on the last Sunday in March. Clocks are put back an hour on the last Sunday in October. Italy operates on a 24-hour clock.

TIPPING

You are not expected to tip on top of restaurant service charges but it is common to leave a small amount, perhaps €1 per person. If there is no service charge, the customer should consider leaving a 10% to 12% tip, but this is by no means obligatory. In bars, Italians often leave any small change as a tip, maybe only €0.10. Tipping taxi drivers is not common practice, but you are expected to tip the porter at top-end hotels.

TOILETS

Public toilets are rare in Naples. Most people use the toilets in bars and cafés, although you might need to buy a coffee first. Department stores are another option and there are public toilets at the main bus and train stations.

TOURIST INFORMATION

The quality of tourist offices in Italy varies dramatically. One office might have enthusiastic staff but no useful printed information, while in another there's indifferent staff but a goldmine of brochures. Most offices will respond to written and telephone requests for information.

Tourist offices are generally open from 8.30am to 12.30pm or 1pm and 3pm to 7pm Monday to Friday. Hours are usually extended in summer, when some offices also open on Saturday or Sunday.

Information booths at most major train stations tend to keep similar hours but in some cases operate only in summer. Staff can usually provide a city map, list of hotels and information on the major sights.

English, and sometimes French or German, is spoken at tourist offices in larger towns and major tourist areas. Printed information is generally provided in a variety of languages.

The national tourist office, **Italian State Tourist Board** (☎ 06 4 97 11; www.enit.it; Via Marghera 2, Rome, 00185) is based in Rome. You'll also get useful information from the Naples **main tourist office** (Map pp248–9; ☎ 081 40 53 11; www.campaniafelix.it in Italian; Piazza dei Martiri 58).

More useful, however, are the information offices at the following locations, which stock the essential tourist brochure *Qui Napoli*, plus a city map and guides to major monuments:

Mergellina train station (Map pp248-9; ☎ 081 761 21 02; 🕑 9am-7.30pm Mon-Sat, 9am-1.30pm Sun)

Piazza del Gesù Nuovo (Map pp244-6; ☎ 081 552 33 28; 🕑 9am-8pm Mon-Sat, 9am-3pm Sun)

Stazione Centrale (Map pp244-6; ☎ 081 20 66 66; 🕑 9am-7.30pm Mon-Sat, 9am-1.30pm Sun)

Via San Carlo 7 (Map pp248-9; ☎ 081 40 23 94; 🕑 9am-8pm Mon-Sat, 9am-3pm Sun)

For local tourist offices outside the city see the relevant town sections in the Bay of Naples & the Amalfi Coast chapter on p163.

VISAS

Italy is among the 15 countries that have signed the Schengen Convention, an agreement where all EU member countries (except the UK and Ireland), plus Iceland and Norway, agreed to abolish checks at common borders. Legal residents of one Schengen country do not require a visa for another. Citizens of the UK and Ireland are also exempt from visa requirements for Schengen countries. Nationals of Australia, Canada, Israel, Japan, New Zealand, Switzerland and the USA do not require visas for tourist visits of up to 90 days to any Schengen country.

The standard tourist visa is valid for up to 90 days. A Schengen visa issued by one Schengen country is generally valid for travel in other Schengen countries. However, individual Schengen countries may impose additional restrictions on certain nationalities. It is therefore worth checking visa regulations with the consulate of each country you plan to visit.

It's now mandatory that you apply for a Schengen visa in your country of residence. You can apply for no more than two Schengen visas in any 12-month period and they are not renewable inside Italy. If you are going to visit more than one Schengen country, you should apply for the visa at a consulate of your main destination country or the first country you intend to visit.

EU citizens do not require any permits to live or work in Italy. They are, however, required to register with a police station if they take up residence and obtain a *permesso di soggiorno*.

Permesso di Soggiorno

If you plan to stay at the same address for more than one week you are obliged to report to the police station to receive a *permesso di soggiorno* (permit to remain in the country). Tourists who are staying in hotels are not required to do this.

A *permesso di soggiorno* only becomes a necessity if you plan to study, work (legally) or live in Italy. Obtaining one is never a pleasant experience; it involves queues and the frustration of arriving at the counter only to find you don't have the necessary documents.

The exact requirements, such as specific documents and *marche da bollo* (official stamps), can change from year to year. In general you will need: a valid passport containing a visa stamp indicating your date of entry into Italy, a special visa issued in your own country if you are planning to study, four passport-style photographs and proof of your ability to support yourself financially.

It is best to obtain precise information on what is required. Sometimes there is a list posted at the police station, otherwise you will need to go to the information counter.

Study Visas

Non-EU citizens who want to study at a university or language school in Italy must have a study visa. These visas can be obtained from your nearest Italian embassy or consulate. You will normally require confirmation of your enrolment, proof of payment of fees and adequate funds to support yourself before a visa is issued. The visa covers only the period of the enrolment. This type of visa is renewable within

Italy but, again, only with confirmation of ongoing enrolment and proof that you are able to support yourself (bank statements are preferred).

WOMEN TRAVELLERS

Lone women may find it difficult to remain alone. Usually the best response is to ignore unwanted approaches, but if that doesn't work politely tell them that you are waiting for your *marito* (husband) or *fidanzato* (boyfriend) and, if necessary, walk away. Avoid becoming aggressive as this may result in an unpleasant confrontation. If all else fails, approach the nearest member of the police.

Watch out for men with wandering hands on crowded buses. Either keep your back to the wall or make a loud fuss if someone starts fondling your backside. A loud '*Che schifo!*' (How disgusting!) will usually do the trick. Similarly, in the case of flashers one should always make a fuss rather than accepting the situation in embarrassed silence. If a more serious incident occurs, make a report to the police who are then required to press charges.

Women on their own should use their common sense. Avoid walking alone in dark streets, and look for hotels that are central (unsafe areas are noted throughout this book). Women should also avoid hitch-hiking alone.

Women will find that the further south they travel, the more likely they are to be harassed. It is advisable to dress more conservatively – skimpy clothing is a sure attention-earner.

WORK
Doing Business

It is illegal for non–EU citizens to work in Italy without a *permesso di lavoro* (work permit), but trying to obtain one can be time-consuming. EU citizens are allowed to work in Italy but they still need a *permesso di soggiorno* from the main police station in the town, ideally before they look for employment. See left for more information.

Immigration laws require all foreign workers to be 'legalised' through their employers, which can apply even to cleaners and babysitters. Employers then pay pension and health-insurance contributions.

This doesn't mean that there aren't employers willing to take people without the right papers.

Work options depend on a number of factors (location, length of stay, nationality and qualifications, for example) but, in the major cities at least, job possibilities for English speakers can be surprisingly plentiful. Go armed with a CV (if possible in Italian) and be persistent.

A very useful guide is *Living, Studying and Working in Italy* by Travis Neighbor Ward and Monica Larner (2003, Owl Books). You could also have a look at *Work Your Way Around the World* by Susan Griffith (2001, Vacation Work Publications), which is now in its 10th edition, and *The Au Pair and Nanny's Guide to Working Abroad* by Susan Griffith and Sharon Legg (2001, Vacation Work Publications).

The most easily secured work is short-term work in bars, hostels and farms, and babysitting. The other obvious source for English-speaking foreigners is teaching English. However, most of the more reputable language schools will only hire people who hold a work permit. The more professional schools will require you to have a TEFL (Teaching English as a Foreign Language) certificate.

Some useful organisations to start the job hunt include:

Au Pair Italy (☎ 05 138 34 66; www.aupairitaly.com) Offers posts from three months to two years, living with an Italian family and working up to 30 hours per week. Italian-language skills are not required.

British Institutes (☎ 02 439 00 41; www.britishinstitutes .org; Via Leopardi 8, Milan) Recruits English-speaking teachers. Knowledge of Italian is essential.

Cambridge School (☎ 0458 00 31 54; www.cambridge school.it; Via Rosmini 6, Verona) A main employer of English teachers.

Center for Cultural Exchange (☎ 630-377 2272; www .cci-exchange.com; 17 North Second Ave, St Charles, Illinois 60174) A nonprofit organisation dedicated to the promotion of cultural understanding. Offers internships in Italy.

Concordia International Volunteer Projects (☎ 01273 422218; www.concordia-iye.org.uk; 20-22 Boundary Rd, Hove, UK) Short-term community-based projects covering the environment, archaeology and the arts. UK applicants only.

Mix Culture Au Pair Service (☎ 06 47 88 22 89; Via Nazionale 204, Rome) Posts from six months to a year. Enrolment in a language school is necessary to obtain the required visa.

Recrultaly (www.recruitaly.it) For graduates looking for long-term employment in Italy this useful website links up to professional employers.

Youth Info Centre (☎ 045 801 0796; Corso Porto Borsari 17, Verona) Finds local employment for travellers.

Volunteer Work

Volunteer work in Naples and southern Italy is fairly thin on the ground for foreigners, especially for those who don't speak Italian. One option is to consult the book *Vacation Work's International Directory of Voluntary Work* by Louise Whetter and Victoria Pybus (2000, Peterson's Thomson Learning).

The following agencies also may be able to help:

Italian Association for Education, Exchanges & Intercultural Activities (AFSAI; ☎ 06 537 03 32; www .afsai.it; Viale dei Colli Portuensi 345, B2) Financed by the EU, this voluntary programme runs projects of six to 12 months for those aged between 16 and 25. Knowledge of Italian is required.

World Wide Opportunities on Organic Farms (www .wwoof.org) For a membership fee of €25 this organisation provides a list of farms looking for volunteer workers. Recommended by LP readers.

Language

Language

It's true – anyone can speak another language. Don't worry if you haven't studied languages before or that you studied a language at school for years and can't remember any of it. It doesn't even matter if you failed English grammar. After all, that's never affected your ability to speak English! And this is the key to picking up a language in another country: you just need to start speaking.

Learn a few key phrases before you go. Write them on pieces of paper and stick them on the fridge, by the bed or even on the computer – anywhere that you'll see them often.

You'll find that locals appreciate travellers trying their language, no matter how muddled you may think you sound. So don't just stand there, say something! If you want to learn more Italian than we've included here, pick up a copy of Lonely Planet's comprehensive but user-friendly *Italian phrasebook*.

PRONUNCIATION

c	as the 'k' in 'kit' before **a**, **o** and **u**; as the 'ch' in 'choose' before **e** and **i**
ch	as the 'k' in 'kit'
g	as the 'g' in 'get' before **a**, **o**, **u** and **h**; as the 'j' in 'jet' before **e** and **i**
gli	as the 'lli' in 'million'
gn	as the 'ny' in 'canyon'
h	always silent
r	a rolled 'rr' sound
sc	as the 'sh' in 'sheep' before **e** and **i**; as 'sk' before **a**, **o**, **u** and **h**
z	as the 'ts' in 'lights', except at the beginning of a word, when it's as the 'ds' in 'suds'

SOCIAL
Meeting People

Hello.
Buon giorno.
Goodbye.
Arrivederci.
Please.
Per favore.
Thank you (very much).
(Mille) Grazie.
Yes/No.
Sì/No.
Do you speak English?
Parla inglese?
Do you understand (me)?
(Mi) capisce?
Yes, I understand.
Sì, capisco.

No, I don't understand.
No, non capisco.

Could you please ...?
Potrebbe ...?
  repeat that   ripeterlo
  speak more   parlare più lentamente
    slowly
  write it down   scriverlo

Going Out

What's on ...?
Che c'è in programma ...?
  locally   in zona
  this weekend   questo fine settimana
  today   oggi
  tonight   stasera

Where are the ...?
Dove sono ...?
  clubs   dei clubs
  gay venues   dei locali gay
  places to eat   posti dove mangiare
  pubs   dei pub

Is there a local entertainment guide?
C'è una guida agli spettacoli in questa città?

PRACTICAL
Question Words

Who?	Chi?
What?	Che?
When?	Quando?
Where?	Dove?
How?	Come?

Numbers & Amounts

1	uno
2	due
3	tre
4	quattro
5	cinque
6	sei
7	sette
8	otto
9	nove
10	dieci
11	undici
12	dodici
13	tredici
14	quattordici
15	quindici
16	sedici
17	diciasette
18	diciotto
19	dicianove
20	venti
21	ventuno
22	ventidue
30	trenta
40	quaranta
50	cinquanta
60	sessanta
70	settanta
80	ottanta
90	novanta
100	cento
1000	mille

Days

Monday	lunedì
Tuesday	martedì
Wednesday	mercoledì
Thursday	giovedì
Friday	venerdì
Saturday	sabato
Sunday	domenica

Accommodation

I'm looking for a ...
Cerco ...

guesthouse	una pensione
hotel	un albergo
youth hostel	un ostello per la gioventù

Do you have any rooms available?
Ha camere libere?

I'd like (a) ...
Vorrei ...

single room	una camera singola
double room	una camera matrimoniale
room with two beds	una camera doppia

with a bathroom	con bagno

How much is it ...?	Quanto costa ...?
per night	per la notte
per person	per ciascuno

Banking

I'd like to ...
Vorrei ...

cash a cheque	riscuotere un assegno
change money	cambiare denaro
change some travellers cheques	cambiare degli assegni di viaggio

Where's the nearest ...?
Dov'è il ... più vicino?

ATM	bancomat
foreign exchange office	cambio

Post

Where is the post office?
Dov'è l'ufficio postale?

I want to send a ...
Voglio spedire ...

fax	un fax
parcel	un pachetto
postcard	una cartolina

I want to buy ...
Voglio comprare ...

an aerogram	un aerogramma
an envelope	una busta
a stamp	un francobollo

Phones & Mobiles

I want to buy a phone card.
Voglio comprare una scheda telefonica.

I want to make ...
Voglio fare ...

a call (to ...)	una chiamata (a ...)
reverse-charge/ collect call	una chiamata a carico del destinatario

Where can I find a/an ...?
Dove si trova ...
I'd like a/an ...
Vorrei ...

adaptor plug	un addattatore
charger for my phone	un caricabatterie
mobile/cell phone for hire	un cellulare da noleggiare
prepaid mobile/cell phone	un cellulare prepagato
SIM card for your network	un SIM card per vostra rete telefonica

Internet

Where's the local Internet cafe?
Dove si trova l'Internet point?

I'd like to ...
Vorrei ...

check my email	controllare le mie email
get online	collegarmi a Internet

Shopping

I'd like to buy ...	Vorrei comprare ...
How much is it?	Quanto costa?

more	più
less	meno
smaller	più piccolo/a (m/f)
bigger	più grande

Do you accept ...?	Accettate ...?
credit cards	carte di credito
travellers cheques	assegni per viaggiatori

Transport

What time does the ... leave?
A che ora parte ...?

boat	la nave
bus	l'autobus
train	il treno

What time's the ... bus?
A che ora passa ... autobus?

first	il primo
last	l'ultimo
next	il prossimo

Are you free? (taxi)
È libero questo taxi?
Please put the meter on.
Usa il tassametro, per favore.
How much is it to ...?
Quant'è per ...?
Please take me to (this address).
Mi porti a (questo indirizzo), per favore.

FOOD

breakfast	prima colazione
lunch	pranzo
dinner	cena
a restaurant	un ristorante
a grocery store	un alimentari

I'd like the set lunch.
Vorrei il menù turistico.
Is service included in the bill?
È compreso il servizio?
What is this?
(Che) cos'è?
I'm a vegetarian.
Sono vegetariano/a.
I'm allergic to nuts.
Sono allergico/a alle noci.

I don't eat ...	Non mangio ...
meat	carne
chicken	pollo
fish	pesce

For more detailed information on food and dining out, see pp29–38.

EMERGENCIES

It's an emergency!
È un'emergenza!
Could you please help me/us?
Mi/Ci può aiutare, per favore?
Call the police/a doctor/an ambulance!
Chiami la polizia/un medico/un'ambulanza!
Where's the police station?
Dov'è la questura?

HEALTH

Where's the nearest ...?
Dov'è ... più vicino?

chemist (night)	la farmacia (di turno)
dentist	il dentista
doctor	il medico
hospital	l'ospedale

I need a doctor (who speaks English).
Ho bisogno di un medico (che parli inglese).

Symptoms

I have (a) ...
Ho ...

diarrhoea	la diarrea
fever	la febbre
headache	mal di testa
pain	un dolore

Glossary

albergo, alberghi (pl) – hotel
alimentari – grocery shop
autostrada, autostrade (pl) – motorway, highway

bagno – bathroom, also toilet
bancomat – ATM (automated teller machine)
biblioteca, biblioteche (pl) – library
biglietto – ticket

calcio – football (soccer)
cambio – currency-exchange bureau
camera – room
campanile – bell tower
carabinieri – police with military and civil duties
carta d'identità – identity card
carta telefonica – phonecard
casa – house, home
castello – castle
catacomba – underground tomb complex
centro – city centre
centro storico – historic centre, old city
chiesa, chiese (pl) – church
cimitero – cemetery
colle/collina – hill
colonna – column
commissariato – local police station
comune – equivalent to a municipality or county; town or city council; historically, a commune (self-governing town or city)
corso – main street
cupola – dome

farmacia – pharmacy
fermo posta – poste restante
ferrovia – train station
festa – feast day; holiday
fiume – river
fontana – fountain
forno – bakery
forte/fortezza – fort
forum, fora (pl) – (Latin) public square
francobolli – stamps

gabinetto – toilet, WC
gasolio – diesel
gelateria – ice-cream parlour
guglia – obelisk

isola – island

lago – lake
largo – small square
lavanderia – laundrette
libreria – bookshop
lido – beach
lungomare – seafront, esplanade

mercato – market
monte – mountain
mura – city wall

orto botanico – botanical gardens
ospedale – hospital
ostello – hostel

palazzo, palazzi (pl) – mansion, palace, large building of any type (including an apartment block)
panetteria – bakery
pasticceria – cake shop
pensione – small hotel or guesthouse, often offering board
pescheria – fish shop
piazza, piazze (pl) – square
piazzale – large open square
pinacoteca – art gallery
piscina – pool
polizia – police
ponte – bridge
porta – city gate

questura – police station

reale – royal

sala – room in a museum or a gallery
salumeria – delicatessen
sedia a rotelle – wheelchair
seggiolone – child's highchair
servizio – service charge in restaurants
stazione – station

tabaccheria – tobacconist's shop
teatro – theatre
tempio – temple
terme – baths
torre – tower
treno – train

via – street, road
vicolo – alley, alleyway

Behind the Scenes

THE LONELY PLANET STORY

The story begins with a classic travel adventure: Tony and Maureen Wheeler's 1972 journey across Europe and Asia to Australia. There was no useful information about the overland trail then, so Tony and Maureen published the first Lonely Planet guidebook to meet a growing need.

From a kitchen table, Lonely Planet has grown to become the largest independent travel publisher in the world, with offices in Melbourne (Australia), Oakland (USA) and London (UK). Today Lonely Planet guidebooks cover the globe. There is an ever-growing list of books and information in a variety of media. Some things haven't changed. The main aim is still to make it possible for adventurous travellers to get out there – to explore and better understand the world.

At Lonely Planet we believe travellers can make a positive contribution to the countries they visit – if they respect their host communities and spend their money wisely. Every year 5% of company profit is donated to charities around the world.

THIS BOOK

This 1st edition of *Naples & the Amalfi Coast* was researched and written by Duncan Garwood and Josephine Quintero. This guidebook was commissioned in Lonely Planet's London office and produced in Melbourne. The project team included:

Commissioning Editor Michala Green
Coordinating Editor Nancy Ianni
Coordinating Cartographer Valentina Kremenchutskaya
Assisting Editor Kate James
Cover Designer Annika Roojun
Layout Designer & Cover Artwork Laura Jane
Managing Editor Kerryn Burgess
Managing Cartographer Mark Griffiths
Project Manager Rachel Imeson
Language Content Coordinator Quentin Frayne

Thanks to Sally Darmody, Adriana Mammarella, Anthony Phelan, Ray Thomson

Cover photographs: Washing drying, Procida, Jeffrey Becom/Lonely Planet Images (top); Statue of Caesar, Capri, Scott Gog/APL Corbis (bottom); Pulcinella, Jean-Bernard Carillet/Lonely Planet Images (back).

Internal photographs by Lonely Planet Images and Jean-Bernard Carillet except for the following: p2 (#3) and p89 (#3) Stephen Saks, p2 (#4) and p89 (#2) Martin Moos, p89 (#1) Bill Wassman, p89 (#4) Jonathan Smith, p90 (#1) Sally Webb, p90 (#2 & 4) Russell Mountford, p90 (#3) Roberto Gerometta. All images are the copyright of the photographers unless otherwise indicated. Many of the images in this guide are available for licensing from Lonely Planet Images: www.lonelyplanetimages.com

THANKS
DUNCAN GARWOOD

Thanks to Nicola and Marco for dinner, to Richard and Duncan for earning a round of applause on Piazza dei Martiri, to Stefano for his tips on the Naples nightlife, and to the staff of the Naples tourist offices who did their best to help. At Lonely Planet, thank you to Michala Green for the commission and Josephine Quintero for her great work. As always, I couldn't have done the job without Lidia's support. *Grazie di cuore*. A final thank you also to Ben for being so good, and to his *nonna* Nicla for helping us out.

JOSEPHINE QUINTERO

Firstly many thanks to Robin Chapman for his sense of humour, map-reading skills and for sharing his expertise on hunting down the ultimate slice of pizza perfection, along with the best wines. Also a mega thank you to my Italy-based daughter, Isabel, for the crash course in Italian and some insider tips. Thanks to the staff of all the tourist offices, particularly those lovely ladies in Salerno who went out of their way to dig out information on Paestum. Thanks also to Duncan Garwood and Michala Green at Lonely Planet for their troop-rallying emails during research.

SEND US YOUR FEEDBACK

We love to hear from travellers – your comments keep us on our toes and help make our books better. Our well-travelled team reads every word on what you loved or loathed about this book. Although we cannot reply individually to postal submissions, we always guarantee that your feedback goes straight to the appropriate authors, in time for the next edition. Each person who sends us information is thanked in the next edition – and the most useful submissions are rewarded with a free book.

To send us your updates – and find out about Lonely Planet events, newsletters and travel news – visit our award-winning website: www.lonelyplanet.com/feedback.

Note: We may edit, reproduce and incorporate your comments in Lonely Planet products such as guidebooks, websites and digital products, so let us know if you don't want your comments reproduced or your name acknowledged. For a copy of our privacy policy visit www.lonelyplanet.com/privacy.

Notes

Notes

Index

See also separate indexes for Eating (p239), Shopping (p239) and Sleeping (p240).

000 map pages
000 photographs

Index

MAP LEGEND

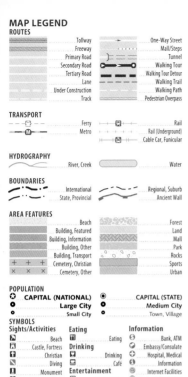

ROUTES

Tollway	One-Way Street
Freeway	Mall/Steps
Primary Road	Tunnel
Secondary Road	Walking Tour
Tertiary Road	Walking Tour Detour
Lane	Walking Trail
Under Construction	Walking Path
Track	Pedestrian Overpass

TRANSPORT

Ferry	Rail
Metro	Rail (Underground)
	Cable Car, Funicular

HYDROGRAPHY

River, Creek	Water

BOUNDARIES

International	Regional, Suburb
State, Provincial	Ancient Wall

AREA FEATURES

Beach	Forest
Building, Featured	Land
Building, Information	Mall
Building, Other	Park
Building, Transport	Rocks
Cemetery, Christian	Sports
Cemetery, Other	Urban

POPULATION

CAPITAL (NATIONAL)	CAPITAL (STATE)
Large City	Medium City
Small City	Town, Village

SYMBOLS

Sights/Activities
- Beach
- Castle, Fortress
- Christian
- Diving
- Monument
- Museum, Gallery
- Ruin

Transport
- Bus Station
- Parking Area

Eating
- Eating

Drinking
- Drinking
- Café

Entertainment
- Entertainment

Shopping
- Shopping

Sleeping
- Sleeping

Information
- Bank, ATM
- Embassy/Consulate
- Hospital, Medical
- Information
- Internet Facilities
- Police Station
- Post Office, GPO
- Telephone
- Toilets

Geographic
- Lookout
- Mountain

Map Section

A **B** **C** **D** (p250)

1 Rione Alto Ⓜ

Materdei

See Capodimonte Map

Tangenziale

Monte Donzelli Ⓜ

See Vomero & Western Naples Map (p247)

Via R Imbriani

2 Materdei Ⓜ

Piazza Medaglie d'Oro Ⓜ Medaglie d'Oro

Via Salvator Rosa Ⓜ S Rosa

Pia
Ta

Piazza
Montesano

Stazio
Cuma
Mont
Pia
Pigna

3 Cilea Ⓜ

Vomero

Montesanto Ⓜ

Via C Bernini

Funicolare di Montesanto

Via Pasqua

Via A Scarlatti

Vanvitelli Ⓜ

Piazza Vanvitelli

Largo San Martino

Via Francesco C

Via F Cilea

Piazza Fuga

Tangenziale di Napoli

Via F Cilea

Parco Lamaro

Funicolare di Chiaia

Corso Vittorio Emanuele

4 Corso Europa

Parco Elena

Villa Floridiana

Funicolare Centrale

Parco Ameno

Amedeo Ⓜ Via del

See Chiaia & Santa Lucia (pp248–9)

Parco Margherita

Piazza Amedeo

Via G Nicotera

Chiaia

Via M Schipa

Corso Vittorio Emanuele

Via Francesco Crispi

Via Martucci

Via dei Mille

Via G Filangieri

Pia
Ple

Mergellina

Via S Pasquale Chiaia

Piazza dei Martiri

Via Monte di Dio

Via Bausan

Riviera di Chiaia

Piazza Carlo Poerio

5 **Piedigrotta**

Mergellina Ⓜ

Via Piedigrotta

Riviera di Chiaia

Piazza della Repubblica

Viale A Dohrn

Villa Comunale

Riviera di Chiaia

Piazza della Vittoria

Via D Morelli

Galleria

Pizzofalcone

17

Piazza Piedigrotta

Via G Bruno

Viale Gramsci

Via Francesco Caracciolo

Via Parten

To Palazzo Donn'Anna (1km); Reginelli (1km);
Stadio San Paolo & Azzuro Service (2.2km);
Mostra d'Oltremare; Piscina Scandone (2.8km); A Lampara;
Al Ciclope (3km); Palapartenope (3.2km); Edenlandia (3.2km);
Villa Rosebery (3.2km); Marechiaro (3.5km);
Grotta di Seiano (3.5km); Parco Virgiliano (3.7km);
Arenile di Bagnoli (5.5km); Città della Scienza (8km);
Campi Flegrei; Pozzuoli (14km); Hotel Terme
Puteolane (14km); Cuma (20km); Baia (21km)

Gulf of Naples
(Golfo di Napoli)

6 Funicolare di Mergellina

Via Mergellina

To Procida;
Ischia; Capri

SIGHTS & ACTIVITIES (pp51–100)
Albergo dei Poveri.................................1 F1
Chiesa San Giovanni a Carbonara......2 F2
Chiesa Santa Caterina a Formiello......3 F2
Chiesa Santa Maria Donnaregina
    Nuova.....................................(see 4)
Chiesa Santa Maria Donnaregina
    Vecchia................................4 F2
Orto Botanico.......................................5 F1
Porta Capuana.....................................6 F2

DRINKING (p130)
Freezer..7 H1

ENTERTAINMENT (p131)
Blu Angels...8 H2

SLEEPING (pp147–60)
B&B Donnaregina..................................9 F2
Hotel Casanova.....................................10 G2
Hotel del Real Orto Botanico............11 F1
Hotel des Artistes..................................12 F2
Hotel Ginevra & Ginevra 2.................13 G2
Hotel Prati...14 G2
Hotel Speranza.....................................15 G2
Hotel Zara...16 G2
Ostello Mergellina.................................17 A5

TRANSPORT (pp205–9)
Alibus...18 E4
Maggiore...19 G2
Stazione Centrale.................................20 G2
Stazione Garibaldi..........................(see 20)

INFORMATION
Agriturist Campania.............................21 G2
Dutch Consulate...................................22 E4

OTHER
Ospedale Loreto-Mare.........................23 G3

CENTRAL NAPLES

VOMERO & WESTERN NAPLES

0		200 m
0		0.1 miles

See Chiaia & Santa Lucia Map (pp248–9)

247

CHIAIA & SANTA LUCIA

See Vomero & Western Naples Map (p247)